Thinking Through the Past

Thinking Through the Past

A Critical Thinking Approach to U.S. History

Volume II: Since 1865

THIRD EDITION

John Hollitz

Community College of Southern Nevada

Houghton Mifflin Company   BOSTON   NEW YORK

Vice President and Publisher: Charles Hartford
Editor-in-Chief: Jean Woy
Sponsoring Editor: Sally Constable
Development Editor: Lisa Kalner Williams
Editorial Assistant: Kisha Mitchell
Associate Project Editor: Teresa Huang
Editorial Assistant: Jake Perry
Senior Art and Design Coordinator: Jill Haber
Senior Photo Editor: Jennifer Meyer Dare
Senior Composition Buyer: Sarah Ambrose
Manufacturing Coordinator: Carrie Wagner
Senior Marketing Manager: Sandra McGuire
Marketing Associate: Ilana Gordon

Cover image: Robert Cottingham, *Barrera-Rosa's* (California), 1985. © Robert Cottingham, Courtesy of Forum Gallery, New York.

Printed in the U.S.A.

Library of Congress Catalog Card Number: 2003110150

ISBN: 0-618-41679-X

89-QF-12 11 10 09 08

Contents

3

Evaluating Primary Sources: "Saving" the Indians in the Late Nineteenth Century   51

6

Ideology and History: Closing the "Golden Door"   **138**

7

History "From the Top Down": Eleanor Roosevelt, First Lady

8

History "From the Bottom Up": The Detroit Race Riot of 1943

9

Popular Culture as History:
The Cold War Comes Home   213

10

History and Popular Memory:
The Civil Rights Movement   239

11

Causation and the Lessons of History: Explaining America's Longest War

12

Gender, Ideology, and Historical Change: Explaining the Women's Movement

300

13

Why Historical Interpretation Matters: The Battle Over Multicultural Education

335

Preface

The encouraging response to the second edition from students and instructors has prompted me to create a third edition of *Thinking Through the Past*. As before, this book is inspired by the idea that interpretation is at the heart of history. That is why learning about the past involves more than mastering facts and dates, and why historians often disagree. As teachers, we know the limitations of the deadly dates-and-facts approach to the past. We also know that encouraging students to think critically about historical sources and historians' arguments is a good way to create excitement about history and to impart understanding of what historians do. The purpose of *Thinking Through the Past*, therefore, is to introduce students to the examination and analysis of historical sources.

FORMAT

To encourage students to think critically about American history, *Thinking Through the Past* brings together primary and secondary sources. It gives students the opportunity to analyze primary sources *and* historians' arguments, and to use one to understand and evaluate the other. By evaluating and drawing conclusions from the sources, students will use the methods and develop some of the skills of critical thinking as they apply to history. Students will also learn about a variety of historical topics that parallel those in U.S. history courses. Unlike most anthologies or collections of primary sources, this book advances not only chronologically, but pedagogically through different skill levels. It provides students the opportunity to work with primary sources in the early chapters before they evaluate secondary sources in later chapters or compare historians' arguments in the final chapters. Students are also able to build on the skills acquired in previous chapters by considering such questions as motivation, causation, and the role of ideas and economic interests in history.

At the same time, this book introduces a variety of approaches to the past. Topics in *Thinking Through the Past* include social, political, cultural, intellectual, economic, diplomatic, and military history. The chapters look at history "from the top down" and "from the bottom up." Thus students have the opportunity to evaluate history drawn from slave quarters as well as from state houses. In the process, they are exposed to the enormous range of sources that historians use to construct arguments. The primary sources in these volumes include portraits, photographs, maps, letters, fiction, music lyrics, laws, oral histories, speeches, movie posters, magazine and newspaper articles, cartoons, and architectural plans.

The chapters present the primary and secondary sources so students can pursue their own investigations of the material. Each chapter is divided into five parts: a brief introduction, which sets forth the problem in the chapter; the Setting, which provides background information pertaining to the topic; the Investigation, which asks students to answer a short set of questions revolving around the problem discussed in the introduction; the Sources, which in most chapters provide a secondary source and a set of primary sources related to the chapter's main problem, and, finally, a brief Conclusion, which offers a reminder of the chapter's main pedagogical goal and looks forward to the next chapter's problem.

CHANGES TO THE THIRD EDITION

In the third edition, there are entirely new chapters in both volumes on provocative topics that have been on the cutting edge of recent historical scholarship. These topics are intended to stimulate student interest in American history. In Volume I, the new chapters focus on the subjects of equality and women. The new Chapter 4 explores the ramifications of equality in the Revolutionary era and the new Chapter 11 examines the role of ideology in accounting for differences between Northern and Southern women before the Civil War. In Volume II, there are new chapters on overseas expansion and multiculturalism. The new Chapter 4 discusses the decision to annex the Philippines at the end of the nineteenth century and the new Chapter 13 explores the impact of multiculturalism on school curricula in the late twentieth century. Overall, the volumes have been revised with an eye toward making the book a more engaging learning tool. To this end, many other chapters contain new sources that provide additional insights for students as they conduct their historical investigations.

INSTRUCTOR'S RESOURCE MANUAL

The format of *Thinking Through the Past* is designed to be effective in various classroom situations. Students in large classes can work through this book with minimal instructor assistance. Yet the format also provides students in seminars, small classes, and discussion sections the opportunity to share with one another the excitement of thinking about the past. The Instructor's Resource Manual is designed to enhance the effectiveness of *Thinking Through the Past* in all these classroom settings. The manual, available online, contains discussion of the sources in each chapter and explanations of how they relate to the chapter's main problem and pedagogical goals. It also contains questions to stimulate classroom discussion and suggestions for evaluating students' learning.

ACKNOWLEDGMENTS

Many people contributed to this book, starting with my own students. Without them, of course, it never would have been created.

I owe many thanks to the people who assisted in various ways with the revisions for this edition. At Houghton Mifflin, Leah Strauss guided the revision process in the initial stages, while Lisa Kalner Williams saw it through to completion. Teresa Huang oversaw the production phase and Peggy Flanagan copyedited the manuscript with a careful eye. I am truly grateful for their help. At the Community College of Southern Nevada, Inter-Library Loan librarian Marion Martin, as always, provided cheerful and invaluable assistance. Numerous colleagues around the country offered useful suggestions regarding revisions and chapter drafts. I am honored by their commitment to *Thinking Through the Past* and thank them for helping to make it a better book. They were Michael D. Wilson, Vanguard University; David A. Canton, Georgia Southern University; Paivi Hoikkala, California State Polytechnic University at Pomona; Kathleen Kennedy, Western Washington University; Monroe H. Little, Jr., Indiana University-Purdue University at Indianapolis; Cathleen Schultz, University of St. Francis; Paul C. Rosier, Villanova University; Marsha L. Weisiger, New Mexico State University; and Katherine A. S. Sibley, St. Joseph's University.

I owe thanks to many others as well for their contribution to the previous editions. Alan Balboni, DeAnna Beachley, Michael Green, Charles Okeke, the late Gary Elliott, colleagues at the Community College of Southern Nevada, offered sources, reviewed portions of the manuscript, shared insights, or simply offered encouragement. Richard Cooper and Brad Nystrom at California State University, Sacramento listened patiently and offered helpful suggestions at the initial stages of this project. Likewise, I remain indebted to numerous people at Houghton Mifflin. Heather Hubbard, Colleen Shanley Kyle, and Leah Strauss oversaw various stages of the revision process for the second edition, while Jay Boggis copyedited the manuscript. Editors Jeffrey Greene, Carol Newman, and copyeditor Susan Zorn performed similar chores on the first edition. In countless ways, this edition continues to reflect their various and invaluable contributions.

The same must be said of the efforts of colleagues around the country who reviewed chapter drafts for the previous editions. These individuals were generous with their time and offered valuable insights and suggestions. The reviewers of the second edition were: Lendol Calder, Augustana College; Gary Daynes, Brigham Young University; Marc Dollinger, Pasadena City College; Kim M. Gruenwald, Kent State University; Penelope Harper, Louisiana State University; Richard E. Herrmann, Dyersburg State Community College; Glenn J.

Kist, Rochester Institute of Technology; Sean O'Neill, Grand Valley State University; Joseph P. Reidy, Howard University; James D. Rice, SUNY Plattsburgh; and Timothy N. Thurber, SUNY Oswego. The reviewers of the first edition were: Karen Blair, Central Washington University; Joan Chandler, University of Texas–Dallas; Myles Clowers, San Diego City College; Julian Del Gaudio, Long Beach City College; Ronald Faircloth, Abraham Baldwin Agricultural College; Gerald Ghelfi, Rancho Santiago College; David Godschalk, Shippensburg University; Robert Goldman, Virginia Union University; Nancy Isenberg, University of Northern Iowa; John Jameson, Kent State University; Benjamin Newcomb, Texas Technological University; Vince Nobile, Chaffey Community College; Mario Perez, University of California–Riverside; Edward Pluth, St. Cloud State University; John Rector, Western Oregon State University; David Schmitz, Whitman College; Luther Spoehr, Lincoln School; Emily Teipe, Fullerton College; Stephen Weisner, Springfield Technical Community College; Marianne Wokeck, Indiana University–Purdue University at Indianapolis; Walter Weare, University of Wisconsin–Milwaukee; and Marli Weiner, University of Maine.

As usual, however, my biggest debt is to Patty. For her enduring support and abiding love, this book is once again dedicated to her.

J. H.

Thinking Through the Past

Introduction

"History," said Henry Ford, "is more or less bunk." That view is still shared by many people. Protests about the subject are familiar. Studying history won't help you land a job. And besides, what matters is not the past but the present.

Such protests are not necessarily wrong. Learning about ancient Greece, the French Revolution, or the Vietnam War will hardly guarantee employment, even though many employers evaluate job candidates on critical thinking skills that the study of history requires. Likewise, who can deny the importance of the present compared to the past? In many ways the present and future are more important than the past. Pericles, Robespierre, and Lyndon Johnson are dead; presumably, anyone reading this is not.

Still, the logic behind the history-as-bunk view is flawed because all of us rely upon the past to understand the present, as did even Henry Ford. Besides building the Model T, he also built Greenfield Village outside Detroit because he wanted to recreate a nineteenth-century town. It was the kind of place the automotive genius grew up in and the kind of place he believed represented the ideal American society: small-town, white, native-born, and Protestant. Greenfield Village was Ford's answer to changes in the early twentieth century that were profoundly disturbing to him and to many other Americans of his generation: growing cities, the influx of non-Protestant immigrants, changing sexual morality, new roles and new fashions for women, and greater freedom for young people.

Ford's interest in the past, symbolized by Greenfield Village, reflects a double irony. It was the automobile that helped to make possible many of the changes, like those in sexual morality, that Ford detested. The other irony is that Ford used history—what he himself called "bunk"—to try to better the world. Without realizing it, he became a historian by turning to the past to explain to himself and others what he disliked about the present. Never mind that Ford blamed immigrants, especially Jews, for the changes he decried in crude, hate-filled tirades. The point is that Ford's view of America was rooted in a vision of the past, and his explanation for America's ills was based on historical analysis, however unprofessional and unsophisticated.

All of us use historical analysis all the time, even if, like Ford, we think we don't. In fact, we all share a fundamental assumption about learning from the past: One of the best ways to learn about something, to learn how it came to be, is to study its past. That assumption is so much a part of us that we are rarely conscious of it.

Think about the most recent time you met someone for the first time. As a way to get to know this new acquaintance you began to ask questions about his or her past. When you asked, "Where did you grow up?" or "How long have you lived in Chicago?" you were relying on information about the past to learn about the present. You were, in other words, thinking as a historian. You assumed that a cause-and-effect relationship existed between this person's past and his or her present personality, interests, and beliefs. Like a historian, you began to frame questions and to look for answers that would help to establish causal links.

Because we all use history to make sense of our world, it follows that we should become more skilled in the art of making sense of the past. Ford did it crudely, and ended up promoting the very things he despised. But how exactly do you begin to think more like a historian? For too many students, this challenge summons up images of studying for history exams: cramming names, dates, and facts and hoping to retain some portion of this information long enough to get a passing grade. History seems like a confusing grab bag of facts and events. The historian's job, in this view, is to memorize as much "stuff" as possible. In this "flash-card" approach, history is reduced to an exercise in the pursuit of trivia, and thinking like a historian is nothing but an exercise in mnemonics—a system of improving the memory.

There is no question that the dates, events, and facts of history are important. Without basic factual knowledge historians could no more practice their craft than biologists, chemists, or astrophysicists could practice theirs. But history is not a static recollection of facts. Events in the past happened only once, but the historians who study those events are always changing their minds about them. Like all humans, historians have prejudices, biases, and beliefs. They are also influenced by events in their own times. In other words, they look at the past through lenses that filter and even distort. Events in the past may have happened only once, but what historians think about them, the meaning they give to those events, is constantly changing. Moreover, because their lenses perceive events differently, historians often disagree about the past. The supposedly "static" discipline of history is actually dynamic and charged with tension.

That brings us to the question of what historians really do. Briefly, historians ask questions about past events or developments and try to explain them. Just as much as biology, chemistry, or astrophysics, therefore, history is a problem-solving discipline. Historians, like scientists, sift evidence to answer questions. Like scientists, whose explanations for things often conflict, historians can ask the same questions, look at the same facts, and come up with different explanations because they look at the past in different ways. Or they may have entirely different questions in mind and so come away with very different "pasts." Thus history is a process of constant revision. As historians like to put it, every generation writes its own history.

But why bother to study and interpret the past in our own way if someone else will only revise it again in the future? The answer is sobering: If we don't write our own history, someone else will write it for us. Who today would accept as historical truth the notion that the Indians were cruel savages whose extermination was necessary to fulfill an Anglo-Saxon destiny to conquer the continent for democracy and civilization? Who today would accept the "truth" that slaves were racially inferior and happy with their lot on southern plantations? If we accept these views of Indians and black slaves, we are allowing nineteenth-century historians to determine our view of the past.

Instead, by reconstructing the past as best we can, we can better understand our own times. Like the amnesia victim, without memory we face a bewildering world. As we recapture our collective past, the present becomes more intelligible. Subject to new experiences, a later generation will view the past differently. Realizing that future generations will revise history does not give us a license to play fast and loose with the facts of history. Rather each generation faces the choice of giving meaning to those facts or experiencing the confusion of historical amnesia.

Finding meaning in the facts of the past, then, is the central challenge of history. It requires us to ask questions and construct explanations—mental activities far different and far more exciting than merely memorizing names, dates, and facts. More important, it enables us to approach history as critical thinkers. The more skilled we become at historical reasoning, the better we will understand our world and ourselves. Helping you to develop skill in historical analysis is the purpose of this volume.

The method of this book reflects its purpose. The first chapter discusses textbooks. History texts have a very practical purpose. By bringing order to the past, they give many students a useful and reassuring "handle" on history. But they are not the Ten Commandments, because, like all works of history, they also contain interpretations. To most readers these interpretations are hard to spot. Chapter 1 examines what a number of college textbooks in American history say and don't say about the role of African Americans during Reconstruction, the period immediately after the Civil War. By examining selections from several texts and asking how and why they differ, we can see that texts are not as objective as readers often believe.

If textbooks are not carved in stone, how can historians know anything? To answer this question, we turn next to the raw material of history. Chapter 2, on the living and working conditions of wage earners in industrializing America, examines the primary sources historians use to reconstruct and interpret the past. What are these sources? What do historians do with them? What can historians determine from them?

With a basic understanding of the nature and usefulness of primary sources, we proceed in Chapter 3 for a closer evaluation. This chapter on late-nineteenth-century efforts to reform the Indians shows how careful historians must be in using primary sources. Does a source speak with one voice or with many? How can historians disagree about the meaning of the same historical facts? By carefully evaluating primary sources in this chapter, you can draw your own conclusions about the nature of these Indian reform efforts. You can also better understand how historians often derive different conclusions from the same body of material.

Chapter 3 is good preparation for the evaluation in Chapter 4 of one historian's argument about the decision to annex the Philippines after the Spanish-American War. In this chapter you can begin to use primary sources to reach a conclusion about a historian's argument. Inasmuch as historians still disagree about the American decision to establish an overseas empire, the essay and the primary sources in this chapter provide another opportunity to see how subjective historical interpretation can be.

One of the most important sources of disagreement among historians is the question of motivation. What drove people to do what they did in the past? The good historian, like the detective in a murder mystery, eventually asks that question. Chapter 5 illustrates the importance of motivation by examining what was behind the promotion of a new housing style in the early twentieth century known as the bungalow. That topic also demonstrates that historians often look in some unlikely places to understand the past.

Motives in history are, of course, related to ideas, the subject of Chapter 6. What power do ideas exert in history? What is their relationship, for example, to the motives examined in the previous chapter? In Chapter 6 we try to answer these questions by examining the role of ideology in closing the doors to large-scale immigration in the early twentieth century.

Chapter 7 turns from the influence of ideas in the past to the influence of a single individual. In this chapter we examine the activities of Eleanor Roosevelt as First Lady. Few First Ladies were more admired, or hated. What can historians learn about an era by focusing on one prominent individual like Eleanor Roosevelt? In the past, many historians believed that history was nothing more than the biography of great people. How much can students of history learn about the past by looking at it this way, that is, "from the top down"? How much do they miss by doing so? Such questions are, of course, related to the topics of previous chapters: historical evidence, motivation, and the influence of ideas.

The next chapter examines history from the opposite perspective—"from the bottom up." What can historians learn by looking at the people at the bottom of a society? What challenges face historians who try? During World War II, a good place for looking at history this way is in the slums of Detroit, one of America's greatest war-production centers. Chapter 8 examines the race riot that occurred there in 1943. We will see who the rioters were and why their lives are important to historians.

Having considered the questions of motivation and ideas in history and examined the past from different perspectives, in Chapter 9 we look at the impact of anticommunist hysteria on postwar popular culture. Aside from the question of causation, this chapter considers the problems historians face when they try to trace the influence of one large force in history. As we shall see, this often requires historians to synthesize, that is, to combine small pieces into a large picture.

Chapter 9 examines the influences shaping popular culture. The next chapter, on the civil rights movement, looks at the way popular culture can influence our views of the past. As with many episodes from the recent American past, popular memories of this movement have been shaped by images conveyed by the media. Those images, however, may distort our view of the past. Often, historians attempt to make more accurate assessments of an event by relying on the accounts of those involved in them. Doing so usually requires that researchers synthesize many *individual* memories into an accurate and coherent *collective* memory. And, as we shall see, using the accounts of many people who participated in such a broad movement again illustrates that the past looks different depending on whether it is presented from the "bottom up" or the "top down."

Many of the preceding chapters have used a single historical essay and an accompanying set of primary sources to examine problems of evidence, motivation, ideology, causation, grand forces, and writing of history from both the "top down" and the "bottom up." The next chapter offers an opportunity to pull together the lessons of previous chapters. Chapter 11 compares what two historians have written about a single topic, the war in Vietnam. We will consider the way the United States fought this war, historians' explanations for the way it turned out, and the lessons they draw from the experience. This requires that we examine the actions of a small but influential set of individuals as well as the attitudes of many ordinary Americans. Thus explaining America's biggest military loss enables us to consider, in a single topic, such questions as motivation, the role of grand historical forces, and the role of the individual in history.

The goal of Chapter 12 is similar to that of Chapter 11: a synthesis, or pulling together, of lessons learned in preceding chapters. Here, however, the emphasis is on the problems of historical evidence, causation, and the role of ideology. Chapter 12 contains two essays on the rise of the women's movement in the 1960s and 1970s and a small collection of primary sources. It asks you to compare and analyze conflicting arguments, using not only primary sources but also insights drawn from previous chapters.

All of the chapters in this volume have a common purpose: to encourage you to think more like a historian and to sharpen your critical thinking skills. Chapter 13 returns to a point emphasized throughout this volume: The pursuit of the past cannot occur apart from a consideration of historical interpretation, and differences in historical interpretation matter not just to historians but to everyone. This final chapter examines differing interpretations about the impact of multiculturalism. It contains two accounts of multiculturalism's significance and primary documents that illuminate both interpretations. In addition, it underscores the way our view of the past can be used to justify policies and practices in a later time.

By the end of this volume, you will have sharpened your ability to think about the past. You will think more critically about the use of historical evidence and about such historical problems as motivation, causation, and interpretation. Moreover, by exploring several styles of historical writing and various avenues to the past—from approaches that emphasize politics or economics to those that highlight social developments or military strategy—you will come to understand better, not only the historian's craft, but also the importance of the past. In short, you will think more like a historian.

Chapter
1

Historians and Textbooks:
The "Story" of Reconstruction

The textbook selections in this chapter illustrate different assumptions about the meaning of post–Civil War Reconstruction history.

Sources

1. Reconstruction (1906), THOMAS W. WILSON
2. The Negro in Reconstruction (1922), CARTER WOODSON
3. The Ordeal of Reconstruction (1966), THOMAS A. BAILEY
4. Reconstruction: An Unfinished Revolution (2001), MARY BETH NORTON ET AL.

*I*n one of the most memorable scenes in movie history, Rhett Butler tells Scarlett O'Hara that he's leaving her. When Scarlett asks what she will do, Rhett answers, "Frankly, my dear, I don't give a damn." It was the climax of *Gone with the Wind,* starring Clark Gable as Rhett and Vivian Leigh as Scarlett. The David O. Selznick film, based on a best-selling novel, was the biggest picture of 1939.

The film's success should have surprised no one. It had all the right elements: strong-willed characters, tempestuous romance, a deathbed scene that left audiences in tears, and courageous people struggling to rebuild lives and fortunes destroyed by war. Yet *Gone with the Wind* also offered an enduring image of life in the Old South and of Reconstruction's "dark days." On the O'Hara plantation, "chivalrous" whites and their loyal ex-slaves confronted "cruel and vicious" Yankee carpetbaggers in cahoots with "traitorous" scalawags. It was a theme that made sense to mostly white movie audiences in 1939. As early as 1915, D. W. Griffith's silent film *The Birth of a Nation* had told the story of the Ku Klux Klan's violent but "valiant" efforts to throw off "carpetbag" rule. Like Griffith's tale, *Gone with the Wind* found a sympathetic audience because it reflected their racial prejudices. As historical drama, it also fit comfortably with what they had learned in school, specifically, with interpretations imparted from history textbooks.

This chapter examines what some twentieth-century textbooks have taught Americans about Reconstruction. We will see if these books always contain the same past or if they, like such powerful movies as *The Birth of a Nation* and *Gone with the Wind,* reflect the biases of their producers. When done, you can judge how well *Gone with the Wind*'s picture of Reconstruction corresponds with those presented in textbooks today.

SETTING

Moviegoers in 1939 may have remembered producer David O. Selznick's name splashed across the screen. Far fewer recalled the author of their American history textbook. More likely than not it was David S. Muzzey, whose *American History* (1911) and *History of the American People* (1927) were bestsellers by the 1930s. Among the most enduring American history textbooks, these books probably taught several generations of Americans more about their nation's past than any other book. If audiences had learned anything about Reconstruction before *Gone with the Wind*'s opening credits, it was probably Muzzey who had taught them.

Muzzey had plenty to say about Reconstruction, and in no uncertain terms. The Republican governments established under congressional Reconstruction he judged to be "sorry affairs." The government "of the negro [*sic*] and his unscrupulous carpetbagger and scalawag patrons was an orgy of extravagance, fraud, and disgusting incompetence." Muzzey, a New Englander, was sympathetic to the efforts of Southerners to "redeem" their states from "negro [*sic*] and carpetbagger rule." Although he called white Southerners' use of violence against black voters "exasperating," their response was understandable. "Congress," he asserted, "did [Southern states] an unpardonable injury by hastening to reconstruct them on the basis of negro [*sic*] suffrage."[1] In short, his view of Reconstruction was that of the white Redeemers themselves.

Muzzey, of course, did not invent this "Redeemer" view of Reconstruction. How, then, had he come to these conclusions? It is impossible to be certain about the intellectual influences on this Columbia University professor. Yet we do know that two other Columbia historians had already written sympathetically about the white South's plight under congressional Reconstruction. Ex-confederate John W. Burgess was an advocate of "Nordic" racial supremacy and the "white man's burden." In *Reconstruction and the Constitution* (1902), he declared that blacks failed to subject "passion to reason." Reconstruction thus put "barbarism in power over civilization."[2] William A. Dunning, a Northerner, agreed. His Reconstruction history was peopled with corrupt carpetbaggers and blacks pursuing "vicious" policies. White Southerners had little choice but to fight back. "All the forces [in the South] that made for civilization," Dunning asserted, "were dominated by a mass of barbarous freedmen."[3]

Burgess and Dunning played a crucial role in transmitting a Southern view of Reconstruction into classrooms nationwide. At Columbia they trained several generations of historians, who wrote more books and trained still other historians. By the time *Gone with the Wind* captivated many moviegoers, the struggle for the hearts and minds of high school and college students was already over. Although a few black historians dissented, most notably W. E. B. Du Bois, the South had triumphed in the historical battle over the theory of Reconstruction. Rather than a new view of the past, *Gone with the Wind* offered white audiences a reassuring version of the past that had been embedded in the popular mind for several decades. In 1939, Hollywood ensured that it would endure for several more.

INVESTIGATION

This chapter contains four selections from American history textbooks published in the twentieth and twenty-first centuries. The first was published in 1906 and the last in 2001. Your primary assignment is to determine how these accounts of Reconstruction differ from one another and which one is most accurate. As you read them, keep in mind the questions that the authors attempt to answer about Reconstruction. These questions, mostly unstated, are not necessarily the same. Also, be careful to note the most important facts of Reconstruction that each presents and the meaning each assigns to them. To see more clearly how these textbook selections differ from one another, it would be helpful to write down brief answers to the following questions as you read each account:

1. **What is the author's view of the integrity and effectiveness of those involved in the Republican governments in the Southern states?** Is the view of the "carpetbaggers" and "scalawags" positive, negative, or neutral?

2. **What is the author's view of blacks?** Is the author's analysis of Reconstruction based on racial assumptions about the character of the freedmen? Are blacks passive or active participants in shaping Reconstruction and their own lives?

3. **What is the author's view of the overturning of Reconstruction?** Is the seizure of power by white Southerners a welcome or regrettable development? What is the author's view of such terrorist organizations as the Ku Klux Klan?

Before you begin, read your own textbook's discussion of Reconstruction. When you are finished, you should be able to explain how these selections differ, which one is closest to the interpretation in your own text, and which one is most plausible.

SOURCES

Reconstruction (1906)

THOMAS W. WILSON

Adventurers swarmed out of the North to cozen, beguile, and use . . . them [negroes]. These men, mere "carpet baggers" for the most part, who brought nothing with them, and had nothing to bring, but a change of clothing and their wits, became the new masters of the blacks. They gained the confidence of the negroes, obtained for themselves the more lucrative offices, and lived upon the public treasury, public contracts, and their easy control of affairs. For the negroes there was nothing but occasional allotments of abandoned or forfeited land, the pay of petty offices, a *per diem* allowance as members of the conventions and the state legislatures which their new masters made business for, or the wages of servants in the various offices of administration. Their ignorance and credulity made them easy dupes. . . .

. . . In Mississippi, before the work of the carpet baggers was done, six

Source: Woodrow Wilson, *A History of the American People* (New York: Harper and Bros., 1906), V: pp. 46, 47–49, 58, 59, 60, 62, 98, 99.

hundred and forty thousand acres of land had been forfeited for taxes, twenty *per cent,* of the total acreage of the State. The state tax levy for 1871 was four times as great as the levy for 1869 had been; that for 1873 eight times as great; that for 1874 fourteen times. The impoverished planters could not carry the intolerable burden of taxes, and gave their lands up to be sold by the sheriff. There were few who could buy. The lands lay waste and neglected or were parcelled out at nominal rates among the negroes. . . .

Taxes, of course, did not suffice. Enormous debts were piled up to satisfy the adventurers. . . . Treasuries were swept clean. . . .

. . . The white men of the South were aroused by the mere instinct of self-preservation to rid themselves, by fair means or foul, of the intolerable burden of governments sustained by the votes of ignorant negroes and conducted in the interest of adventurers: governments whose incredible debts were incurred that thieves might be enriched, whose increasing loans and taxes went to no public use but into the pockets of party managers and corrupt contractors. . . .

They took the law into their own hands, and began to attempt by intimidation what they were not allowed to attempt by the ballot or by any ordered course of public action. They began to do by secret concert and association what they could not do in avowed parties. Almost by accident a way was found to succeed which led insensibly farther and farther afield into the ways of violence and outlawry. In May, 1866, a little group of young men in the Tennessee village of Pulaski, finding time hang heavy on their hands after the excitements of the field, so lately abandoned, formed a secret club for the mere pleasure of association, for private amusement—for anything that might promise to break the monotony of the too quiet place. . . .

. . . Year by year the organization spread, from county to county, from State to State. Every country-side wished to have its own Ku Klux, founded in secrecy and mystery like the mother "Den" at Pulaski, until at last there had sprung into existence a great *Ku Klux Klan,* an "Invisible Empire of the South," bound together in loose organization to protect the southern country from some of the ugliest hazards of a time of revolution. . . .

It was impossible to keep such a power in hand. Sober men governed the counsels and moderated the plans of those roving knights errant; but it was lawless work at best. They had set themselves, after the first year or two of mere mischievous frolic had passed, to right a disordered society through the power of fear. Men of hot passions who could not always be restrained carried their plans into effect. . . .

The reconstruction of the southern States had been the undoing of the Republican party. The course of carpet bag rule did not run smooth. Every election fixed the attention of the country upon some serious question of fraud or violence in the States where northern adventurers and negro majorities were in control. . . . Before [Ulysses S. Grant's] term was out the white voters of the

South had rallied strong enough in every State except South Carolina, Florida, and Louisiana to take their governments out of the hands of the men who were preying upon them.

2   The Negro in Reconstruction (1922)
CARTER WOODSON

Reconstruction began in the schoolhouses not in the State houses, as uninformed persons often say. . . . As the Union armies gradually invaded that area the soldiers opened schools for Negroes. Regular teachers came from relief societies and the Freedmen's Bureau. These enlightened a fair percentage of the Negroes by 1870. The illiteracy of the Negroes was reduced to 79.9 by that time. When about the same time these freedmen had a chance to participate in the rehabilitation of State governments in the South, they gave that section of the first free public school system, the first democratic education it ever had. . . .

The [majority of] other States in the South, from 1868 to about 1872, became subjected to what is commonly known as "Negro carpet-bag rule."

To call this Negro rule, however, is very much of a mistake. As a matter of fact, most of the local offices in these commonwealths were held by the white men, and those Negroes who did attain some of the higher offices were usually about as competent as the average whites thereto elected. Only twenty-three Negroes served in Congress from 1868 to 1895. The Negroes had political equality in the Southern States only a few years, and with some exceptions their tenure in Congress was very short. . . .

The charge that all Negro officers were illiterate, ignorant of the science of government, cannot be sustained. In the first place, the education of the Negro by Union soldiers in the South began in spots as early as 1861. Many of the Negro leaders who had been educated in the North or abroad returned to the South after the war. Negro illiteracy had been reduced to 79.9 by 1870, just about the time the freedmen were actually participating in the reconstruction. The masses of Negroes did not take a part in the government in the beginning of the reconstruction.

It is true that many of them were not prepared to vote, and decidedly disqualified for the positions which they held. In some of the legislatures, as in Louisiana and South Carolina, more than half of the Negro members could scarcely read or write. They, therefore, had to vote according to emotions or the dictates of the demagogues. This, of course, has been true of legislatures composed entirely of whites. In the local and State administrative offices, how-

Source: Carter G. Woodson and Charles H. Wesley, *The Negro in Our History* (Washington, D.C.: The Associated Publishers, Inc., 1962). Excerpted by permission of the Association for the Study of African American Life and History, Inc.

ever, where there were frequent chances for corruption, very few ignorant Negroes ever served. . . .

Most of the local, State and Federal offices, however, were held not by Negroes but by southern white men, and by others who came from the North and profited by the prostration of the South. They were in many respects selfish men, but not always utterly lacking in principle. The northern whites, of course, had little sympathy for the South. They depended for their constituency upon the Negroes, who could not be expected to placate the ex-slaveholders. Being adventurers and interested in their own affairs, the carpet-baggers became unusually corrupt in certain States. They administered affairs selfishly. Most Negro officers who served in the South came out of office with an honorable record. . . .

Reconstruction history, however, was distorted by J. W. Burgess, a slaveholder of Giles County, Tennessee, who was educated in the North and finally attained distinction as a teacher and writer at Columbia University; and by W. A. Dunning, the son of an industrialist of Plainfield, New Jersey, who became the disciple of Burgess. The two trained or influenced in the same biased way the sons and sympathizers of former slaveholders who prostituted modern historiography to perpetuate the same distortion. These pseudo-historians refused to use the evidence of those who opposed slavery, discredited the testimony of those who favored Congressional Reconstruction, and ignored the observations of travellers from the North and from Europe. These makers of history to order were more partial than required by the law of slavery, for they rejected the evidence from Negro sources and thus denied the Negro not only the opportunity to testify against the white man but even to testify in favor of himself. . . .

Wherever they could, the native whites instituted government by investigation to expose all shortcomings of Negro officials. The general charge was that they were corrupt. The very persons who complained of the corruption in the Negro carpet-bag governments and who effected the reorganization of the State governments in the South when the Negroes were overthrown, however, became just as corrupt as the governing class under the preceding régime. In almost every restored State government in the South, and especially in Mississippi, the white officers in control of the funds defaulted. These persons who had been so long out of office came back so eager to get the most out of it that they filled their own pockets from the coffers of the public. No exposure followed. . . .

The attack on the policies of the carpet-bag governments, moreover, had the desired effect among the poor and ignorant whites. Reared under the degrading influences of slavery, they could not tolerate the blacks as citizens. The Negroes thereafter were harassed and harried by disturbing elements of anarchy, out of which soon emerged an oath-bound order called the Ku Klux Klan, established to terrorize the Negroes with lawlessness and violence.

3 The Ordeal of Reconstruction (1966)
THOMAS A. BAILEY

Enfranchised Freedmen

The sudden thrusting of the ballot unto the hands of the ex-slaves, between 1867 and 1870, set the stage for stark tragedy. As might have been foreseen, it was a blunder hardly less serious than thrusting overnight freedom upon them. Wholesale liberation was probably unavoidable, given the feverish conditions created by war. But wholesale suffrage was avoidable, except insofar as the Radicals found it necessary for their own ends, both selfish and idealistic.

The bewildered Negroes were poorly prepared for their new responsibilities as citizens and voters. Democracy is a delicate mechanism, which requires education and information. Yet about nine-tenths of the 700,000 adult Negro males were illiterate. When registering, many did not know their ages; and boys of sixteen signed the rolls. Some of these voters could not even give their last name, if indeed they had any. Bob, Quash, Christmas, Scipio, Nebuchadnezzar would take any surname that popped into their heads, often that of "massa." Sometimes they chose more wisely than they knew. On the voting lists of Charleston, South Carolina, there were forty-six George Washingtons and sixty-three Abraham Lincolns.

The tale would be amusing were it not so pathetic and tragic. After the Negroes were told to come in for registration, many appeared with boxes or baskets, thinking that registration was some new kind of food or drink. Others would mark their ballots and then carefully deposit them in mail boxes.

While these pitiable practices were going on, thousands of the ablest Southern whites were being denied the vote, either by act of Congress or by the new state constitutions. . . .

Enthroned Ignorance

Some of the new Southern legislatures created in 1867–1870, not unlike some Northern legislatures, presented bizarre scenes. They were dominated by newly arrived carpetbaggers, despised scalawags, and pliant Negroes. Some of the ex-bondsmen were remarkably well educated, but many others were illiterate. In a few of the states the colored legislators constituted a strong minority. In once-haughty South Carolina, the tally stood at 88 Negroes to 67 whites; and ex-slaves held offices ranging from speaker to doorkeeper. Negroes who had been raising cotton under the lash of the overseer were now raising points of order under the gavel of the speaker. As a Negro song ran:

Source: Thomas A. Bailey, *The American Pageant*, 3rd ed., pp. 475, 476–478. Copyright © 1966 by D. C. Heath and Company. By permission of Houghton Mifflin Company.

De bottom rail's on de top
And we's gwine to keep it dar.

Greatly to their credit, these Negro-white legislatures passed much desirable legislation and introduced many overdue reforms. In some states a better tax system was created, state charities were established, public works were launched, property rights were guaranteed to women, and free public schools were encouraged—for Negroes as well as whites. Some of these reforms were so welcome that they were retained, along with the more enlightened state constitutions, when the Southern whites finally strong-armed their way back into control.

But the good legislation, unhappily, was often obscured by a carnival of corruption and misrule. Graft and theft ran wild, especially in states like South Carolina and Louisiana, where designing whites used naive Negroes as cats-paws. The worst black-and-tan legislatures purchased, under "legislative supplies," such items as hams, perfumes, suspenders, bonnets, corsets, champagne, and a coffin. One "thrifty" carpetbag governor in a single year "saved" $100,000 from a salary of $8000.

The public debt of the Southern states doubled and trebled, as irresponsible carpetbag legislatures voted appropriations and bond issues with light-hearted abandon. Burdensome taxes were passed in Mississippi, where some 6,000,000 acres were sold for delinquent taxes. The disfranchised and propertied whites had to stagger along under a tax burden that sometimes rose ten or fifteenfold. . . .

One should also note that during this hectic era corruption was also rampant in the North, among Republicans as well as Democrats. The notorious Tweed Ring of New York City probably stole more millions, though with greater sophistication, than the worst of the carpetbag legislatures combined. And when the Southern whites regained the whip hand, graft by no means disappeared under Democratic auspices.

The Rule of Night Riders

Goaded to desperation, once-decent Southern whites resorted to savage measures against Negro-carpetbag control. A number of secret organizations blossomed forth, the most notorious of which was the Ku Klux Klan, founded in Tennessee in 1866. Besheeted night riders, their horses' hoofs muffled, would hammer on the cabin door of a politically ambitious Negro. In ghoulish tones one thirsty horseman would demand a bucket of water, pour it into a rubber attachment under pretense of drinking, smack his lips, and declare that this was the first water he had tasted since he was killed at the battle of Shiloh. If fright did not produce the desired effect, force was employed.

Such tomfoolery and terror proved partially effective. Many Negroes and carpetbaggers, quick to take a hint, were scared away from the polls. But those stubborn souls who persisted in their forward ways were flogged, mutilated, or even murdered. In one Louisiana parish in 1868, the whites in two days killed or wounded two hundred victims; a pile of twenty-five bodies was found half-buried in the woods. By such atrocious practices was the Negro "kept in his place."

4 Reconstruction: An Unfinished Revolution (2001)
MARY BETH NORTON ET AL.

Reconstruction Politics in the South

From the start, Reconstruction encountered the resistance of white southerners. In the black codes and in private attitudes, many whites stubbornly opposed emancipation, and the former planter class proved especially unbending. In 1866 a Georgia newspaper frankly observed that "most of the white citizens believe that the institution of slavery was right, and . . . they will believe that the condition, which comes nearest to slavery, that can now be established will be the best."

White Resistance   Fearing loss of control over their slaves, some planters attempted to postpone freedom by denying or misrepresenting events. Former slaves reported that their owners "didn't tell them it was freedom" or "wouldn't let [them] go." Agents of the Freedmen's Bureau reported that "the old system of slavery [is] working with even more rigor than formerly at a few miles distant from any point where U.S. troops are stationed." To hold onto their workers, some landowners claimed control over black children and used guardianship and apprentice laws to bind black families to the plantation.

Whites also blocked blacks from acquiring land. A few planters divided up plots among their slaves, but most condemned the idea of making blacks landowners. A Georgia woman whose family was known for its support of religious education for slaves was outraged that two property owners planned to "rent their lands to the Negroes!" Such action was, she declared, "injurious to the best interest of the community."

Adamant resistance by propertied whites soon manifested itself in other ways, including violence. In one North Carolina town a local magistrate clubbed a black man on a public street, and bands of "Regulators" terrorized blacks in parts of that state and in Kentucky. Such incidents were predictable in a defeated society in which many planters believed, as a South Carolinian put it, that blacks "can't be governed except with the whip."

After President Johnson encouraged the South to resist congressional Reconstruction, white conservatives worked hard to capture the new state governments. Many whites also boycotted the polls in an attempt to defeat Congress's plans; by sitting out the elections, whites might block the new constitutions, which had to be approved by a majority of registered voters. This tactic was tried in North Carolina and succeeded in Alabama, forcing Congress to base ratification of the Fourteenth Amendment and of new state constitutions on a majority of "votes cast" (the provision of the Fourth Reconstruction Act).

Black Voters and Emergence of a Southern Republican Party   Very few black men stayed away from the polls. Enthusiastically and hopefully, they voted Republican. Most agreed with one man who felt he should "stick to the end with the party that freed me." Illiteracy did not prohibit blacks (or uneducated whites) from making intelligent choices. Although Mississippi's William Henry could read only "a little," he testified that he and his friends had no difficulty selecting the Republican ballot. "We stood around and watched," he explained. "We saw D. Sledge vote; he owned half the county. We knowed he voted Democratic so we voted the other ticket so it would be Republican." Women, who could not vote, encouraged their husbands and sons, and preachers exhorted their congregations to use the franchise. With such group spirit, zeal for voting spread through the entire black community.

Thanks to a large black turnout and the restrictions on prominent Confederates, a new southern Republican Party came to power in the constitutional conventions of 1868–1870. Republican delegates consisted of a sizable contingent of blacks (265 out of the total of just over 1,000 delegates throughout the South), some northerners who had moved to the South, and native southern whites who favored change. Together these Republicans brought the South into line with progressive reforms adopted earlier in the rest of the nation. The new constitutions were more democratic. They eliminated property qualifications for voting and holding office, and they turned many appointed offices into elective posts. They provided for public schools and institutions to care for the mentally ill, the blind, the deaf, the destitute, and the orphaned. . . .

The Myth of "Negro Rule"   Within a few years, as centrists in both parties met with failure, white hostility to congressional Reconstruction began to dominate. Some conservatives had always desired to fight Reconstruction through pressure and racist propaganda. They put economic and social pressure on blacks: one black Republican reported that "my neighbors will not employ me, nor sell me a farthing's worth of anything." Charging that the South had been turned over to ignorant blacks, conservatives deplored "black domination," which became a rallying cry for a return to white supremacy.

Such attacks were inflammatory propaganda, and part of the growing myth of "Negro rule," which would serve as a central theme in battles over the memory of Reconstruction. African Americans participated in politics but hardly dominated or controlled events. They were a majority in only two out of ten state constitutional writing conventions (transplanted northerners were a majority in one). In the state legislatures, only in the lower house in South Carolina did blacks ever constitute a majority; among officeholders, their numbers generally were far fewer than their proportion in the population. Sixteen blacks won seats in Congress before Reconstruction was over, but none was ever elected governor. Only eighteen served in a high state office such as lieutenant governor, treasurer, superintendent of education, or secretary of state. In all, some four hundred blacks served in political office during the Reconstruction era. Although they never dominated the process, they established a rich tradition of government service and civic activism. Elected officials, such as Robert Smalls in South Carolina, labored tirelessly for cheaper land prices, better healthcare, access to schools, and the enforcement of civil rights for their people. The black politicians of Reconstruction are lost in the mists, the forgotten heroes of this seedtime of America's long civil rights movement.

Carpetbaggers and Scalawags   Conservatives also assailed the allies of black Republicans. Their propaganda denounced whites from the North as "carpetbaggers," greedy crooks planning to pour stolen tax revenues into their sturdy luggage made of carpet material. Immigrants from the North, who held the largest share of Republican offices, were all tarred with this brush.

In fact, most northerners who settled in the South had come seeking business opportunities or a warmer climate and never entered politics. Those who did enter politics generally wanted to democratize the South and to introduce northern ways, such as industry, public education, and the spirit of enterprise. Carpetbaggers' ideals were tested by hard times and ostracism by white southerners.

In addition to tagging northern interlopers as carpetbaggers, Conservatives invented the term "scalawag" to discredit any native white southerner who cooperated with the Republicans. A substantial number of southerners did so, including some wealthy and prominent men. Most scalawags, however, were yeoman farmers, men from mountain areas and nonslaveholding districts who had been restive under the Confederacy. They saw that they could benefit from the education and opportunities promoted by Republicans. Banding together with freedmen, they pursued common class interests and hoped to make headway against the power of long-dominant planters. Cooperation even convinced a few scalawags that "there is but little if any difference in the talents of the two races," as one observed, and that all should have "an equal start." Yet this black-white coalition was vulnerable to the race issue, and most scalawags did not support racial equality. Republican tax policies also cut into upcountry yeoman support because reliance on the property tax hit many small landholders hard.

Tax Policy and Corruption as Political Wedges   Taxation was a major problem for the Reconstruction governments. Republicans wanted to maintain prewar services, repair the war's destruction, stimulate industry, and support important new ventures such as public schools. But the Civil War had destroyed much of the South's tax base. One category of valuable property—slaves—had disappeared entirely. And hundreds of thousands of citizens had lost much of the rest of their property—money, livestock, fences, and buildings—to the war. Thus an increase in taxes was necessary even to maintain traditional services, and new ventures required still higher taxes. Inevitably, Republican tax policies aroused strong opposition, especially among the yeomen.

Corruption was another serious charge levied against the Republicans. Unfortunately, it often was true. Many carpetbaggers and black politicians engaged in fraudulent schemes, sold their votes, or padded expenses, taking part in what scholars recognize was a nationwide surge of corruption in an age ruled by "spoilsmen." Corruption carried no party label, but the Democrats successfully pinned the blame on unqualified blacks and greedy carpetbaggers among southern Republicans.

Ku Klux Klan   All these problems hurt the Republicans, whose leaders also allowed factionalism along racial and class lines to undermine party unity. But in many southern states the deathblow came through violence. The Ku Klux Klan, a secret veterans' club that began in Tennessee in 1866, spread through the South and rapidly evolved into a terrorist organization. Violence against African Americans occurred from the first days of Reconstruction but became far more organized and purposeful after 1867. Klansmen rode to frustrate Reconstruction and keep the freedmen in subjection. Nighttime harassment, whippings, beatings, and murder became common, and terrorism dominated some counties and regions. . . .

Klan violence injured Republicans across the South. No fewer than one-tenth of the black leaders who had been delegates to the 1867–1868 state constitutional conventions were attacked, seven fatally. In one judicial district of North Carolina the Ku Klux Klan was responsible for twelve murders, over seven hundred beatings, and other acts of violence, including rape and arson. A single attack on Alabama Republicans in the town of Eutaw left four blacks dead and fifty-four wounded. In South Carolina five hundred masked Klansmen lynched eight black prisoners at the Union County jail, and in nearby York County the Klan committed at least eleven murders and hundreds of whippings. According to historian Eric Foner, the Klan "made it virtually impossible for Republicans to campaign or vote in large parts of Georgia."

Failure of Reconstruction   Thus a combination of difficult fiscal problems, Republican mistakes, racial hostility, and terror brought down the Republican regimes. In most southern states, "Radical Reconstruction" lasted only a few years. The most enduring failure of Reconstruction, however, was not political; it was social and economic. Reconstruction failed to alter the South's social structure or its distribution of wealth and power. Without land of their own, freed men and women were dependent on white landowners who could and did use their economic power to compromise blacks' political freedom. Armed only with the ballot, freed men in the South had little chance to effect major changes.

CONCLUSION

These discussions of Reconstruction should make it clear that history textbooks contain interpretations. They are no different from other historical writing in that regard. Modern texts are also written by people with biases and opinions, although their interpretations may be as difficult to spot today as Muzzey's were for his students. In part that's because historians often do not reveal their most important assumptions, as the selection from *The American Pageant,* another best-selling American history textbook, demonstrates. The original author, Stanford University historian Thomas A. Bailey, approached his task in much the same spirit as Muzzey; he wrote history as a lively story, with the accomplishments of prominent people giving direction to the narrative. Behind this approach was the unspoken assumption that the lives of people at the bottom of the society mattered less than the bold actions of diplomats, generals, and politicians. Moreover, Bailey wrote *The American Pageant* before the growing civil rights protests began to assault legal segregation and the racial attitudes that upheld it. Thus the earlier editions of *The American Pageant* reflect the continuing hold of the Dunning view of Reconstruction. On the other hand, Mary Beth Norton and the other authors of *A People and a Nation* are of the generation of scholars who came of age in the 1960s. Not only do many of these historians incorporate ordinary people into their accounts, but their racial assumptions differ from those of most historians earlier in the twentieth century.

It is usually easier to spot interpretations in older textbooks because their authors do not share our premises. The first textbook selection, written with an unquestioned assumption of black inferiority, is a good example. Its author, Thomas W. Wilson, was probably as unfamiliar to you as were William Dunning and David Muzzey. He is better known today as Woodrow Wilson, the Princeton historian who later became the twenty-eighth president of the United States. If Wilson's text reflects the racist assumptions at the heart of the triumphant Southern view of Reconstruction, the second selection reveals that not all historians accepted this dominant view, even in the early twentieth century. Its author, Carter Woodson, was a Virginia-born African American who earned a Ph.D. from Harvard University in 1912. Like the work of fellow Harvard-trained black historian W. E. B. Du Bois, Woodson's *The Negro in Our History* and his other Negro history textbooks were largely ignored by white historians and students. In its own way, of course, Woodson's text also demonstrates the importance of racial assumptions in shaping interpretations about Reconstruction. It also illustrates that historians are more than mouthpieces for the dominant views of their day.

Together, all of these texts remind us that Americans' social views have not remained frozen since the early twentieth century. And although the questions historians ask are not entirely dependent on whatever social views happen to be popular, historians are surely influenced by their times. However, these selections also make clear that historians do not simply mirror what happened in the past but instead give meaning to the "facts" of history. To do that, they study primary sources—the materials left to us by people in the past. We turn to them next.

FURTHER READING

W. E. B. Du Bois, *Black Reconstruction* (New York: Russell and Russell, 1935).
Frances FitzGerald, *America Revised: History Schoolbooks in the Twentieth Century* (New York: Random House, 1979).
Eric Foner, *A Short History of Reconstruction, 1863–1977* (New York: Harper and Row, 1990).
James W. Loewen, *Lies My Teacher Told Me: Everything Your American History Textbook Got Wrong* (New York: The New Press, 1995).

NOTES

1. David Saville Muzzey, *History of the American People* (New York: Ginn and Company, 1935), pp. 408, 410.
2. John W. Burgess, *Reconstruction and the Constitution, 1866–1876* (New York: Da Capo Press, 1970; reprint of 1902 edition), p. viii.
3. William A. Dunning, *Reconstruction, Political and Economic* (New York: Harper and Brothers, 1907), p. 212.

Chapter

2

Using Primary Sources: Industrialization and the Condition of Labor

This chapter introduces primary sources. The documents presented give information on nineteenth-century working conditions.

Sources

1. Testimony of Workingmen (1879)
2. "Earnings, Expenses and Conditions of Workingmen and Their Families" (1884)
3. Wages in the Iron and Steel Industry, 1858–1900
4. Price Indexes, 1866–1890
5. Why We Struck at Pullman (1895)
6. Colored Workmen and a Strike (1887)
7. Women Make Demands (1869)
8. Summary of Conditions Among Women Workers Found by the Massachusetts Bureau of Labor (1887)
9. Work in a Garment Factory (1902)
10. Gainful Workers by Age, 1870–1920
11. Breaker Boys (1906), JOHN SPARGO
12. Night Shift in a Glass Factory (1906)

*I*n 1873 a financial panic sparked a severe depression. Four years later business was still stagnant, and, with unemployment at perhaps one million, working people grew restless. In Pennsylvania's coal mining regions the militia was called on repeatedly to keep order. Then in 1877 wage cuts and layoffs on the railroads exploded into a paralyzing railroad strike. After the violent confrontation was over, many people lay dead, millions of dollars of property had been destroyed, and dazed Americans stared at the specter of class warfare.

In 1878 Congress appointed a committee to investigate the causes of the "General Depression in Labor and Business." One of the witnesses called to testify was the Yale University professor William Graham Sumner. Sumner was a proponent of what would be known as Social Darwinism, a theory that applied Darwin's theories of evolution to society in an attempt to justify uncontrolled economic competition. Sumner later shared his views about the "survival of the fittest" through books and a stream of popular magazine articles. Now, he responded to Congress with answers that many middle-class Americans found reassuring. When asked by one congressman what effect the spread of machinery had on workers, Sumner admitted that they suffered a loss of income and "a loss of comfort." Asked if there was any way to help, Sumner responded, "not at all." And when pressed to admit that there was "distress among the laboring classes," Sumner shot back, "I do not admit any such thing. I cannot see any evidence of it."[1]

Many of Sumner's contemporaries eagerly embraced his conclusion that industrialization caused no real suffering. Yet it would be foolish for us to do so. Instead, we can rely on a wide variety of primary sources—the historical evidence and artifacts that survive from the past—to understand the ways industrialization influenced the lives of workers. Without them, historians are at the mercy of other people's interpretations of the past. With them, they can make direct contact with the past. In this chapter, therefore, we turn to these sources to examine the same question about the "laboring classes" posed to William Graham Sumner in 1878.

SETTING

Historians who study workers in the late nineteenth century have a wealth of primary sources. They include "literary" or *written* sources, *statistical* sources relating to such information as wages and the cost of living, and such *nonwritten* sources as sketches and photographs. Many of these sources are available because a variety of bureaus, commissions, and committees in the late nineteenth century began to investigate the effects of industrial growth on labor. By the 1880s, for instance, a number of states had set up bureaus of labor statistics to assess the living and working conditions of wage earners. In 1884, Congress established the Bureau of Labor, which two years later began to issue annual reports related to the conditions of workers. At about the same time, the U.S. Senate issued a five-volume *Report upon the Relations Between Capital and Labor.* In addition, in 1901 and 1902 its Industrial Commission produced a massive report on the effects of industrial growth. Meanwhile, other investigators also began to produce valuable sources. Often armed with only pens and cameras, such reformers as Jacob Riis, Lewis Hine, John Spargo, and Upton Sinclair recorded the conditions in the industrial workplace at the turn of the century. The *Atlantic Monthly, Independent, Outlook,* and other popular magazines also published articles on the living and working conditions of laborers. Added to these sources are newspaper accounts, diaries, songs, and documents from such organizations as charities, labor unions, corporations, and business associations. In short, the sources reflecting the condition of labor in industrial America are as varied as they are numerous.

INVESTIGATION

The main problem we investigate in this chapter is the question posed to William Graham Sumner in the congressional investigation in 1878: Was there "distress" among the "laboring classes" as the United States industrialized in the late nineteenth century? That question is a very broad one, and, given the abundance of primary sources, it might seem easy to answer. Yet it is not. First, by 1900 there were more than 13 million nonagricultural wage earners in the United States, and their working conditions varied greatly. Second, we must define *distress* and determine whether our definition is the same as that of industrial wage earners themselves. We need to know the "objective" conditions as defined by wages, hours of labor, and cost of living, as well as what people at the time thought about them. That might depend, in turn, on workers' expectations. The question Sumner answered with such certainty is thus more complicated than it first appears. A good answer must be based on a careful consideration of the evidence. It should also address the following questions:

1. **Overall, do conditions appear to be improving or getting worse?** What important qualifications must be made to any generalizations about the conditions of workers? Do these qualifications involve certain groups or classes of workers?

2. **What do workers think about their conditions?** Which sources are especially valuable in understanding what it was like to be a wage earner in the late nineteenth century? Are some of the sources more biased than others?

3. **Many late-nineteenth-century commentators like William Graham Sumner argued that it was not the role of government to improve the condition of the working classes. The claim of some writers that employers treated workers as a mere commodity, Sumner also asserted, was "ludicrous" in the "cold light of reason." Do you agree?** What does the "cold light" of your reason applied to this evidence suggest to you about the validity of Sumner's assertions?

Before you begin, read the sections in your textbook on the condition of labor in the late nineteenth century and its response to industrial growth. See if you can detect a point of view regarding the living and working conditions of industrial workers.

SOURCES

1   In 1878 the Massachusetts Bureau of the Statistics of Labor sent a questionnaire to working men and women throughout the state to solicit their opinions about their own work. According to the report, many of the respondents "expressed themselves at length upon some phase of the labor question."[2] Does this report show that workers were content or unhappy with their jobs? What were their primary complaints?

Testimony of Workingmen (1879)

Hours of Labor

From a Carpet-Mill Operative   I am satisfied with sixty hours a week: it is plenty time for any man, although there are some employed in the same place over that time, and get nothing extra for it. I know of one young man under age who was absent two Saturday afternoons, and his overseer gave him his bill on Monday morning when he went in. If there is any inspector of the ten-hour law, he would do well to call round, and see for himself.

From a Shoemaker   I think there ought to be an eight-hour law all over the country. There is not enough work to last the year round, and work over eight hours a day, or forty-eight hours a week. There can be only about so much work to do any way: and, when that is done, business has got to stop, or keep dragging the year round, so that a man has to work for almost any price offered; when, if there was an eight-hour law, things would be more even, and

Source: John A. Garraty, *The Transformation of American Society, 1870–1890* (Columbia: University of South Carolina Press, 1968). Reprinted by permission of the University of South Carolina Press.

a man could get what his labor was worth, according to the price of living, and there would be plenty of work for all, and business would be good the year round. . . .

Overwork

From a Harness-Maker   In answer to the question, "Do you consider yourself overworked?" I answered, "Yes"; and it is my honest and firm conviction that I am, by at least two hours a day. With the great increase in machinery within the last fifteen or twenty years, I think, in justice, there ought to be some reduction in the hours of labor. Unless the hours of labor are shortened in proportion to the increase of machinery, I consider machinery an injury rather than a benefit to humanity. I tell you that ten hours a day, hard, steady work, is more than any man can stand for any length of time without injuring his health, and therefore shortening his life. For my own part, although my work is not very laborious, when I stop work in the evening, I feel completely played out. I would like to study some; but I am too fatigued. In fact it is as much as I can do to look over the evening paper; and I am almost certain that this is the condition of a majority of workingmen. . . .

From a Quarryman   In filling this blank, there are a good many questions which I did not answer relative to men with families; but, however, I would say, on behalf of married men in this locality, that they are poorly situated, working hard eleven and a half hours a day for $1.25 in summer, and 80 cents a day in winter, and obliged to purchase merchandise in company stores, and pay enormous rents for tenements. Merchandise being thirty per cent above market price, and being paid monthly, they are obliged to purchase at supply store; if not, they will be discharged, and starvation is the result. It is ridiculous in a free country that the laws are not more stringent, whereby the capitalist cannot rule and ruin his white slaves. I would draw your attention carefully to this matter, and I lay before you all truth, not hearsay, but from experience, I am a single man, and I would not be so if times were better than they are now. . . .

From a Machinist   In reply to your question concerning overwork, I wish to say, that, in employment requiring close application of mind or body, to be successful, the diligent and conscientious workman often, I might say always, finds his energy exhausted long before his ten hours are up. Then he is obliged to keep up an appearance to get the pay for his day's work, which he might do in eight hours as well as ten. If we are to have our pay by the hour, I should not advocate the eight-hour system. I think the employer would be the gainer, and the employé the loser. In the shop I work a little less than ten hours. To do that I have to leave home at 5:30 A.M., and arrive home again at

7 P.M.; so you see it makes a pretty long day. I travel not less than thirty-four miles daily, and pay $28.50 per quarter for car-fare. If I want to have a garden, I must do the work nights, or hire it done. I do not think I should be able to follow up work in this way until the age of sixty-five. Hope to find some way to avoid some of the long hours and some of the heavy work before then. I do not mean to complain; but it does seem as if the burdens and the pleasures of this world were very unequally divided. It is a hard matter to say what is right in every case. If my answers and statements should be of any service in improving the condition, prospects, or possibilities of the toiling thousands in our State, I shall be well paid for the same. . . .

The Use of Machinery

From a Boot and Shoe Cutter   Tax machinery. Bring it in common with hand labor, so a man can have twelve months' work in a year, instead of six or eight months. Protect hand labor, same as we protect trade from Europe, by tax or tariff.

From a Machinist   Machinery and the swarms of cheap foreign labor are fast rendering trades useless, and compelling the better class of mechanics to change their occupation, or go to farming. . . .

Habits of Industry

From a Shoe-Cutter   There is no way I think I could be paid more fairly than I now am. I do not consider that my employers profit unfairly by my labor. My labor is in the market for sale. My employers buy it just as they buy a side of leather, and expect, and I think are willing to pay, a fair market price for it. The miller who makes a grade of flour up to the very highest point in excellence will command the highest price for it in the market. The workingman who makes his labor of the most value will generally command the highest market price for it, and sharp business men are quick to discover its value. I consider all legislation in regard to any thing connected with labor as injurious. All trades-unions and combinations I also consider as injurious to the mass of working-people. A few profit by these associations, and the many pay the bills. If working-people would drop the use of beer, tobacco, and every thing else that is not of real benefit, and let such men as _____ and a host of others earn their own living, they would have far more money for the general expenses of a family than they now have. I live in a village of about two thousand inhabitants; and I do not know of a family in destitute circumstances which has let alone vicious expenditures, and been industrious. It is the idle, unthrifty, beer-drinking, don't-care sort of people, who are out at the elbows, and waiting for some sort of legislation to help them. The sooner working-people get rid of the idea that somebody or something is going to help them, the better it will be for them. In this country, as a general thing, every man has an equal chance to rise. In our village there are a number of successful business men, and all began in the world without any thing but their hands and a will to succeed. The best way for working-people to get help is to help themselves . . . .

2   In 1884 the Illinois Bureau of Labor Statistics conducted an investigation of the standard of living of Illinois workers and their families. One result was a tabulation of the amount of money that 2,139 families in a number of communities actually earned and spent. As the bureau's report put it, "this minute catalogue of the details governing the life of each family portrays more vividly than any mere array of figures the common current of daily life among the people."[3] As you study these summaries, pay attention to the standard of living of families in this sample. Note the characteristics of the families who earned the most money or had the highest standard of living and of those who earned the least or had the lowest standard of living.

"Earnings, Expenses and Conditions of Workingmen and Their Families" (1884)

No. 35   LABORER   *Italian*

EARNINGS—Of father $270

CONDITION—Family numbers 5—parents and three children, all boys, aged one, three and five. Live in one room, for which they pay $4 per month rent. A very dirty and unhealthy place, everything perfectly filthy. There are about fifteen other families living in the same house. They buy the cheapest kind of meat from the neighboring slaughter houses and the children pick up fuel on the streets and rotten eatables from the commission houses. Children do not attend school. They are all ignorant in the full sense of the word. Father could not write his name.

FOOD—*Breakfast*—Coffee and bread.
        Dinner—Soups.
        Supper—Coffee and bread.

COST OF LIVING—
    Rent $ 48
    Fuel   5

Source: Illinois Bureau of Labor Statistics, "Earnings, Expenses and Conditions of Workingmen and Their Families," *Third Biennial Report* (Springfield, Ill., 1884), pp. 164, 267–271, 357–362, 365, 369–370, 373, 375, 383–385, 390–393, 395, 401–402, 404, 406–407, 410.

Meat and groceries	100	
Clothing, boots and shoes and dry goods	15	
Sickness	5	
Total		$173

| No. 46 | LABORER | *American* |

EARNINGS—Of father	$360	
Of wife	100	
Total		$460

CONDITION—Family numbers 7—parents and five children, aged from six months to eight years. They live in a house which they rent, and pay rental of $10 per month. Two of the children attend school. House is situated in good, respectable neighborhood. The furniture and carpets are poor in quality, but substantial. The father is not a member of a labor organization, but subscribes for the labor papers. Their living expenses exceed their income.

FOOD—*Breakfast*—Salt meat, bread, butter and coffee.
     Dinner—Bread, meat and vegetables.
     Supper—Bread, coffee, etc.

COST OF LIVING—

Rent	$120	
Fuel, meat and groceries	225	
Clothing, boots and shoes and dry goods	85	
Books, papers, etc.	2	
Sundries	75	
Total		$507

| No. 47 | LABORER | *Irish* |

| EARNINGS—Of father | $343 |

CONDITION—Family numbers 5—parents and three children, two girls, aged seven and five, and boy, aged eight. They occupy a rented house of 4 rooms, and pay a rental, monthly of $7. Two of the children attend school. Father complains of the wages he receives, being but $1.10 per day, and says it is extremely difficult for him to support his family upon that amount. His work consists in cleaning yards, basements, out-buildings, etc., and is, in fact, a regular scavenger. He also complains of the work as being very unhealthy, but it seems he can procure no other work.

FOOD—*Breakfast*—Black coffee, bread and potatoes.
　　　Dinner—Corned beef, cabbage and potatoes.
　　　Supper—Bread, coffee and potatoes.

COST OF LIVING—

Rent	$ 84
Fuel	15
Meat and groceries	180
Clothing, boots and shoes and dry goods	40
Sundries	20
Total	$339

No. 51	MACHINIST	*American*

EARNINGS—Of father　　　　　$540
　　　　　Of mother　　　　　255
　　　　　Of son, aged sixteen　255
　　　　　　Total　　　　　　　　$1,050

CONDITION—Family numbers 10—parents and eight children, five girls and three boys, aged from two to sixteen. Four of the children attend school. Father works only 30 weeks in the year, receives $3 per day for his services. They live in a comfortably furnished house, of 7 rooms, have a piano, take an interest in society and domestic affairs, are intelligent, but do not dress very well. Their expenditures are equal, but do not exceed their income. Father belongs to trades union, and is interested and benefited by and in it.

FOOD—*Breakfast*—Bread, meat and coffee.
　　　Dinner—Bread, meat, vegetables and tea.
　　　Supper—Bread, meat, vegetables and coffee.

COST OF LIVING—

Rent	$300
Fuel	50
Meat	100
Groceries	200
Clothing	160
Boots and shoes	50
Dry goods	25
Books, papers, etc.	15
Trades unions	10
Sickness	50

| Sundries | 90 |
| Total | $1,050 |

No. 105   BRAKEMAN   *Irish*

EARNINGS—Of father $360

CONDITION—Family numbers 10—parents and eight children, six girls and two boys, aged one year to fifteen. Four of them attend public school. Family occupy a house of 3 rooms, for which they pay $5 per month rental. The house presents a most wretched appearance. Clothes ragged, children half dressed and dirty. They all sleep in one room regardless of sex. The house is devoid of furniture, and the entire concern is as wretched as could well be imagined. Father is shiftless and does not keep any one place for any length of time. Wife is without ambition or industry.

FOOD—*Breakfast*—Bread, coffee and syrup.
    Dinner—Potatoes, soup and bread, occasionally meat.
    Supper—Bread, syrup and coffee.

COST OF LIVING—

Rent	$ 60
Fuel	25
Meat	20
Groceries	360
Clothing	50
Boots and shoes	15
Dry goods	30
Books, papers, etc.	20
Sickness	5
Total	$585

No. 112   COAL MINER   *American*

EARNINGS—Of father $250

CONDITION—Family numbers 7—husband, wife, and five children, three girls and two boys, aged from three to nineteen years. Three of them go to the public school. Family live in 2 rooms tenement, in healthy locality, for which they pay $6 per month rent. The house is scantily furnished, without carpets, but is kept neat and clean. They are compelled to live very economically, and every cent they earn is used to the best advantage.

Father had only thirty weeks work during the past year. He belongs to trades union. The figures for cost of living are actual and there is no doubt the family lived on the amount specified.

FOOD—*Breakfast*—Bread, coffee and salt meat.
　　　Dinner—Meat, bread, coffee and butter.
　　　Supper—Sausage, bread and coffee.

COST OF LIVING—

Rent	$72
Fuel	20
Meat	20
Groceries	60
Clothing	28
Boots and shoes	15
Dry goods	20
Trades union	3
Sickness	10
Sundries	5
Total	$252

No. 130　　　　　　　　　　COAL MINER　　　　　　　　　　*Irish*

EARNINGS—Of father	$420
Of son, twenty-one years of age	420
Of son, eighteen years of age	420
Of son, sixteen years of age	150
Total	$1,410

CONDITION—Family numbers 6—parents and four children, three boys and one girl. The girl attends school, and the three boys are working in the mine. Father owns a house of six rooms, which is clean and very comfortably furnished. Family temperate, and members of a church, which they attend with regularity. They have an acre of ground, which they work in summer, and raise vegetables for their consumption. They have their house about paid for, payments being made in installments of $240 per year. Father belongs to mutual assessment association and to trades union.

FOOD—*Breakfast*—Steak, bread, butter, potatoes, bacon and coffee.
　　　Dinner—Bread, butter, meat, cheese, pie and tea.
　　　Supper—Meat, potatoes, bread, butter, puddings, pie and coffee.

COST OF LIVING—

Rent	$240
Fuel	10
Meat	200
Groceries	700
Clothing	80
Boots, shoes and dry goods	70
Books, papers, etc.	15
Life insurance	18
Trades unions	3
Sickness	4
Sundries	75
Total	$1,415

No. 131   COAL MINER   *German*

EARNINGS—Of father $200

CONDITION—Family numbers 6—parents and four children, two boys and two girls, aged two, four, nine and eleven years. Two of them attend school. Family occupy a house containing 3 rooms, for which they pay $60 per annum. Father works all he can, and only receives $1 per day for his labor. He has only been in this country two and one half years and is anxious to get back to Germany. The house is miserably furnished, and is a wretched affair in itself. They have a few broken chairs and benches and a bedstead. Father is a shoemaker by trade, and does some cobbling which helps a little toward supporting his family. He receives the lowest wages in the shaft.

FOOD—*Breakfast*—Bread and coffee.
          Dinner—Bread, meat and coffee.
          Supper—Bread, meat, potatoes and coffee.

COST OF LIVING—

Rent	$60
Meat	36
Groceries	84
Clothing	12
Boots and shoes and dry goods	15
Sickness	1
Sundries	20
Total	$228

No. 137   IRON AND STEEL WORKER   *English*

EARNINGS—Of father $1,420
        Of son, aged fourteen   300
           Total $1,720

CONDITION—Family numbers 6—parents and four children; two boys and two girls, aged from seven to sixteen years. Three of them attend school, and the other works in the shop with his father. Family occupy their own house, containing 9 well-furnished rooms, in a pleasant and healthy locality. They have a good vegetable and flower garden. They live well, but not extravagantly, and are saving about a thousand dollars per year. Father receives an average of $7 per day of twelve hours, for his labor, and works about thirty-four weeks of the year. Belongs to trades union, but carries no life insurance. Had but little sickness during the year.

FOOD—*Breakfast*—Bread, butter, meat, eggs, and sometimes oysters.
        Dinner—Potatoes, bread, butter, meat, pie, cake or pudding.
        Supper—Bread, butter, meat, rice or sauce, and tea or coffee.

COST OF LIVING—
  Fuel $ 55
  Meat   100
  Groceries   300
  Clothing   75
  Boots and shoes   50
  Dry goods   50
  Books, papers, etc.   10
  Trades unions   6
  Sickness   12
  Sundries   50
    Total $708

No. 159   ROLLER BAR MILL   *American*

EARNINGS—Of father $2,200

CONDITION—Family numbers 5—parents and three children, two boys and one girl, aged four, six and eight years. Do not attend school. Family occupy house containing 3 rooms, well furnished in healthy locality, but the surroundings are not of the best. Family ordinarily intelligent. Father works eleven hours per day for 37 weeks in the year, and receives $10 per day for his labor; he saves about $1,400 per year, which he deposits in the bank. Family live well, but not extravagantly.

FOOD—*Breakfast*—Bread, meat, eggs, and coffee.
       Dinner—Bread, meat, vegetables, fruits and coffee.
       Supper—Bread, fruits, coffee and meat.

COST OF LIVING—

Rent	$120
Fuel	40
Groceries	200
Clothing	55
Boots and shoes	35
Dry goods	60
Books, papers, etc.	8
Sickness	50
Sundries	75
Total	$768

3   The iron and steel industry was central to the economic growth of the United States in the late nineteenth century. The table on the following pages, from the United States Bureau of Labor Statistics, illustrates the wages of blast furnace keepers. Keeping in mind that workers often did not work full-time or year-round, note the general trend of their wages and hours. Were they better or worse off as time went on? Using information in the previous source, determine what living standard the average furnace keeper most likely had.

Wages in the Iron and Steel Industry, 1858–1900

Furnace keepers, pig-iron blast furnaces, 1858–1900, by year and state

Year and State	Sex	Hours per week	Lowest, highest, and average— Rate per day (dollars)	Year and State	Sex	Hours per week	Lowest, highest, and average— Rate per day (dollars)
1858:				1866:			
Pennsylvania	M	(1)	1.70–1.70–1.70	Pennsylvania	M	(1)	2.41–2.41–2.41
1859:				1867:			
Pennsylvania	M	(1)	1.67–1.67–1.67	Pennsylvania	M	(1)	2.53–2.53–2.53
1860:				1868:			
Pennsylvania	M	(1)	1.85–1.85–1.85	Pennsylvania	M	(1)	2.53–2.53–2.53
1861:				1869:			
Pennsylvania	M	(1)	1.90–1.90–1.90	Pennsylvania	M	(1)	2.77–2.77–2.77
1862:				1870:			
Pennsylvania	M	(1)	1.68–1.68–1.68	Pennsylvania	M	(1)	2.77–2.77–2.77
1863:				1871:			
Pennsylvania	M	(1)	1.90–1.90–1.90	Pennsylvania	M	(1)	2.78–2.78–2.78
1864:				1872:			
Pennsylvania	M	(1)	2.70–2.70–2.70	Pennsylvania	M	(1)	3.15–3.15–3.15
1865:				1873:			
Pennsylvania	M	(1)	2.49–2.49–2.49	Pennsylvania	M	(1)	2.58–3.27–2.81

(cont. on next page)

Source: United States Department of Labor, Bureau of Labor Statistics, *History of Wages in the United States from Colonial Times to 1928*, Revision of Bulletin No. 499 (Washington, D.C., 1934), pp. 247–248.

Year and State	Sex	Hours per week	Rate per day (dollars)
1874:			
Pennsylvania	M	(1)	1.25–4.00–1.94
1875:			
Pennsylvania	M	(1)	1.60–1.94–1.71
1876:			
Pennsylvania	M	(1)	.85–2.37–1.67
1877:			
Ohio	M	60–84–77	.86–1.90–1.32
Pennsylvania	M	(1)	1.56–1.56–1.56
1878:			
Ohio	M	(1)	.86–1.75–1.37
Pennsylvania	M	67–84–82	.79–2.25–1.36
1879:			
Ohio	M	(1)	.86–2.80–1.51
Pennsylvania	M	84–84–84	.79–2.50–1.59
Do*	M	(1)	[2].66– .66– .66
1880:			
Ohio	M	60–84–78	1.07–2.50–1.63
Pennsylvania	M	84–84–84	1.30–1.78–1.62
1881:			
Ohio	M	70–84–77	1.00–2.65–1.65
Pennsylvania	M	84–84–84	1.78–1.90–1.84
1882:			
Pennsylvania	M	84–84–84	1.90–2.00–1.95
1883:			
Pennsylvania	M	(1)	2.25–2.25–2.25
1884:			
Michigan	M	(1)	1.85–1.85–1.85
New Jersey	M	(1)	1.59–2.53–1.82
Ohio	M	70–84–80	1.00–2.25–1.64
Pennsylvania	M	(1)	2.25–2.25–2.25
1885:			
Indiana	M	70–70–70	1.85–1.85–1.85
Maryland	M	84–84–84	1.50–1.50–1.50
New York	M	84–84–84	1.67–1.85–1.79
Ohio	M	72–84–84	1.35–2.00–1.64
Pennsylvania	M	84–84–84	1.80–2.25–2.02
Tennessee	M	84–84–84	1.80–1.80–1.80
Virginia	M	84–84–84	1.50–2.30–1.93

(cont. on next page)

Furnace keepers, pig-iron blast furnaces, 1858–1900, by year and state

Year and State	Sex	Lowest, highest, and average—		Year and State	Sex	Lowest, highest, and average—	
		Hours per week	Rate per day (dollars)			Hours per week	Rate per day (dollars)
1886:				1889 (cont.):			
Pennsylvania	M	(1)	2.05–2.05–2.05	Illinois	M	84–84–84	3.10–3.25–3.21
1887:				Indiana	M	84–84–84	1.70–1.70–1.70
Ohio	M	70–84–74	1.40–2.25–1.91	Maryland	M	72–72–72	1.58–1.58–1.58
Pennsylvania	M	84–84–84	2.10–2.25–2.18	Michigan	M	84–84–84	2.00–2.00–2.00
Wisconsin	M	(1)	3.10–3.10–3.10	Missouri	M	84–84–84	1.70–1.70–1.70
1888:				New York	M	84–84–84	1.85–2.15–1.98
Illinois	M	84–84–84	3.25–3.25–3.25	Ohio	M	84–84–84	1.80–2.50–2.07
Michigan	M	84–84–84	1.80–2.00–1.90	Pennsylvania	M	56–84–83	1.08–3.00–1.91
New York	M	70–84–75	1.88–2.15–1.98	Tennessee	M	77–84–82	1.75–2.00–1.89
Ohio	M	84–84–84	2.40–2.40–2.40	Virginia	M	84–84–84	1.50–2.00–1.83
Pennsylvania	M	84–84–84	1.85–2.25–2.04	West Virginia	M	84–84–84	1.65–2.40–2.01
Tennessee	M	(1)	1.85–1.85–1.85	1890:			
Virginia	M	84–84–84	1.40–2.00–1.67	Alabama	M	84–84–84	2.00–2.00–2.00
West Virginia	M	84–84–84	2.40–2.40–2.40	New York	M	(1)	2.00–2.00–2.00
1889:				Ohio	M	72–84–76	1.00–2.30–1.43
Alabama	M	84–84–84	1.25–2.00–1.89	Pennsylvania	M	84–84–84	1.90–2.25–2.02
Georgia	M	84–84–84	1.65–1.65–1.65	Wisconsin	M	84–84–84	3.00–3.00–3.00

(cont. on next page)

| Year and State | Sex | Lowest, highest, and average— | | Year and State | Sex | Lowest, highest, and average— | |
		Hours per week	Rate per day (dollars)			Hours per week	Rate per day (dollars)
1891:				1897:			
New York	M	(1)	1.75–2.20–1.93	Ohio	M	84–84–84	.75–2.20–1.50
Pennsylvania	M	(1)	2.00–2.00–2.00	Pennsylvania	M	(1)	2.00–2.10–2.06
1892:				1898:			
Ohio	M	58–84–72	1.00–3.00–1.69	Pennsylvania	M	(1)	2.10–2.20–2.17
Pennsylvania	M	(1)	2.25–2.25–2.25	1899:			
1893:				Alabama	M	84–84–84	1.75–1.84–1.82
New Jersey	M	84–84–84	1.75–1.75–1.75	Pennsylvania	M	(1)	2.40–2.50–2.47
1895:				1900:			
Ohio	M	84–84–84	.75–2.25–1.70	Alabama	M	84–84–84	1.80–1.85–1.83
1896:							
Pennsylvania	M	84–84–84	1.68–1.69–1.69				

[1]Not reported.
[2]And rent.
*Ditto.

4   Prices did not remain stable in the late nineteenth century. Before concluding that wage earners' material conditions were improving or declining, it is necessary to determine if prices were rising (inflation) or declining (deflation). With inflation, the same wages purchase less over time;

Price Indexes, 1866–1890

(1910–14 = 100)

Year	All commodities	Farm products	Foods	Hides and leather products	Textile products	Fuel and lighting
	1	2	3	4	5	6
1890	82	71	86	74	103	72
1889	81	67	79	80	99	71
1888	86	75	86	86	98	72
1887	85	71	86	92	98	70
1886	82	68	78	101	100	70
1885	85	72	84	105	105	72
1884	93	82	93	111	109	77
1883	101	87	103	107	116	89
1882	108	99	114	108	119	92
1881	103	89	106	109	119	91
1880	100	80	96	113	128	92
1879	90	72	90	100	114	80
1878	91	72	93	95	115	93
1877	106	89	115	109	125	108
1876	110	89	113	104	138	127
1875	118	99	120	123	141	128
1874	126	102	126	128	151	135
1873	133	103	122	132	175	148
1872	136	108	121	130	177	153
1871	130	102	130	126	170	152
1870	135	112	139	128	179	134
1869	151	128	154	134	194	166
1868	158	138	171	126	197	149
1867	162	133	167	132	220	144
1866	174	140	173	146	245	160

Source: Historical Statistics of the United States: Colonial Times to 1957 (Washington, D.C.: Bureau of the Census, 1960), p. 115.

with deflation, the same wages purchase more. The indexes shown (which are best read from bottom to top) reveal wholesale prices for basic commodities between 1866 and 1890. They use the average wholesale prices between 1910 and 1914 as a base (100). A base is a convenient tool for determining how much prices rose above or fell below a fixed point. Note the general course of prices in the late nineteenth century—that is, whether commodities became more or less expensive. Consider how these price changes corresponded to the changes in workers' wages in the previous source. Taking into account the changes in prices, would you say that workers were better or worse off than they would have been if prices for major commodities had remained the same?

Metals and metal products	Building materials	Chemicals and drugs	House-furnishing goods	Spirits	Miscellaneous
7	8	9	10	11	12
123	84	90	91	—	89
116	81	101	94	74	80
121	80	103	94	80	73
119	81	97	92	77	75
110	82	99	94	79	74
109	81	100	99	79	78
124	84	105	105	81	78
144	85	110	110	83	93
157	88	114	109	80	93
150	83	120	109	81	90
166	81	120	117	83	91
134	74	120	105	82	90
126	72	127	109	82	88
141	80	136	118	86	95
157	84	140	123	86	98
175	90	149	134	88	98
194	101	176	149	78	111
243	106	181	160	75	115
257	107	175	159	73	125
203	102	177	154	74	120
200	101	199	164	78	128
227	110	227	178	86	136
225	116	204	178	117	153
248	120	229	196	146	162
278	128	283	220	154	170

Workers Respond

Workers did not react passively to the conditions they confronted in the late nineteenth century. What do the following sources reveal about the conditions workers faced and what they thought about those conditions? What challenges did workers confront in attempting to improve their conditions?

 In 1894, workers at George Pullman's "model" company town went on strike. This is a statement of a Pullman striker at the Chicago convention of the American Railway Union.

Why We Struck at Pullman (1895)

We struck at Pullman because we were without hope. We joined the American Railway Union because it gave us a glimmer of hope. Twenty thousand souls, men, women, and little ones, have their eyes turned toward the convention today, straining eagerly through dark despondency for a glimmer of the heaven-sent message you alone can give us on this earth.

In stating to this body our grievances it is hard to tell where to begin. . . . Five reductions in wages, work, and in conditions of employment swept through the shops at Pullman between May and December 1893. The last was the most severe, amounting to nearly 30 percent and our rents had not fallen. . . . No man or woman of us all can ever hope to own one inch of George Pullman's land. Why even the streets are his. . . .

Pullman, both the man and the town, is an ulcer on the body politic. He owns the houses, the schoolhouses, the churches of God. . . . The revenue he derives from these, the wages he pays out with one hand—the Pullman Palace Car Company, he takes back with the other—the Pullman Land Association. He is able by this to bid under any contract car shop in the country. His competitors in business, to meet this, must reduce the wages of their men. . . . And thus the merry war—the dance of skeletons bathed in human tears—goes on, and it will go on, brothers, forever, unless you, the American Railway Union, stop it; end it; crush it out.

Source: Joshua Freeman et al., *Who Built America? Working People and the Nation's Economy, Politics, Culture, and Society* (New York: Pantheon Books, 1992), II: p. 140; originally from U.S. Strike Commission, *Report on the Chicago Strike of June–July 1894* (1895).

This letter was written by an African American iron worker at the Black
Diamond Steel Works.

Colored Workmen and a Strike (1887)

To the Editor:

As a strike is now in progress at the Black Diamond Steel Works, where
many of our race are employed, the colored people hereabouts feel a deep interest in its final outcome. As yet few colored men have taken part in it, it
having been thus far thought unwise to do so. It is true our white brothers,
who joined the Knights of Labor and organized the strike without conferring
with, or in any way consulting us, now invite us to join with them and help
them to obtain the desired increase in wages and control by the Knights of
Labor of the works. But as we were not taken into their schemes at its inception, and as it was thought by them that no trouble would be experienced in
obtaining what they wanted without our assistance, we question very much
the sincerity and honesty of this invitation. Our experience as a race with
these organizations has, on the whole, not been such as to give us either great
satisfaction or confidence in white men's fidelity. For so often after we have
joined them, and the desired object has been attained, we have discovered
that sinister and selfish motives were the whole and only cause that led them
to seek us as members.

A few years ago a number of colored men working at this mill were in-
duced to join the Amalgamated Association, thereby relinquishing the positions which they held at these works. They were sent to Beaver Falls, Pa., to
work in a mill there controlled by said Association, and the men there, brothers too, mark you, refused to work with them because they were black. It
is true Mr. Jaret, then chairman of that Association, sat down upon those
skunks, but when that mill closed down, and those men went out from there
to seek employment in other mills governed by the Amalgamated, while the
men did not openly refuse to work with them, they managed always to find
some pretext or excuse to keep from employing them.

Now, Mr. Editor, I am not opposed to organized labor. God forbid that I
should be when its members are honest, just and true! But when I join any society, I want to have pretty strong assurance that I will be treated fairly. I do
not want to join any organization the members of which will refuse to work
by my side because the color of my skin happens to be of a darker hue than
their own. Now what the white men in these organizations should and must
do, if they want colored men to join with and confide in them, is to give them

Source: Philip S. Foner and Ronald L. Lewis, eds., *Black Workers: A Documentary History from
Colonial Times to the Present* (Philadelphia: Temple University Press, 1989), pp. 220–221; originally from *New York Freeman,* August 13, 1887.

a square deal—give them a genuine white man's chance—and my word for it they will flock into them like bees into a hive. If they will take Mr. B. F. Stewart's advice! "take the colored man by the hand and convince him by actual fact that you will be true to him and not a traitor to your pledge," he will be found with them ever and always; for there are not under heaven men in whose breasts beat truer hearts than in the breast of the Negro.

John Lucus Dennis
Colored Puddler at Black Diamond
Steel Works, Pittsburgh, Pa., Aug. 8.

Women at Work

By 1900 five million of the 25 million Americans in the work force were women, most of whom worked at wages far below those of male workers. Note what the following sources reveal about the conditions confronting many female wage earners. How do they compare to conditions confronting male workers?

7   In 1869, a group of women petitioned the Massachusetts legislature to have the state help finance homes for them. Their demands were discussed in a meeting held in Boston. This account is from the *Workingman's Advocate,* an influential labor paper.

Women Make Demands (1869)

A convention of Boston work women was held in that city on the 21st ult. at which some extraordinary developments were made. We append some of the discussions:

Opening Address by Miss Phelps

Miss Phelps said: the subject of this meeting is to bring out the purpose of the petition just read, and the facts whereon it is based. We do not think the men of Massachusetts know how the women live. We do not think if they did they would allow such a state of things to exist. Some of us who signed the petition have had to work for less than twenty-five cents a day, and we know that many others have had to do the same. True, many get good wages comparatively for women. There are girls that get from $1 to $1.50 per day, either because they are superior laborers or have had unusual opportunities. But

Source: Rosalyn Baxandall et al., *America's Working Women: A Documentary History—1600 to the Present* (New York: Vintage Books, 1976), pp. 105–106; originally from *Workingman's Advocate* 5, No. 41 (May 8, 1869), p. 3.

many of these poor girls among whom it has been my fortune to live and work, are not skilled laborers. They are incapable of going into business for themselves, or carrying on for themselves, and incapable of combination; they are uneducated, and have no resource but the system that employs them. There are before me now women who I know to be working at the present time for less than twenty-five cents a day. Some of the work they do at these rates from the charitable institutions of the city. These institutions give out work to the women with the professed object of helping them, at which they can scarcely earn enough to keep them from starving; work at which two persons, with their utmost exertions cannot earn more than forty-five cents a day. These things, I repeat, should be known to the public. . . .

8   Summary of Conditions Among Women Workers Found by the Massachusetts Bureau of Labor (1887)

Feather-sorters, fur-workers, cotton-sorters, all workers on any material that gives off dust are subject to lung and bronchial troubles. In soap-factories the girls' hands are eaten by the caustic soda, and by the end of the day the fingers are often raw and bleeding. In making buttons, pins, and other manufactures . . . there is always liability of getting the fingers jammed or caught. For the first three times the wounds are dressed without charge. After that the person injured must pay expenses. . . .

In food preparation girls who clean and pack fish get blistered hands and fingers from the saltpetre. . . . Others in "working stalls" stand in cold water all day. . . .

In match-factories . . . necrosis often attacks the worker, and the jaw is eaten away. . . .

Source: Barbara M. Wertheimer, *We Were There: The Story of Working Women in America* (New York: Pantheon Books, 1977), pp. 212–213.

9   A garment worker wrote this description for *The Independent* magazine.

Work in a Garment Factory (1902)

At seven o'clock we all sit down to our machines and the boss brings each one the pile of work that he or she is to finish during the day. . . . This pile is

Source: Joshua Freeman et al., *Who Built America? Working People and the Nation's Economy, Politics, Culture, and Society* (New York: Pantheon Books, 1992), II: p. 173; originally from *The Independent* (1902).

put down beside the machine and as soon as a skirt is done it is laid on the other side of the machine. Sometimes the work is not all finished by six o'clock and then the one who is behind must work overtime. . . . The machines go like mad all day, because the faster you work the more money you get. Sometimes in my haste I get my finger caught and the needle goes right through it. . . . The machines are all run by foot power, and at the end of the day one feels so weak that there is a great temptation to lie right down and sleep. But you must go out and get air, and have some pleasure. . . .

Children at Work

Industrial growth in the late nineteenth century had an impact on working children. Note what these sources reveal about the numbers of children working full-time and about the conditions under which they labored.

 Gainful Workers by Age, 1870–1920

(In thousands of persons 10 years old and over)

		Age (in years)				
Year	Total Workers	10 to 15	16 to 44	45 to 64	65 and over	Unknown
1930	48,830	667	33,492	12,422	2,205	44
1920	42,434	1,417	29,339	9,914	1,691	73
1910	37,371	1,622	26,620	7,606	1,440	83
1900	29,073	1,750	20,223	5,804	1,202	94
1890	23,318	1,504	16,162	4,547	1,009	97
1880	17,392	1,118		16,274		
1870	12,925	765		12,160		

Source: Historical Statistics of the United States: Colonial Times to 1957 (Washington, D.C.: Bureau of the Census, 1960), p. 72.

Spargo was the author of *The Bitter Cry of the Children,* a major exposé of child labor.

Breaker Boys (1906)

JOHN SPARGO

According to the census of 1900, there were 25,000 boys under sixteen years of age employed in and around the mines and quarries of the United States. In the state of Pennsylvania alone,—the state which enslaves more children than any other,—there are thousands of little "breaker boys" employed, many of them not more than nine or ten years old. The law forbids the employment of children under fourteen, and the records of the mines generally show that the law is "obeyed." Yet in May, 1905, an investigation by the National Child Labor Committee showed that in one small borough of 7000 population, among the boys employed in breakers 35 were nine years old, 40 were ten, 45 were eleven, and 45 were twelve—over 150 boys illegally employed in one section of boy labor in one small town! During the anthracite coal strike of 1902, I attended the Labor Day demonstration at Pittston and witnessed the parade of another at Wilkesbarre. In each case there were hundreds of boys marching, all of them wearing their "working buttons," testifying to the fact that they were *bona fide* workers. Scores of them were less than ten years of age, others were eleven or twelve.

Work in the coal breakers is exceedingly hard and dangerous. Crouched over the chutes, the boys sit hour after hour, picking out the pieces of slate and other refuse from the coal as it rushes past to the washers. From the cramped position they have to assume, most of them become more or less deformed and bent-backed like old men. When a boy has been working for some time and begins to get round-shouldered, his fellows say that "He's got his boy to carry round wherever he goes." The coal is hard, and accidents to the hands, such as cut, broken, or crushed fingers, are common among the boys. Sometimes there is a worse accident: a terrified shriek is heard, and a boy is mangled and torn in the machinery, or disappears in the chute to be picked out later smothered and dead. Clouds of dust fill the breakers and are inhaled by the boys, laying the foundations for asthma and miners' consumption. I once stood in a breaker for half an hour and tried to do the work a twelve-year-old boy was doing day after day, for ten hours at a stretch, for sixty cents a day. The gloom of the breaker appalled me. Outside the sun shone brightly, the air was pellucid, and the birds sang in chorus with the trees and the rivers. Within the breaker there was blackness, clouds of deadly dust enfolded everything, the harsh, grinding roar of the machinery and the ceaseless rushing of coal through the chutes filled the ears. I tried to pick out the pieces of slate from the hurrying stream of coal,

Source: John Spargo, *The Bitter Cry of the Children* (New York: The Macmillan Company, 1915).

often missing them; my hands were bruised and cut in a few minutes; I was covered from head to foot with coal dust, and for many hours afterwards I was expectorating some of the small particles of anthracite I had swallowed.

I could not do that work and live, but there were boys of ten and twelve years of age doing it for fifty and sixty cents a day. Some of them had never been inside of a school; few of them could read a child's primer. True, some of them attended the night schools, but after working ten hours in the breaker the educational results from attending school were practically *nil*. "We goes fer a good time, an' we keeps de guys wots dere hoppin' all de time," said little Owen Jones, whose work I had been trying to do. How strange that barbaric patois sounded to me as I remembered the rich, musical language I had so often heard other little Owen Joneses speak in faraway Wales. As I stood in that breaker I thought of the reply of the small boy to Robert Owen. Visiting an English coal-mine one day, Owen asked a twelve-year-old lad if he knew God. The boy stared vacantly at his questioner: "God?" he said, "God? No, I don't. He must work in some other mine." It was hard to realize amid the danger and din and blackness of that Pennsylvania breaker that such a thing as belief in a great All-good God existed.

12   Night Shift in a Glass Factory (1906)

Source: Photo by Lewis Hine for the National Child Labor Committee, 1906. Reprinted in John Spargo, *The Bitter Cry of the Children,* 1906.

CONCLUSION

When he was a graduate student, the future historian and president Woodrow Wilson protested that he had to learn "one or two hundred dates and one or two thousand minute particulars" about "nobody knows who." He took comfort in knowing that he would easily forget this "mass of information."[4] The sources in this chapter represent another set of "minute particulars." From them we can learn any number of forgettable facts, from the daily wage of steel workers to the amount of money a coal miner's family spent on rent. By themselves these facts are not useful; contrary to the cliché, they do not "speak for themselves." Rather, they have meaning and interest only when historians order and arrange them. Moreover, what they tell us is often influenced by contemporary concerns. Americans still debate the proper role of the government in their society, the regulation of business, the value of labor unions, the usefulness of "schemes" for helping people, and the desirability of letting people rise or fall on their own. Just as such debates help to frame the questions historians ask about the past, answers to these questions lend historical perspective to the debates. The questions in this chapter are thus part of the ongoing dialogue between the past and present. And if you compare your answers to this chapter's questions to those of your classmates, you will see that all of you did not come to the same conclusions. Historians do not always agree about the answers to their inquiries either. In fact, debate is at the heart of their discipline.

These sources further demonstrate that historians must do more than just select certain facts; they must also know what people in the past perceived and believed. In this case, we need to understand workers' circumstances as well as what they thought about those circumstances. In fact, as we shall see in the next chapter, primary sources are often more valuable to historians for the opinions and biases they reflect than for the facts that they contain.

FURTHER READING

Margaret F. Byington, *Homestead: The Households of a Mill Town* (1910; repr., Pittsburgh, Pa.: University Center for International Studies, 1974).

Lizabeth A. Cohen, "Embellishing a Life of Labor: An Interpretation of the Material Culture of American Working-Class Homes, 1885–1915," in *Common Places: Readings in American Vernacular Culture,* ed. Dell Upton and John Michael Vlach (Athens: University of Georgia Press, 1986).

Melvyn Dubofsky, *Industrialism and the American Worker, 1865–1920* (Arlington Heights, Ill.: AHM Publishing Corp., 1975).

Joshua Freeman et al., *Who Built America? Working People and the Nation's Economy, Politics, Culture, and Society,* Vol. II (New York: Pantheon Books, 1992).

John Spargo, *The Bitter Cry of the Children* (London: Macmillan and Co., 1906).

NOTES

1. *Investigation by a Select Committee of the House of Representatives Relative to the Causes of the General Depression in Labor and Business,* 45th Cong., 3d sess., Misc. House Doc. No. 29 (Washington, D.C.: U.S. Government Printing Office, 1879), pp. 310–321.
2. *Massachusetts Bureau of the Statistics of Labor Reports* (1878, 1881), in *The Transformation of American Society, 1870–1890,* ed. John A. Garraty (Columbia: University of South Carolina Press, 1968), p. 88.
3. *Illinois Bureau of Labor Statistics Report* (1884), in *The Transformation of American Society, 1870–1890,* ed. John A. Garraty (Columbia: University of South Carolina Press, 1968), p. 120.
4. Quoted in James A. Henretta, *The Origins of American Capitalism* (Boston: Northeastern University Press, 1991), pp. xv, xvi.

Chapter

3

Evaluating Primary Sources: "Saving" the Indians in the Late Nineteenth Century

The primary sources in this chapter were produced by late-nineteenth-century Indian reformers and by Native Americans. They illustrate the biases often found in primary source material.

Sources

1. "Land and Law as Agents in Educating Indians" (1885)
2. The Dawes Act (1887)
3. A Cheyenne Tells His Son About the Land (ca. 1876)
4. Cheyennes Try Farming (ca. 1877)
5. A Sioux Recalls Severalty (ca. 1900)
6. Supervised Indian Land Holdings by State, 1881–1933
7. A Proposal for Indian Education (1888)
8. Instructions to Indian Agents and Superintendents of Indian Schools (1889)
9. The Education of Indian Students at Carlisle (1891)
10. Luther Standing Bear Recalls Carlisle (1933)
11. Wohaw's Self-Portrait (1877)
12. Taking an Indian Child to School (1891)
13. A Crow Medicine Woman on Teaching the Young (1932)
14. Percentage of Population Over Ten Illiterate, 1900–1930

*T*he guests of the rambling hotel had chosen a perfect spot to gather in October 1883. While strolling along Lake Mohonk, less than a hundred miles north of New York City, they could take in autumn's splendor in a landscape punctuated by cliffs, boulders, and caverns. The main attraction, though, was the hotel itself. Built of wood and rock, the multistoried Mohonk House arose at the end of the lake in a forest of chimneys, turrets, and gables. In proper Victorian style, gingerbread frills adorned the exterior, while inside an air of quiet gentility prevailed. The hotel's Quaker proprietors prohibited strong drink, card playing, and dancing, but these guests did not seem to mind. They could relax in a large parlor tastefully filled with wicker chairs, writing desks, books, and flowers freshly cut from the hotel's gardens. Besides, they had come to Lake Mohonk for work, not play. And their work, they knew, was of utmost importance.

Here on the fringe of New York's peaceful Catskills a hundred or so people gathered for four days to discuss and—they hoped—influence the fate of the Native Americans. The Lake Mohonk Conference of the Friends of the Indian, the first of many such meetings held each October at the resort, attracted delegates from the country's leading Indian reform organizations as well as members of Congress and federal officials. Mostly Easterners, the conferees had been stirred into action by distressing reports out of the West. From the Great Plains to the Pacific, Indians and their reservation lands were under a massive assault. After years of white-Indian warfare that raged from the Dakotas to California, reformers grew more determined by the 1880s to save America's 250,000 or so indigenous inhabitants from total destruction. This gathering at Lake Mohonk marked a growing unity among them.

The objects of the reformers' concern, of course, were far removed from this tranquil setting. And although some of these "friends" of the Indians could claim first-hand knowledge of the Western tribes, Native American representatives were not present at Lake Mohonk. Their absence, however, did not seem to trouble the conferees, who were imbued with a sense of high moral purpose and a conviction that they knew what was best for the Indians. Nor were these reformers disturbed that their campaign to "save" the Indian—and Native Americans' responses to it—reflected conflicting cultural assumptions. In ways that *neither* group could clearly perceive, competing values lay at the heart of late-nineteenth-century Indian reform. What people in the past missed, however, modern students of history *can* see. The historical sources left by reformers and Native Americans alike may give us a better understanding of America's solution to the "Indian problem" than possessed even by people at the time.

SETTING

Like the organized efforts to save the Indians of the West, the assault on them began at the Civil War's end. After 1865, the spread of the iron rail opened up large portions of the country to white settlers. At the same time, the military began a concerted effort to confine the Indians to reservations. The nomadic tribes of the Great Plains became the military's primary target. By the 1870s, scores of battles had bloodied the prairie from Texas to Montana. After Appomattox, soldiers and hunters also launched a relentless campaign of slaughter against millions of buffalo, pushing the animal to the brink of extinction by the early 1880s. Bloodshed, however, was not confined to the plains. From the verdant Northwest to the sun-bleached southwestern deserts, tribes were assaulted and gradually stripped of their lands as prior treaties were renegotiated in favor of encroaching settlers. Wherever they lived, Indians discovered the same thing: resistance to military force only inflamed whites. Even events in remote northern California could stoke anti-Indian sentiment in the rest of the nation. There, in 1873, the Modoc Indians fled their reservation and fought off the Army for seven months before surrendering. Three years later, hatred of the Indian reached a fever pitch when Americans in the midst of their nation's centennial celebration received news of the Sioux Indians' shocking annihilation of Colonel George Custer and his Seventh Cavalry detachment at Little Big Horn in Montana.

In the years following Custer's "Last Stand," however, intense white animosity toward the Indians began to wane as their resistance was gradually broken. In addition, several events covered widely in the Eastern press contributed to a more favorable view of Native Americans by the late 1870s. In 1877, Chief Joseph led the Nez Perces on a dramatic 1,500-mile trek through Idaho, Wyoming, and Montana while heroically fighting off Army troops. By the time Chief Joseph and his harried band surrendered, their determined effort to secure the return of the Nez Perces' northwest homeland had won the sympathy of many Americans. So too did the struggle of Nebraska's Ponca Indians about the same time to get back *their* land, which had been inadvertently included in a Sioux reservation by an earlier treaty. When the Sioux attempted to force the Poncas off their land in the 1870s, the government intervened and shipped the Poncas against their will to the Indian Territory of present-day Oklahoma, where many died of disease. Then when Chief Standing Bear led a Ponca band back to its homeland in 1879, the Army moved in to stop them. Meanwhile, popular sentiments had also been aroused by the flight of Cheyennes from the Indian Territory to their traditional tribal lands in Montana. Led by Dull Knife and Little Wolf, the band eluded troops across Kansas and Nebraska, only to be cut down by soldiers after attempting to break out of their eventual confinement at Fort Robinson, Nebraska, in 1878.

Such determined efforts to return to lost homes drew a sympathetic white response and swelled the ranks of Indian reformers by 1880. In 1879, the

Philadelphia-based Woman's National Indian Association and the Boston Indian Citizenship Committee were formed in the wake of the Ponca affair. Three years later, the Indian Rights Association was organized in Philadelphia, and the year after that representatives of these and other Indian-reform groups came together on the shores of Lake Mohonk to discuss the Indians' future. Indeed, not since the end of the Civil War had prospects looked better for the advocates of reform. They would be boosted further when New England–born Helen Hunt Jackson decided to write a book after attending a lecture by Ponca chief Standing Bear on the tribe's heartbreaking loss of its ancestral land. Published in 1881, *A Century of Dishonor* provided a record of the government's "shameful record of broken treaties and unfulfilled promises" regarding the Indians.[1] Jackson, who sent copies of the book to every member of Congress, helped win even greater support for resolving once and for all the country's long-standing "Indian problem."

Increasingly organized, and armed with Jackson's exposé, reformers set their sights on government policy toward the Indian. It was an issue with which these mostly well-to-do Protestants were already familiar. In 1869, the Grant administration brought religious denominations into the administration of Indian policy through the Board of Indian Commissioners, established to help oversee a scandal-ridden Office of Indian Affairs. The commissioners—one of whom owned the Mohonk House and many of whom represented Protestant religious groups—for a time administered Indian policy and disbursed reservation funds. Meanwhile, various missionary organizations took over the appointment of reservation agents. Like other reformers who initially supported the reservation system, the commissioners had put great faith in its power to reform the Indian. By the late 1870s, however, Protestant reformers came to view the reservation itself as the chief obstacle in the way of Native American progress. There they saw a still-corrupt federal Indian service, increasing Native American dependence on government largesse, and stubborn resistance to a new way of life. The solution to the "Indian problem," they concluded, required breaking up the reservations. And that was not all. This radical change in policy had to be accompanied by a program to educate Indian children. By the time of the first Lake Mohonk conference, these determined reformers were devoting their efforts almost exclusively to promoting these goals. Before the end of the decade, their labors would begin to bear fruit.

INVESTIGATION

This chapter contains a variety of primary sources relating to late-nineteenth-century Indian reform. Produced both by white reformers and Native Americans, the sources are as useful for the opinions and biases that they reveal as for the facts that they contain. As you analyze them, your main job is to evaluate the Indian reform program and its impact on Native Americans. In other words, you must determine in what ways late-nineteenth-century reformers' efforts to "save" the Indian succeeded or failed and the reasons why their fruits proved bitter or sweet to Native Americans themselves. A good analysis of this reform movement will address these questions:

1. **What did white reformers hope to achieve with the breakup of the reservations and with schools for Indian children?** What problems were these reforms designed to solve? Were their goals and remedies appropriate?

2. **What were the reformers' attitudes toward the Indians and their culture?** How did their views or beliefs influence their proposals?

3. **What impact did the reformers' solutions to the "Indian problem" have on the Indians and their culture?** How did the Native Americans' views or beliefs influence their response to these reforms?

4. **What circumstances or factors would have altered the nature and impact of Indian reform?** Was the ultimate outcome inevitable?

As you evaluate the sources in this chapter, look not only for the stated beliefs but also the unstated assumptions of white reformers and Native Americans. Before you begin, read the sections in your textbook on the opening of the West and white-Indian relations after the Civil War as well as any discussion of the Indian reform movement. Pay particular attention to your text's interpretation of the last development, for you may want to use the evidence in this chapter to assess it.

SOURCES

Reformers and the Reservation

This section contains a selection by a prominent Indian reformer on the need to abandon the reservation system (Source 1) and an excerpt from the General Allotment Law of 1887, commonly known as the Dawes Act (Source 2). As you evaluate these sources, look for evidence of the way reformers defined the "Indian problem," their views about the reservation, and their attitudes toward the Indians. Also consider the ways in which the Dawes Act reflected these views.

 Merrill E. Gates was one of the most prominent late-nineteenth-century Indian reformers. The president of Rutgers College and, later, Amherst College, Gates was appointed by President Chester A. Arthur to the Board of Indian Commissioners in 1884. For many years, he also presided over the Lake Mohonk conferences. In 1885, he presented a paper to the Board of Indian Commissioners that advanced his solution to the Indian problem. What are his views on the nature of Indian society?

"Land and Law as Agents in Educating Indians" (1885)

Two peculiarities which mark the Indian life, if retained, will render his progress slow, uncertain and difficult. These are:

1. The tribal organization.
2. The Indian reservation.

I am satisfied that no man can carefully study the Indian question without the deepening conviction that these institutions must go if we would save the Indian from himself. . . .

A false sentimental view of the tribal organization commonly presents itself to those who look at this question casually. It takes form in such objections as this:

> The Indians have a perfect right to bring up their children in the old devotion to the tribe and the chief. To require anything else of them is unreasonable. These are their ancestral institutions. We have no right to meddle with them.

The correction for this false view seems to me to come from the study of the tribe and its actual effects upon the family and upon the manhood of the individual.

The highest right of man is the right to be a man, with all that this involves. The tendency of the tribal organization is constantly to interfere with and frustrate the attainment of his highest manhood. The question whether parents have a right to educate their children to regard the tribal organization as supreme, brings us at once to the consideration of the family.

And here I find the key to the Indian problem. More than any other idea, this consideration of the family and its proper sphere in the civilizing of races and in the development of the individual, serves to unlock the difficulties which surround legislation for the Indian.

The family is God's unit of society. On the integrity of the family depends that of the State. There is no civilization deserving of the name where the family is not the unit of civil government. . . .

The tribal organization, with its tenure of land in common, with its constant divisions of goods and rations per capita without regard to service

Source: Merrill E. Gates, "Land and Law as Agents in Educating Indians," in Francis Paul Prucha, ed., *Americanizing the American Indians: Writings by the "Friends of the Indian," 1880–1900* (Cambridge, Mass.: Harvard University Press, 1973), pp. 48–52; originally from *Seventeenth Annual Report of the Board of Indian Commissioners* (1885).

rendered, cuts the nerve of all that manful effort which political economy teaches us proceeds from the desire for wealth. True ideas of property with all the civilizing influences that such ideas excite are formed only as the tribal relation is outgrown. . . .

But the tribal system paralyzes at once the desire for property and the family life that ennobles that desire. Where the annuities and rations that support a tribe are distributed to the industrious and the lazy alike, while almost all property is held in common, there cannot be any true stimulus to industry. . . .

As the allegiance to tribe and chieftain is weakened, its place should be taken by the sanctities of family life and an allegiance to the laws which grow naturally out of the family! Lessons in law for the Indian should begin with the developing and the preservation, by law, of those relations of property and of social intercourse which spring out of and protect the family. First of all, he must have land in severalty.

Land in severalty, on which to make a home for his family. This land the Government should, where necessary, for a few years hold in trust for him or his heirs, inalienable and unchargeable. But it shall be his. It shall be patented to him as an individual. He shall hold it by what the Indians who have been hunted from reservation to reservation pathetically call, in their requests for justice, "a paper-talk from Washington, which tells the Indian what land is his so that a white man cannot get it away from him." "There is no way of reaching the Indian so good as to show him that he is working for a home. Experience shows that there is no incentive so strong as the confidence that by long, untiring labor, a man may secure a home for himself and his family." The Indians are no exception to this rule. There is in this consciousness of a family-hearth, of land and a home in prospect as permanently their own, an educating force which at once begins to lift these savages out of barbarism and sends them up the steep toward civilization, as rapidly as easy divorce laws are sending some sections of our country down the slope toward barbaric heathenism. . . .

We must as rapidly as possible break up the tribal organization and give them law, with the family and land in severalty as its central idea. We must not only give them law, we must force law upon them. We must not only offer them education, we must force education upon them. Education will come to them by complying with the forms and the requirements of the law.

---

2   The passage of the General Allotment Law, or Dawes Act, in 1887 represented a major victory for reformers. Sponsored by Massachusetts Republican Senator Henry L. Dawes, the act allotted reservation lands in severalty (that is, with individual ownership rights) to Indians. How do the specific provisions of this law reflect widespread assumptions about the Indians and their culture?

The Dawes Act (1887)

An act to provide for the allotment of lands in severalty to Indians on the various reservations, and to extend the protection of the laws of the United States and the Territories over the Indians, and for other purposes.

Be it enacted by the Senate and House of Representatives of the United States of America in Congress assembled, That in all cases where any tribe or band of Indians has been, or shall hereafter be, located upon any reservation created for their use, either by treaty stipulation or by virtue of an act of Congress or executive order setting apart the same for their use, the President of the United States be, and he hereby is, authorized, whenever in his opinion any reservation or any part thereof of such Indians is advantageous for agricultural and grazing purposes, to cause said reservation, or any part thereof, to be surveyed, or resurveyed if necessary, and to allot the lands in said reservation in severalty to any Indian located thereon in quantities as follows:

To each head of a family, one-quarter of a section;

To each single person over eighteen years of age, one-eighth of a section;

To each orphan child under eighteen years of age, one-eighth of a section; and

To each other single person under eighteen years now living, or who may be born prior to the date of the order of the President directing an allotment of the lands embraced in any reservation, one-sixteenth of a section: *Provided,* That in case there is not sufficient land in any of said reservations to allot lands to each individual of the classes above named in quantities as above provided, the lands embraced in such reservation or reservations shall be allotted to each individual of each of said classes pro rata in accordance with the provisions of this act: *And provided further,* That where the treaty or act of Congress setting apart such reservation provides for the allotment of lands in severalty in quantities in excess of those herein provided, the President, in making allotments upon such reservation, shall allot the lands to each individual Indian belonging thereon in quantity as specified in such treaty or act: *And provided further,* That when the lands allotted are only valuable for grazing purposes, an additional allotment of such grazing lands, in quantities as above provided, shall be made to each individual.

Sec. 2.   That all allotments set apart under the provisions of this act shall be selected by the Indians, heads of families selecting for their minor children, and the agents shall select for each orphan child, and in such manner as to embrace the improvements of the Indians making the selection. Where the improvements of two or more Indians have been made on the same legal subdivision of

Source: United States Statutes at Large, 24 (1887): pp. 388–391.

land, unless they shall otherwise agree, a provisional line may be run divid-
ing said lands between them, and the amount to which each is entitled shall
be equalized in the assignment of the remainder of the land to which they are
entitled under this act: Provided, That if any one entitled to an allotment
shall fail to make a selection within four years after the President shall direct
that allotments may be made on a particular reservation, the Secretary of the
Interior may direct the agent of such tribe or band, if such there be, and if
there be no agent, then a special agent appointed for that purpose, to make a
selection for such Indian, which election shall be allotted as in cases where
selections are made by the Indians, and patents shall issue in like manner . . . .

Sec. 5.   That upon the approval of the allotments provided for in this
act by the Secretary of the Interior, he shall cause patents to issue therefor in
the name of the allottees, which patents shall be of the legal effect, and declare that the United States does and will hold the land thus allotted, for the
period of twenty-five years, in trust for the sole use and benefit of the Indian
to whom such allotment shall have been made, or, in case of his decease, of
his heirs according to the laws of the State or Territory where such land is located, and that at the expiration of said period the United States will convey
the same by patent to said Indian, or his heirs as aforesaid, in fee, discharged
of said trust and free of all charge or incumbrance whatsoever . . . .

Sec. 6.   That upon the completion of said allotments and the patenting
of the lands to said allottees, each and every member of the respective bands
or tribes of Indians to whom allotments have been made shall have the benefit of and be subject to the laws, both civil and criminal, of the State or Territory in which they may reside; and no Territory shall pass or enforce any law
denying any such Indian within its jurisdiction the equal protection of the
law. And every Indian both within the territorial limits of the United States to
whom allotments shall have been made under the provisions of this act, or
under any law or treaty, and every Indian born within the territorial limits of
the United States who has voluntarily taken up, within said limits, his resi-
dence separate and apart from any tribe of Indians therein, and has adopted
the habits of civilized life, is hereby declared to be a citizen of the United
States, and is entitled to all the rights, privileges, and immunities of such citizens, whether said Indian has been or not, by birth or otherwise, a member
of any tribe of Indians within the territorial limits of the United States without in any manner, impairing or otherwise affecting the right of any such Indian to tribal or other property . . . .

Sec. 8.   That the provision of this act shall not extend to the territory occupied by the Cherokees, Creeks, Choctaws, Chickasaws, Seminoles, and
Osage, Miamies and Peorias, and Sacs and Foxes, in the Indian Territory, nor

to any of the reservations of the Seneca Nation of New York Indians in the State of New York, nor to that strip of territory in the State of Nebraska adjoining the Sioux Nation on the south added by executive order.

Native Americans and Severalty

This section contains sources that reflect Native Americans' views about the land and their experience with severalty and farming of reservation lands. As you examine these sources, consider what they reveal about the Dawes Act as a solution to the Indian problem.

---

3   Wooden Leg was a Northern Cheyenne who fought George Custer and his forces at Little Big Horn, Montana, in 1876. In the early twentieth century, he recounted his early life to a white physician who was practicing among the Cheyennes. In the following passage, he recalls his father's views about the land. What do Wooden Leg's recollections suggest about the forces working against the reformers' plans for the Indians?

A Cheyenne Tells His Son About the Land (ca. 1876)

After we had been driven from the Black Hills and that country was given to the white people my father would not stay on any reservation. He said it was no use trying to make farms as the white people did. In the first place, that was not the Indian way of living. All of our teachings and beliefs were that land was not made to be owned in separate pieces by persons and that the plowing up and destruction of vegetation placed by the Great Medicine and the planting of other vegetation according to the ideas of men was an interference with the plans of the Above. In the second place, it seemed that if the white people could take away from us the Black Hills after that country had been given to us and accepted by us as ours forever, they might take away from us any other lands we should occupy whenever they might want these other lands. In the third place, the last great treaty had allowed us to use all of the country between the Black Hills and the Bighorn river and mountains as hunting grounds so long as we did not resist the traveling of white people through it on their way to or from their lands beyond its borders. My father decided to act upon this agreement to us. He decided we should spend all of our time in the hunting region. We could do this, gaining our own living in this way, or we could be supported by rations given to us at the agency. He chose to stay away from all white people. His family all agreed with him.

Source: Thomas B. Marquis, *Wooden Leg: A Warrior Who Fought Custer* (Lincoln: University of Nebraska Press, 1965), pp. 155–156.

4   John Stands-in-Timber was a Northern Cheyenne who related his tribe's experience with farming in the late 1870s. What do his recollections reveal about the difficulties of transforming the Indian into a yeoman farmer?

Cheyennes Try Farming (ca. 1877)

The government started the Indians raising gardens as soon as they surrendered. Some had gardens of corn and other crops. . . . They had forgotten how, though they all used to garden in the old days before they hunted buffalo. Now they were learning about new crops as well, things they had never seen before. The Dull Knife people got to Oklahoma in 1877 about the time the watermelons ripened, and when the Southern Cheyennes gave them some they cut them up and boiled them like squash. They did not know you could eat them raw. But later when they planted their own they put sugar with the seeds. They said it would make them sweeter when they grew.

When they reached Tongue River every man was supposed to have a garden of his own. A government farmer went around to teach them. And many of them worked hard, even carrying buckets of water from the river by hand. One man, Black White Man, wanted to raise cotton. He had seen it in Oklahoma. He plowed a piece of ground and smoothed it up, and when it was ready he took his wife's quilt and made little pieces from the inside and planted them with a garden hoe. When his wife missed the quilt, she got after him. He was afraid to tell her, but finally he said, "I got it and took out the cotton and planted it. We will have more quilts than we need, as soon as it grows."

When they first learned to plow in Oklahoma the farmer told them to get ready and come to a certain place and he would show them. They did not understand. They thought "Get ready" meant fancy costumes and not their new pants and shirts. So everybody had feathers on their heads and necklaces and leggings and fancy moccasins. It looked like a dance, not a farming lesson. And all the women and children went along to see them.

The farmer told one man to grab the handles while he started ahead with the team. But the plow jumped out of the ground and turned over, and the Indian fell down. But he tried again, and by the time they got back around he was doing pretty well. Then they all tried. At last they came to one man who had been watching closely. When he started off the dirt rolled right over and he went clear around that way, and the criers started announcing, "Ha-aah! See that man!" The women made war cries and everybody hollered just as if he had counted coup.*

Another time when they practiced plowing down there, one man plowed

Source: John Stands-in-Timber and Margo Liberty, *Cheyenne Memories* (New Haven, Conn.: Yale University Press, 1967), pp. 276–278.

up a bull snake and the next man plowed up a rattlesnake, and after that they were all afraid to go.

In Montana they began to help each other. The government issued plows to quite a few men, and in Birney the Fox Military Society used to plow together as soon as the frost was out. They would all gather at the farthest place up the river and work together until that was done, and then move to the next. They had seven or eight plows and it went faster that way. Besides, it was more fun. . . .

*To ceremoniously recount one's exploits in battle.

Ella C. Deloria, a Yankton Sioux, recalled the impact of the division of reservation lands into individual allotments. What does her account reveal about the Dawes Act's impact on traditional patterns of life?

A Sioux Recalls Severalty (ca. 1900)

At length there came the time when individual allotments of land were made. Families were encouraged to live out on them and start to be farmers forthwith. Equipment for this, as well as some essential furniture, was given the most docile ones by way of inducement. But again, it wasn't easy to make the spiritual and social adjustment. The people were too used to living in large family groups, cooperatively and happily. Now, here they were in little father-mother-child units (with an occasional grandparent, to be sure), often miles from their other relatives, trying to farm an arid land—the very same land from which, later on, white farmers of Old World tradition and training could not exact even a subsistence living. Enduring frightful loneliness and working at unfamiliar tasks just to put himself ahead financially were outside the average Dakota's ken. For him there were other values. The people naturally loved to foregather; and now the merest excuse for doing so became doubly precious. For any sort of gathering it was the easiest thing to abandon the small garden, leave the stock to fend for themselves, and go away for one to four weeks. On returning, they might find the place a wreck. That was too bad; but to miss getting together with other Dakotas was far worse. . . .

The man was the tragic figure. Frustrated, with his age old occupation suddenly gone, he was left in a daze, unable to overcome the strange and passively powerful inertia that stayed him from doing anything else. And so he sat by the hour, indifferent and inactive, watching—perhaps envying—his wife, as she went right on working at the same essential role of woman that had been hers since time immemorial. In such a mental state, what did he

Source: Ella C. Deloria, *Speaking of Indians* (Vermillion, S.Dak.: Dakota Press, 1979), pp. 60, 62–63.

care that unsympathetic onlookers called him "lazy Indian" and accused him of driving his wife, like a slave, while "he took his ease"! As though he enjoyed it! If, as he sat there, someone had called, "Hey! There's a herd of buffalo beyond that hill! Come quick!" he would have sprung into life instantly again. But, alas, no such thing would ever happen now. All he could do, or thought he could do, on his "farm" was to water the horses mechanically, bring in fuel and water, cut a little hay, tend a little garden. He did it listlessly, almost glad when the garden died on his hands for lack of rain. His heart was not in what he was doing anyway—until something human came up: a gathering of the people, where he could be with many relatives again; or a death, when he must go to help with the mourning; or a cow to be butchered, reminiscent of the hunt; or time to go to the agency for the biweekly issue of rations. That he must not miss. For him and his family, that was what still gave meaning to life.

6   The following table relates to land holding among Indians subject to the Dawes Act in the late nineteenth and early twentieth centuries. What does it reveal about one impact of severalty on Native Americans? Do previous sources provide any explanations for the pattern revealed in this table?

Supervised Indian Land Holdings by State, 1881–1933

	1881	1890	1900	1911[a]	1933
Idaho	2,748,981	2,273,421	1,364,500	770,706	803,239
Kansas	137,747	102,026	28,279	273,408	34,821
Michigan	66,332	27,319	8,317	153,910	20,233
Minnesota	5,026,447	2,254,781	1,566,707	1,480,647	549,320
Montana	29,356,800	10,591,360	9,500,700	6,263,151	6,055,009
Nebraska	436,252	136,947	74,592	344,375	69,280
North Dakota		5,861,120	3,701,724	2,786,162	1,034,123
South Dakota	36,616,448	11,661,360	8,991,791	7,221,939	5,544,424
Washington	7,779,348	4,045,248	2,333,574	2,948,708	2,712,915
Wisconsin	526,026	512,129	381,061	590,094	395,919
Total	82,694,381	37,465,711	27,951,245	22,833,100[a]	17,219,283
Oklahoma	41,100,915	39,156,040	27,397,237	22,736,473[a]	2,919,886
Arizona	3,092,720	6,603,191	15,150,757	17,358,741	18,657,984
California	415,841	494,045	406,396	437,629	625,354
Colorado	12,467,200	1,094,400	483,750	556,621	443,751
Nevada	885,015	959,135	954,135	696,749	866,176
New Mexico	7,228,731	10,002,525	1,667,485	4,520,652	6,188,964
Oregon	3,853,800	2,075,240	1,300,225	1,719,561	1,718,510
Utah	2,039,040	3,972,480	2,039,040	219,101	1,571,020
Wyoming	2,342,400	2,342,400	1,810,000	318,543	2,249,576
Total U.S.	156,120,043	104,314,349	78,372,185	71,464,393[a]	52,651,393

[a]Totals include all allotted land.

Source: Indians, Bureaucrats, and Land: The Dawes Act and the Decline of Indian Farming, by Leonard A. Carlson. Copyright © 1981 by Leonard A. Carlson. Reproduced with permission of Greenwood Publishing Group, Inc., Westport, CT. Data from "Statistical Supplement to the Annual Report of the Commissioner of Indian Affairs, for the Fiscal Year ended June 30, 1940," p. 37.

Reformers and Indian Education

Reformers did not believe that the Indian problem could be solved only by breaking up the reservation. Instead, education had to supplement severalty. After the breakup of the reservations, therefore, the education of Native American children was the chief interest of most "friends of the Indian" in the late nineteenth century. This section contains sources that reflect their concerns. As you examine them, note the reformers' goals and methods. Also consider what these sources reveal about the reformers' values—and what they thought about the Indians' values.

7 The Reverend Lyman Abbott, one of the most committed Indian reformers, advanced a plan for a universal system of education for Indian children at the Lake Mohonk Conference in 1888. On what grounds does Abbott argue that education must accompany severalty?

A Proposal for Indian Education (1888)

The Indian problem is three problems—land, law, and education. The country has entered upon the solution of the land problem. It has resolved to break up the reservation system, allot to the Indians in severalty so much land as they can profitably occupy, purchase the rest at a fair valuation, throw it open to actual settlers, and consecrate the entire continent to civilization, with no black spot upon it devoted to barbarism. Upon that experiment the country has entered, and it will not turn back. The law problem, also, has been put in the way of solution. It is safe to assume that it will not be long before the existing courts are open to the Indians; and it is reasonable to hope that special courts will be provided for their special protection, in accordance with the general plan outlined by the law committee of the Lake Mohonk Conference. But nothing has yet been done toward the solution of the educational problem. A great deal has been done toward the education of individual Indians, something, perhaps, toward the education of single tribes, but no plan has been agreed upon; and it is hardly too much to say that no plan has even been proposed for solving the educational problem of the Indian race,—for converting them from groups of tramps, beggars, thieves, and sometimes robbers and murderers, into communities of intelligent, industrious, and self-supporting citizens. But this is by far the most important problem of the three. Put an ignorant and imbruted savage on land

Source: Francis Paul Prucha, ed., *Americanizing the American Indians: Writings by the "Friends of the Indian," 1880–1900* (Cambridge, Mass.: Harvard University Press, 1973), pp. 208–210, 212; originally from *Proceedings of the Sixth Annual Meeting of the Lake Mohonk Conference of Friends of the Indian* (1888).

of his own, and he remains a pauper, if he does not become a vagrant and a thief. Open to him the courts of justice, and make him amenable to the laws of the land, and give him neither knowledge nor a moral education, and he will come before those courts only as a criminal; but inspire in him the ambition of industry, and equip him with the capacity of self-support, and he will acquire in time the needful land and find a way to protect his personal rights. These reforms must move on together. Certain it is that without the legal and the educational reform the land reform will be death to the Indian, and burden, if not disaster, to the white race. My object in this paper is simply to set before the Lake Mohonk Conference the outlines of a possible educational system, in the hope that the principles here announced, and the methods here suggested, may at least be found worthy of discussion, out of which may be evolved a plan worthy to be presented to the country for its adoption.

At present we have no system of Indian education. Some Christian and philanthropic individuals and societies are attempting, in various fragmentary ways, to do a work of education in special localities. The Government is doing some educational work under teachers whom it has appointed and whom it supports; but the efficacy of these governmental efforts depends largely upon the ability and character of the agent of the reservation on which the school is situated. . . .

Nor is this the only vice of the present essentially vicious no-system of Indian education. A minority of Indian children are taught more or less feebly the rudiments of civilization, some in boarding schools, some in day schools, some on the reservation, some off it, some under one, others under another sectarian influence. When a little smattering of education has been given them, they drift back, or are sent back to the reservation, to forget what they have learned,—to take off the beaver and put on the feathers, to lay aside the hoe and take up the hatchet, and resume the war paint which they had washed from their faces at the schoolhouse door. That so many Indians are able to resist the evil influences of their savage environments, and interpenetrate their tribe with any civilizing influences whatever, affords a singular testimony to the stability of character which goes along with a saturnine disposition. What the country should do, what the friends of Indian emancipation—rather let me say of justice, humanity, and equal rights—should do, is to substitute for this chaotic congeries of fragmentary efforts, a system which shall secure within a generation the education of all Indian children within the borders of the United States in the essentials of American civilization. Certain propositions looking to this ultimate result I desire to put before the Lake Mohonk Conference for its discussion.

1. The United States Government must undertake to provide this education, not to supplement provision made by others. . . .

2. The education thus to be afforded must not merely be offered as a gift; it must be imposed by superior authority as a requirement. In other words, the

education of Indian children must be made compulsory. It is a great mistake to suppose that the red man is hungering for the white man's culture, eager to take it if it is offered to him. The ignorant are never hungry for education, nor the vicious for morality, nor barbarism for civilization; educators have to create the appetite as well as to furnish the food. The right of Government to interfere between parent and child must indeed be exercised with the greatest caution; the parental right is the most sacred of all rights; but a barbaric father has no right to keep his child in barbarism, nor an ignorant father to keep his child in ignorance.

<hr>

8   Soon after he was appointed Commissioner of Indian Affairs in 1889, Thomas J. Morgan issued instructions to Indian agents in charge of reservation schools. What did he see as the main goal of Indian education? How did he propose to achieve it?

Instructions to Indian Agents and Superintendents of Indian Schools (1889)

The great purpose which the Government has in view in providing an ample system of common school education for all Indian youth of school age, is the preparation of them for American citizenship. The Indians are destined to become absorbed into the national life, not as Indians, but as Americans. They are to share with their fellow-citizens in all the rights and privileges and are likewise to be called upon to bear fully their share of all the duties and responsibilities involved in American citizenship.

It is in the highest degree important, therefore, that special attention should be paid, particularly in the higher grades of the schools, to the instruction of Indian youth in the elements of American history, acquainting them especially with the leading facts in the lives of the most notable and worthy historical characters. While in such study the wrongs of their ancestors can not be ignored, the injustice which their race has suffered can be contrasted with the larger future open to them, and their duties and opportunities rather than their wrongs will most profitably engage their attention.

Pupils should also be made acquainted with the elementary principles of the Government under which they live, and with their duties and privileges as citizens. To this end, regular instructions should be given them in the form of familiar talks, or by means of the use of some elementary text-book in civics. Debating societies should be organized in which may be learned the

Source: Francis Paul Prucha, ed., *Americanizing the American Indians: Writings by the "Friends of the Indian," 1880–1900* (Cambridge, Mass.: Harvard University Press, 1973), pp. 257–259; originally from "Instructions to Indian Agents in Regard to Inculcation of Patriotism in Indian Schools," in *House Executive Document* No. 1, part 5, vol. II, 51st Cong., 2d sess, serial 2841, p. clxvii.

practical rules of procedure which govern public assemblies. Some simple manual of rules of order should be put into the hands of the more advanced students, and they should be carefully instructed in its use.

On the campus of all the more important schools there should be erected a flagstaff, from which should float constantly, in suitable weather, the American flag. In all schools of whatever size and character, supported wholly or in part by the Government, the "Stars and Stripes" should be a familiar object, and students should be taught to reverence the flag as a symbol of their nation's power and protection.

Patriotic songs should be taught to the pupils, and they should sing them frequently until they acquire complete familiarity with them. Patriotic selections should be committed and recited publicly, and should constitute a portion of the reading exercises.

National holidays—Washington's birthday, Decoration Day, Fourth of July, Thanksgiving, and Christmas—should be observed with appropriate exercises in all Indian schools. It will also be well to observe the anniversary of the day upon which the "Dawes bill" for giving to Indians allotments of land in severalty became a law, viz, February 8, 1887, and to use that occasion to impress upon Indian youth the enlarged scope and opportunity given them by this law and the new obligations which it imposes.

In all proper ways, teachers in Indian schools should endeavor to appeal to the highest elements of manhood and womanhood in their pupils, exciting in them an ambition after excellence in character and dignity of surroundings, and they should carefully avoid any unnecessary reference to the fact that they are Indians.

They should point out to their pupils the provisions which the Government has made for their education, and the opportunities which it affords them for earning a livelihood, and for achieving for themselves honorable places in life, and should endeavor to awaken reverence for the nation's power, gratitude for its beneficence, pride in its history, and a laudable ambition to contribute to its prosperity.

Agents and school superintendents are specially charged with the duty of putting these suggestions into practical operation.

---

9   Captain Richard Henry Pratt was an Army officer who fought the Indians on the southern plains and then devoted many years to Indian education. After supervising an experiment in the education of Indian prisoners at Fort Marion, Florida, Pratt established a school for Native American students in some old army barracks at Carlisle, Pennsylvania, in 1879 and served as its superintendent until 1904. A vocational training school, Carlisle was considered a model institution by many Indian reformers. What parallels does Pratt see between Indians and African Americans? What is his argument for educating Indian students off the reservation?

The Education of Indian Students at Carlisle (1891)

A great general has said that the only good Indian is a dead one, and that high sanction of his destruction has been an enormous factor in promoting Indian massacres. In a sense, I agree with the sentiment, but only in this: that all the Indian there is in the race should be dead. Kill the Indian in him, and save the man. . . .

"Put yourself in his place" is as good a guide to a proper conception of the Indian and his cause as it is to help us to right conclusions in our relations with other men. For many years we greatly oppressed the black man, but the germ of human liberty remained among us and grew, until, in spite of our irregularities, there came from the lowest savagery into intelligent manhood and freedom among us more than seven millions of our population, who are to-day an element of industrial value with which we could not well dispense. However great this victory has been for us, we have not yet fully learned our lesson nor completed our work; nor will we have done so until there is throughout all of our communities the most unequivocal and complete acceptance of our own doctrines, both national and religious. . . .

Inscrutable are the ways of Providence. Horrible as were the experiences of its introduction, and of slavery itself, there was concealed in them the greatest blessing that ever came to the Negro race,—seven millions of blacks from cannibalism in darkest Africa to citizenship in free and enlightened America; not full, not complete citizenship, but possible—probable—citizenship, and on the highway and near to it.

There is a great lesson in this. The schools did not make them citizens, the schools did not teach them the language, nor make them industrious and self-supporting. Denied the right of schools, they became English-speaking and industrious through the influences of association. Scattered here and there, under the care and authority of individuals of the higher race, they learned self-support and something of citizenship, and so reached their present place. No other influence or force would have so speedily accomplished such a result. Left in Africa, surrounded by their fellow-savages, our seven millions of industrious black fellow-citizens would still be savages. Transferred into these new surroundings and experiences, behold the result. They became English-speaking and civilized, because forced into association with English-speaking and civilized people; became healthy and multiplied, because they were property; and industrious, because industry, which brings contentment and health, was a necessary quality to increase their value.

The Indians under our care remained savage, because forced back upon

Source: Francis Paul Prucha, ed., Americanizing the American Indians: Writings by the "Friends of the Indian," 1880–1900 (Cambridge, Mass.: Harvard University Press, 1973), pp. 260–261, 262, 263–264, 269; originally from Proceedings of the Ninth Annual Meeting of the Lake Mohonk Conference of Friends of the Indian (1891).

themselves and away from association with English-speaking and civilized people, and because of our savage example and treatment of them. . . .

This ponderous Indian question relates to less than two hundred and fifty thousand people, numerically less than double the population of this city. They are divided into about seventy tribes and languages. Their plane of life has always been above that of the African in his native state. That they have not become civilized and incorporated in the nation is entirely our fault. We have never made any attempt to civilize them with the idea of taking them into the nation, and all of our policies have been against citizenizing and absorbing them. Although some of the policies now prominent are advertised to carry them into citizenship and consequent association and competition with other masses of the nation, they are not, in reality, calculated to do this.

We are after the facts. Let us take the Land in Severalty Bill. Land in severalty, as administered, is in the way of the individualizing and civilization of the Indians, and is a means of holding the tribes together. Land in severalty is given to individuals adjoining each other on their present reservations. And experience shows that in some cases, after the allotments have been made, the Indians have entered into a compact among themselves to continue to hold their lands in common as a reservation. The inducement of the bill is in this direction. The Indians are not only invited to remain separate tribes and communities, but are practically compelled to remain so. The Indian must either cling to his tribe and its locality, or take great chances of losing his rights and property.

The day on which the Land in Severalty Bill was signed was announced to be the emancipation day for the Indians. The fallacy of that idea is so entirely demonstrated that the emancipation assumption is now withdrawn.

We shall have to go elsewhere, and seek for other means besides land in severalty to release these people from their tribal relations and to bring them individually into the capacity and freedom of citizens. . . .

As we have taken into our national family seven millions of Negroes, and as we receive foreigners at the rate of more than five hundred thousand a year, and assimilate them, it would seem that the time may have arrived when we can very properly make at least the attempt to assimilate our two hundred and fifty thousand Indians. . . .

The school at Carlisle is an attempt on the part of the government to do this. Carlisle has always planted treason to the tribe and loyalty to the nation at large. It has preached against colonizing Indians, and in favor of individualizing them. It has demanded for them the same multiplicity of chances which all others in the country enjoy. Carlisle fills young Indians with the spirit of loyalty to the stars and stripes, and then moves them out into our communities to show by their conduct and ability that the Indian is no different from the white or the colored, that he has the inalienable right to liberty and opportunity that the white and the negro have. Carlisle does not dictate to him what line of life he should fill, so it is an honest one. It says to him that, if he gets his living by the sweat of his brow, and demonstrates to the nation that he is a man, he does more good for his race than hundreds of his fellows who cling to their tribal communistic surroundings. . . .

Indians and the White Man's Education

This section contains sources that reflect Native American experience at Indian schools and some of the effects of reformers' efforts to educate the Indian. As you examine these sources, consider what they reveal about Indian culture, the Indians' views about their own education, and the effectiveness of reformers' educational efforts.

10 In 1879, when he was eleven years old, Plenty Kill, the son of Standing Bear, left his South Dakota home with other Sioux boys and girls to enroll at Captain Richard Pratt's new school for Indians at Carlisle, Pennsylvania, where he received a new name: Luther Standing Bear. Later, he recalled his experiences as a student at Carlisle. What does this account reveal about Pratt's methods and their impact?

Luther Standing Bear Recalls Carlisle (1933)

At the age of eleven years, ancestral life for me and my people was most abruptly ended without regard for our wishes, comforts, or rights in the matter. At once I was thrust into an alien world, into an environment as different from the one into which I had been born as it is possible to imagine, to remake myself, if I could, into the likeness of the invader.

By 1879, my people were no longer free, but were subjects confined on reservations under the rule of agents. One day there came to the agency a party of white people from the East. Their presence aroused considerable excitement when it became known that these people were school teachers who wanted some Indian boys and girls to take away with them to train as were white boys and girls. . . .

At last at Carlisle the transforming, the "civilizing" process began. It began with clothes. Never, no matter what our philosophy or spiritual quality, could we be civilized while wearing the moccasin and blanket. The task before us was not only that of accepting new ideas and adopting new manners, but actual physical changes and discomfort had to be borne uncomplainingly until the body adjusted itself to new tastes and habits. Our accustomed dress was taken and replaced with clothing that felt cumbersome and awkward. Against

Source: Reprinted from *Land of the Spotted Eagle* by Luther Standing Bear by permission of the University of Nebraska Press. Copyright, 1933, by Luther Standing Bear. Renewal copyright, 1960, by May Jones.

trousers and handkerchiefs we had a distinct feeling—they were unsanitary and the trousers kept us from breathing well. High collars, stiff-bosomed shirts, and suspenders fully three inches in width were uncomfortable, while leather boots caused actual suffering. We longed to go barefoot, but were told that the dew on the grass would give us colds. That was a new warning for us, for our mothers had never told us to beware of colds, and I remember as a child coming into the tipi with moccasins full of snow. Unconcernedly I would take them off my feet, pour out the snow, and put them on my feet again without any thought of sickness, for in that time colds, catarrh, bronchitis, and *la grippe* were unknown. But we were soon to know them. Then, red flannel undergarments were given us for winter wear, and for me, at least, discomfort grew into actual torture. I used to endure it as long as possible, then run upstairs and quickly take off the flannel garments and hide them. When inspection time came, I ran and put them on again, for I knew that if I were found disobeying the orders of the school I should be punished. My niece once asked me what it was that I disliked the most during those first bewildering days, and I said, "red flannel." Not knowing what I meant, she laughed, but I still remember those horrid, sticky garments which we had to wear next to the skin, and I still squirm and itch when I think of them. Of course, our hair was cut, and then there was much disapproval. But that was part of the transformation process and in some mysterious way long hair stood in the path of our development. For all the grumbling among the bigger boys, we soon had our heads shaven. How strange I felt! Involuntarily, time and time again, my hands went to my head, and that night it was a long time before I went to sleep. If we did not learn much at first, it will not be wondered at, I think. Everything was queer, and it took a few months to get adjusted to the new surroundings.

Almost immediately our names were changed to those in common use in the English language. Instead of translating our names into English and calling Zinkcaziwin, Yellow Bird, and Wanbli K'leska, Spotted Eagle, which in itself would have been educational, we were just John, Henry, or Maggie, as the case might be. I was told to take a pointer and select a name for myself from the list written on the blackboard. I did, and since one was just as good as another, and as I could not distinguish any difference in them, I placed the pointer on the name Luther. I then learned to call myself by that name and got used to hearing others call me by it, too. By that time we had been forbidden to speak our mother tongue, which is the rule in all boarding-schools. This rule is uncalled for, and today is not only robbing the Indian, but America of a rich heritage. The language of a people is part of their history. Today we should be perpetuating history instead of destroying it, and this can only be effectively done by allowing and encouraging the young to keep it alive. A language unused, embalmed, and reposing only in a book, is a dead language. Only the people themselves, and never the scholars, can nourish it into life.

Of all the changes we were forced to make, that of diet was doubtless the most injurious, for it was immediate and drastic. White bread we had for the first meal and thereafter, as well as coffee and sugar. Had we been allowed our own simple diet of meat, either boiled with soup or dried, and fruit, with perhaps a few vegetables, we should have thrived. But the change in clothing, housing, food, and confinement combined with lonesomeness was too much, and in three years nearly one half of the children from the Plains were dead and through with all earthly schools. In the graveyard at Carlisle most of the graves are those of little ones.

11 Wohaw, a Kiowa Indian, was imprisoned along with other warriors of the southern plains tribes at Fort Marion, Florida. There he and many of the other prisoners produced numerous drawings that depicted their earlier lives. After his release in 1878, Wohaw continued to draw scenes that reflected the experience of many Plains Indians who, like himself, had been educated by whites. As you examine this drawing, notice the way Wohaw represented his two worlds. (The small structure next to his left foot represents a church. The offering of a pipe was a sign of respect, while the smoke from the animals was an indication of power.) In which direction is Wohaw being pulled?

Wohaw's Self-Portrait (1877)

Source: Missouri Historical Society, St. Louis. Art Acc.# 1882.18.32. Reprinted in Evan M. Maurer et al., *Visions of the People: A Pictorial History of Plains Indian Life* (Minneapolis: Minneapolis Institute of Arts, 1992), p. 183.

12   According to a Bureau of Indian Affairs clerk at the Crow reservation, this drawing was made by Carlisle school boys. His notes on the drawing read: "Major Wyman, U.S. Ind[ian] Agent at Crow Agency Mont. with his chief of Police 'Boy that Grabs' trying to get Indian children for the school. A Crow Indian squaw leading her little girl by the hand to deliver her to the Capt. of Police."[2] What is the view here of the cigar-smoking agent? What do the gesture and facial expression of the mother indicate about her attitude toward the captain of police?

Taking an Indian Child to School (1891)

Source: 1930.51. Drawing by Boys from Carlisle Indian School. Crow, 1981. Charles H. Barstow Collection, Special Collections Library, Montana State University-Billings. Reprinted in Evan M. Maurer et al., *Visions of the People: A Pictorial History of Plains Indian Life* (Minneapolis: Minneapolis Institute of Arts, 1992), p. 284.

13   Pretty-Shield, a Crow medicine woman, reflected in the early twentieth century on relations between adults and children in the old days. What does her account reveal about the impact of white culture on those relations? On the lives of Indian adults and children?

A Crow Medicine Woman on Teaching the Young (1932)

"We were a happy people when I came onto this world, Sign-talker. There was plenty to eat, and we could laugh. Now all this is changed. But I will try to begin with the first things I remember.

"About the time when I came to live on this world my aunt, Strikes-with-an-axe, lost two little girls. They had been killed by the Lacota; and so had her man. This aunt, who was my mother's sister, mourned for a long time, growing thinner, and weaker, until my mother gave me to her, to heal her heart. This aunt, Strikes-with-an-axe, was a River Crow. You know that because of a quarrel, just before my time [about 1832], the Crows divided into two tribes, the Mountain Crows, and the River Crows? Well, I was born a Mountain Crow, and this aunt was a River Crow.

"I can remember going away to live with my aunt, and the River Crows, although I could not have been three years old. This separation from my mother and my sisters was in fact not a very real one, because all the Crows came together often. These meetings gave me opportunities to see my family, so that I was happy, perhaps happier than I should have been at home. My aunt's lodge was large, and she lived alone, until I came to stay with her. She needed me, even though I was at first too young to help her.

"I well remember the first time that the Crow clans gathered after I had left my mother to live with my aunt. It was in the springtime. A crier, on a beautiful bay horse, rode through the big village telling the people to get ready to move to the mountains. His words set thoughts of again seeing my mother and sisters and brothers dancing in my young head. I felt very happy. Almost at once my aunt began to pack up; and then she took down her lodge.

"How I loved to move, especially when the clans were going to meet at some selected place, always a beautiful one." She turned to look out of the window at the wide plains, screened by the giant cottonwoods that surround Crow Agency, her eyes wistful.

"A crier would ride through the village telling the people to be ready to move in the morning. In every lodge the children's eyes would begin to shine. Men would sit up to listen, women would go to their doors to hear where the next village would be set up, and then there would be glad talking until it was time to go to sleep. Long before the sun came the fires would be going in every lodge, the horses, hundreds of them, would come thundering in, and then everybody was very busy. Down would come the lodges, packs would be made, travois loaded. Ho! Away we would go, following the men, to some new camping ground, with our children playing around us. It was good hard work to get things packed up, and moving; and it was hard, fast

Source: Pages 20–24 from *Pretty-Shield: Medicine Woman of the Crows* by Frank Linderman. Copyright 1932 by Frank B. Linderman, renewed © 1960 by Norma Waller, Verne Linderman, and Wilda Linderman. Reprinted by permission of HarperCollins Publishers, Inc.

work to get them in shape again, after we camped. But in between these times we rested on our traveling horses. Yes, and we women visited while we traveled. There was plenty of room on the plains then, so that many could ride abreast if they wished to. There was always danger of attack by our enemies, so that far ahead, on both sides, and behind us, there were our wolves who guarded us against surprise as we traveled. The men were ever watching these wolves, and we women constantly watched the men.

"I have been dreaming," she said, smiling, "not telling stories. I will try to stay awake after this."

Just here a boy of about sixteen years entered the room with an air of assurance. Decked out in the latest style of the "movie" cowboy, ten-gallon hat, leather cuffs and all, he approached Pretty-shield, spoke a few words to her in Crow, and then stood waiting while the old woman dug down into a hidden pouch for a silver dollar, which she gave him without a word.

"My grandson," said Pretty-shield, when the boy had gone. "I have told you that I have raised two families of grandchildren. This one is of the first lot. They never get over *needing* me, though," she smiled, her kind face again merry.

"I wonder how my grandchildren will turn out," she said, half to herself, a dazed look coming into her eyes. "They have only me, an old woman, to guide them, and plenty of others to lead them into bad ways. The young do not listen to the old ones now, as they used to when I was young. I worry about this, sometimes. I may have to leave my grandchildren any day now."

"Did you ever whip your own children?" I asked.

"No, Sign-talker, you know that my people never did such things. We talked to our children, told them things they needed to know, but we never struck a child, never."

She stopped short, her lips pressed tightly together. "Lately I *did* strike a child," she said, grimly. "There seemed to be nothing else to do. Times and children have changed so. One of my grand-daughters ran off to a dance with a bad young man after I had told her that she must not go. I went after her. It was a long way, too, but I got her, and in time. I brought her home to my place, and used a saddle-strap on her. I struck hard, Sign-talker. I hope it helped her, and yet I felt ashamed of striking my grandchild. I am trying to live a life that I do not understand.

"Young people know nothing about our old customs, and even if they wished to learn there is nobody now to teach them."

As you examine this table, compare the illiteracy levels and trends for different population groups in the early twentieth century. Do Sources 7–13 offer explanations for the level and trend of Indian illiteracy?

Percentage of Population Over Ten Illiterate, 1900–1930

Class	1900	1910	1920	1930
All classes	10.7	7.7	6.0	4.3
Indian	56.2	45.3	34.9	25.7
White	6.2	5.0	4.0	3.0
Native	4.6	3.0	2.0	1.6
Foreign-born	12.9	12.7	13.1	10.8
Negro	44.5	30.4	22.9	16.3
All others	26.6	13.1	14.5	12.3

Source: Indians, Bureaucrats, and Land: The Dawes Act and the Decline of Indian Farming, by Leonard A. Carlson. Copyright © 1981 by Leonard A. Carlson. Reproduced with permission of Greenwood Publishing Group, Inc., Westport, CT. Data from The Indian Population of the United States and Alaska, 1930, p. 143.

CONCLUSION

The sources in this chapter demonstrate that historians' primary material is often biased, reflecting not only objective conditions but also what people thought about them. The sources also make clear that these biases and views are as important as historical facts. In this case, historians can learn a great deal about white-Indian relations because their sources reflect the beliefs and perceptions of both Indian reformers and Native Americans.

Similarly, historians' writings—called secondary sources—contain different views of the past, even when they rely on the same primary sources. Thus, historians' debates often hinge less on matters of fact than on their own assumptions and values. By shaping the questions that historians ask, such assumptions and values often determine the facts they choose to emphasize. Remembering that will make it easier in the following chapters to evaluate both primary and secondary sources and to use one kind of historical source to appraise the other.

FURTHER READING

Frederick E. Hoxie, A Final Promise: The Campaign to Assimilate the Indians, 1880–1920 (Lincoln: University of Nebraska Press, 1984).

Arnold Krupat, ed., Native American Autobiography: An Anthology (Madison: University of Wisconsin Press, 1994).

Robert W. Mardock, *The Reformers and the American Indian* (Columbia: University of Missouri Press, 1971).

Janet A. McDonnell, *The Dispossession of the American Indian, 1887–1934* (Bloomington: Indiana University Press, 1991).

Robert M. Utley, *The Indian Frontier of the American West, 1846–1890* (Albuquerque: University of New Mexico Press, 1983).

NOTES

1. Helen Hunt Jackson, *A Century of Dishonor* (New York: Harper & Row, Publishers, 1965), p. 339.
2. Quoted in Evan M. Maurer et al., *Visions of the People: A Pictorial History of Plains Indian Life* (Minneapolis: The Minneapolis Institute of Arts, 1992), p. 284.

Chapter

4

Evaluating a Historical Argument:
American Manhood and Philippine Annexation

This chapter presents one secondary source, an argument concerning the American decision to annex the Philippines after the Spanish-American War, and primary sources that can be used to evaluate that argument.

Secondary Source

Primary Sources

*I*n early 1899, many Americans could agree with Secretary of State John Hay that the just-concluded conflict with Spain was "a splendid little war." The previous summer, the United States had defeated Spain in a matter of months. Fewer than four hundred American troops died in combat in the Spanish-American War. The American experience in the Philippines seemed especially splendid. In May 1898, Commodore George Dewey's fleet steamed into Manila Bay and sunk the entire Spanish fleet without suffering a single casualty. American troops now occupied Manila and it appeared likely that the former Spanish colony in the Far East—recently ceded to the United States by a defeated Spain—would become a permanent American overseas possession.

Before the war, most Americans cared little about this distant place across the Pacific. In fact, most probably would have had difficulty locating it on the map. Few knew much more about it when the war ended. But with American forces in possession of the country's principal city, many influential Americans began calling for the United States to keep the entire Philippines—a sprawling chain of some seven thousand islands. The matter would be settled in February 1899, when the Senate voted on the treaty signed with Spain two months earlier. After a fierce debate in and outside the halls of Congress, the Senate made its decision: The United States would annex the Philippines and, in effect, turn it into an American colony in the Far East.

Few Americans foresaw the consequences of this decision, even though some Filipinos had already turned their guns from the Spanish to the American occupation forces. For the next two years, the United States would be tied down in a bloody conflict with Filipino nationalists that was marred by atrocities on both sides. Certainly, there was nothing splendid about American operations in the Philippines, which claimed more lives than had the Spanish-American War itself. By 1902, more than 126,000 American troops had been committed to the Philippines and more than 4,200 had died. Meanwhile, perhaps as many as two hundred thousand civilians had perished. Although President Theodore Roosevelt declared the fighting over in the summer of 1902, Filipino Muslim fighters actually continued their armed opposition to American occupation for more than a decade. Their resistance was finally quelled, but American military forces would still be in the Philippines four decades later when invading Japanese troops drove them out and took over the islands at the start of World War II. In fact, only after this war would the Philippines finally achieve independence. Long before the Stars and Stripes were finally lowered, historians sought explanations for the American decision to establish an overseas empire at the end of the nineteenth century. At the beginning of another century, that search goes on. As the United States continues to assert its power around the globe, few topics from the turn of a previous century could be more timely.

SETTING

Historians have been drawn to the decision to annex the Philippines for several important reasons. When the United States took control of the country, it broke with its own revolutionary past and anti-colonial ideals. The decision for empire also provides a powerful case study—for some, a cautionary tale—regarding the unintended consequences of intervening in foreign lands. In this case, of course, that consequence was a prolonged, bloody military struggle far from American shores. Finally, Philippine annexation occurred just as the United States had arrived as a great power, a status it holds more than a century later. To many historians, then, American imperialism at the turn of the twentieth century represents an important key for understanding the rise of the United States as a global power.

If historians do not dispute the importance of Philippine annexation, they do not necessarily agree about the reasons for it. Often their explanations reflect conflicting views about the most important influences on foreign policy. Some scholars argue that democratic or popular influences play an important role in shaping policy; others contend that elites dominate decision making. Still others insist that American foreign policy has been shaped primarily by powerful ideas and cultural forces. For the better part of a century, explanations for Philippine annexation have reflected these competing views about influence. The result has been a fierce debate among historians not only about the forces propelling American imperialism at the turn of the twentieth century, but about the nature of foreign policy in a democratic society.

One argument, an extension of President William McKinley's own explanation at the time, emphasized a humanitarian impulse behind American overseas expansion at the end of the nineteenth century. In this view, the decision to go to war with Spain so as to liberate Cuba from the oppressive Spanish rule naturally spilled over to a desire to keep the Philippines once the war was over. Annexation would "uplift" the Filipinos and prevent another oppressive power from seizing an independent but weak Philippines. Proponents of this view maintain that the American empire was thus "accidental" in nature. An unthinking response to events in Cuba and the Philippines, it was carried out without forethought or assessments about American strategic or economic interests. In other words, the decision for empire was an "aberration" that was unrelated to the needs of America's expanding industrial economy.

That view did not long go unchallenged. In fact, early in the twentieth century many historians believed that the search for overseas markets explained both the war with Spain and the subsequent decision for empire. In the 1930s, for example, historian Charles Beard argued that McKinley's decision for war reflected his close ties to expansionist business leaders. This interpretation was especially popular during the Great Depression, when economic issues were on the minds of many people. Americans generally held business responsible for the country's economic ills, and "war profiteers" were under investigation by the U.S. Senate for their role in World War I. At the same time, historian Julius Pratt argued that another influential, elite group was more responsible for American imperialism than profit-minded businessmen. In *Expansionists of 1898* (1936), Pratt concluded that many prominent business leaders actually opposed going to war with Spain. Vocal and well-placed officials such as Assistant Secretary of the Navy Theodore Roosevelt, Navy Captain Alfred Thayer Mahan, and Senator Henry Cabot Lodge pushed McKinley to war with Spain. Only when these expansionists pressed for retaining the Philippines, Pratt concluded, did the business community finally join the annexationist chorus.

Later, many historians rejected arguments about the responsibility of these elite groups for American overseas expansion. Reminded by World War II of the powerful effects of mass hysteria, in the postwar years they emphasized the emotional or irrational nature of American overseas expansion at the end of the nineteenth century. In their view, McKinley and the Congress were swept toward war and colonialism by a public whipped to a frenzy by so-called yellow journalism—the sensationalist coverage of Spanish oppression in Cuba. The decision for war, then, was an "unthinking" response by political leaders to popular passion. As historian Ernest May argued in *Imperial Democracy* (1961), William McKinley was simply unable to withstand the tide of public opinion and "led his country unwillingly toward a war that he did not want."[1] A little later, historian Richard Hofstadter extended this thesis when he concluded that Americans were suffering from a collective "psychic crisis" in the 1890s brought on by economic depression and social turmoil related to industrialization. Increasingly frightened about their own prospects at home, Hofstadter concluded, Americans were especially susceptible to manipulation by the yellow press, which offered them the prospect of overseas conquests as a cure for their own frustrations. As in the humanitarian-impulse interpretation, America's unthinking decisions for war and empire were aberrations that had more to do with popular influence on the government than with concerns for overseas markets.

It was not long before some historians questioned these conclusions too. By the 1960s the Vietnam War had created doubts among many Americans about popular influence on government policy and the motives of elite policy makers. At the same time, "New Left"* historians began to emphasize the economic influences on American foreign policy and the expansionist nature of capitalism. These historians downplayed the role of the yellow press and public opinion. They pointed instead to the desire of American leaders to find commercial outlets abroad. In *The New Empire* (1963), for instance, Walter LaFeber argued that American leaders realized the economic benefits of overseas expansion and led the nation to war with Spain to build a commercial empire. Historian Thomas McCormick agreed in *China Market* (1967), which concluded that the

---

*The label was applied to distinguish these historians from the "Old Left" of the 1930s.

acquisition of the Philippines was essential to realizing profits in China—potentially a huge market for American goods in the Far East.

Closer to our own time, many historians have stressed the important role of culture in shaping the past, even in the field of foreign relations. These historians emphasize the ideological rather than purely economic motives behind American overseas expansion, in particular the belief in the duty of the "Anglo-Saxon race" to uplift "uncivilized" peoples. In *Spreading the American Dream* (1982), for instance, Emily Rosenberg argued that assumptions about the superiority of Anglo-Saxons and of American political, religious, and economic institutions propelled American expansion at the turn of the century. In *Ideology and U.S. Foreign Policy* (1987), historian Michael Hunt likewise argued that an ideological stew containing generous portions of chauvinism and racism led many Americans to assume that they could simply remake other societies.

This emphasis on the cultural roots of expansionism has given rise even more recently to a renewed focus on changes in late-nineteenth-century American society, especially those affecting Americans' own views about themselves and their nation. In *The United States and Imperialism* (2001), for instance, historian Frank Ninkovich argues that agrarian unrest, immigration, and labor unrest helped to create a national "identity crisis" in the late nineteenth century. To many influential Americans, the cure was for the United States to become a leading player in a new "global community" by adhering to a European "standard of civilization"—one that emphasized the need to "civilize" the "backward" areas of the world. By emphasizing mass psychology, the role of elites, and the idea of cultural uplift, such explanations are in some ways an extension of older arguments about American expansion. They serve as reminders that historians build on the work of those who came before them and that their interpretations are not necessarily mutually exclusive. By pointing to developments far from the steamy jungles of the Philippines to explain the presence of American troops there, they also remind us that studying American involvement in other countries promises to tell us much about our own.

INVESTIGATION

Unlike the previous chapters, this one presents a *secondary source*—the work of a historian—as well as the usual set of primary sources. You will be able to use the evidence from the primary sources to evaluate the argument in the secondary source. The main question presented by the secondary and primary sources is why the United States annexed the Philippines following the Spanish-American War. Like many contemporary historians, the author of the secondary source traces the roots of American expansionism at the turn of the twentieth century to an aspect of American culture—in this case, late-nineteenth-century conceptions about masculinity. First determine the argument presented in this source, paying attention to the evidence it presents to support it. Then assess what light the primary sources shed on the argument offered in the secondary source. A good analysis of the American decision for annexation will address the following questions:

1. **According to the essay (Source 1), how did concerns about American masculinity influence the decision to annex the Philippines?** What developments in American society reinforced these concerns by the time Americans debated the fate of the Philippines? According to the essay, were annexationists' concerns about masculinity an important independent factor in the American decision to hold the Philippines or important only because they reinforced the influence of other factors?

2. **Do the primary sources indicate that views about gender played a role in the debate over the Philippines?** Is there evidence that annexationists' fears about masculinity were connected to other concerns or desires?

3. **Do you agree with the author's explanation for the American annexation of the Philippines?** Compared to other factors, how important were the gender concerns that she identifies? Were there more important issues in the minds of expansionists?

4. **Based on the sources in this chapter, what explanation would you offer to account for the American decision to take the Philippines?** What is the most important evidence to support it?

Before you begin, read the sections in your textbook on American overseas expansion in the late nineteenth century and on the Spanish-American War. Note what factors or forces it points to in explaining this expansion and, in particular, American annexation of the Philippines. When you are finished with this assignment you will be able to compare your text's conclusions with the interpretation offered in Source 1 of this chapter.

SECONDARY SOURCE

In this selection, historian Kristin Hoganson argues that while a number of influences were evident in the American decision to annex the Philippines, they were related to overriding fears about declining masculinity. Note how she connects fears about masculinity to other concerns or desires on the part of annexationists. How in the minds of expansionists would annexing the Philippines help to restore American masculinity, according to Hoganson?

Male Degeneracy and the Allure of the Philippines (1998)

KRISTIN L. HOGANSON

Begun as a chivalrous crusade to redeem American honor and liberate the Cubans from Spanish oppression, the Spanish-American War ended as a self-aggrandizing war, a war that resulted not only in the temporary occupation of Cuba but also in the annexation of Puerto Rico and Guam. Most ironic of all, it ended in a bloody colonial war in the Philippines that involved over 126,000 American soldiers, more than 4,000 of whom lost their lives. For years, historians have grappled with the question, Why did the United States finish one war, waged in the name of liberty, only to start another, waged in behalf of empire?

The United States initially became involved in the Philippines as part of the war effort against Spain. After Commodore Dewey sank the Spanish fleet in Manila Bay, President McKinley sent reinforcements, who took the city of Manila from the Spaniards in an attack on August 13, 1898. (During the hostilities the Filipino nationalists who ringed the city established a foothold in some of its suburbs.) The peace treaty with Spain, signed on December 10, ceded the Philippines along with Guam and Puerto Rico to the United States. The treaty, known as the Treaty of Paris, then went to the U.S. Senate for ratification. But the Filipinos who had been fighting for independence from Spain did not want to be ceded. On February 4, 1899, shortly before the Senate voted on the treaty, fighting broke out between Filipino troops and American soldiers when a private from Nebraska fired at Filipinos who refused to obey his command to halt. The Senate went ahead and narrowly ratified the treaty ending the war with Spain on February 6, leaving the nation to confront an even greater issue: whether to wage a war against the Filipino nationalists.

Economic motives certainly played a significant role in the decision to fight for the control of the Philippines, which were located close to the hotly contested and potentially lucrative China market. Those who believed the nation needed strategic bases to secure its share of eastern profits regarded the Philippines as a stepping-stone. Yet a troubling question remains: What led Americans to set their democratic scruples aside and wage a trans-Pacific war of conquest? To answer this question, a number of historians have turned to the racial assumptions of the time. Imperialists generally thought the Filipinos unfit for self-government. They viewed them as even less adept than the Cubans, who at least had enjoyed a favorable image as heroic fighters prior to the Spanish-American War. . . .

Source: Kristin L. Hoganson, *Fighting for American Manhood: How Gender Politics Provoked the Spanish-American and Philippine-American Wars* (New Haven, Conn.: Yale University Press, 1998), pp. 133–134, 138–140, 142–143, 149–150, 153–154, 176–177, 178–179. Copyright © 1998. Reprinted by permission of the publisher, Yale University Press.

Unlike the anti-imperialists, who drew on negative stereotypes of the Filipinos to argue that the United States should not admit the islands into the Republic, imperialists employed images of savage, childish, and feminine Filipinos to argue that the United States had humanitarian obligations in the Philippines. Claiming that the seemingly unmanly Filipinos were unfit to govern themselves, imperialists held that the United States had a duty to do it for them. Yet given the brutality of the war (an estimated sixteen to twenty thousand Filipino soldiers and two hundred thousand civilians died in the conflict) such humanitarian assertions seem more a justification of imperialist policies than a reflection of a guiding spirit of altruism. But if assessments of the Filipinos served primarily to make U.S. policies seem more palatable, we are left with the original question: Why did the United States wage a lengthy war for control of the Philippines? What explains the imperialist impulse?

To more fully understand the imperialist impulse, meaning the desire to take and govern the Philippines, it is necessary to turn the spotlight from perceptions of the Filipinos to American self-perceptions. Imperialists' comments on American men and American democracy indicate that they wanted to govern the Philippines not only because they doubted the Filipinos' governing capacity, but, just as important, because they doubted their own. In addition to being motivated by markets (and the military bases that seemed necessary to secure them), imperialists were driven by another fundamentally self-interested motive: the conviction that holding colonies would keep American men and their political system from degenerating.

Although a number of Americans believed that, by creating a new cohort of veterans, the Spanish-American War had ensured the well-being of the nation's political system for another generation, some men continued to be plagued by anxieties that an extended peace would lead to, as one author put it, "effeminate tendencies in young men," foremost among them the middle- and upper-class white men who enjoyed the many comforts of industrial society. Rather than easing their minds, the post-Spanish-American War valorization of the serviceman as the ideal citizen and political leader only underscored the question that had troubled them before the war: What would happen if the martial spirit dissipated in the United States? Theodore Roosevelt mentioned some of these concerns in 1901 in a letter to his English friend Cecil Arthur Spring Rice: "I do not wonder that you sometimes feel depressed over the future both of our race and of our civilization," he wrote. ". . . I should be a fool if I did not see grave cause for anxiety in some of the social tendencies of the day: the growth of luxury throughout the English-speaking world; and especially the gradual diminishing birth rate; and certain other signs of like import are not pleasant to contemplate." Fearful that the short Spanish-American War had not permanently rectified the softness wrought by industrialization, Roosevelt turned to empire as a more lasting remedy.

Imperialists like Roosevelt believed that holding colonies could prove to be a longer-term solution to modern civilization's seemingly dangerous tendency to make young, middle-class, and wealthy men soft, self-seeking, and materialistic. They thought that the experience of holding colonies would create the kind of martial character so valued in the nation's male citizens and political leaders (especially in the aftermath of the Spanish-American War), and that, in so doing, it would prevent national and racial degeneracy. James C. Fernald, who in less militant moments worked on abridging the *Standard Dictionary,* conveyed this idea in his expansionist tract *The Imperial Republic,* published in 1898. Imperial pursuits, he wrote, would "provide adventurous occupation for a host of sturdy men," thereby preventing the United States from retrograding "toward Chinese immobility and decay." Fervent imperialists joined with Fernald to contend that American men must embrace rigorous overseas challenges lest they lose their privileged position in a Darwinian world. "The law of evolution is pitiless and he who gets in its way will be run over," wrote one expansionist to his senator. "There is no standing still, forward or backward we must go." Sen. Jonathan Ross (R, Vt.) drew on similar logic in a speech advocating retention of the Philippines: "Stagnation is decay and ultimate death. Honest struggle, endeavor, and discussion bring light, growth, development, and strength." To such men, colonies held the key to character.

Imperialists wanted to build manly character not only because they were concerned about American men's standing relative to other races and nations but also because they were worried about American men's position vis-à-vis women. Fernald illustrates this point. Seven years before publishing *The Imperial Republic,* he published a tract titled *The New Womanhood* that deplored women who did not devote themselves to maternity and homemaking. In this tract, Fernald said that "for high manly health," boys needed "a certain roughness and severity of exercise," but that women would be destroyed by such strenuous endeavors. He was so committed to womanly delicacy that he deplored the style of dress that tried to give women the "high, square shoulders which are the beauty of the manly figure." He went on, "The tendency of man is toward authority, command, and penalty; of woman, toward tenderness, persuasion and reward" and concluded that women should be sheltered from the wider world for their moral well-being. From Fernald's point of view, women who ceased to devote themselves to men and instead competed with them, who preferred "manly" self-assertion to "womanly" self-sacrifice, threatened the health of the race. But just as worrisome was women's threat to traditional male prerogatives. Warning that softness in men and assertiveness in women indicated degeneracy, Fernald offered imperial policies as a solution. He looked to overseas policies to solve domestic problems because he believed that the rigors of combat and challenges of establishing colonial control would test American men more thoroughly than domestic pursuits. Beyond that, they seemed certain to separate American men from effeminizing domestic influences. . . .

As the nation celebrated its victory, some observers concluded that American men had done more than prove their manhood in war—they had improved it. Manhood, they opined, was the greatest legacy of the war. The newspaper editor Henry Watterson conveyed this idea in his *History of the Spanish-American War.* "Above all, it [the war] elevated, broadened, and vitalized the manhood of the rising generation of Americans," he wrote. Similarly, an article in *Century Magazine* held that "exhibitions of the finer and rarer qualities of manhood, added to the record of bravery made by white and black, regular and volunteer, all these are national possessions that can never be taken away from us, that can never work us injury; they are of more real value than any territorial possessions that the war has brought or may bring to these United States. For it remains forever true that it is the manhood, the nobility, the character of its people, and not the extent of its territory, that makes a country great." Such statements implied that the war had been, above all, a wonderful and ultimately successful opportunity for American men to "vitalize" their manhood and then flaunt it before everyone who had doubted it. This included American men themselves. In the Republican convention of 1900, Sen. Chauncey M. Depew (R, N.Y.) applauded the war's effects on American men's psyches. Thinking of charges such as those made by Theodore Roosevelt on the eve of the war that "shilly-shallying and half-measures at this time merely render us contemptible in the eyes of the world; and what is infinitely more important in our own eyes too," Depew declared, "There is not a man here who does not feel four hundred percent bigger in 1900 than he did in 1896. Bigger intellectually, bigger hopefully, bigger patriotically, bigger in the grasp of the fact that he is a citizen of a country which has become a world power."

It was against this martial backdrop that the United States confronted the Philippine issue. The ascendant belief that martial endeavors were good for the nation because they vitalized American men made overseas colonies appear desirable not only for their economic and strategic benefits but also for their character-building potential. This assumption was particularly noticeable in the thought of the prominent imperialists Theodore Roosevelt, Albert Beveridge, and Henry Cabot Lodge, all of whom regarded manly character as the bedrock of American democracy. . . .

Roosevelt, Beveridge, and Lodge had plenty of company in glorifying imperial policies for their effects on character. Similar strains of thought can be seen in the statements made by many of their fellow imperialists, including even President McKinley. After resisting the pressures for war with Spain in the early months of 1898, McKinley caught a mild dose of war fever. "What a wonderful experience," he said of the Spanish-American War. The success of the war and his own increased status made McKinley more receptive to taking and holding the Philippines. Though never an ardent imperialist, McKinley went along with the affirmations put forth by such imperialists as Roosevelt, Beveridge, and Lodge. Echoing their assertions, he explained his decision to take the Philippines by saying, "The progress of a nation can alone prevent degeneration. There must be new life or there will be weakness and decay." McKinley proffered the Philippines as a challenge with great potential, as "the mightiest test of American virtue and capacity." Like a number of other imperialists, he concluded that aggressive Philippine policies would build character in American men. "We have not only been adding territory to the United States," he declared in 1899, "but we have been adding character and prestige to the American name (continued applause)."

Driven by a desire to build character in American men, imperialists welcomed the Philippine War as a great challenge. Behind their noble-sounding talk of U.S. obligations to the Filipinos lay a self-serving motive: the belief that the Filipinos were opportunities as well as responsibilities. The imperialists' calls to duty, calculated to appeal to Americans' sense of mission, masked the less benevolent idea that conquering and governing the Philippines would benefit American men. The stereotypes of the Filipinos [mentioned] earlier can reveal much about these self-interested concerns if they are interpreted with their implications for American men foremost in mind. . . .

At the turn of the century, Lodge, Beveridge, and Roosevelt worried that American men were abdicating their domestic authority, thus causing women to become more active in public life. Like Fernald, the imperial publicist and exponent of domesticity for women, all three deplored women's growing political presence and insisted that electoral politics should remain a male preserve. . . .

Believing that the refinement and purity of such women as [his wife] Anna Lodge depended on their distance from ugly political and commercial struggles, Henry Cabot Lodge and his like-minded allies on the imperial issue preached men's responsibility to shelter and protect women. . . . For his part, Roosevelt maintained that a healthy state relied on women's domesticity as well as men's heroism. "The woman must be the housewife, the helpmeet of the homemaker, the wise and fearless mother of many healthy children," he wrote in "The Strenuous Life." "When men fear work or fear righteous war, when women fear motherhood, they tremble on the brink of doom." Fearing that "race suicide" would enfeeble the nation, Roosevelt told his turn-of-the-century audiences that women's primary political role was to bear and raise children.

Roosevelt, Beveridge, and Lodge wanted to build American men's governing capacity in part to counter women's increasing political activism. They believed that more authoritative men would dispel the pernicious "propaganda" of women's equality and cause women to return to domestic pursuits. These objectives contributed to their commitment to martial policies, for they assumed that by teaching American men to wield authority, such policies would teach them to govern their households with a firm, though benevolent, hand. Arduous struggles, they believed, would enable men to regain women's respect, devotion, and admiration. The same logic which held that an inability to govern household dependents served as evidence of Filipino men's political incapacity led Beveridge and other imperialists to think that shouldering responsibility for childlike or feminine colonial dependents would demonstrate American men's political fitness. . . .

By imperialist accounts, the [anti-annexationists] deserved little credibility in political debate because they were effeminate, homebound critics, not bold men of action. In "The Strenuous Life," Roosevelt blamed the "silly, mock humanitarianism of the prattlers who sit at home in peace" for costing the lives of American men in the Philippines. The timid antis, he maintained, spoke of liberty and the consent of the governed merely to "excuse themselves for their unwillingness to play the part of men." Roosevelt continued this theme in another address: "We need display but scant patience with those who, sitting at ease in their own homes, delight to exercise a querulous and censorious spirit of judgment upon their brethren who, whatever their shortcomings, are doing strong men's work as they bring the light of civilization into the world's dark places. . . .

As they struggled to stigmatize antis as womanly, imperialists benefited from the widespread tendency to construe opposition to war as a sign of cowardice, weakness, or other supposedly unmanly attributes. Especially in the frenzy of militarism that followed the Spanish-American War, militance seemed to indicate manly character, and a lack thereof, effeminacy. Imperialists also benefited from the composition of the anti-imperialist forces. Women were, indeed, important to the anti-imperialist cause. Although the Anti-Imperialist League had no women in its elected leadership, women were highly visible among the ranks. In the first mass meeting to protest imperialism, held in June 1898, half of the people in attendance were women. The antis' campaign to recall volunteer troops from the Philippines in the spring of 1899 relied heavily on the energies of women, who lobbied to have the troops returned. Women also helped sustain the anti-imperialist movement financially. In the second meeting of the New England Anti-Imperialist League, an officer reported that "noble-hearted ladies in Boston and New York" had contributed "ten or a dozen times each" to the league. . . .

By depicting the antis as women, imperialists suggested that the elderly, peaceable, seemingly female (if not literally female) antis did not represent the [founding] fathers as much as themselves, for, although older, the antis lacked the fathers' manly character. Despite their relative youthfulness, imperialists could say that they resembled the manly fathers more than the womanly antis did. Because of the martial ideal of citizenship that flourished in the aftermath of the Spanish-American War and the more fundamental assumption that manhood mattered in politics, these claims significantly benefited imperialists. The valorization of manly character in late-nineteenth-century U.S. politics meant that the "aunties," as the "old lady element" in public affairs, appeared less qualified to judge whether American policies were consistent with American principles than the imperialists, who might have seemed boyish but always seemed male.

PRIMARY SOURCES

The primary sources fall into several categories: cartoons from the popular press, writings of expansionists regarding the Philippines, selections from the congressional debates over Philippine annexation, and statistical tables related to U.S. overseas trade. As you evaluate these sources, remember that they may support different conclusions about the decision to annex the Philippines and thus may reinforce or contradict Kristin Hoganson's argument in Source 1. They will also help you come to your own conclusion about why the United States decided to keep the Philippines.

Cartoons on Philippine Annexation

This section contains cartoons related to the issue of the annexation of the Philippines. As you study them, note the issues that they emphasize. Pay particular attention to images revealing attitudes toward masculinity or gender. Do these images reveal that proponents of annexation attempted to use gender as an effective weapon in the debate over the Philippines? Do any of these images suggest that the need to assert masculinity was connected in annexationists' minds to other issues?

This cartoon, originally published in the *Minneapolis Tribune,* comments on the opposition of Massachusetts senator George Hoar to Philippine annexation.

"Recommended by Hoar" (1899)

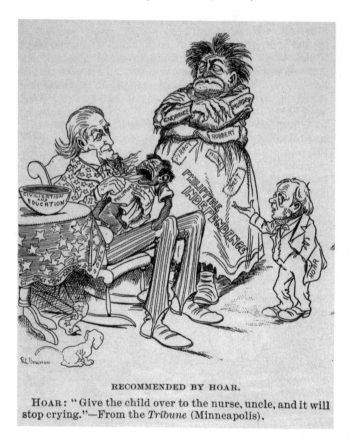

RECOMMENDED BY HOAR.

HOAR: "Give the child over to the nurse, uncle, and it will stop crying."—From the *Tribune* (Minneapolis).

Source: Review of Reviews. Volume 20, June 15, 1899. Reprinted in Kristin L. Hoganson, *Fighting for American Manhood: How Gender Politics Provoked the Spanish-American and Philippine-American Wars* (New Haven, Conn.: Yale University Press, 1998), p. 136.

3   This cartoon from *Judge* magazine also focuses on George Hoar's opposition to annexation. The figure on the lower left is John P. Altgeld, the former governor of Illinois who gained nationwide attention by freeing three of the accused bombers in Chicago's Haymarket Square bombing.

"The Anti-Expansion Ticket for 1900" (1899)

Source: Judge. Volume 37, July 8, 1899. Reprinted in Kristin L. Hoganson, *Fighting for American Manhood: How Gender Politics Provoked the Spanish-American and Philippine-American Wars* (New Haven, Conn.: Yale University Press, 1998), p. 177.

4   English poet Rudyard Kipling penned the poem "The White Man's Burden" in celebration of the U.S. Senate's ratification of the treaty with Spain. This cartoon originally from the *Detroit Journal* and reprinted in the *Literary Digest* illustrates the same theme.

"The White Man's Burden" (1899)

THE WHITE MAN'S BURDEN.—*The Journal, Detroit.*

Source: Literary Digest, February 18, 1899. Courtesy Harvard College Library. Reprinted in Frank Ninkovich, *The United States and Imperialism* (Malden, Mass.: Blackwell Publishers, Inc., 2001), between p. ix and p. 1.

Also from *Judge* magazine, this cartoon makes an obvious connection between cultural uplift and annexation. Note, too, the contrasting images of McKinley and Cuba, Puerto Rico, and the Philippines.

"The Filipino's First Bath" (1899)

Source: Judge. Volume 37, No. 947. June 10, 1899. Courtesy Harvard College Library. Reprinted in Franklin Odo, ed., *The Columbia Documentary History of the Asian American Experience* (New York: Columbia University Press, 2002), p. 125.

Statements by Expansionists

Even before the start of the Spanish-American War, many American expansionists were vocal in their desire to see American influence expand overseas. After the U.S. Senate voted to ratify the treaty with Spain, which turned over the Philippines to the United States, they were equally vocal in support of a war against Fil- ipino nationalists upset with the American decision to keep their country. This section contains excerpts from speeches, articles, and books written by some of the most prominent expansionists. As you read them, note the various justifica- tions offered for taking—and then fighting to keep—the Philippines. Do any of these sources equate manliness with such a policy?

6   There was no more ardent or vocal expansionist than Theodore Roo- sevelt. As Assistant Secretary of the Navy, Roosevelt ordered Com- modore Dewey several months before the Spanish-American War started to keep his fleet together and, in the event of war with Spain, engage the Spanish fleet in the Philippines. Roosevelt also wrote and spoke widely on the desirability of American overseas expansion. His essay "The Strenuous Life," originally delivered as a speech in April 1899, offers an especially forceful statement of Roosevelt's thinking about America's role in the world. It is also a vivid demonstration of his thinking about manliness and gender.

"The Strenuous Life" (1899)
THEODORE ROOSEVELT

A life of slothful ease, a life of that peace which springs merely from lack either of desire or of power to strive after great things, is as little worthy of a nation as of an individual. I ask only that what every self-respecting American de- mands from himself and from his sons shall be demanded of the American na- tion as a whole. Who among you would teach your boys that ease, that peace is to be the first consideration in their eyes—to be the ultimate goal after which they strive? . . . We do not admire the man of timid peace. We admire the man who embodies victorious effort; the man who never wrongs his neighbor, who is prompt to help a friend, but who has those virile qualities necessary to win in the stern strife of actual life. . . .

In the last analysis a healthy state can exist only when the men and women who make it up lead clean, vigorous, healthy lives; when the children are so trained that they shall endeavor, not to shirk difficulties, but to over- come them; not to seek ease, but to know how to wrest triumph from toil and risk. The man must be glad to do a man's work, to dare and endure and to la- bor; to keep himself, and to keep those dependent upon him. The woman must be the housewife, the helpmeet of the homemaker, the wise and fearless mother of many healthy children. . . .

When men fear work or fear righteous war, when women fear mother-

Source: Theodore Roosevelt, *The Strenuous Life: Essays and Addresses* (New York: The Century Co., 1903), pp. 1–4, 6–8, 9–10, 17–18; original copyright 1899 by The Century Company.

hood, they tremble on the brink of doom; and well it is that they should vanish from the earth, where they are fit subjects for the scorn of all men and women who are themselves strong and brave and high-minded. . . .

. . . In 1898 we could not help being brought face to face with the problem of war with Spain. All we could decide was whether we should shrink like cowards from the contest, or enter into it as beseemed a brave and high-spirited people; and, once in, whether failure or success should crown our banners. So it is now. We cannot avoid the responsibilities that confront us in Hawaii, Cuba, Porto [sic] Rico, and the Philippines. All we can decide is whether we shall meet them in a way that will redound to the national credit, or whether we shall make of our dealings with these new problems a dark and shameful page in our history. To refuse to deal with them at all merely amounts to dealing with them badly. We have a given problem to solve. If we undertake the solution, there is, of course, always danger that we may not solve it aright; but to refuse to undertake the solution simply renders it certain that we cannot possibly solve it aright. The timid man, the lazy man, the man who distrusts his country, the over-civilized man, who has lost the great fighting, masterful virtues, the ignorant man, and the man of dull mind, whose soul is incapable of feeling the mighty lift that thrills "stern men with empires in their brains"—all these, of course, shrink from seeing the nation undertake its new duties; shrink from seeing us build a navy and an army adequate to our needs; shrink from seeing us do our share of the world's work, by bringing order out of chaos in the great, fair tropic islands from which the valor of our soldiers and sailors has driven the Spanish flag. These are the men who fear the strenuous life, who fear the only national life which is really worth leading. They believe in that cloistered life which saps the hardy virtues in a nation, as it saps them in the individual; or else they are wedded to that base spirit of gain and greed which recognizes in commercialism the be-all and end-all of national life, instead of realizing that, though an indispensable element, it is, after all, but one of the many elements that go to make up true national greatness. . . .

. . . It is worse than idle to say that we have no duty to perform, and can leave to their fates the islands we have conquered. Such a course would be the course of infamy. It would be followed at once by utter chaos in the wretched islands themselves. Some stronger, manlier power would have to step in and do the work, and we would have shown ourselves weaklings, unable to carry to successful completion the labors that great and high-spirited nations are eager to undertake. . . .

The problems are different for the different islands. Porto [sic] Rico is not large enough to stand alone. We must govern it wisely and well, primarily in the interest of its own people. Cuba is, in my judgment, entitled ultimately to settle for itself whether it shall be an independent state or an integral portion of the mightiest of republics. . . . The Philippines offer a yet graver problem. Their population includes half-caste and native Christians, warlike Moslems, and wild pagans. Many of their people are utterly unfit for self-government, and show no signs of becoming fit. Others may in time become fit but at present can only take part in self-government under a wise supervision, at once firm and beneficent. We have driven Spanish tyranny from the islands. If we now let it be replaced by savage anarchy, our work has been for harm and not for good. I have scant patience with those who fear to undertake the task of governing the Philippines, and who openly avow that they do fear to undertake it, or that they shrink from it because of the expense and trouble; but I have even scanter patience with those who make a pretense of humanitarianism to hide and cover their timidity, and who cant about "liberty" and the "consent of the governed," in order to excuse themselves for their unwillingness to play the part of men. Their doctrines, if carried out, would make it incumbent upon us to leave the Apaches of Arizona to work out their own salvation, and to decline to interfere in a single Indian reservation. Their doctrines condemn your forefathers and mine for ever having settled in these United States.

 In a meeting with a group from the Methodist Episcopal Church, President William McKinley explained how he came to a decision about the desirability of annexing the Philippines.

William McKinley on Annexation (1899)

Hold a moment longer! Not quite yet, gentlemen! Before you go I would like to say just a word about the Philippine business. I have been criticized a good deal about the Philippines, but don't deserve it. The truth is I didn't want the Philippines, and when they came to us, as a gift from the gods, I did not know what to do with them. When the Spanish War broke out [Admiral George] Dewey was at Hongkong, and I ordered him to go to Manila and to capture or destroy the Spanish fleet, and he had to; because, if defeated, he had no place to refit on that side of the globe, and if the Dons were victorious they would likely cross the Pacific and ravage our Oregon and California coasts. And so he had to destroy the Spanish fleet, and did it! But that was as far as I thought then.

When I next realized that the Philippines had dropped into our laps I confess I did not know what to do with them. I sought counsel from all sides—Democrats as well as Republicans—but got little help. I thought first we would take only Manila; then Luzon; then other islands perhaps also. I walked the floor of the White House night after night until midnight; and I am not ashamed to tell you, gentlemen, that I went down on my knees and prayed Almighty God for light and guidance more than one night. And one night late it came to me this way—I don't know how it was, but it came: (1) That we could not give them back to Spain—that would be cowardly and dishon-

Source: Charles S. Olcott, *William McKinley* (Boston: Houghton Mifflin Company, 1916; reprinted in 1972 by AMS Press, New York), Vol. II, pp. 110–111.

orable; (2) that we could not turn them over to France and Germany—our commercial rivals in the Orient—that would be bad business and discreditable; (3) that we could not leave them to themselves—they were unfit for self-government—and they would soon have anarchy and misrule over there worse than Spain's was; and (4) that there was nothing left for us to do but to take them all, and to educate the Filipinos, and uplift and civilize and Christianize them, and by God's grace do the very best we could by them, as our fellow-men for whom Christ also died. And then I went to bed, and went to sleep, and slept soundly, and the next morning I sent for the chief engineer of the War Department (our map-maker), and I told him to put the Philippines on the map of the United States (pointing to a large map on the wall of his office), and there they are, and there they will stay while I am President!

8   Senator Albert J. Beveridge of Indiana was another vocal defender of American imperialism. In this speech before the Senate in January 1900, Beveridge defends the American effort to keep the Philippines in the face of both armed Filipino resistance and vocal critics at home of an increasingly costly Philippine-American War.

"In Support of an American Empire" (1900)
ALBERT J. BEVERIDGE

The Philippines are ours forever, "territory belonging to the United States," as the Constitution calls them. And just beyond the Philippines are China's illimitable markets. We will not retreat from either. We will not repudiate our duty in the archipelago. We will not abandon our opportunity in the Orient. We will not renounce our part in the mission of our race, trustee under God, of the civilization of the world. And we will move forward to our work, not howling out regrets like slaves whipped to their burdens, but with gratitude for a task worthy of our strength, and thanksgiving to Almighty God that He has marked us as His chosen people, henceforth to lead in the regeneration of the world.

This island empire is the last land left in all the oceans. If it should prove a mistake to abandon it, the blunder once made would be irretrievable. If it proves a mistake to hold it, the error can be corrected when we will. Every other progressive nation stands ready to relieve us.

But to hold it will be no mistake. Our largest trade henceforth must be with Asia. The Pacific is our ocean. More and more Europe will manufacture the most it needs, secure from its colonies the most it consumes. Where shall

Source: U.S. Congress, Senate, "In Support of an American Empire," speech by Senator Albert J. Beveridge of Indiana, 56th Cong., 1st sess., *Congressional Record* 33 (January 9, 1900): pp. 704–712 passim.

we turn for consumers of our surplus? Geography answers the question. China is our natural customer: She is nearer to us than to England, Germany, or Russia, the commercial powers of the present and the future. They have moved nearer to China by securing permanent bases on her borders. The Philippines gives us a base at the door of all the East.

Lines of navigation from our ports to the Orient and Australia; from the Isthmian Canal to Asia; from all Oriental ports to Australia, converge at and separate from the Philippines. They are a self-supporting, dividend-paying fleet, permanently anchored at a spot selected by the strategy of Providence, commanding the Pacific. And the Pacific is the ocean of the commerce of the future. Most future wars will be conflicts for commerce. The power that rules the Pacific, therefore, is the power that rules the world. And, with the Philippines, that power is and will forever be the American Republic.

China's trade is the mightiest commercial fact in our future. Her foreign commerce was $285,738,300 in 1897, of which we, her neighbor, had less than 9 per cent, of which only a little more than half was merchandise sold to China by us. We ought to have 50 per cent, and we will. And China's foreign commerce is only beginning. Her resources, her possibilities, her wants, all are undeveloped. She has only 340 miles of railway. I have seen trains loaded with natives and all the activities of modern life already appearing along the line. But she needs, and in fifty years will have, 20,000 miles of railway.

Who can estimate her commerce then? That statesman commits a crime against American trade—against the American grower of cotton and wheat and tobacco, the American manufacturer of machinery and clothing—who fails to put America where she may command that trade. . . .

It will be hard for Americans who have not studied them to understand the people. They are a barbarous race, modified by three centuries of contact with a decadent race. The Filipino is the South Sea Malay, put through a process of three hundred years of superstition in religion, dishonesty in dealing, disorder in habits of industry, and cruelty, caprice, and corruption in government. It is barely possible that 1,000 men in all the archipelago are capable of self-government in the Anglo-Saxon sense.

My own belief is that there are not 100 men among them who comprehend what Anglo-Saxon self-government even means, and there are over 5,000,000 people to be governed. . . .

Mr. President, reluctantly and only from a sense of duty am I forced to say that American opposition to the war has been the chief factor prolonging it. Had Aguinaldo* not understood that in America, even in the American Congress, even here in the Senate, he and his cause were supported; had he not known that it was proclaimed on the stump and in the press of a faction in the United States that every shot his misguided followers fired into the breasts of American soldiers was like the volleys fired by Washington's men

*Filipino nationalist Emilio Aguinaldo was the leader of the armed resistance to American occupation.

against the soldiers of King George his insurrection would have dissolved before it entirely crystallized. . . .

Mr. President, this question is deeper than any question of party politics; deeper than any question of the isolated policy of our country even; deeper even than any question of constitutional power. It is elemental. It is racial. God has not been preparing the English-speaking and Teutonic peoples for a thousand years for nothing but vain and idle self-contemplation and self-admiration. No! He has made us the master organizers of the world to establish system where chaos reigns. He has given us the spirit of progress to overwhelm the forces of reaction throughout the earth. He has made us adept in government that we may administer government among savage and senile peoples. Were it not for such a force as this the world would relapse into barbarism and night. And of all our race He has marked the American people as his chosen nation to finally lead in the regeneration of the world. This is the divine mission of America, and it holds for us all the profit, all the glory, all the happiness possible to man. We are trustees of the world's progress, guardians of its righteous peace. The judgment of the Master is upon us: "Ye have been faithful over a few things; I will make you rule over many things."

Senate Debate on the Treaty with Spain

In early 1899, the U.S. Senate debated the ratification of the Treaty of Paris, negotiated with Spain at the end of the Spanish-American War. The treaty called for the Philippines to be turned over to the United States, a key issue in the debates on the treaty in the Senate and the country at large. As you read the following excerpts from these debates, notice how annexationists counter objections to taking the Philippines. How did racial attitudes influence each side's arguments? What issues seem most important in the minds of the expansionist senators?

 ## 9   Selections from the Treaty Debate (1899)

Sen. [Donelson] Caffery (*D, Louisiana*)

In the first place, any people that we take jurisdiction over, by taking the territory in which they live, ought not to be, and, in my opinion, can not be, incorporated into our midst, to be bone of our bone and flesh of our flesh, without their free consent.

In the second place, if such a people are unfit and in all human probability never will be fit for the glorious privileges, franchises, and functions of an American citizen, we ought not in that case to even think of incorporating

Source: Congressional Record, 55th Cong., 3rd sess., January through early February 1899, Vol. 32, pts. 1 and 2, pp. 436–1481 passim.

them into the United States, for we can not establish the principle of despotic sway in America. . . .

Sir, when I look at the condition of the world to-day, when I review the history of the past, I am unalterably convinced that no permanent sway can ever be held by the white man over the colored races of the Tropics; and if sway is held, it is held under the power of unlimited, cruel despotism. That is the only way the white man can rule in the Tropics. It is the only way he has ever ruled. Whether it is providential or whether it is not, it is a fact. . . .

Sen. [Orville H.] Platt *(R, Connecticut)*

Mr. President, what did we do with the Indians of this country? I said that that doctrine would have turned back the *Mayflower* from Plymouth Rock. We found here a continent in the hands of the Indians, aborigines, who did not want us to come here, who did not want to be governed by us without their consent, and with them incapable of consenting, we have, nevertheless, gone on and legislated for them and governed them, and now, at last, have brought many of them to a state where they have become citizens and incorporated with us. If you attempt to make a literal application of this doctrine, what answer have you to make when the Indian raises his voice and says: "I did not want to be legislated for, I did not consent to be governed by the United States; you violated your Declaration of Independence when you attempted to legislate for and to govern me without my consent"? . . .

. . . I am one who believes that we shall not have done a great wrong to humanity, that we shall not have imperiled our institutions, that we shall not have rung the doom knell of republican institutions if we extend over the people who reside in the territory which we may acquire those principles which protect them in their lives, which protect them in their property, which protect them in their efforts to secure happiness, and the American Senate and the American House of Representatives are not going to legislate in any other spirit, Mr. President. . . .

I believe in Providence. I believe the hand of Providence brought about the conditions which we must either accept or be recreant to duty. I believe that those conditions were a part of the great development of the great force of Christian civilization on earth. I believe the same force was behind our army at Santiago and our ships in Manila Bay that was behind the landing of the Pilgrims on Plymouth Rock. I believe that we have been chosen to carry on and to carry forward this great work of uplifting humanity on earth. From the time of the landing on Plymouth Rock in the spirit of the Declaration of Independence, in the spirit of the Constitution, believing that all men are equal and endowed by their Creator with inalienable rights, believing that governments derive their just powers from the consent of the governed, we have spread that civilization across the continent until it stood at the Pacific Ocean looking ever westward.

> Westward the course of empire takes its way.

The English-speaking people, the agents of this civilization, the agency through which humanity is to be uplifted, through which despotism is to go down, through which the rights of man are to prevail, is charged with this great mission. Providence has put it upon us. We propose to execute it. We propose to proclaim liberty in the Philippines Islands, if they are ours. We propose to proclaim liberty and justice and the protection of life and human rights wherever the flag of the United States is planted. Who decries that? Who will haul down those principles? . . .

Sen. [John Lowndes] McLaurin *(D, South Carolina)*

I feel that a representative from South Carolina is peculiarly qualified to speak upon one phase of the question, and it is that pertaining to the incorporation of a mongrel and semibarbarous population into our body politic, a population that, so far as I can ascertain, is inferior to but akin to the negro in moral and intellectual qualities and incapacity for self-government. The experience of the South for the past thirty years with the negro race, is pregnant with lessons of wisdom for our guidance in the Philippines. It is passing strange that Senators who favored universal suffrage and the full enfranchisement of the negro should now advocate imperialism.

In other words, that territory can be acquired by conquest, held as a colony, and its inhabitants treated as vassals rather than citizens—governed by military rule or legislation not authorized by the Constitution. There is a glaring inconsistency in these positions. If they are sincere in their views as to the Philippines, they should propose an amendment to the Constitution which will put the inferior races in this country and the inhabitants of the Philippines upon an equality as to their civil and political rights, and thus forever settle the vexed race and suffrage questions in this country as well as the outlying territories.

How can they consistently, justly, and, I might add, constitutionally advocate a policy for outlying territories, embracing races so nearly akin to the negro, which differs so radically from the policy adopted as to that race in the South? There can be but one answer to that question, and that is that they substantially admit, in the light of a third of a century's experience, that universal suffrage is a monumental failure and that the time has come for the correction of this stupendous government error. . . .

Therefore, if the Philippine Islands were annexed and formed into States, this Chamber and the other House would contain about one-seventh Japanese, Malays, Chinese, or whatever mixture they have out there. We would have representatives with a voice in directing the affairs of this country from another continent, speaking another language, different in race, religion, and civilization—a people with whom we have nothing in common. For me, I can not tolerate the thought. The great strength of our country is not merely its isolated position, washed on each side by the waters of a great ocean, but in a homogeneous population, speaking a common language, and with similar aspirations and ideas of liberty and civilization.

In a commercial point of view, I believe the importance of the Philippines per se is greatly exaggerated. They are chiefly valuable as the key to the Orient, but we need not colonize to obtain that advantage. The exports of the Philippines, according to the Statistical Abstract, in 1896 amounted to $30,806,250. If this entire trade was monopolized by us it would be insignificant. We will have to teach them to wear shirts and breeches before we can trade with them much. But England and Germany have large trade interests in the Philippines, and under our agreement with Spain she must have equal trade privileges with the United States. As a matter of dollars and cents, I doubt its advantage. . . .

If we embark in a colonial system, it means the inauguration of a despotic power in Washington. It means a large standing army that will not only be used to rule outlying territories with an iron hand, but that sooner or later will be used at home to overawe and override the popular will. An imperialistic democracy, like an atheistic religion, is an impossible hybrid. . . .

Sen. [Henry Cabot] Lodge (R, *Massachusetts*)

What our precise policy shall be I do not know, because I for one am not sufficiently informed as to the conditions there to be able to say what it will be best to do, nor, I may add, do I think anyone is. But I believe that we shall have the wisdom not to attempt to incorporate those islands with our body politic, or make their inhabitants part of our citizenship, or set their labor alongside of ours and within our tariff to compete in any industry with American workmen. I believe that we shall have the courage not to depart from those islands fearfully, timidly, and unworthily and leave them to anarchy among themselves, to the brief and bloody domination of some self-constituted dictator, and to the quick conquest of other powers, who will have no such hesitation as we should feel in crushing them into subjection by harsh and repressive methods. It is for us to decide the destiny of the Philippines, not for Europe, and we can do it alone and without assistance. I believe that we shall have the wisdom, the self-restraint, and the ability to restore peace and order in those islands and give to their people an opportunity for self-government and for freedom under the protecting shield of the United States until the time shall come when they are able to stand alone, if such a thing is possible, and if they do not themselves desire to remain under our protection. This is a great, a difficult, and a noble task. I believe that American civilization is entirely capable of fulfilling it, and I should not have that profound faith which I now cherish in American civilization and American manhood if I did not think so.

Take now the other alternative. Suppose we reject the treaty or strike out the clause relating to the Philippines. That will hand the islands back to Spain; and I can not conceive that any American should be willing to do that. Suppose we reject the treaty; what follows? Let us look at it practically. We continue the state of war, and every sensible man in the country, every business interest, desires the reestablishment of peace in law as well as in fact. At the same time we repudiate the President and his action before the whole world, and the repudiation of the President in such a matter as this is, to my mind, the humiliation of the United States in the eyes of civilized mankind and brands us as a people incapable of great affairs or of taking rank where we belong, as one of the greatest of the great world powers. . . .

There is much else involved here, vast commercial and trade interests, which I believe we have a right to guard and a duty to foster. But the opponents of the treaty have placed their opposition on such high and altruistic grounds that I have preferred to meet them there, and not to discuss the enormous material benefits to our trade, our industries, and our labor dependent upon a right settlement of this question, both directly and indirectly. For this reason I have not touched upon the commercial advantages to the country involved in the question of these islands, or the far greater question of the markets of China, of which we must have our share for the benefit of our workingmen. I have confined myself solely to the question which has been brought to the front here, and to the proposition that we could not be trusted to deal honestly with those islands of the East, for that is what the argument of the opposition, stripped of rhetoric and ornament, amounts to.

Tables on American Exports

As you examine these tables (which are better read from bottom to top), note the trend in manufactured exports and in the exports to particular nations or regions. Are these trends relevant in understanding the decision to annex the Philippines?

 ## Value of Manufactured Exports, 1866–1900

[In millions of dollars]

Year	Manufactured foodstuffs[a]	Semi manufactures[b]	Finished manufactures
1900	320	153	332
1899	305	118	263
1898	285	102	223
1897	235	98	213

(cont. on next page)

Year	Manufactured foodstuffs[a]	Semi manufactures[b]	Finished manufactures
1896	219	76	182
1895	219	62	144
1894	250	67	136
1893	247	49	130
1892	250	50	133
1891	226	48	140
1890	225	46	133
1889	175	43	123
1888	170	40	114
1887	176	37	112
1886	163	34	112
1885	202	39	111
1884	195	38	118
1883	186	38	122
1882	178	37	125
1881	226	33	102
1880	193	29	93
1879	174	30	103
1878	170	29	110
1877	150	32	113
1876	122	31	74
1875	110	27	75
1874	114	26	81
1873	101	25	76
1872	84	21	65
1871	67	14	76
1870	51	14	56
1869	44	14	47
1868	42	17	43
1867	34	15	44
1866	41	12	39

[a]Processed food.
[b]Partially finished manufactured goods.

Source: Historical Statistics of the United States: Colonial Times to 1957 (Washington, D.C.: U.S. Bureau of the Census, 1960), pp. 544–545.

11 Value of U.S. Exports by Country of Destination, 1866–1900

[In millions of dollars]

Year	Total value	America						Europe					Asia				Australia and Oceania	Africa
		Total	Canada	Cuba	Mexico	Brazil	Other	Total	United Kingdom	France	Germany	Other	Total	China	Japan	Other		
1900	1,394	227	95	26	35	12	59	1,040	534	83	187	236	68	15	29	24	41	19
1899	1,227	194	88	19	25	12	50	937	512	61	156	208	49	14	17	18	29	19
1898	1,231	174	84	10	21	13	46	974	541	95	155	183	45	10	20	15	22	18
1897	1,051	159	65	8	23	12	51	813	483	58	125	147	39	12	13	14	23	17
1896	883	153	60	8	19	14	52	673	406	47	98	122	26	7	8	11	17	14
1895	808	143	53	13	15	15	47	628	387	45	92	104	18	4	5	9	13	6
1894	892	153	57	20	13	14	49	701	431	55	92	123	22	6	4	12	12	5
1893	848	152	47	24	20	12	49	662	421	47	84	110	17	4	3	10	11	5
1892	1,030	139	43	18	14	14	50	851	499	99	106	147	20	7	3	10	16	5
1891	884	131	38	12	15	14	52	705	445	61	93	106	26	9	5	12	18	5
1890	858	133	40	13	13	12	55	684	448	50	86	100	20	3	5	12	16	5
1889	742	125	41	12	11	9	52	579	383	46	68	82	19	8	5	6	16	4
1888	696	110	36	10	10	7	47	549	362	39	56	92	20	5	4	11	15	3
1887	716	104	35	11	8	8	42	575	366	57	59	93	20	6	3	11	14	3
1886	680	98	33	10	8	7	40	541	348	42	62	89	23	8	3	12	15	3
1885	742	104	38	9	8	7	42	599	398	47	62	92	21	6	3	12	14	4

(cont. on next page)

Source: Historical Statistics of the United States: Colonial Times to 1957 (Washington, D.C.: U.S. Bureau of the Census, 1960), pp. 550–551.

	Total value	America						Europe					Asia				Australia and Oceania	Africa
Year		Total	Canada	Cuba	Mexico	Brazil	Other	Total	United Kingdom	France	Germany	Other	Total	China	Japan	Other		
1884	741	123	44	11	13	9	46	584	386	51	61	86	17	5	3	9	13	3
1883	824	129	44	15	17	9	44	660	425	59	66	110	17	4	3	10	14	4
1882	751	113	37	12	15	9	40	600	408	50	54	88	19	6	3	10	13	6
1881	902	108	38	11	11	9	39	766	481	94	70	121	13	5	1	7	10	5
1880	836	93	29	11	8	9	36	719	454	100	57	108	12	1	3	8	7	5
1879	712	91	30	13	7	8	33	594	349	90	57	98	12	3	3	6	10	5
1878	710	100	37	12	7	9	35	584	387	55	55	87	12	4	2	6	9	4
1877	645	99	37	13	6	8	35	525	346	45	58	76	10	2	1	7	8	3
1876	610	96	33	13	6	7	37	497	336	40	51	70	8	1	1	6	5	4
1875	574	100	35	15	6	8	36	459	317	34	50	58	7	1	2	4	5	3
1874	651	110	42	17	6	8	37	528	345	43	63	77	5	1	1	3	5	3
1873	594	102	33	16	6	7	40	479	317	34	62	66	5	1	1	3	5	3
1872	492	89	29	14	6	6	34	393	265	31	41	56	4	3	1	—	4	2
1871	493	89	32	15	8	6	28	394	273	27	35	59	3	2	1	1	4	3
1870	471	79	25	14	6	6	28	381	248	46	42	45	4	3	1	—	5	2
1869	382	74	23	12	5	6	28	291	185	33	38	35	7	5	1	1	6	3
1868	383	81	24	15	6	6	30	287	198	26	31	32	6	4	1	1	6	3
1867	398	77	21	14	5	5	32	307	225	34	22	26	5	4	1	—	6	3
1866	479	80	24	15	5	6	30	386	288	51	22	25	5	3	1	2	7	2

CONCLUSION

Whatever your conclusions about the reasons for the American decision to annex the Philippines, you probably have discovered that it may not necessarily be easy for historians to prove broad assertions. The U.S. Senate, of course, made the ultimate decision about the retention of the Philippines after the Spanish-American War, but that decision was not made in a vacuum. Senators may have been subject to numerous influences, including an assessment about markets for American goods, notions about the responsibilities of "civilized" nations toward "backward" ones, or even concerns about the character of the American people. The sources in this chapter suggest that these and other influences were present in 1899.

The sources also illustrate some important axioms of historical inquiry. First, historians seek the causes of things. They do not just want to know that the United States decided to keep the Philippines for itself in 1899, but why. The search for causes leads historians to consider the influence of ideas. In this case, that search has led historians to consider the influence of an American sense of mission and even ideas about gender and masculinity. It also requires them to ask whether history is better written "from the top down" or "from the bottom up," that is, from the point of view of leaders or followers. Thus historians attempt to determine if the influence of elite individuals like William McKinley and Theodore Roosevelt or of a voting public aroused by press accounts, political cartoons, or speeches was more important in explaining the decision for annexation. Finally, the sources in this chapter make clear that the question of motivation is central to historical inquiry. Your conclusion about the role of fears regarding American masculinity or other factors in the decision for annexation involve a corresponding view about the motives of annexationists in and outside the Congress. The chapters that follow will consider these problems: historical causation, ideology and history, history written from the top and bottom of society, and, as we will see next, motivation in history.

FURTHER READING

H. W. Brands, *Bound to Empire: The United States and the Philippines* (New York: Oxford University Press, 1992).

Frank Hindman Golay, *Face of Empire: United States–Philippine Relations, 1898–1946* (Madison, Wisc.: Center for Southeast Asian Studies, 1998).

Robert E. Hannigan, *The New World Power: American Foreign Policy, 1898–1917* (Philadelphia: University of Pennsylvania Press, 2002).

Stanley Karnow, *In Our Image: America's Empire in the Philippines* (New York: Random House, 1989).

Stuart Creighton Miller, *"Benevolent Assimilation": The American Conquest of the Philippines, 1899–1903* (New Haven, Conn.: Yale University Press, 1982).

Frank Ninkovich, *The United States and Imperialism* (Malden, Mass.: Blackwell Publishers Inc., 2001).

NOTE

1. Ernest R. May, *Imperial Democracy: The Emergence of America as a Great Power* (New York: Harcourt, Brace and World, 1961), p. 159.

Chapter

5

The Problem of Historical Motivation: The Bungalow as the "Progressive" House

The documents in this chapter present various kinds of information on the craze for the bungalow style in the Progressive era.

Secondary Source

Primary Sources

*I*n the first decades of the twentieth century, the bungalow transformed the appearance of neighborhoods throughout the United States. With its wide, low-pitched roof, overhanging eaves, prominent front porch, straight lines, "modern" kitchen, and economical use of space, it was the new ideal home for middle-class Americans. In drawings and photographs, it filled the pages of *Architectural Record, Ladies' Home Journal, Good Housekeeping,* and other magazines. One book on bungalows published in 1908 went through five editions in two years. To Progressive-era critics, the older Victorian house was now "aesthetically repulsive," an "architectural atrocity," "hideous," and a reflection of a "fatuous craze for the crudely ornate."[1] Suddenly nineteenth-century styles were out of date.

The bungalow was more than a fad. Many housing crusaders—architects, craftsmen, social reformers, home economists, feminists, and home builders—promoted this architectural style as a powerful means to transform American society. What exactly did the bungalow promoters hope to achieve with new designs and furnishings? What motivated them to assault older "Victorian" aesthetic standards? What values did they seek to promote? In this chapter, we examine the motives of the early-twentieth-century housing reformers and the middle-class Americans whose tastes they influenced.

SETTING

The bungalow craze did not arise in a cultural vacuum, but was one expression of a broader artistic movement at the turn of the century known as Arts and Crafts. English Arts and Crafts enthusiasts in the late nineteenth century promoted simple architectural styles and handicraft production. In response to the spread of the factory, they drew inspiration from Oxford artist John Ruskin and his student William Morris, who argued that machines robbed work of its creativity and pleasure. By the early twentieth century the Arts and Crafts movement had come to America. It was taken up by a number of influential reformers, including Jane Addams, labor reformer Ellen Gates Starr, architect Frank Lloyd Wright, and naturalist Charles Keeler.

Middle-class magazines also popularized the bungalow. *Ladies' Home Journal* editor Edward Bok campaigned relentlessly to replace the "repellently ornate" Victorian home and its "machine-made ornamentation" with simplified home designs and decorations.[2] So did Gustav Stickley, founder of *The Craftsman* magazine, which published dozens of bungalow plans and promoted the Arts and Crafts style as the key to "right living." Other magazines, including *House Beautiful, House and Garden,* and *Country Life in America,* also publicized the Arts and Crafts style. As one observer put it, the nation seemed to have been swept by a "craftsman craziness."[3]

Although craftsmen promoters helped to popularize the bungalow, "craftsman craziness" was not foisted on an unsuspecting public by a cultural elite. Influenced by a variety of social and economic trends, an expanding middle class was very receptive to the new style. For instance, as the army of white-collar workers swelled between 1860 and 1900, so did the anxiety about loss of independence and masculinity. One popular magazine observed in 1903 that "the middle class is becoming a salaried class, and rapidly losing the economic and moral independence of former days."[4] Promoters of Arts and Crafts associated its rugged style with creative manual work, independence, and "the return of manhood to common work."[5] Theodore Roosevelt, who fretted about the decline of America's virility, was an enthusiastic supporter of the new style and called for "the overcivilized man" to cultivate "hardy virtues." Gustav Stickley was in turn an ardent supporter of Roosevelt and reprinted Roosevelt's "The Strenuous Life" in *The Craftsman*.

The bungalow's appeal was also related to dramatic changes overtaking women in the late nineteenth century. By the turn of the century the weight of household chores had been lightened by such technological innovations as water heaters, running water, and washing machines. Moreover, urbanization had led to both lower middle-class birthrates and the ability to purchase more household goods outside the home. Gradually, the housewife's role had been transformed from producer to consumer. At the same time, smaller families and labor-saving products created greater opportunities for women to work outside the home. As work at typewriters and telephone switchboards drew the daughters of the middle class out of the house, the supply of domestic servants declined and fears about a household "crisis" rose.

These changes in women's roles stimulated varied responses, from alarm about the fate of the family to proposals for completely reorganizing the family. Some commentators called on housewives to become experts in spending. The new profession of home economics moved to transform housekeeping into a profession, a domestic science requiring special training in household and scientific management. Settlement house pioneer Jane Addams advocated public kitchens for working mothers. Feminist Charlotte Perkins Gilman, who believed that domestic architecture kept women enslaved, proposed new living arrangements involving cooperative housekeeping and homes without kitchens to free women to pursue careers outside the home.

To many Progressive-era Americans, however, the bungalow was the answer to the "woman question." Within its walls they could project their ideal middle-class woman and family. It was not an accident that bungalow "craziness" swept Americans in the midst of a discussion about work, families, and the role of women in society. Progressive-era Americans, from Edward Bok and Gustav Stickley to Theodore Roosevelt and Charlotte Perkins Gilman, had a deep desire to reshape institutions and values and an enormous faith in the power of the domestic environment to reform people. As one commentator put it: "Our works and our surroundings corrupt or refine our souls. The dwelling, the walls, the windows, the roof, the furniture, the pictures, the ornaments . . . all act constantly upon the imagination and determine its contents."[6] Like the tenement house movement, bungalow "craziness" reflected a Progressive impulse to view the home as an instrument of uplift. Examining this infatuation with the bungalow is thus a good way for historians to understand one generation's domestic hopes and fears.

INVESTIGATION

Americans embraced the bungalow for many reasons. Examining the ideas and designs of its promoters can reveal what they thought about family life and what they hoped to achieve by adopting this new style. One of their concerns was the changing status of women. The essay in this chapter examines the relationship between the popularity of the bungalow and changing gender roles. It is accompanied by a variety of primary sources, including house plans, illustrations of home decorations, and the writings of Progressive-era housing reformers. As you read the essay and study the primary sources, your main task is to determine what motivated Americans to adopt the bungalow style in the early twentieth century. To complete this assignment, use the secondary and primary sources to answer the following main questions:

1. **According to historian Gwendolyn Wright in Source 1, why were many Americans receptive to the bungalow style at the turn of the century?** What social and economic developments influenced their tastes in housing?

2. **Is Wright's argument supported by the primary sources?** What evidence do the primary sources provide about the motives of bungalow promoters? What family problems do they identify, and how do they think the bungalow would solve them?

3. **Was the bungalow craze prompted mostly by radical or conservative motives?** Did the bungalow hold out the promise of revamping domestic life completely, or of solving social problems without drastic change?

Before you begin, read the sections in your textbook on Progressive reform and cultural changes at the turn of the century. Although these sections may not mention the bungalow, they will provide additional background on the economic, social, and cultural trends in the Progressive era and about the goals of Progressive reformers.

SECONDARY SOURCE

1 In *Building the Dream: A Social History of Housing in America* (1981), from which the following selection was drawn, Gwendolyn Wright argues that Americans have long used domestic architecture to encourage certain kinds of family and home life and that the bungalow was no exception. As you read this excerpt, note Wright's argument about the impact of changing gender roles on the popularity of the bungalow. What kind of home life did bungalow enthusiasts envision? Were they motivated by a desire to keep women in the home or to free her from it? How did their house plans reflect their desires?

The Progressive Housewife and the Bungalow (1981)
GWENDOLYN WRIGHT

In the early twentieth century, many different groups were campaigning for what they called a progressive approach to house design and upkeep. While their social goals often were based on conflicting values, public-health nurses, arts and crafts advocates, feminists, domestic scientists, and settlement-house workers favored the same simplified, standardized home to represent those values. . . .

In the arts and crafts movement of the early 1900s, architects and designers mixed with poets and writers, housewives and reformers, combining a sentimental reverence for hand-crafted goods with a more up-to-date endorsement of simplified, wholesome environments. Some designers acclaimed a self-consciously rustic aesthetic for the home, using massive tree trunks and uncut stone for structural elements, which they left exposed. While the fashionable family might display Indian handicrafts or folk art in the living room, most American arts and crafts enthusiasts simply called for "good taste" through quiet lines and minimal ornament. In contrast to their English counterparts who had initiated the arts and crafts movement as a reaction against the abuses of industrialization, most members of the numerous American organizations claimed that it was possible to produce pleasing forms in a factory as well as in a crafts workshop. They focused predominantly on the final product rather than on the actual conditions of making that product.

One of the most prominent popularizers of the arts and crafts movement in the United States was Gustav Stickley of Syracuse, New York. A furniture maker, Stickley had first redesigned the practices in his shop so that all work

was done with hand tools. Simple, rectilinear lines and unvarnished oak became characteristic of his "Craftsman" furniture. In 1901 Stickley began publication of a magazine, *The Craftsman,* hoping to lead a social and artistic
revolution in America. The journal featured articles on tenements in New
York City, . . . utopian anarchism, factory working conditions, flower arrang-
ing, and glass blowing. The following year, Stickley began to offer his readers model house designs, and continued to feature both interior and exterior
plans until the magazine's demise in 1916. In 1903 he established the Craftsman Home Builder's Club, which gave free advice on "well-built, democratic, well-planned homes."

According to Stickley, "The Craftsman type of building is largely the result
not of elaboration, but of elimination." The houses in his magazine had simple, rectilinear, built-in furniture, plain surfaces of native stone or wood, unpretentious plans and elevations. Stickley did not insist that every dwelling
be a highly personalized design, even though he clearly enjoyed experiment-
ing with the texture and variety of materials. To him, "democratic architecture" meant good homes available to all Americans through economy of
construction and materials, together with necessary standardization. Though
Craftsman designs suggested time-consuming construction techniques, the
exposed beams were often simply tacked on under the eaves and the rough
"clinker brick," produced in a factory to look like hand-molded brick.

Stickley claimed that his approach to design could remedy almost every
problem facing the middle-class family, from lack of servants to the increased
divorce rate. He also saw the well-crafted home as a key to solving larger social problems, such as crime and civil disorder. Small, inexpensive versions
of the Craftsman house would make working-class families homeowners.
Apprentice training programs in house construction and furniture making,
run by the state and by private business, would provide uplifting employment for young men. The pages of *The Craftsman* carried the message that
housing and social issues were related in their need for good design. Though
Stickley's expectations of immediate, lasting social harmony through aesthetic reform were obviously unrealistic, he found a sizable audience that regarded residential architecture as the preferred American approach to reform.

Other magazines also offered detailed specifications for modern model
houses, as well as more general advice on decoration and domesticity. By the
time Edward Bok retired in 1919 as editor of *Ladies' Home Journal,* this magazine had a circulation of 2 million largely because of Bok's crusade for
"model *Journal* houses." Bok wanted to encourage middle-class women to
become more involved with the home, thereby relinquishing their recent tendencies to abandon domestic duties for jobs or women's club activities. He
was emphatic about architectural standards for the modern home. The house
should be free from "senseless ornamentation"; it should be equipped with
the latest sanitary fixtures; it should be decorated with unpretentious furnishings and a few handmade niceties. These dicta did not, by any means,

imply a spartan setting. The *Journal*'s 1901 series of room designs by the St. Louis artist Will Bradley were opulent Art Nouveau décors. Yet Bok's taste was not all-embracing. He laid down exacting specifications for every detail, from pillows to room dimensions, often showing comparisons of "Good Taste vs. Bad Taste" in furnishings.

At first, no architects would deign to accept Bok's offer to design "model *Journal* houses," but with the depression of the 1890s, they became more willing. Beginning in 1895, suburban dwellings in Colonial Revival, Elizabethan, and Queen Anne styles, costing between $3,500 and $7,000, regularly appeared. In 1901, Bok launched the first of a series of modern model dwellings by Frank Lloyd Wright and his associates in Chicago. Thousands of readers sent in $5 for a complete set of plans and specifications, which would enable them to build duplicates of these model houses. As Theodore Roosevelt supposedly said of the *Journal*'s editor "Bok is the only man I ever heard of who changed, for the better, the architecture of an entire nation, and he did it so quickly and yet so effectively that we didn't know it was begun before it was finished."

While there were many words for the new house of the early twentieth century, "bungalow" was certainly the most widely used. It usually referred to a relatively unpretentious small house, although more exotic, expansive, hand-crafted dwellings created by architects like Charles and Henry Greene in southern California were also called bungalows. In general, though, the term implied a one-story or story-and-a-half dwelling of between six hundred and eight hundred square feet. Bedrooms were only bunk spaces. The kitchen, fitted like a ship's galley, accommodated a single person, and she (it was assumed) had a squeeze, . . .

. . . The kitchen replaced the parlor as the focus of attention in many builders' pattern books, and certainly in domestic science textbooks and women's magazines. Isabell McDougall, describing "An Ideal Kitchen" for readers of *The House Beautiful* in 1902, evoked the by-now familiar metaphors of impeccable laboratory order to be enforced by the housewife, or household administrator. "Everything in her temple is clean," she explained, "with the scientific cleanliness of a surgery, which we all know to be far ahead of any mere housewifely neatness."

The average kitchen in the turn-of-the-century bungalow or larger house was compact and carefully planned. It measured approximately 120 square feet, and everything had its place. The commodious Hoosier cabinet, with numerous wooden drawers and bins, stood against one wall. Wooden worktables were positioned to cut down on unnecessary steps—a principle that domestic scientists borrowed from Taylorism. By 1910, the built-in breakfast nook had become popular; and in many houses, the kitchen had been reduced to a Pullman kitchen, or "kitchenette."

New appliances held center stage. The sink and drainboard were of shiny white porcelain or enameled iron. An automatic pump supplied hot and cold running water. If there was no brine-cooled or ammonia-cooled icebox on the back porch, where the iceman had easy access, a metal basin in one corner sufficed. A hood hung over the gas range to cut smells, and porcelain-enameled cookware hung on wall hooks. Unfortunately, the new appliances were not necessarily reliable. As one textbook on domestic architecture admitted, most laundry machines "are not economical on account of the severity of the process on the clothes being washed." Most households still used a washboard and hung the clothes in the yard to dry.

To many Americans, mechanical devices for the home were the essence of progressive improvements and a bright future. Writing in the *Congregationalist,* Henry Demarest Lloyd, the Chicago muckraking journalist, extolled the benefits he envisioned:

> Equal industrial power will be as invariable a function of citizenship as the equal franchise. Power will flow in every house and shop as freely as water. All men will become capitalists and all capitalists co-operators. . . . Women, released from the economic pressure which has forced them to deny their best nature and compete in unnatural industry with men, will be re-sexed. . . . Every house will be a center of sunshine and scenery.

According to Lloyd, technology promised individual freedom and social equality. Men and women of all classes would share the infinite power of electricity, the "modern servant." Lloyd envisioned women returning to their homes, leaving their jobs because of increased economic abundance brought about by electrical power. But other reformers, especially feminists, foresaw a future wherein more women would be able to take on jobs outside the home because electricity had freed them from household drudgery. . . .

In more and more cases, the housewife worked alone in her kitchen. Between 1900 and 1920, the number of domestic servants in the United States declined by half—from eighty per thousand families to thirty-nine. (Most of these were day workers, usually black married women rather than live-in servants.) Yet no builders considered opening up the kitchen and ending the housewife's isolation there. Rather, they praised the smaller, better-equipped kitchen, planned for the domestic scientist who had no need of a servant, since she had learned the most efficient techniques for housework. The kitchen was not to be a place for playing with children or visiting with neighbors but a modern "home laboratory."

One of the principal justifications for the smaller kitchen and the minimum-upkeep materials of the progressive house was the middle-class woman's demand for more time of her own outside the house. By 1900, women held jobs in almost every occupation listed in the census. Although most of these women were unmarried, and a quarter of them domestics or factory workers, college-educated women did enter the professions. Other young women donned the starched shirtwaist and ankle-length skirt of the Gibson girl and entered offices as receptionists, clerical workers, and typewriters (the same word was used for the machine and the person working at it).

Middle-class women who did not hold regular jobs often worked as volunteers in charity or civic organizations, promoting the numerous improvement campaigns of the National Consumers' League or their local women's club, lobbying for reform legislation or neighborhood parks. These women still considered domestic issues their primary concern, but now the entire city was their home. In 1910, the president of the General Federation of Women's Clubs declared that their platform was based on protecting "women and children, and the home, the latter meaning the four walls of the city as well as the four walls of brick and mortar."

Private homes were often the focus of debate, all the same. In order for women to have time for their non-domestic activities, they wanted both simpler houses that were easier to keep clean and more labor-saving appliances. The single-family dwelling was condemned in the pages of *Harper's Bazaar* as "a prison and a burden and a tyrant." The Philadelphia economist Robert E. Thompson and Charlotte Perkins Gilman and other radical feminists demanded kitchenless houses and public childcare facilities to ease the domestic demands on women.

There was some reservation about architectural changes that were tied to new sex roles. The restlessness that characterized "the modern woman" caused a stir among many conservatives. Journalists, physicians and politicians raised the issues of "race suicide" and "desexualization," which they connected to the declining birth rate among white women. In *The Foes of Our Own Household* (1917) and in articles for *Ladies' Home Journal*, Theodore Roosevelt spoke about the dangers of women abandoning the traditional roles of wife and mother for more exciting challenges outside the home. Higher education for women came under attack, since college-educated women often did not marry, and when they did, they had one or two children at most. The modern home and, even worse, the apartment, requiring as little time as they did, seemed to encourage these tendencies.

Despite their misgivings, architects, builders, and the editors of women's magazines recognized the growing market of working women. Even the married woman who worked was not necessarily considered a pariah. *Ladies' Home Journal* carried several articles on ways to earn one's living both inside and outside the home; and a full-page color spread in February 1911 considered the best house plan for a woman with a family and a career at home. Her bungalow had two separate entrances, a living room that doubled as a reception room for clients, and many built-in conveniences to accelerate housekeeping chores. Bungalows designed for single "business-girls" or "girl-bachelors" were featured in magazines and home-economics texts in the 1910s. Space allotted for cooking and laundering was minimal, for it was assumed that such tasks were done commercially, outside the private home. . . .

An elaboration of this model was the bungalow court—a group of ten or twenty almost identical dwellings, first designed as winter housing in southern California—which appeared in all parts of the country in the 1910s. Since the bungalows were quite small, there was usually a community "play-house," where residents entertained guests and organized evening enter-tainments. Those who promoted the bungalow court as a modern living environment suggested that it could domesticate single working women, demonstrating to them the progressive side of home life. According to many advocates, this setting also represented "The Community Problem Solved." The harmonious uniform aesthetic and the shared outdoor spaces, play-house, and garages were evidence that the residents had established strong social ties among themselves. . . .

While more than half the nation's farmers owned their homes in 1910, only one third of non-farm households did. . . . It was increasingly difficult for Americans to afford to become homeowners. In particular, the growing number of unmarried women and men usually rented rather than owned. The smaller, plainer dwelling, especially one set on a common court rather than on a large private yard, was an attempt to find a solution to the eco-nomic problem and to the seemingly related problem of a growing popula-tion of unmarried persons. Participants at the annual National Conference on City Planning, whose meetings began in 1909, and the National Confer-ence on Housing, which commenced in 1911, hoped to find innovative ways to increase home-ownership without moving toward any sort of federal sub-sidies. They endorsed architectural solutions to economic and social dilem-mas. The Model Street display at the St. Louis Exposition of 1904, the Model Bungalow installed at the Indiana State House for the 1913 National Conser-vation Congress, and the flurry of competitions for model suburban develop-ments were all expressions of a nationwide enthusiasm for the "progressive house," which began to look much the same, wherever it appeared.

The uniform image appealed to a range of people who hoped that domes-tic architecture would encourage social cooperation. The Victorian suburb was branded as a "labyrinth of unreason," reflecting a time of "rabid democ-racy," of social and aesthetic license. Settlement workers Jane Addams and Graham R. Taylor, Jr., the domestic scientist Marion Talbot, the statistician Adna Weber, and the political journalist Herbert Croly concurred: houses conceived as individualistic display encouraged class differences and com-petition among neighbors. They argued for common architectural standards that would visually reinforce their ideal of a balanced, egalitarian social life for women and men. Both feminists and conservatives asserted that it was possible to solve "the woman question" through a more rational approach toward living environments. In 1912, Grosvenor Atterbury, who designed the model suburb of Forest Hills Gardens in Queens and championed planned industrial towns, wrote an appeal for progressive residential plan-ning in *Scribner's*. He too argued that domestic architecture could reinforce the higher social values of residents, subordinating individual desires to the general good. "[T]he truth is that with any kind of control anarchy ceases,"

Atterbury claimed. "With the elimination of lawless eccentricity and disregard of architectural decency, the good elements begin to count."

PRIMARY SOURCES

There are several types of primary sources in this chapter: sketches and floor plans of a Victorian house and a Progressive-era bungalow, illustrations of old and new styles of household furnishings, and the writings of housing reformers and others. They may reflect a variety of motives for embracing a new architectural style.

Victorian and Craftsman Home Designs

The Craftsman magazine offered house plans and suggestions for home decorations to "simplify the work of home life." Compared to Victorian houses, such as those illustrated in Sources 2 and 4, what might Progressive-era Americans have found especially appealing about the features of Craftsman houses and their interiors? *The Craftsman* magazine publisher Gustav Stickley suggested that his own home reflected the personality of a man, in contrast to "the majority of modern houses . . . built to meet the ideas of women."[7] Why may this have been one of the appealing features of the Craftsman house?

2   A Victorian House (1881)

Perspective View.

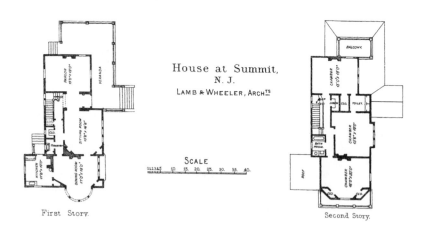

First Story.

House at Summit,
N. J.
LAMB & WHEELER, ARCH^{TS}

SCALE

Second Story.

Source: William T. Comstock, *Victorian Domestic Architectural Plans and Details* (New York: Dover Publications, Inc., 1987); reprint of 1881 edition, Plate 1.

3 A Craftsman Cottage (1909)

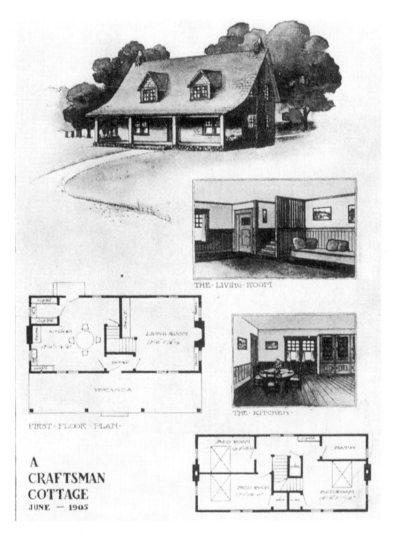

THE · LIVING · ROOM

THE · KITCHEN ·

FIRST · FLOOR · PLAN ·

A
CRAFTSMAN
COTTAGE
JUNE — 1905

Note the division of space so that the greatest amount of freedom and convenience is obtained within a small area. The illustrations of the interior serve to show how the structural features, although simple and inexpensive, give to each room an individual beauty and charm. The kitchen is arranged to serve also for a dining room.

Source: Gustav Stickley, *Craftsman Homes* (New York: Craftsman Publishing Co., 1909).

4 *The Craftsman* Contrasts Complexity and Confusion with Cohesion and Harmony (1907)

Source: Gustav Stickley, *The Craftsman*, 1907.

Gustav Stickley was one of the most influential promoters of the bungalow. Note the social ills that Stickley suggests will be solved by the adoption of this simple home style.

Gustav Stickley on the Craftsman Home (1909)

That the influence of the home is of the first importance in the shaping of character is a fact too well understood and too generally admitted to be offered here as a new idea. One need only turn to the pages of history to find abundant proof of the unerring action of Nature's law, for without exception the people whose lives are lived simply and wholesomely, in the open, and who have in a high degree the sense of the sacredness of the home, are the people who have made the greatest strides in the development of the race. When luxury enters in and a thousand artificial requirements come to be regarded as real needs, the nation is on the brink of degeneration. . . . Even in the rush and hurry of life in our busy cities we remember well the quality given to the growing nation by such men and women a generation or two ago and, in spite of the chaotic conditions brought about by our passion for money-getting, extravagance and show, we have still reason to believe that the dominant characteristics of the pioneer yet shape what are the salient qualities in American life.

To preserve these characteristics and to bring back to individual life and work the vigorous constructive spirit which during the last half-century has spent its activities in commercial and industrial expansion, is, in a nut-shell, the Craftsman idea. We need to straighten out our standards and to get rid of a lot of rubbish that we have accumulated along with our wealth and commercial supremacy. It is not that we are too energetic, but that in many ways we have wasted and misused our energy precisely as we have wasted and misused so many of our wonderful natural resources. All we really need is a change in our point of view toward life and a keener perception regarding the things that count and the things which merely burden us. This being the case, it would seem obvious that the place to begin a readjustment is in the home, for it is only natural that the relief from friction which would follow the ordering of our lives along more simple and reasonable lines would not only assure greater comfort, and therefore greater efficiency, to the workers of the nation, but would give the children a chance to grow up under conditions which would be conducive to a higher degree of mental, moral and physical efficiency.

Therefore we regard it as at least a step in the direction of bringing about better conditions when we try to plan and build houses which will simplify the work of home life and add to its wholesome joy and comfort. We have

Source: Excerpted from Gustav Stickley, *Craftsman Homes: Architecture and Furnishings of the American Arts and Crafts Movement* (Mineola, NY: Dover Publications, 1979) by permission of Dover Publications.

already made it plain to our readers that we do not believe in large houses with many rooms elaborately decorated and furnished, for the reason that these seem so essentially an outcome of the artificial conditions that lay such harassing burdens upon modern life and form such a serious menace to our ethical standards. Breeding as it does the spirit of extravagance and of discontent which in the end destroys all the sweetness of home life, the desire for luxury and show not only burdens beyond his strength the man who is ambitious to provide for his wife and children surroundings which are as good as the best, but taxes to the utmost the woman who is trying to keep up the appearances which she believes should belong to her station in life. Worst of all, it starts the children with standards which, in nine cases out of ten, utterly preclude the possibility of their beginning life on their own account in a simple and sensible way. Boys who are brought up in such homes are taught, by the silent influence of their early surroundings, to take it for granted that they must not marry until they are able to keep up an establishment of equal pretensions, and girls also take it as a matter of course that marriage must mean something quite as luxurious as the home of their childhood or it is not a paying investment for their youth and beauty. Everyone who thinks at all deplores the kind of life that marks a man's face with the haggard lines of anxiety and makes him sharp and often unscrupulous in business, with no ambition beyond large profits and a rapid rise in the business world. Also we all realize regretfully the extravagance and uselessness of many of our women and admit that one of the gravest evils of our times is the light touch-and-go attitude toward marriage, which breaks up so many homes and makes the divorce courts in America a by-word to the world. But when we think into it a little more deeply, we have to acknowledge that such conditions are the logical outcome of our standards of living and that these standards are always shaped in the home.

That is why we have from the first planned houses that are based on the big fundamental principles of honesty, simplicity and usefulness,—the kind of houses that children will rejoice all their lives to remember as "home," and that give a sense of peace and comfort to the tired men who go back to them when the day's work is done. Because we believe that the healthiest and happiest life is that which maintains the closest relationship with out-of-doors, we have planned our houses with outdoor living rooms, dining rooms and sleeping rooms, and many windows to let in plenty of air and sunlight.

---

6   As the editor of the *Ladies' Home Journal,* Edward Bok promoted a variety of Progressive causes. He also used the magazine to publicize the simple bungalow style. Note the ills Bok hoped to cure with the reform of home design, especially for women.

Edward Bok on Simplicity (1900)

There are no people on the face of the earth who litter up the rooms of their homes with so much useless, and consequently bad, furnishing as do the Americans. The curse of the American home to-day is useless bric-a-brac. A room in which we feel that we can freely breathe is so rare that we are instinctively surprised when we see one. It is the exception, rather than the rule, that we find a restful room.

As a matter of fact, to this common error of overfurnishing so many of our homes are directly due many of the nervous breakdowns of our women. The average American woman is a perfect slave to the useless rubbish which she has in her rooms. This rubbish, of a costly nature where plenty exists, and of a cheap and tawdry character in homes of moderate incomes, is making housekeeping a nerve-racking burden. A goodly number of these women are conscious of their mistakes. Others, if not absolutely conscious, feel that something is wrong in their homes, yet they know not exactly what it is. But all are loath, yes, I may say afraid, to simplify things. They fear the criticism of the outside world that their homes are sparsely furnished; they dread the possibility that their rooms may be called "bare." They fear to give way to common-sense. It is positively rare, but tremendously exhilarating, to find a woman, as one does now and then, who is courageous enough to furnish her home with an eye single to comfort and practical utility, and who refuses to have her home lowered to a plane of mediocrity by filling it with useless bric-a-brac and jimcracks, the only mission of which seems to be to offend the eye and accumulate dust. . . .

More simplicity in our homes would make our lives simpler. Many women would live fuller lives because they would have more time. As it is, hundreds of women of all positions in life are to-day the slaves of their homes and what they have crowded into them. Instead of being above inanimate objects of wood and clothes and silks, their lives are dominated by them. They are the slaves of their furniture and useless bric-a-brac. One hears men constantly complain of this. The condition is not a safe one for wives. No woman can afford to allow a lot of unnecessary furnishings to rule her life. . . . We need only to be natural: to get back to our real, inner selves. Then we are simple. It is only because we have got away from the simple and the natural that so many of our homes are cluttered up as they are, and our lives full of things that are not worth the while. We have bent the knee to show, to display, and we have lowered ourselves in doing it: surrounded ourselves with the trivial and the useless: and filling our lives with the poison of artificiality and the unnatural, we have pushed the Real: the Natural: the Simple: the Beautiful—the best and most lasting things—out of our lives. Now, I ask, in all fairness: Is it worth while?

Source: Reprinted from David E. Shi, *In Search of the Simple Life* (Layton, Utah: Gibbs M. Smith, 1986), by permission of the author.

The *Bungalow Magazine* provided readers with plans for inexpensive bungalows. What does this cover illustration suggest about the benefits of a simpler home style?

Cover from *The Bungalow Magazine* (1909)

Source: The Bungalow Magazine, October 1909.

Christine Frederick on the Efficient Homemaker

Frederick was one of the leaders of the home economics movement at the turn of the century. In numerous articles and books she preached the need to apply the principles of scientific management to housekeeping. She was a vocal advocate of simple designs, and her ideal home closely resembled the Arts and Crafts bungalow. As you read and examine these selections, note what Frederick hoped to achieve by applying the principles of efficiency and simplicity to the home. Did she advocate a change in gender roles?

8   Putting the American Woman and Her Home on a Business Basis (1914)
CHRISTINE FREDERICK

Is the American housewife facing a great revolution? Is the efficiency idea, which has already revolutionized many industrial plants, now going to attack that last stronghold of tradition—the American Home?

Signs point that way. The ideas of motion study, standardized conditions of work, scientific management of servants, had simply to be announced to strike a responsive chord among intelligent home-makers. Efficiency is in the air, and has permeated to the kitchen no less than to the counting-room, and to general homemaking—even to woman herself. . . .

The most serious evidences of decay of the home such as it used to be are seen on every side. From scores of points the home has been, and is being attacked. The chief of these are:

1. Decided drift to large cities, where more and more of the original functions of the home, even to cooking, are being diminished.
2. Increasing demands of sanitation and modern ideas in homemaking, which compel progress upward with, or downward from, accepted standards.
3. Greatly increased cost of living, compelling either disastrous extravagances or lowered standards, or increased brain management on the part of housewives to meet the situation.
4. General broadening of woman's horizon and making the entire line of human endeavor her sphere, with the home becoming more incidental, as with men. . . .

If the home is to survive it must do so on a reorganized basis. No industry founded upon admittedly unwilling, uninterested millions can continue to operate; yet everybody admits the tremendous discontent among home women. As at present operated, American housekeeping is distasteful to admittedly the liveliest and most intelligent portion of housekeepers, and is only endured in a dull way by the masses of women. Its grave faults have been that it lacked mental interest, that it was without the spur of competition, and that it did not possess the dignity of a serious profession. Degradation has more and more attached itself to housework as ambition has raised other standards of living. Every other member of the family hastened to rise

Source: The American Review of Reviews, 64 (February 1914), pp. 199, 200.

from the drudgery state of his chosen work, but the woman who merely "kept house" has felt her wings clipped.

9 The Efficient and Inefficient Kitchen (1920)
CHRISTINE FREDERICK

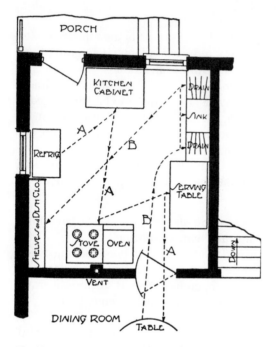

"Badly Grouped Kitchen Equipment." A: preparation route; B: clearing-away route. A and B intersect with no apparent order.

Source: Household Engineering (Chicago: American School of Home Economics, 1920).

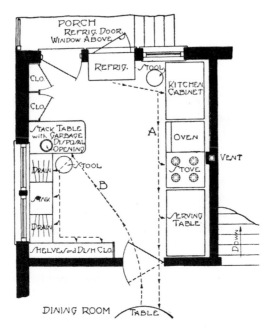

"Efficient Grouping of Kitchen Equipment." Preparing and clearing away do not intersect; each activity is clearly organized.

Charlotte Perkins Gilman and the Bungalow

Feminist Charlotte Perkins Gilman wrote extensively on the need to revamp domestic architecture. She advocated the replacement of traditional household arrangements so that women could enjoy work outside the home and the economic independence it would bring. Gilman called for the replacement of the traditional home with its isolated kitchen by kitchenless houses and apartments connected to central kitchens staffed by paid professionals. She also suggested the advantages of husbands and wives living in "separate establishments" such as those at Bowen Court, constructed in Pasadena, California, in 1910. Known as a bungalow court, Bowen Court contained twenty-two bungalows bordering a center garden. It also featured a sewing room and laundry for women tenants. Some of the units were double bungalows "planned for two or more persons who may wish to live under the same roof, but desire separate establishments."[8] Bowen Court was designed by architects who had been influenced by Gilman. As you read and examine these sources, note Gilman's response to the home economists' solution to the problem of "domestic economy." How do the motives behind the bungalow court compare to those of Stickley, Bok, and other bungalow promoters?

10 Domestic Economy (1904)
CHARLOTTE PERKINS GILMAN

One of the strongest intrenchments of our piously defended system of household industry is its supposed economy. "The careful housewife" is our ideal of a wise and judicious expender of money, some even going so far as to call her a "partner" in the business of housekeeping. . . .

Let us give a fair examination to this particular point, the economy of domestic industry. . . .

Merely as a matter of business, is it good business?

What is, exactly, the business we are to study?

It is that of catering to the personal physical needs of the human animal, caring for the health of the body, providing shelter, warmth, food and cleanliness. . . .

The home is intended to furnish shelter and protection to the family—sleeping accommodations, food, and those cleansing processes so essential to all civilized life. The business of the home is in the rent or purchase and replenishment of the place and plant; the provision of supplies for consumption; the preparation and service of food, and all kinds of cleaning. What is commonly called "housekeeping" really embraces this group of industries, arbitrarily connected by custom, but in their nature not only diverse, but grossly incompatible. . . .

Yet we carry on all these contradictory trades in one small building, and also live in it!

Not only do we undertake to have all these labors performed in one house, but by one person.

In full ninety per cent of our American homes there is but one acting functionary to perform these varied and totally dissimilar functions—to be cook, laundress, chambermaid, charwoman, seamstress, nurse and governess. . . .

The person who is expected to achieve this miracle is not some specially selected paragon of varied ability, but merely the average woman; neither is she prepared for her herculean tasks (Hercules was never required to perform his twelve labors all at once!) by a rigorous course of training, but is supposed to be fitted by nature for their successful achievement, aided perhaps by instruction from a similarly well prepared predecessor. Under these circumstances the wonder is that even half of us live to grow up, that our average of intelligence and ability is so good, and that our common standard of comfort and cleanliness, of health, vigor and peace of mind is as high as it is; that any degree of family happiness remains to us; and it is no wonder what-

Source: Charlotte Perkins Gilman, "Domestic Economy," *The Independent,* June 16, 1904, pp. 1359–1363.

ever, but an inevitable consequence, that the waste and incompetence manifested in this pitiful business constitute so huge a loss and injury. . . .

Double Bungalow Plan, Bowen Court

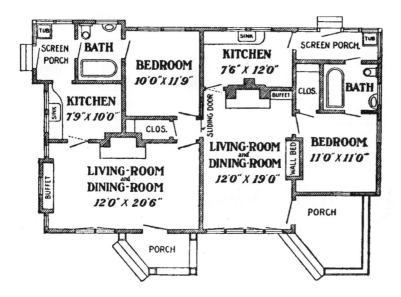

Source: Ladies' Home Journal 30 (April 1913).

Changes in Middle-Class Life

By the turn of the century industrial growth had had a profound impact on middle-class life. What changes do these tables reveal that may have made the bungalow more attractive to middle-class Americans?

Average Daily Servants' Wage Rates, Chicago, 1890–1910

Year	Wage	Year	Wage	Year	Wage
1890	$3.82	1897	$3.60	1904	$5.10
1891	4.15	1898	4.12	1905	5.08
1892	4.23	1899	4.08	1906	5.36
1893	4.50	1900	4.28	1907	5.77
1894	3.99	1901	4.40	1908	5.60
1895	4.16	1902	4.57	1909	5.68
1896	3.83	1903	4.93	1910	6.16

Source: Seven Days a Week: Women and Domestic Service in Industrializing America, edited by David M. Katzman. Copyright © 1978 by David M. Katzman. Used by permission of Oxford University Press, Inc.

 Female Servants by Regions, per 1,000 Families, 1880–1920

	Per 1,000 families		
United States	**1880**	**1900**	**1920**
The North	92	80	39
New England	105	96	45
Middle Atlantic	121	99	49
Eastern North Central	74	68	32
Western North Central	61	61	32
The South	78	63	46
Northern South Atlantic	131	104	64
Southern South Atlantic	70	59	51
Eastern South Central	68	61	42
Western South Central	51	43	36
The West	43	49	28
Mountain, Basin, and Plateau	33	43	25
Pacific	49	53	29

Source: Seven Days a Week: Women and Domestic Service in Industrializing America, edited by David M. Katzman. Copyright © 1978 by David M. Katzman. Used by permission of Oxford University Press, Inc.

14 **Clerical Workers in the United States, by Sex, 1870–1920**

Job Category	1870	1880	1890	1900	1910	1920
Bookkeepers, cashiers, and accountants						
Total	38,776	74,919	159,374	254,880	486,700	734,688
Male	37,892	70,667	131,602	180,727	299,545	375,564
Female	884	4,252	27,772	74,153	187,155	359,124
% Female	2.0	5.7	17.4	29.1	38.5	48.4
Office clerks						
Total	29,801	59,799	187,969	248,323	720,498	1,487,905
Male	28,878	59,484	163,686	229,991	597,833	1,015,742
Female	923	315	24,283	18,332	122,665	472,163
% Female	3.1	.5	12.9	7.4	17.0	31.7
Messenger, errand, and office boys/girls						
Total	8,046	12,818	47,183	66,009	108,035	113,022
Male	7,967	12,421	44,294	59,392	96,748	98,768
Female	79	397	2,889	6,617	11,287	14,254
% Female	.9	3.1	6.1	10.0	10.4	12.6
Stenographers and typists						
Total	154	5,000	33,418	112,364	316,693	615,154
Male	147	3,000	12,148	26,246	53,378	50,410
Female	7	2,000	21,270	86,118	263,315	564,744
% Female	4.5	40.0	63.6	76.6	83.1	91.8

Source: Alba M. Edwards, *Comparative Statistics for the United States, 1870 to 1940.* Part of the *Sixteenth Census of the United States: 1940* (Washington, D.C.: U.S. Government Printing Office, 1943), Tables 9 and 10.

CONCLUSION

As the bungalow craze illustrates, historians must often sort out a variety of motives. Housing reformers expressed fears about inflation, declining middle-class birthrates, rising divorce rates, women leaving the home, and the confinement of women in the home. They saw new housing styles as a way to reform domestic life. Because their views about domestic problems varied, so too did their motives for promoting the bungalow.

The sources in this chapter also illustrate that we cannot escape the influence of ideas. The bungalow reflected the influence of a Progressive ideology characterized by a belief in efficiency, faith in the power of the environment to transform people, and a distrust of concentrated wealth, class divisions, and urban life. It led Progressive reformers to take up such diverse causes as trust busting, housing reform, and conservation. It also led them to see common solutions for social problems. It was no coincidence, for instance, that Progressive conservationists promoted contact with nature at the same time that Progressive-era bungalow designers found rugged, natural houses aesthetically pleasing. As we shall see next, historians cannot fully understand motivations or any historical change without reference to ideologies.

FURTHER READING

Polly Wynn Allen, *Building Domestic Liberty: Charlotte Perkins Gilman's Architectural Feminism* (Amherst: University of Massachusetts Press, 1988).

Eileen Boris, "The Gendered Meaning of Arts and Crafts," in *The Ideal Home, 1900–1920: The History of Twentieth-Century American Craft,* ed. Janet Kardon (New York: Harry N. Abrams, 1993).

Clifford Edward Clark, Jr., *The American Family Home, 1800–1960* (Chapel Hill: The University of North Carolina Press, 1986).

David E. Shi, "Progressive Simplicity," in *The Simple Life: Plain Living and High Thinking in American Culture* (New York: Oxford University Press, 1985).

Gustav Stickley, *Craftsman Homes: Architecture and Furnishings of the American Arts and Crafts Movement* (New York: Dover Publications, 1979; reprint of 1909 edition).

NOTES

1. Quoted in Clifford Edward Clark, Jr., *The American Family Home* (Chapel Hill: University of North Carolina Press, 1986), pp. 132, 144.
2. Quoted in David E. Shi, *The Simple Life: Plain Living and High Thinking in American Culture* (New York: Oxford University Press, 1985), p. 186.
3. Quoted in Eileen Boris, *Art and Labor: Ruskin, Morris, and the Craftsman Idea in America* (Philadelphia: Temple University Press, 1986), p. 75.
4. Quoted in Eileen Boris, "Crossing Boundaries: The Gendered Meaning of Arts and Crafts," in *The Ideal Home: The History of Twentieth-Century American Craft,* ed. Janet Kardon (New York: Harry N. Abrams, 1993), p. 35.

5. Quoted in ibid., p. 36.
6. Quoted in Clark, *American Family Home,* p. 153.
7. Quoted in Eileen Boris, "The Gendered Meaning of Arts and Crafts," in Kardon, *The Ideal Home,* p. 44.
8. Quoted in Dolores Hayden, *The Grand Domestic Revolution: A History of Feminist Designs for American Homes, Neighborhoods, and Cities* (Cambridge, Mass.: MIT Press, 1981), p. 239.

Chapter

6

Ideology and History:
Closing the "Golden Door"

The sources in this chapter offer information on the attitude of Americans toward immigrants in the early twentieth century.

Secondary Source

1. Racism and Immigration Restriction (1984), JOHN HIGHAM

Primary Sources

2. The Passing of the Great Race (1916), MADISON GRANT
3. Whose Country Is This? (1921), CALVIN COOLIDGE
4. The Klan's Fight for Americanism (1926), HIRAM W. EVANS
5. Because You're a Jew (1908)
6. Her Father's Daughter (1921), GENE STRATTON-PORTER
7. A Congressman Calls for Restriction (1921)
8. The Bootleggers (1925)
9. Immigrant Occupation Groups, 1899–1924
10. Unemployment Rates, 1900–1924

"Give me your tired, your poor,
Your huddled masses yearning to breathe free,
The wretched refuse of your teeming shore.
Send these, the homeless, tempest tossed to me,
I lift my lamp beside the golden door!"
—Emma Lazarus

The majestic statue commemorated in Emma Lazarus's poem was the first glimpse many immigrants had of their new home. Despite its welcoming words, many of the newcomers were also aware of other attitudes in their new country, since news, letters, and even immigrants traveled both ways across the Atlantic. They might not know that native-born Americans did not see the Statue of Liberty as a national symbol of refuge, yet some of them surely suspected that they might not be welcome.

Their suspicions were well founded. Growing numbers of Americans at the turn of the century were convinced that there was too much "wretched refuse" pouring in from the Old World's "teeming shores." Such sentiments had already led Congress to exclude Chinese immigrants and soon thereafter led it to restrict Japanese immigration. The doors to European immigration—through most of the nineteenth century white, overwhelmingly Christian, and mostly Protestant—remained wide open. Yet that too would change when Congress severely restricted European immigration in the early 1920s.

Although restrictions on immigration and hostility toward immigrants remain today, by World War II intense hostility toward European immigrants had subsided. Only then did Lazarus's poem, engraved on Lady Liberty's pedestal and in the minds of countless schoolchildren, help to transform the Statue of Liberty into an enduring symbol of asylum. Today the national self-image embodied in the statue still obscures other images Americans have had of immigrants. We often forget that in the early twentieth century many Americans looked at newcomers through a filter of beliefs, values, fears, and prejudices that historians call an ideology. This powerful ideological filter prevented many people in this country from seeing it as a haven for all of the oppressed. In this chapter we examine the nature of this ideology and its role in closing the "golden door" after World War I.

SETTING

America had never experienced the sheer numbers of immigrants that arrived in the first fifteen years of the twentieth century. Between 1900 and 1914, more than 13 million immigrants arrived, mostly from Europe. Yet this European im-migration was changing. Since the mid-1880s, the percentage of southern and eastern European immigrants had risen steadily, from about 16 percent of total immigration in 1885 to 75 percent in 1914. This dramatic shift alarmed many observers, especially after the U.S. Immigration Commission concluded in 1911 that the "new" southern and eastern European immigrants differed from the "old" northern European immigrants. The commission declared that the old immigrants had "entered practically every line of activity" and had "mingled freely" with native-born Americans. On the other hand, the new immigrants were mostly unskilled laborers who "congregated together in sections apart from native Americans."[1] They seemed unable to become American.

Doubts about the ability or willingness of immigrants to assimilate were nothing new. Nativism—hostility to groups because of their foreignness—had a long history in the United States. In the 1790s Federalists pointed to foreign rad-icals as a threat to the republic. When Irish immigrants fled oppression and famine in their homeland a half century later, many Americans flocked into the Know-Nothing party to battle the "menace" of Catholicism. In 1882, a growing fear of a "yellow menace" on the West Coast led Congress to exclude the Chinese from further entry. A Gentleman's Agreement between the United States and Japan denied entry to Japanese laborers in 1907. Asian immigrants were also denied the benefits of citizenship.

Meanwhile European immigration policy reflected a demand for cheap labor and optimism about America's ability to absorb white newcomers. But here too doubts were growing at the end of the century. In 1894, the Immigration Restric-tion League began a campaign to close America's doors even to European immi-grants. The league's immediate goal was to impose a literacy test on immigrants, a goal it achieved in 1917. Then in 1921 Congress enacted a provisional mea-sure that established annual quotas on European immigration, and in 1924 it passed the Johnson-Reed Act, which set a total annual limit of European immi-grants at 150,000. The act distributed annual quotas on the basis of the proportion of each nationality in the existing American population, and it also banned Japa-nese immigration entirely, making Asian exclusion virtually complete. Since southern and eastern European nationalities made up far smaller percentages of the population than northern European groups, their quotas were tiny. At the same time, the larger quotas of more prosperous northern European countries went mostly unfilled. By closing the doors to the worrisome Asians and "new" immi-grants, restrictionists had ended a century of massive immigration to America.

INVESTIGATION

Historians point to many reasons for growing hostility to immigrants in the first decades of the twentieth century: fears about radical influence, the fact that most new immigrants were Catholics or Jews, a perception that they took jobs from native-born Americans, and the general hostility to foreigners aroused by the loyalty campaigns during World War I. Others insist that immigration restriction cannot be understood apart from a nativist ideology that led many Americans to see racial distinctions among immigrant groups. Your main job in this chapter is to explain why the United States ended Japanese and unrestricted European immigration after World War I. To do that, you must analyze the role that ideology—a complex of values, fears, interests, and prejudices— played in immigration restriction. Answering the following questions will make it easier to assess this ideology:

1. **What is historian John Higham's explanation in Source 1 for the restriction of European immigration?** What role did a racist ideology play in closing the doors? What does Higham mean when he says that race was a "vehicle for thinking about culture"?

2. **What do the primary sources reveal about the racial differences many native-born Americans saw among immigrants?** What qualities did nativists assign to "racially inferior" groups? What other factors contributed to restrictionist sentiment after World War I?

3. **Were the fears about "inferior racial stock" deeply held or simply a convenient weapon for nativists who were interested in closing the doors for other reasons?** Do you agree that the "race-menace" argument actually reflected deeper fears about maintaining cultural homogeneity?

Before you begin, read the sections in your textbook on immigration. Pay special attention to the role it assigns to racial thought in the restriction of immigration.

SECONDARY SOURCE

1   John Higham is a leading immigration scholar. In the following essay, he discusses the role that racial theory in the early twentieth century played in defining a nativist ideology and in closing the gates to unrestricted European immigration. Note how ideas about race change in the late nineteenth century, according to Higham. What influences transformed the concept of race from a simple notion of white supremacy to something much more elaborate? What is Higham's evidence that Americans became increasingly concerned about the "unity of their culture" after World War I?

Racism and Immigration Restriction (1984)

JOHN HIGHAM

In the decade from 1905 to 1914 an average of more than a million people annually crowded past the immigration inspectors. After 1896 the great majority derived from southern and eastern Europe. Thereafter, the outflow from the more highly developed countries of northwestern Europe declined as the movement from distant lands increased. . . . Whereas nativists in the nineties had very generally disliked the foreigner as such, the "new immigration" now stood out sharply as the heart of the problem. All of the regressive and antisocial qualities once imputed to the immigrants in general could now be fixed upon this more specific category. In fact, the major theoretical effort of restrictionists in the twentieth century consisted precisely in this: the transformation of relative cultural differences into an absolute line of cleavage, which would redeem the northwestern Europeans from the charges once leveled at them and explain the present danger of immigration in terms of the change in its sources. . . .

. . . The earliest attacks stressed a social and economic peril. Pennsylvania coal miners denounced the Italian, Hungarian, and Polish labor arriving among them as a degraded, servile class whose presence frustrated efforts to improve wages and conditions. Economists and a growing number of labor leaders generalized the argument into a plea for saving "the American standard of living." The economic case was systematized by the United States Immigration Commission of 1907–11, whose forty-two-volume report comprised the most massive investigation of immigration ever made. The Commission worked out, in vast detail, an unfavorable contrast between the northwestern and southeastern Europeans in the United States *at that time.* The latter were more highly concentrated in cities and in unskilled jobs and were more inclined to return to Europe. These figures obscured significant differences between particular nationalities and did not take account of a marked improvement in the social-economic caliber of northwestern European immigration since the time when it had led the way. Other critics, beginning with the Immigration Restriction League, produced even more misleading figures, correlating the new immigration with the growth of slums and with a high incidence of crime, disease, and insanity.

A second line of argument concerned a racial menace. Here, the case against the new nationalities was harder to build. In popular parlance, race meant color. Since no very clear-cut difference of complexion was apparent between native Americans and any European group, the old instincts of

Source: John Higham, *Send These to Me: Immigrants in Urban America*, pp. 43–50, 53–56. Reprinted by permission of The Estate of John Higham.

white supremacy did not extend to the new immigration as easily as they did to the Chinese. To a large extent, race lines would have to be manufactured. Their construction was a gradual process, long impeded by the democratic tradition. Ultimately, however, the racial attack on the new immigration emerged as a powerful ideological weapon of the restriction movement.

For a starting point, restrictionist intellectuals had a romantic, traditionalist concept of race that was different from the popular spirit of white supremacy. Throughout the nineteenth century patrician writers often acclaimed the American people as the finest branch of the Anglo-Saxon race. The Anglo-Saxon myth was somewhat inconsistent with the cosmopolitan ideal of nationality; but originally no race feelings (in the sense of biological taboos) were involved. In the Anglo-Saxon sense "race" meant essentially the persistence of national character; it expressed a cultural nationalism. In time, however, Anglo-Saxonism expanded and sharpened. It became permeated with race feelings. Increasingly, Anglo-Saxon culture seemed to depend on the persistence of a physical type. Nationalism was naturalized; and "race" in every sense came to imply a biological determinism.

Darwinism was a preliminary influence in the confusion of natural history with national history. By suggesting that a biological struggle underlies all of life, Darwinism encouraged Anglo-Saxon theorists to think of nations as species engaged in a desperate battle for survival. Toward the end of the nineteenth century, a number of patrician intellectuals turned the Anglo-Saxon tradition into a defensive attack on immigrants and an aggressive doctrine in foreign policy. They summoned Anglo-Saxon America to protect herself at home and to demonstrate her mastery abroad. Consequently, the victory of imperialism in 1898 gave racial nationalism an unprecedented vogue. Ideas that had been the property of an intellectual elite permeated public opinion.

Yet, race thinking still did not satisfactorily define the danger of the new immigration. Why would they or their children not respond favorably to the American environment? Indeed, what were the racial differences between southeastern Europeans and old-stock Americans? Darwinism was little help in answering these questions. Answers came only in the early twentieth century through new scientific and pseudoscientific ideas imported from Europe. The dazzling development of modern genetics around 1900 revealed principles of heredity that seemed entirely independent of environmental influences. Genetics inspired many scientists, led by Sir Francis Galton in England and Charles B. Davenport in the United States, to hope for the improvement of society by preventing the inheritance of bad traits. Under the banner of "eugenics," these biological reformers gave a presumably scientific validation to immigration restriction; for how could a nation protect and improve its genes without keeping out "degenerate breeding stock"?

Simultaneously, a new school of anthropology was reeducating Anglo-Saxon nationalists on the racial composition of European man. William Z.

Ripley's *The Races of Europe* (1899) conveyed to American readers a tripartite classification of white men recently developed by European scholars. The new race lines conformed not to national groups, but to physical types: the Nordics of northern Europe, the Alpines of central Europe, and the Mediterraneans of southern Europe. The latter two corresponded roughly to the new immigration. A number of writers combined the new anthropology with eugenics to produce a racist philosophy of history. Probably the most influential of these was Madison Grant, whose pretentious tract, *The Passing of the Great Race* (1916), delivered a solemn warning that the Nordics were making their last stand against the inferior races pouring in from southern and eastern Europe.

These ideas did not develop autonomously. Their importance was chiefly in giving clarity, definition, and some intellectual substance to fears and anxieties that were much more broadly based. The new racism seems to have reflected a wider tendency to make racial categories ever more rigid and impermeable; for this was also the period when lynchings and other measures to degrade and isolate southern Negroes reached an all-time high. Moreover, allegations of a racial peril in the new immigration rationalized an underlying concern about cultural homogeneity. At the deepest level, what impelled the restriction movement in the early decades of the twentieth century was the discovery that immigration was undermining the unity of American culture and threatening the accustomed dominance of a white Protestant people of northern European descent. The science of the day, together with America's traditional susceptibility to race feelings, made the language of race an impelling vehicle for thinking and talking about culture.

The mounting sense of danger—even dispossession—among millions of native-born white Protestants in the period 1910–30 is not hard to understand. A people whose roots were in the towns and farms of the early republic saw great cities coming more and more under the control of strangers whose speech and values were not their own. A people who unconsciously identified Protestantism with Americanism saw Catholic voters and urban bosses gaining control of the industrialized states. A people whose religion was already badly damaged by modern ideas saw the compensating rigors of their lifestyle flouted in the saloons and cabarets of a more expressive, hedonistic society. In reaction, the older America mounted a cultural counteroffensive through the prohibition movement, immigration restriction, and a sharpened racism.

At first the counteroffensive made headway slowly. Statewide prohibition took hold in the South after 1907 but spread widely in the Midwest only after 1912. In Congress an effort to pass the literacy test failed in 1906. No further attempt was made until six years later. Not until 1914 did the restriction movement regain the momentum it had in the mid-nineties. The main reason for this slow recovery was the generally optimistic spirit of the first years of the twentieth century—an optimism reflected in the progressives' absorption with internal reform and the industrialists' unconcern with foreign radicalism. Another constraint was imposed by the ballots of the new immigrants. By the early twentieth century their voting strength in northeastern industrial areas was attracting Republican as well as Democratic politicians. Republicans could sometimes offset Democratic strength in the big cities by appealing to Jews, Slavs, Italians, and French Canadians who fell out with the Irish. Consequently, the G.O.P. could not afford to identify itself with restriction as openly as it had in the nineties. The immigrants made use of their growing influence whenever restriction bills came up. No legislative issue was closer to their hearts, and congressional committees had to face troops of immigrant representatives whenever hearings opened. Jews generally took the lead; a National Liberal Immigration League under Jewish auspices did much to rally the opposition to the literacy bill in 1906 and in succeeding years.

Against this opposition, the restrictionist forces drew on three centers of strength. Patrician race thinkers supplied intellectual leadership. A stream of books and articles urged the eugenic implications of immigration policy and the danger of "race suicide." Meanwhile, a second group, the trade unions, lobbied energetically against the business apologists for immigration. The American Federation of Labor had moved far enough from its immigrant past by the early twentieth century to adopt an uncompromisingly restrictionist position. But its agitation did not count for much in actuality. The Congressmen who might have done labor's bidding were swayed by the stronger pressure of the immigrants; the big cities and industrial centers voted regularly and overwhelmingly against restriction.

Most of the support for restriction in Congress came from a third sector. From 1910 to 1952, the common people of the South and West formed a massive phalanx in favor of rigid legislation. This regional grouping represented a major shift in the alignment of forces. Initially, restriction sentiment had congealed in the Northeast, where the impact of immigration was most quickly and directly felt. In the 1890's the South and West had responded to the issue slowly and uncertainly. But in the twentieth century, while industrial and immigrant opposition thwarted northeastern restrictionists, the South and West emerged into the forefront of the movement. Appropriately, the political leadership passed from Henry Cabot Lodge of Massachusetts, who retired into the background after 1906, to more demagogic men like "Cotton Ed" Smith of South Carolina, Albert Johnson of Washington, and Pat McCarran of Nevada.

The essential explanation is to be found in racial and cultural defensiveness. The Deep South and the Far West, where the new regional lineup started, had long been the areas of most intense race feelings. Even without the sophisticated rationale of the new racial science, southerners and westerners could regard the unfamiliar peoples of southeastern Europe as less than completely white. Moreover, the Deep South and the western frontier had long been the sections with the most militant consciousness of having to fight to maintain a culture against external enemies. As racial lines hardened in the early twentieth century and the torrent of immigration mounted, community leaders from Seattle to Savannah raged at the great alien cities of the East and Midwest for polluting the purity of an Anglo-Saxon country and corrupting an individualistic, Protestant culture.

The first operative demonstration of the new racial emphasis came in 1905 with the outbreak of an anti-Japanese movement on the West Coast. Restrictionist leaders sensed that the Japanese issue might enable them to get the kind of general legislation they wanted. As matters turned out, the immigration law enacted in 1907 began the process of Japanese exclusion but otherwise contained only administrative reforms. Nevertheless, it was significant that Asiatic and European immigration were now, and would henceforth be, treated as different phases of a single question, not as entirely separate from one another. . . .

From 1911 (when the United States Immigration Commission made its report) to 1917, a general bill that included a watered-down literacy test was continually before an increasingly race-conscious Congress. Despite vociferous support from the South and West, the bill did not become law until the eve of America's entry into the war. In even years, Congress stalled for fear of antagonizing the foreign vote in the November elections. In odd years, the bill passed by large majorities but succumbed to a presidential veto. Taft, in 1913, argued that America needed the immigrants' labor and could supply the literacy. Wilson, in 1915 and 1917, appealed to the cosmopolitan ideal of America as a haven for the oppressed.

Enacted finally over Wilson's second veto, the immigration law of 1917 was the first general and sweeping victory for the restrictionists in their thirty-five-year crusade. . . .

Though the whole law grew out of prewar trends, the First World War created the extra margin of support that carried it past a veto. And before long, the war generated a climate of opinion that made these restrictions seem perilously inadequate. Although the war temporarily deferred further action by interrupting migration automatically, the European holocaust unleashed the forces that brought immigration restriction to its historic culmination.

The struggle with Germany stirred public opinion like a cyclone. America's isolation from European affairs, taken for granted in 1914, dissolved. Though statesmen tried to restore it after the war, henceforth it would have to be a deliberate contrivance rather than a natural condition. No longer could the American people feel providentially exempted from any international crisis. The new sense of danger came with such devastating force that it produced very little of the caution and restraint that had marked Roosevelt's Japanese policy. Instead, in every section of the country, men reacted toward all ethnic minorities as Californians had reacted toward the Japanese. Suddenly conscious of the presence of millions of unassimilated people in their midst,

Americans quaked with fear of their potential disloyalty. Roosevelt himself signalized the change; for now he led the clamor for repressing any kind of divided loyalty.

The chief victims during the war years, the German-Americans, were soon thereafter restored to public favor, but the new emotional climate was not a passing phenomenon. Other minorities inherited the hysteria because it arose from a structural change in American nationalism. Known at the time as 100-percent Americanism, the new spirit demanded an unprecedented degree of national solidarity; loyalty and social conformity became virtually synonymous. The slack and gradual processes of assimilation characteristic of the past no longer seemed tolerable. Thus the war destroyed most of what remained of the old faith in America's capacity to fuse all men into a "nation of nations." The development of social stratification had weakened that faith; racial and cultural cleavage had narrowed it; and international stresses dealt it a final blow.

Once immigration revived in 1920, stringent restrictions seemed instantly imperative. Outside of immigrant groups and a few sympathetic social workers, the question no longer concerned the desirability of restriction, but simply the proper degree and kind. Even big business conceded the value of a "selective" policy. Furthermore, the 100-per-cent-American impulse created by the war greatly intensified the racial attitudes evolved in earlier years. For the first time the demand for Japanese exclusion met a general sympathy in eastern opinion; and everywhere a large sector of both the public and the intelligentsia echoed Madison Grant's pleas for preserving Nordic America from the mongrel hordes of southeastern Europe.

Two laws resulted. The first of them, though frankly a makeshift designed to hold the gate while a permanent plan was worked out, established the underlying principle of national quotas based on the preexisting composition of the American population. The law of 1921 limited European immigration to 3 per cent of the number of foreign-born of each nationality present in the United States at the time of the last available census, that of 1910. This would hold the transatlantic current to a maximum of 350,000 and assign most of that total to northwestern Europe. Ethnic affiliation became the main determinant for admission to the United States.

Restrictionists remained dissatisfied, partly because of administrative snarls in the law but chiefly because it was not sufficiently restrictive. In fact, a good many people were pressing for complete suspension of immigration. After three years of bickering, a permanent law passed on a landslide of southern, western, and rural votes. The only opposition came from industrial areas in the Northeast and Midwest. Owing to considerations of Pan-American goodwill and to the southwestern desire for Mexican "stoop-labor," the act of 1924 left immigration from the western hemisphere unrestricted; but it perfected the structure of Oriental exclusion and drastically tightened the quota system for the rest of the world.

PRIMARY SOURCES

The primary sources in this section illustrate nativism in the late nineteenth and early twentieth centuries. They also reflect developments that may have influenced perceptions of immigrants. As you analyze these sources, keep in mind the argument you just read about the role of racial thought as an "ideological weapon" to restrict immigration. One approach is to make a brief list of the most important immigrant characteristics that the primary sources mention, and then determine if nativists saw them as racial traits. What evidence is there that a racist ideology helped to define deeper fears among many Americans?

2   Madison Grant's book, which helped popularize turn-of-the-century theories about "race suicide," went through four editions by 1921. His discussion is based on the assumption that "Nordics" or northern Europeans were racially superior to other "racial stocks." What fears about immigrants does Grant reveal?

The Passing of the Great Race (1916)
MADISON GRANT

The prosperity that followed the [Civil War] attracted hordes of newcomers who were welcomed by the native Americans to operate factories, build railroads and fill up the waste spaces—"developing the country" it was called.

These new immigrants were no longer exclusively members of the Nordic race as were the earlier ones who came of their own impulse to improve their social conditions. The transportation lines advertised America as a land flowing with milk and honey and the European governments took the opportunity to unload upon careless, wealthy and hospitable America the sweepings of their jails and asylums. The result was that the new immigration . . . contained a large and increasing number of the weak, the broken and the mentally crippled of all races drawn from the lowest stratum of the Mediterranean basin and the Balkans, together with hordes of the wretched, submerged populations of the Polish Ghettos. Our jails, insane asylums and almshouses are filled with this human flotsam and the whole tone of American life, social, moral and political has been lowered and vulgarized by them.

With a pathetic and fatuous belief in the efficacy of American institutions and environment to reverse or obliterate immemorial hereditary tendencies, these newcomers were welcomed and given a share in our land and pros-

Source: Excerpted from Madison Grant, The Passing of the Great Race, third edition (New York: Charles Scribner's Sons, 1916) as in Oscar Handlin, ed., Immigration as a Factor in American History (Englewood Cliffs, N.J.: Prentice-Hall, Inc., 1959), pp. 184–185.

perity. The American taxed himself to sanitate and educate these poor helots and as soon as they could speak English, encouraged them to enter into the political life, first of municipalities and then of the nation. . . .

These immigrants adopt the language of the native American, they wear his clothes, they steal his name and they are beginning to take his women, but they seldom adopt his religion or understand his ideals and while he is being elbowed out of his own home the American looks calmly abroad and urges on others the suicidal ethics which are exterminating his own race. . . .

As to what the future mixture will be it is evident that in large sections of the country the native American will entirely disappear. He will not inter-marry with inferior races and he cannot compete in the sweat shop and in the street trench with the newcomers. Large cities from the days of Rome, Alexandria, and Byzantium have always been gathering points of diverse races, but New York is becoming a *cloaca gentium* which will produce many amazing racial hybrids and some ethnic horrors that will be beyond the pow-ers of future anthropologists to unravel.

One thing is certain: in any such mixture, the surviving traits will be de-termined by competition between the lowest and most primitive elements and the specialized traits of Nordic man; his stature, his light colored eyes, his fair skin and light colored hair, his straight nose and his splendid fighting and moral qualities, will have little part in the resultant mixture.

---

3 Calvin Coolidge quickly signed the Johnson-Reed Act when it passed Congress in 1924. Three years earlier, Vice President Coolidge had ex-pressed his views on immigration in this *Good Housekeeping* article. Does his warning about racial "deterioration" reveal other anxieties that Amer-icans may have had after World War I?

Whose Country Is This? (1921)
CALVIN COOLIDGE

We want no such additions to our population as those who prey upon our in-stitutions or our property. America has, in the popular mind, been an asylum for those who have been driven from their homes in foreign countries be-cause of various forms of political and religious oppression. But America cannot afford to remain an asylum after such people have passed the portals and begun to share the privileges of our institutions.

These institutions have flourished by reason of a common background of experience; they have been perpetuated by a common faith in the righteousness of their purpose; they have been handed down undiminished in effectiveness

Source: Lewis H. Carlson and George A. Colburn, *In Their Place: White America Defines Her Mi-norities, 1850–1950* (New York: John Wiley & Sons, Inc., 1972), pp. 342–343.

from our forefathers who conceived their spirit and prepared the foundations. We have put into operation our faith in equal opportunity before the law in exchange for equal obligation of citizenship.

All native-born Americans, directly or indirectly, have the advantage of our schools, our colleges, and our religious bodies. It is our belief that America could not otherwise exist. Faith in mankind is in no wise inconsistent with a requirement for trained citizenship, both for men and women. No civilization can exist without a background—an active community of interest, a common aspiration—spiritual, social, and economic. It is a duty our country owes itself to require of all those aliens who come here that they have a background not inconsistent with American institutions.

Such a background might consist either of a racial tradition or a national experience. But in its lowest terms it must be characterized by a capacity for assimilation. . . . It would not be unjust to ask of every alien: What will you contribute to the common good, once you are admitted through the gates of liberty? Our history is full of answers of which we might be justly proud. But of late, the answers have not been so readily or so eloquently given. Our country must cease to be regarded as a dumping ground. Which does not mean that it must deny the value of rich accretions drawn from the right kind of immigration.

Any such restriction, except as a necessary and momentary expediency, would assuredly paralyze our national vitality. But measured practically, it would be suicidal for us to let down the ban for the inflowing of cheap manhood, just as, commercially, it would be unsound for this country to allow her markets to be overflooded with cheap goods, the product of cheap labor. There is no room either for the cheap man or the cheap goods. . . .

If we believe, as we do, in our political theory that the people are the guardians of government, we should not subject our government to the bitterness and hatred of those who have not been born of our tradition and are not willing to yield an increase to the strength inherent in our institutions. American liberty is dependent on quality in citizenship. Our obligation is to maintain that citizenship at its best. We must have nothing to do with those who would undermine it. The retroactive immigrant is a danger in our midst. His discontent gives him no time to seize a healthy opportunity to improve himself. His purpose is to tear down. There is no room for him here. He needs to be deported, not as a substitute for, but as a part of his punishment.

We might avoid this danger were we insistent that the immigrant, before he leaves foreign soil, is temperamentally keyed for our national background. There are racial considerations too grave to be brushed aside for any sentimental reasons. Biological laws tell us that certain divergent people will not mix or blend. The Nordics propagate themselves successfully. With other races, the outcome shows deterioration on both sides. Quality of mind and body suggests that observance of ethnic law is as great a necessity to a nation as immigration law. . . .

4   By 1923, the Ku Klux Klan had attracted millions of members. Hiram Evans's article, published in the *North American Review* in 1926, offers some clues about the fears of many of them. Does his article support John Higham's contention that race was only a "vehicle" for expressing anxieties about culture?

The Klan's Fight for Americanism (1926)

HIRAM W. EVANS

The Klan, therefore, has now come to speak for the great mass of Americans of the old pioneer stock. We believe that it does fairly and faithfully represent them, and our proof lies in their support. To understand the Klan, then, it is necessary to understand the character and present mind of the mass of old-stock Americans. The mass, it must be remembered, as distinguished from the intellectually mongrelized "Liberals."

These are, in the first place, a blend of various peoples of the so-called Nordic race, the race which, with all its faults, has given the world almost the whole of modern civilization. The Klan does not try to represent any people but these. . . .

[T]hese Nordic Americans for the last generation have found themselves increasingly uncomfortable, and finally deeply distressed. There appeared first confusion in thought and opinion, a groping and hesitancy about national affairs and private life alike, in sharp contrast to the clear, straightforward purposes of our earlier years. There was futility in religion, too, which was in many ways even more distressing. Presently we began to find that we were dealing with strange ideas; policies that always sounded well but somehow always made us still more uncomfortable.

Finally came the moral breakdown that has been going on for two decades. One by one all our traditional moral standards went by the boards or were so disregarded that they ceased to be binding. The sacredness of our Sabbath, of our homes, of chastity, and finally even of our right to teach our own children in our own schools fundamental facts and truths were torn away from us. Those who maintained the old standards did so only in the face of constant ridicule. . . .

One more point about the present attitude of the old-stock American: he has revived and increased his long-standing distrust of the Roman Catholic Church. It is for this that the native Americans, and the Klan as their leader, are most often denounced as intolerant and prejudiced. . . .

There are three of these great racial instincts, vital elements in both the historic and the present attempts to build an America which shall fulfill the aspirations and justify the heroism of the men who made the nation. These are

Source: Hiram W. Evans, "Klan's Fight for Americanism," from *North American Review,* March/April/May 1926, pp. 37–63. Reprinted by permission of the Univeristy of Northern Iowa.

the instincts of loyalty to the white race, to the traditions of America, and to the spirit of Protestantism, which has been an essential part of Americanism ever since the days of Roanoke and Plymouth Rock. They are condensed into the Klan slogan: "Native, white, Protestant supremacy."

---

5   The author of this article, published in *The Independent* magazine, asked several Gentiles why anti-Semitism existed. What stereotypes are evident in the responses? How do the stereotypes here compare to group stereotypes in the other sources?

Because You're a Jew (1908)

It was not easy to get frank testimony. Merchants, officials, hotel men, did not care to speak out. When they spoke at all they stipulated that their names should not be mentioned. It was only by putting many testimonies together that one was enabled to get the Gentile side of the case, which may be fairly presented in this manner:

"We have no prejudice against the Jews. We do dislike them but it is dislike based on knowledge and evidence which is so widespread and so general that it has resulted in an instinctive dislike. It is because of qualities which are manifested by Jews. The dishonest among them are out of all proportion to their numbers. No other people so persistently, shrewdly, cunningly, constantly, skim the very verge of crime, and many go over the verge." . . .

"There is another thing against the Jew. They are too prosperous. Where they contest they win. Five or six years ago, after the French Ball, there was a fight and the victor stood over the body of his antagonist and proudly proclaimed: 'The Jew is always on top.' The fact that the man whom he had defeated was also a Jew did not affect the truth he had uttered. The Jew is winning everywhere. By fair means or by foul means he wins. He has the commerce of the city in his hands now, and the signs on Broadway make one think of the main street in New Jerusalem and make Gentiles curse Titus* and wish that he had never been born. Why couldn't he leave them alone in Judea? Perhaps he might have stayed there? As to the possibility of a great Zionist movement, it's too good to be true!

"One tentacle of the Hebrew octopus has caught our newspapers now, and we also see Jews running our theaters and giving us a drama that never before was so low. We see the Hebrew octopus seizing one enterprise after the other, and we can't stop it. They are beating us. . . ."

"Two or three Jews at a summer resort utterly spoil the place for the Gen-

---

*The Roman who conquered Jerusalem, destroyed the great temple, and sold many of the city's residents into slavery.

Source: Lewis H. Carlson and George A. Colburn, *In Their Place: White America Defines Her Minorities, 1850–1950* (New York: John Wiley & Sons, Inc., 1972), pp. 255, 256–257.

tiles. The first thing that the Jew does when he gets in a hotel is to bribe the head waiter. He must have the best steak, the best of everything, and be served first, and he is so persistent, so acute, so eager and so willing to resort to anything to get his way that he does get his way and makes every less strenuous person about him so uncomfortable that they'd sooner leave the place than contend. If he sits at a table near you and you have secured something especially good, his greedy eyes boring into you utterly spoil your repast. If you give your children new toys and send them out to play you will find in half an hour that the Jew children have the new toys while your youngsters are looking on. The young Jews are not violent, but they get what they want by reason of their greater appetite for it. They're insatiable and can only be repressed by force . . ."

"How foolish, then, to associate with these people when there can by no means be any real assimilation."

6   Gene Stratton-Porter was a best-selling novelist whose works were popular with young readers in the early twentieth century. In *Her Father's Daughter,* heroine Linda Strong bore a striking resemblance to Stratton-Porter herself. In this excerpt, Linda advises a fellow student at a Los Angeles high school how to overtake a Japanese American student at the head of the class. How does the fear of the Japanese compare to the fear of Jews in the previous source?

Her Father's Daughter (1921)

GENE STRATTON-PORTER

An angry red rushed to the boy's face. It was an irritating fact that in the senior class of that particular Los Angeles high school a Japanese boy stood at the head. This was embarrassing to every senior.

Shortly after this, Sweet Linda is discussing the problem with a fellow student:

"I am getting at the fact that a boy as big as you and as strong as you and with as good brain and your opportunities has allowed a little brown Jap to cross the Pacific Ocean and in a totally strange country to learn a language foreign to him, and with the same books and the same chances, to beat you at your game. You and every other boy in your class ought to be thoroughly ashamed of yourselves. Before I would let a Jap, either boy or girl, lead in my class, I would give up going to school and go out and see if I could beat him growing lettuce and spinach." . . .

"For God's sake, Linda, tell me how I can beat that little coconut-headed Jap."

Source: Lewis H. Carlson and George A. Colburn, *In Their Place: White America Defines Her Minorities, 1850–1950* (New York: John Wiley & Sons, Inc., 1972), pp. 225–227.

Linda slammed down the lid to the lunch box. Her voice was smooth and even but there was battle in her eyes and she answered decisively: "Well, you can't beat him calling him names. There is only one way on God's footstool that you can beat him. You can't beat him legislating against him. You can't beat him boycotting him. You can't beat him with any tricks. He is as sly as a cat and he has got a whole bag full of tricks of his own, and he has proved right here in Los Angeles that he has got a brain that is hard to beat. All you can do, and be a man commendable to your own soul, is to take his subject and put your brain on it to such purpose that cut pigeon wings around him. . . . There is just one way in all this world that we can beat Eastern civilization and all that it intends to do to us eventually. The white man has dominated by his color so far in the history of the world, but it is written in the Books that when the men of colour acquire our culture and combine it with their own methods of living and rate of production, they are going to bring forth greater numbers, better equipped for the battle of life, than we are. When they have got our last secret, constructive or scientific, they will take it, and living in a way that we would not, reproducing in numbers we don't, they will beat us at any game we start, if we don't take warning while we are in the ascendency, and keep there." . . .

"I'll do anything in the world if you will only tell me how," said Donald. "Maybe you think it isn't grinding me and humiliating me properly. Maybe you think Father and Mother haven't warned me. Maybe you think Mary Louise isn't secretly ashamed of me. How can I beat him, Linda?" . . .

"I have been watching pretty sharply," she said. "Take them as a race, as a unit—of course there are exceptions, there always are—but the great body of them are mechanical. They are imitative. They are not developing anything great of their own in their own country. They are spreading all over the world and carrying home sewing machines and threshing machines and automobiles and cantilever bridges and submarines and aeroplanes—anything from eggbeaters to telescopes. They are not creating one single thing. They are not missing imitating everything that the white man can do anywhere else on earth. They are just like the Germans so far as that is concerned." . . .

Donald started up and drew a deep breath.

"Well, some job I call that," he said. "Who do you think I am, The Almighty?"

"No," said Linda quietly, "you are not. You are merely His son, created in his own image, like Him, according to the Book, and you have got to your advantage the benefit of all that has been learned down through the ages. . . . All Oka Sayye knows how to do is to learn the lesson in his book perfectly, and he is 100 per cent. I have told you what you must do to add the plus, and you can do it if you are that boy I take you for. People have talked about the 'yellow peril' till it's got to be a meaningless phrase. Somebody must wake up to the realization that it's the deadliest peril that ever has menaced white civilization. Why shouldn't you have your hand in such wonderful work?"

7   Speeches by members of Congress often reflected popular attitudes toward immigrants. In this selection, Representative Lucian W. Parish, a Democrat from Texas, compares old and new immigrants. How does he compare them? Look for evidence of anxieties about postwar American society.

A Congressman Calls for Restriction (1921)

We should stop immigration entirely until such a time as we can amend our immigration laws and so write them that hereafter no one shall be admitted except he be in full sympathy with our Constitution and laws, willing to declare himself obedient to our flag, and willing to release himself from any obligations he may owe to the flag of the country from which he came.

It is time that we act now, because within a few short years the damage will have been done. The endless tide of immigration will have filled our country with a foreign and unsympathetic element. Those who are out of sympathy with our Constitution and the spirit of our Government will be here in large numbers, and the true spirit of Americanism left us by our fathers will gradually become poisoned by this uncertain element.

The time once was when we welcomed to our shores the oppressed and downtrodden people from all the world, but they came to us because of oppression at home and with the sincere purpose of making true and loyal American citizens, and in truth and in fact they did adapt themselves to our ways of thinking and contributed in a substantial sense to the progress and development that our civilization has made. But that time has passed now; new and strange conditions have arisen in the countries over there; new and strange doctrines are being taught. The Governments of the Orient are being overturned and destroyed, and anarchy and bolshevism are threatening the very foundation of many of them, and no one can foretell what the future will bring to many of those countries of the Old World now struggling with these problems.

Our country is a self-sustaining country. It has taught the principles of real democracy to all the nations of the earth; its flag has been the synonym of progress, prosperity, and the preservation of the rights of the individual, and there can be nothing so dangerous as for us to allow the undesirable foreign element to poison our civilization and thereby threaten the safety of the institutions that our forefathers have established for us.

Now is the time to throw about this country the most stringent immigration laws and keep from our shores forever those who are not in sympathy with the American ideas. It is the time now for us to act and act quickly, because every month's delay increases the difficulty in which we find ourselves and renders the problems of government more difficult of solution. We must protect ourselves from the poisonous influences that are threatening the very foundation of the Governments of Europe; we must see to it that those who

Source: Congressional Record, April 20, 1921, p. 450.

come here are loyal and true to our Nation and impress upon them that it means something to have the privileges of American citizenship. We must hold this country true to the American thought and the American ideals. . . .

 As you examine this cartoon, pay attention to the fears about immigrants that it reflects. What developments after World War I reinforced the fear of immigrants?

The Bootleggers (1925)

Source: The Independent, March 14, 1925.

Tables on Unemployment and Immigrant Occupations

Do these tables provide evidence for additional reasons why many Americans, including organized labor, supported immigration restriction after World War I?

 ## Immigrant Occupation Groups, 1899–1924

Year	Total	Professional, technical, and kindred workers	Farmers and farm managers	Managers, officials, and proprietors, exc. farm	Clerical, sales, and kindred workers
1924	706,896	20,926	20,320	15,668	27,373
1923	522,919	13,926	12,503	12,086	17,931
1922	309,556	9,696	7,676	9,573	10,055
1921	805,228	12,852	22,282	18,286	18,922
1920	430,001	10,540	12,192	9,654	14,054
1919	141,132	5,261	3,933	4,247	6,524
1918	110,618	3,529	2,583	3,940	4,239
1917	295,403	7,499	7,764	8,329	10,554
1916	298,826	9,024	6,840	8,725	9,907
1915	326,700	11,453	6,518	10,728	9,377
1914	1,218,480	13,454	14,442	21,903	17,933
1913	1,197,892	12,552	13,180	19,094	15,173
1912	838,172	10,913	7,664	14,715	13,782
1911	878,587	11,275	9,709	15,416	14,723
1910	1,041,570	9,689	11,793	14,731	12,219
1909	751,786	7,603	8,914	11,562	8,467
1908	782,870	10,504	7,720	16,410	11,523
1907	1,285,349	12,016	13,476	20,132	12,735
1906	1,100,735	13,015	15,288	23,515	12,226
1905	1,026,499	12,582	18,474	27,706	12,759
1904	812,870	12,195	4,507	26,914	11,055
1903	857,046	6,999	13,363	15,603	7,226
1902	648,743	2,937	8,168	9,340	3,836
1901	487,918	2,665	3,035	8,294	3,197
1900	448,572	2,392	5,433	7,216	2,870
1899	311,715	1,972	3,973	6,815	2,473

(cont. on next page)

Source: "Occupations," *Historical Statistics of the United States: Colonial Times to 1957* (Washington, D.C.: U.S. Bureau of the Census, 1960), p. 60.

Craftsmen, foremen, operatives, and kindred workers	Private household workers	Service workers, exc. private household	Farm laborers and foremen	Laborers, exc. farm and mine	No occupation
123,923	51,680	29,261	27,492	112,344	277,909
87,899	52,223	22,244	25,905	86,617	191,585
40,309	44,531	12,340	10,529	33,797	131,050
109,710	102,478	24,298	32,400	162,859	301,141
55,991	37,197	18,487	15,257	83,496	173,133
21,671	6,277	11,571	4,412	18,922	58,314
17,501	7,816	6,367	4,538	15,142	44,963
38,660	31,885	11,784	22,328	52,182	104,418
36,086	29,258	10,989	26,250	56,981	104,766
45,591	39,774	11,976	24,723	49,620	116,940
149,515	144,409	19,621	288,053	228,935	320,215
139,091	140,218	17,609	320,105	223,682	297,188
107,893	116,529	13,580	184,154	137,872	231,070
128,717	107,153	11,051	176,003	158,518	246,022
121,847	96,658	8,977	288,745	216,909	260,002
75,730	64,568	5,849	171,310	176,490	221,293
106,943	89,942	10,367	138,844	147,940	242,677
169,394	121,587	13,578	323,854	293,868	304,709
156,902	115,984	10,439	239,125	228,781	285,460
159,442	125,473	5,849	142,187	290,009	232,018
133,748	104,937	6,400	85,850	212,572	214,692
110,644	92,686	11,482	77,518	321,824	199,701
71,131	69,913	6,298	80,562	243,399	153,159
57,346	42,027	5,352	54,753	162,563	148,686
54,793	40,311	4,406	31,949	164,261	134,941
38,608	34,120	4,580	17,343	92,452	109,379

10 Unemployment Rates, 1900–1924

Year	Unemployed*	Percent of civilian labor force
1924	2,440	5.5
1923	1,380	3.2
1922	3,220	7.6
1921	5,010	11.9
1920	1,670	4.0
1919	950	2.3
1918	560	1.4
1917	1,920	4.8
1916	1,920	4.8
1915	3,840	9.7
1914	3,110	8.0
1913	1,680	4.4
1912	1,960	5.2
1911	2,290	6.2
1910	2,150	5.9
1909	1,870	5.2
1908	2,960	8.5
1907	600	1.8
1906	280	0.8
1905	1,000	3.1
1904	1,490	4.8
1903	800	2.6
1902	800	2.7
1901	710	2.4
1900	1,420	5.0

*In thousands.

Source: "Unemployment," Historical Statistics of the United States: Colonial Times to 1957 (Washington, D.C.: U.S. Bureau of the Census, 1960), p. 73.

CONCLUSION

Like the newcomers sailing through the Golden Gate, steaming by the Statue of Liberty, or crossing the Rio Grande, historians often find themselves strangers in the land. As we saw in the last chapter, houses and furniture in the past were often different from ours. More important, the ideological "filter"—the complex of beliefs, values, fears, prejudices, and interests that people in the past used to make sense of their world—was also different from ours. Because these differences make the past a foreign place for us, we cannot expect to get very far without understanding what people thought—their ideology. Although that alone may not make their motives clear, no explanation of motivation is complete without it. And when historians know the motives of people in the past they can better comprehend historical causes—one theme of the coming chapters.

FURTHER READING

Leonard Dinnerstein and David Reimers, *Ethnic Americans and Assimilation* (New York: Harper and Row, 1975).

Maldwyn A. Jones, *American Immigration* (Chicago: University of Chicago Press, 1960).

Alan M. Kraut, *The Huddled Masses: The Immigrant in American Society, 1880–1921* (Arlington Heights, Ill.: Harlan Davidson, 1982).

Wayne Moquin, ed., *Makers of America—Hyphenated Americans, 1914–1924* (Chicago: Encyclopaedia Britannica Educational Corp., 1971).

Dale Steiner, *Of Thee We Sing: Immigrants and American History* (San Diego: Harcourt Brace Jovanovich, 1987).

NOTE

1. Maldwyn Allen Jones, *American Immigration* (Chicago: University of Chicago Press, 1960), p. 177.

Chapter

7

History "From the Top Down": Eleanor Roosevelt, First Lady

The sources in this chapter enable the reader to evaluate the activities of Eleanor Roosevelt and to assess their relevance to the times.

Secondary Source

1. Eleanor Roosevelt as First Lady (1996), ALLIDA M. BLACK

Primary Sources

2. Letter to Lorena Hickok (1933)
3. Transcripts of Eleanor Roosevelt's Press Conferences (1933–1938)
4. "The Negro and Social Change" (1936)
5. Letter to Her Daughter (1937)
6. This I Remember (1949), ELEANOR ROOSEVELT
7. Letter from Barry Bingham to Marvin McIntyre (1934)
8. Excerpts from Letters to Franklin Roosevelt (1935)
9. It's Up to the Women (1933)
10. News Item, "Definition of Feminism" (1935)
11. News Item, "Opposes Amendment" (1938)

*D*uring the Great Depression in 1932, unemployed World War I veterans marched on Washington, D.C., to demand early payment of their service bonuses. In response Herbert Hoover called out the army, which routed the desperate marchers out of their shantytown and then burned it down. Shortly after Franklin Roosevelt took office in 1933, a second "bonus army" descended on Washington. This time the First Lady drove out to talk to them. When she arrived, they asked her who she was and what she wanted. She told them her name and that she wanted to see how they were doing. "I did not spend as much as an hour there; then I got into my car and drove away," she said. "Everyone waved and I called, 'Good luck,' and they answered, 'good-by and good luck to you.'"[1]

Before the Depression was over, Eleanor Roosevelt had visited coal miners, Civilian Conservation Corps boys, women in Works Progress Administration sewing rooms, tenant farmers, and many others. As she traveled around the country, the First Lady gave a human face to numerous New Deal relief programs. At the same time she was her paralyzed husband's eyes and ears, reporting to him Americans' struggles to survive the Depression. She was also his conscience, fighting amid much criticism to extend the boundaries of the New Deal to blacks and women.

By sharing the public spotlight with her husband, Eleanor Roosevelt was the first "modern" First Lady. As a political activist, she redefined the role of the president's wife. At the same time, there was also something old-fashioned about her. A Victorian upbringing gave her what one historian called "an uncynical sense of duty and moral purpose."[2] It also left her with a traditional view of women as mothers and wives. Eleanor believed that women were agents of moral good and needed protection more than equality. She never went to college or pursued a career. Self-reliance grew only slowly, nurtured by the pain of rejection.

Eleanor Roosevelt's struggle for independence is a compelling story for biographers, but there is another reason to examine her life. Like her, there is something "old-fashioned" about biography itself. Traditionally it was written about people at the "top" of their society, wealthy and influential people like Eleanor. Moreover, as one writer put it, biography "moves to the pace and powers of individual human beings and not to the impersonal dictates of markets and masses."[3] During the Depression, of course, few Americans had escaped the dictates of either. FDR was president because markets had collapsed and the "masses" had chosen him to lead the nation. At first glance, biography's personal approach to history might seem ill-suited to a time dominated by such impersonal forces. Yet the Depression era is actually a good time to see how one person's life illuminates the past, because biographers deal with the important historical developments as well as with individual lives. Biographies show us the forces that shaped their subjects' lives and how, in turn, their lives influenced history. This chapter, therefore, examines how one exceptional woman both reflected and affected her times.

SETTING

Anna Eleanor Roosevelt was born in 1884 into a world of privilege. The daughter of two families that could trace their wealth to colonial times, she grew up sheltered from both the masses and the marketplace. Yet her childhood was hardly blissful. Eleanor's mother was cold, distant, and disappointed by her only daughter's plain appearance. As Eleanor later realized, she grew up shy and lonely, "entirely lacking in the spontaneous joy and mirth of youth."[4] Her affectionate but alcoholic father was the one bright spot in her childhood. Unfortunately, he died when she was ten, two years after diphtheria had claimed her mother. Eleanor and her younger brother lived with their grandmother, who reared them "on the principle that 'no' was easier to say than 'yes.'"[5]

Escape came in the form of an English finishing school. There Eleanor learned more than the social graces that upper-class Americans considered "education" for their daughters. Headmistress Marie Souvestre encouraged her students to think critically and to challenge conventional ideas. Souvestre took special interest in Eleanor, who seemed burdened with a sense of inferiority. She taught her to champion the underdog. Together they traveled through Europe. "Whatever I have become since," Eleanor later confided, "had its seeds in those three years of contact with a liberal mind and strong personality."[6]

Still, exposure to Madame Souvestre's "liberal" ideas did not prevent Eleanor from becoming a New York society debutante when she returned home, or from being depressed about her appearance. "I was the first girl in my mother's family who was not a belle," she confessed, "and . . . I was deeply ashamed."[7] Eleanor had not forgotten Souvestre's lessons, however. After her debut, she joined the National Consumers' League, which fought for better conditions for female workers in sweatshops and clothing factories. She also joined the Junior League, recently founded by charity-minded socialites. She taught classes at a community center on the Lower East Side, where she was at first terrified at the sight of "foreign-looking people, crowded and dirty."[8] In time, however, Eleanor discovered she preferred social work to the social whirl.

Marriage to distant cousin Franklin in 1905 ended Eleanor's trips to the tenements. For the next fifteen years she was occupied with her five children and her husband's budding political career. Gradually, though, she was again drawn out of her private sphere. After World War I, Eleanor joined the League of Women Voters and the Women's Trade Union League, which fought for legislation regulating women's wages and hours of labor. Personal shocks furthered a growing sense of independence and self-confidence. In 1918 she discovered Franklin's affair with her personal secretary. "The bottom dropped out of my . . . world and I faced myself, my surroundings, my world honestly for the first time," she later wrote.[9] Their marriage continued, but marital relations did not. Eleanor began to spend more time in reform causes and discovered her own political skills. Franklin's paralyzing bout with polio four years later further encouraged her independence.

Eleanor began to represent her husband in public and became active in New York Democratic party politics. She organized women voters, fought for numerous social reforms, and developed associations with many female reformers. In 1928, while teaching part-time at a private girls' school in New York City, Eleanor worked for Al Smith's unsuccessful campaign for the presidency, running the New York headquarters of the Democratic Party's National Women's Committee. When Franklin was elected governor of New York the same year, Eleanor decided to keep her teaching job and be First Lady in Albany only part-time.

Eleanor nevertheless played an influential role as the governor's wife, advising him on policies and appointments, and when FDR ran for the presidency four years later she put her experience to work campaigning around the country. It was on the campaign that she also began an intimate friendship with reporter Lorena Hickok. During Eleanor's years in the White House, the two women sustained a furtive relationship that was both passionate and romantic. To Hickok, Eleanor shared her fears about becoming First Lady. Eleanor was fearful for her husband and children, but mostly she was worried about her own fate. She knew that, far more than in the governor's mansion, she would have to sacrifice her autonomy and tend to social obligations as the nation's First Lady. Right after FDR's sweeping victory in 1932, Eleanor confided to Hickok that she was "sincerely" glad for her husband. "Now," she added, "I shall have to work out my own salvation."[10]

INVESTIGATION

This chapter examines Eleanor Roosevelt's efforts to "work out" her "salvation" as First Lady. Thus your main task is to evaluate Eleanor Roosevelt as an activist First Lady during the Depression. Your evaluation should address the following main questions:

1. **What do Eleanor Roosevelt's activities reveal about the limitations on women in the early twentieth century?** Do the sources reveal that she had power, or only influence with other people?

2. **Do the sources reveal that Eleanor challenged or reinforced traditional conceptions of women's proper role?** Did she challenge her role as helpmate to her husband or channel her energies in only socially acceptable directions?

3. **In what ways was Eleanor Roosevelt's struggle unique and how did it reflect**

the situation of women generally? What do the sources reveal about the influence of Eleanor's social background on her attitudes?

4. **Do you agree with historian Allida Black's conclusions in Source 1 about Eleanor's achievements?** What were her greatest achievement and biggest failure as First Lady? Was she able to change the lives of women and blacks, or only her own?

Before you begin, review the sections in your textbook on the status and role of women in American society in the first decades of the twentieth century, as well as the chapter on the New Deal. Although Eleanor Roosevelt may not be mentioned, these sections will provide useful background for evaluating her activities and achievements.

SECONDARY SOURCE

1   In this selection, historian Allida M. Black examines Eleanor Roosevelt's role as First Lady during the 1930s. Note how Black uses ER's life to examine important social issues during the Depression. What impact did she have on these issues? Do you think a biography of an exceptional, upperclass woman like Eleanor Roosevelt reveals a lot or a little about historical developments and the lives of ordinary Americans in the early twentieth century?

Eleanor Roosevelt as First Lady (1996)

ALLIDA M. BLACK

Questions "seethed" in ER's mind about what she should do after March 4, 1933. Realizing that FDR would not allow her the same mobility she had when he was governor, ER worried that she would be confined to a schedule of teas and receptions and tried to create a less restrictive place for herself within the White House. She volunteered to "do a real job" for FDR. . . . The president rebuffed the first lady's offer. Trapped by convention, she begrudgingly recognized that "the work [was FDR's] work and the pattern his pattern." Frustrated and disappointed, she acknowledged that she "was one of those who served his purposes."

Nevertheless, ER refused to accept a superficial and sedentary role. She wanted "to do things on my own, to use my own mind and abilities for my own aims" and struggled to carve out an active contributory place for herself in the New Deal. This was not to be a challenge easily met. Dejected, she found it "hard to remember that I was not just 'Eleanor Roosevelt,' but the 'wife of the President.'" Yet within her first two years in the White House, she had turned her "joblessness" into the freedom to investigate a variety of issues and the power to advance specific programs which she hoped would ease the problems she detected. . . .

She was lonely. . . . "First Friend" Hickok, who continued to travel as an investigative reporter for the Federal Emergency Relief Administration after she resigned her position with the Associated Press, tried to fill the gap. By May, ER's frustration had given way to immense depression. "My zest in life is rather gone for the time being," ER confessed to Hickok. "If anyone looks at me, I want to weep . . . my mind goes round and round like a squirrel in a cage. I want to run and I can't, and I despise myself. . . .

. . . On March 6, two days after her husband became president, Eleanor Roosevelt held her own press conference to announce that she would "get together" with women reporters once a week. She asked for the reporters' cooperation. ER hoped that together they not only could discuss her duties as first lady but also explain "what goes on politically in the legislative national life" and encourage women to become active in the New Deal programs in their community. "The idea," she said, "largely is to make an understanding between the White House and the general public."

Initially ER tried to weight the discussion more in favor of her traditional social duties and away from her views of the problems the nation confronted. However, as she expanded her role, the topics covered during the press conferences also expanded. Her statements to the press notwithstanding, political issues soon became a central part of the weekly briefings.

FDR, at [his adviser Louis] Howe's urging, had asked his wife to travel the nation as his "ambassador." Within three months, ER had logged 40,000 miles. Her observations during these tours only reinforced the impressions she had formed during the final days of the campaign. She returned to Washington convinced that relief programs alone could not counteract the Depression and that basic economic reforms were essential. She began to share these views with the women assigned to cover her.

By May she discussed the White House protocol for serving 3.2 percent beer, her opposition to sweat shops and child labor, the problem confronting those living in the Bonus Army encampment and poverty-stricken Appalachia, and her support for the Veterans National Liaison Committee and higher salaries for teachers. By early June she proclaimed that "very few women know how to read the newspapers," argued that they should pay close attention to international economic news, and delivered a tutorial on how "a busy woman" could keep track of the news "at a time when every one of us ought to be on [our] toes."

These pronouncements, when coupled with the image she made when she visited those the Depression affected most, encouraged political reporters to cover her. This fostered an in-house rivalry between reporters assigned to cover hard news and those assigned to the women's pages. Society reporters complained that her meetings with the press did not cover enough social news and many eventually stopped attending her weekly briefings.

Some political journalists, worried that such unorthodox comments would encourage criticism, urged ER to go off the record when she discussed political issues. Grateful for their concern, she nevertheless rejected their advice and argued that she knew that some of her statements would "cause unfavorable comment in some quarters," but, she told Emma Bugbee, "I am making these statements on purpose to arouse controversy and thereby get the topics talked about."

By 1934 ER's press conferences had become one of the major ways she defended her own activity and the programs she championed. Although she never issued a formal statement to the reporters and met with the press only to answer their questions, she soon learned to use these conferences as a way to appeal directly to the people. As [reporter] Bess Furman later recalled, "at the President's press conference, all the world's a stage, at Mrs. Roosevelt's, all the world's a school. . . . Give Mrs. Roosevelt a roomful of newspaper women, and she conducts classes on scores of subjects, always seeing beyond her immediate hearers to the 'women of the country.'"

ER, not satisfied with just disseminating information, also wanted to know how the public responded to the positions she advocated and those positions promoted by FDR's major critics, Huey Long and Father Charles Coughlin. Consequently, when *Women's Home Companion* asked her to write a monthly column, she gladly accepted. Announcing that she would donate her monthly thousand dollar fee to charity, ER then proceeded to ask her readers to help her establish "a clearinghouse, a discussion room" for "the particular problems which puzzle you or sadden you" and to share "how you are adjusting yourself to new conditions in this amazing changing world." Entitling the article "I Want You to Write to Me," ER reinforced the request throughout the piece. "Do not hesitate," she wrote in August 1933, "to write to me even if your views clash with what you believe to be my views." Only a free exchange of ideas and discussion of problems would help her "learn of experiences which may be helpful to others." By January 1934, 300,000 Americans had responded to this solicitation, more than the total number of letters received by Abraham Lincoln and Woodrow Wilson in their first year in office and equal to the weekly circulation of Long's *American Progress.*

This was not a token offer. ER had personal and political reasons for appealing for public input. Worried that Long and Coughlin supporters felt neglected by the New Deal, she wanted to make herself available to them. Also concerned that the Federal Emergency Relief Administration programs did meet enough of people's needs, she pressured FERA administrator Harry Hopkins to hire Hickok to tour different parts of the nation, observe FERA programs, and report to him on their effectiveness. Hickok sent copies of these honest, harsh field reports to ER, daily confirming the many obstacles those seeking relief encountered. Plus, she was bored. "Your job is much more interesting than mine," she complained to Hickok that winter. She desperately wanted an assignment that was hers alone, an arena in which she could judge for herself the effectiveness of her husband's programs.

Yet her appeal to the public was not motivated solely by her dissatisfaction. Her commitment to free and unrestricted public discussion was heartfelt and intense. She considered the free exchange of information and ideas central to democracy's success. The more informed the public about the issues it confronted, the more educated the society would become, and the more opportunities democracy would have to be realized. . . .

The cornerstone of ER's emerging political philosophy was as simple as it was powerful: if the nation was to flourish, Americans must accept the responsibility of living in a democracy. They must study the issues and develop informed opinions about the best ways to solve the nation's problems because "knowledge will forever govern ignorance." Americans "must arm themselves. with the power that knowledge gives" because government could only be as good as its people. Democracy was a two-way street. It not only "must have leaders who have the power to see farther, to imagine a better life but it must also have a vast army of men and women capable of understanding these leaders." . . .

Although most historians focus on ER's enthusiastic support for the model subsistence homestead community in Arthurdale, West Virginia, as the clearest example of ER's pressuring FDR toward a more encompassing relief effort, other New Deal programs, when examined as a group, offer a more thorough illustration of ER's democratic principles. While she doggedly advocated programs which would ensure "that a family shall have sufficient means of livelihood and the assurance of an ability to pay their expenses covering a stand which we hope to establish as something to shoot at," in her vision, the responsibilities of a democratic state were not to be confined to improving the lot of only one socioeconomic group. . . .

The huge numbers of unemployed youth of the 1930s underscored several fears adults had about society. Conservatives saw disgruntled young people as a fertile ground for revolutionary politics while progressives mourned the disillusionment and apathy spreading among American youth. Indeed, concern over the political susceptibility of youth concerned some within the administration so much that they wondered "whether the New Deal ought to establish a democratic alternative to the Hitler Youth." Educators feared that without some type of financial aid, colleges would suffer irreversible damage. Eleanor Roosevelt agreed with the progressives, telling the *New York Times* that "I live in real terror when I think we may be losing this generation. We have got to bring these young people into the active life of the community and make them feel that they are necessary."

ER insisted that government had the responsibility to keep these young people from becoming even more "stranded." Although many in the White House agreed with her, New Deal officials differed over the means to reduce joblessness among high school and college-age youth and debated whether or not student aid should be provided as part of the relief package. Public opinion, fearful that students would take jobs that might otherwise help adult workers, was ambivalent over which course the government should pursue. Moreover, understanding the sensitivity of this issue, FDR proved reluctant to institute a program which might backfire. Although he wanted to put young people to work and believed that action must be taken to shore up youth's commitment to democracy, the president "never approved of ideological training for American youth." Furthermore, he did not want to be accused of favoritism or despotism. While everyone agreed there was a major problem, there was no consensus on how to address it.

FDR signed the executive order creating the National Youth Administration (NYA) in the summer of 1935, two years after telling the press that he objected to "channeling direct federal aid to high school graduates or their teachers." He insisted that he had "pretty serious" disagreements with a program that would "do anything in the way of sending boys and girls to college." And lastly, he categorically rejected any proposal which would provide widespread vocational training. Instead he championed a more traditional approach that emphasized physical labor, strict supervision, and limited job training. In short, FDR promoted the Civilian Conservation Corps (CCC) as the model agency for youth relief.

ER, who could not have disagreed more strongly with her husband, emphatically rejected the CCC model. Although it certainly helped adults, she argued that it failed youth. Its camps were too militaristic to encourage independence and its instruction was limited to forestry. This was no way to bring disgruntled and disillusioned youth back into society. The specific problem facing youth needed to be recognized, but in a way that not only fostered self-worth but also encouraged faith in democratic capitalism. The government must show American youth that they had more options than the military and the dole.

By 1934, ER decided that the government had to develop a program tailored to the special economic, educational, and vocational needs of youth, and she dedicated herself to seeing a comprehensive program implemented. She lobbied the press and administration officials, appealed to the public to recognize the social and political benefits the program could offer, and coaxed student leaders into setting realistic goals. Having met regularly with student leaders and relief officials, she understood both sides of the argument. And she strove to form a consensus that could satisfy most needs of both groups. . . .

Although not the legislative architect of the NYA, ER nevertheless helped establish its priorities, and in so doing left an indelible imprint upon the agency's development. When FDR issued the executive order June 26, 1935, he authorized the NYA to administer programs in five areas: work projects, vocational guidance, apprenticeship training, educational and nutritional guidance camps for unemployed women, and student aid. Clearly ER's preference for vocational guidance and education triumphed over his earlier support of the CCC relief model. Even historian James Kearney, who believed that the first lady's sole contribution to political thought was her "goodness," acknowledged that over time, "the NYA moved toward [her] preferences." As the agency progressed from its initial emphasis on relief to placing more emphasis on recreation and clerical training to providing educational loans, this shift in emphasis was "more than coincidental." . . .

Indeed, ER took such satisfaction in the NYA that when she briefly acknowledged her role in forming the agency, she did so with an uncharacteristic candor. "One of the ideas I agreed to present to Franklin," she wrote in *This I Remember,* "was that of setting up a national youth administration. . . . It was one of the occasions on which I was very proud that the right thing was done regardless of political consequences." . . .

Despite the fervor with which ER campaigned for a more democratic administration of relief through the NYA . . . , these efforts paled in comparison to the unceasing pressure she placed upon the president and the nation to confront the economic and political discrimination facing Black America. In seeking to educate the public on the evils of racial discrimination, she underscored the moral imperative of the civil rights agenda. Although the first lady did not become an ardent proponent of integration until the 1950s, throughout the thirties and forties she nevertheless persistently labeled racial prejudice as undemocratic and immoral. Black Americans recognized the depth of her commitment and consequently kept faith with FDR because his wife kept faith with them. . . .

ER's racial policies attracted notice almost immediately. Less than a week after becoming first lady, she shocked conservative Washington society by announcing she would have an entirely black White House domestic staff. And even though the staff would be supervised by the "bigoted" Henrietta Nesbit, White House maid Lillian Rogers Parks recalled that "it was the first time it was great to be black. It meant you could hang on to your job at the White House."

By late summer 1933, photographs appeared showing ER discussing living conditions with black miners in West Virginia and the press treated her involvement in the anti-lynching campaign as front page news. Rumors of ER's "race-baiting" actions sped across the South with hurricane force. In August 1934, Barry Bingham, son of the publisher of the *Louisville Courier-Journal,* wrote FDR aide Marvin McIntyre that ER "has made herself offensive to Southerners by a too great affection for Negroes." Although Bingham claimed not to believe the rumor, he needed reassurance. The first lady refused to comply completely, responding that while she was "very much interested in the Negroes and their betterment," the story that she "drove through the streets of a town with a negro woman beside me happens to be untrue." Yet she warned Bingham that while she "probably would not do it in North Carolina," she "would, however, not have a single objection to doing so if I found myself in a position where it had to be done."

ER refused to be intimidated by rumor. In 1935, she visited Howard University's Freedman Hospital, attended the University's fundraising banquet, lobbied Congress for increased appropriations, and praised the institution in her press conferences. After intensive briefing by [NAACP secretary] Walter White ER toured the Virgin Islands with Lorena Hickok investigating conditions for herself only to return agreeing with White's initial assessments. When White asked her to address the 1934 and 1935 national NAACP conventions, FDR vetoed her appearance, fearing political backlash from southern Democrats. ER acceded to his wishes; however, FDR's cautiousness did not affect her support of the organization. "I deeply regret that I was obliged to refuse to attend the conference," she telegraphed the delegates. Her commitment had not waned. She continued, "I am deeply interested . . . [and] I hope that ways can be found to accomplish some of the things that you and I both desire." She then joined the local chapter of the NAACP and the National Urban League, becoming the first white District of Columbia resident to respond to the membership drives.

She mobilized cabinet and congressional wives for a walking tour of the slum alleys of Southeast Washington to increase support for housing legislation then before Congress. Lady Bird Johnson* accompanied ER on this tour and recalled that as accustomed as she was to rural poverty, she "hadn't seen anything like this." The first lady strode "along streets . . . [which] you usually kept off" and shamed her companions into following her example, hoping that if they saw such deprivation, they would be spurred to action. And, in a truly unique outreach, enlisted her mother-in-law's assistance in pressuring FDR to speak out in favor of the Costigan-Wagner anti-lynching bill. FDR's refusal to make anti-lynching legislation a priority did not dissuade her from actively seeking its passage. Indeed, when the bill finally came to the floor for a vote in 1937, ER's presence in the Senate gallery throughout the entire seven-day filibuster stood in stark contrast to FDR's cautious endorsement of the bill.

Unlike his wife, the president saw civil rights as more a political than a moral issue. Therefore, as the 1936 election approached and Eleanor Roosevelt continued her very public inspections, she finally convinced FDR to let her address the NAACP and National Urban League annual conventions by arguing that he needed the black vote. When *The New Yorker* published the famous cartoon of miners awaiting her visit, ER aggressively defended her outreach to minorities and the poor in a lengthy article for *The Saturday Evening Post*. Directly she attacked those who mocked her interest. "In strange and subtle ways," she began, "it was indicated to me that I should

*Wife of the congressman and future president, Lyndon Baines Johnson.

feel ashamed of that cartoon and that there was certainly something the matter with a woman who wanted to see so much and know so much." She refused to be so limited, she responded to those "blind" critics who refused to be interested in anything outside their own four walls. In a more subdued tone, she argued the same point when questioned by high school students about her "excitement" over discrimination. "People say I become 'too excited' about conditions," she replied. "Not at all. It is simply that I prefer to have my excitement in advance when it may do some good." . . .

By 1939, ER's support of civil rights was so well known that she could have dodged the controversy surrounding [singer] Marian Anderson's [proposed] performance [at Constitution Hall] and have few question her commitment to racial justice. But she did not sidestep the affair. Indeed, her bold actions on the diva's behalf not only "gave her opponents something [more] to talk about" but also provided her with unquestionable proof of her own political power.

Marian Anderson, the world's greatest contralto, was black. She had entertained all the crowned heads and elected officials of Europe, had won the highest awards her profession could bestow, and entertained the Roosevelts in the White House. Her previous performances in the District of Columbia before sold-out racially mixed audiences had received rave reviews. In January, Howard University had asked Anderson to perform a benefit concert for its School of Music on Easter weekend 1939. Anderson gladly accepted.

The problem surfaced when the Daughters of the American Revolution (DAR) refused to rent its auditorium, Constitution Hall, to Anderson because she was black. While at first the DAR denied that race was the reason preventing her leasing the hall, the truth soon emerged; and the University and the NAACP launched an immense lobbying campaign to force the DAR to change its policy. The DAR refused. Prominent black and white Washingtonians then formed the Marian Anderson Citizens Committee and petitioned the District of Columbia School Board for permission to use the Armstrong High School Auditorium for the concert. Following the DAR's lead, the school board denied the request.

ER debated what action to take on Anderson's behalf. By early January, she already had agreed to present the Spingarn Medal to the artist at the National NAACP convention, met with NAACP Secretary Walter White and conference chair Dr. Elizabeth Yates Webb to discuss the broadcast of the awards ceremony, invited Anderson to perform for the British King and Queen at the White House in June, and telegraphed her support to Howard University. Although initially she thought she should not attack the DAR's decision, she changed her mind and resigned from the organization in late February. Still angry and embarrassed at the treatment Anderson received, ER worked behind the scenes to arrange for the concert to be held at the Lincoln Memorial.

As important as ER's interventions on Anderson's behalf were they pale in comparison to the pivotal role she played in highlighting the discriminatory conduct of such a prestigious organization as the DAR. The power of understatement displayed in her "My Day" column of February 28, 1939, revealed ER's hand on the pulse of the nation. Carefully portraying the situation in impersonal, nonthreatening terms with which the majority of her readers would identify, she refrained from naming the issue or the organization that had caused her distress.

She introduced the dilemma simply: "I have been debating in my mind for some time a question which I have had to debate with myself once or twice before in my life. Usually I have decided differently from the way in which I am deciding now." She then outlined the problem and her response to it. "The question is, if you belong to an organization and disapprove of an action which is typical of a policy, shall you resign or is it better to work for a changed point of view within the organization?" Telling her readers that she preferred to work for change, she "usually stayed in until I had at least made a fight and been defeated." When she lost, she "accepted my defeat and decided either that I was wrong or that I was perhaps a little too far ahead of the thinking of the majority of that time." Indeed, she "often found that thing in which I was interested was done some years later." But this case did not fit that pattern because this organization is one "in which I do no active work." Moreover, "they have taken an action which has been widely talked of in the press. To remain as a member implies approval of that action, and therefore, I am resigning."

The next day, the column splashed across the front pages of American newspapers from San Francisco to New York City. Although others had resigned from the DAR over this issue, although other major public figures had publicly lamented the DAR's policy, Eleanor Roosevelt put Marian Anderson, the DAR, and racial discrimination on a national stage. By placing her political clout and personal popularity squarely behind Anderson and in front of the DAR, she moved the conflict into another arena. . . .

Although the history of Eleanor Roosevelt's actions as first lady is far from complete, all studies of both her life and the Roosevelt Administration agree that she redefined the role of president's wife and set the standard by which all future presidential spouses would be judged. So strong an imprint on contemporary American culture did this woman's struggle for self-reliance and independent action leave that when Katharine Hepburn was struggling to find the appropriate demeanor with which to approach her most famous character, the prim, but feisty missionary Rose Sayer who rode the rapids on *The African Queen*, her director John Huston simply instructed, "Play her like Eleanor Roosevelt."

PRIMARY SOURCES

Many of the sources in this section are the kinds of evidence that biographers often use to learn about people's lives: personal letters, autobiographies, memoirs, and speeches or transcriptions. They will help you evaluate Eleanor Roosevelt's effectiveness as First Lady, the challenges she faced in that role, and whether she challenged or reinforced traditional conceptions of women's proper role.

2   By the time FDR and ER moved into the White House in early 1933, the First Lady was corresponding regularly with her friend, journalist Lorena Hickok. What does this letter reveal about ER's views on her new role as First Lady? What does it reveal about her relationship with Hickok?

Letter to Lorena Hickok (1933)

[March 9]

THE WHITE HOUSE
Washington

Hick dearest, It was good to talk to you & you sounded a bit happier. I hated to have Nan* go to-night & yet it is rather nice to have a few hours alone, so I know how you feel but I shall miss Nan to-morrow. She has been such a help & apparently enjoyed herself. The one thing which reconciles me to this job is the fact that I think I can give a great many people pleasure & I begin to think there may be ways in which I can be useful. I am getting some ideas which I want to talk over with you—

Life is pretty strenuous—one or two A.M. last night & 12:15 now & people still with F.D.R. but this should settle things more or less.

My pictures are nearly all up & I have you in my sitting room where I can look at you most of my waking hours! I can't kiss you [in person] so I kiss your *picture* good night & good morning! This is the first day I've had no let-ter & I missed it sadly but it is good discipline.

Now for the diary! Out with Meggie [the dog] as usual. Breakfast 8:30, 9:30 housekeeper, 10:30 got splint for my [sprained] finger & went to kitchen. Put books ornaments etc. around left at 11:40 for Capitol, back at 1:40 for lunch & [son] James brought a California congressman making us 10 instead of 8 at last minute which was good training in our ways for the staff! After lunch some went back to Capitol. I took Nan to Mt. Vernon, back 4:40 saw 2 ladies for 5 minutes each, one brought gifts, one wanted to reorganize all govern-ment cafeterias! Tea, took [FDR advisor] Louis [Howe] to garage to see his car back, dressed for dinner & to-night dictated to Tommy [Malvina Thomp-son, ER's secretary], signed oodles of mail, took Nan to train & Tommy

*Nan Cook, a friend of ER who lived in Greenwich Village with Marion Dickerman, another friend of the First Lady.

home. [FDR's bodyguard] Gus [Gennerich] paid me a long visit while I signed & now 12:35 & to bed! . . .

One more day marked off my dear. My dear if you meet me [in public] may I forget there are other reporters present or must I behave? I shall want to hug you to death. I can hardly wait!

A world of love to you & good night & God bless you "light of my life,"

E.R.

---

3 In 1933, Eleanor Roosevelt began to hold regular press conferences limited to female reporters. What do Eleanor's answers to reporters' questions reveal about her efforts to change the role of women during the Depression?

Transcripts of Eleanor Roosevelt's Press Conferences (1933–1938)

June 15, 1933

TOPIC: Need for women to understand news.

Mrs. Roosevelt: "It is an awfully good thing to stress that this is a time when women have a special stake in watching national and international news. Every woman should have a knowledge of what is going on in economic conferences. It does affect the future amicable relations between the nations of the world. It has been stated the debt question is not to be discussed. But whatever does come out will be vitally important to every woman in her own home. Very few women know how to read newspapers and they miss what could give a new point of view. If more women would get in the habit of reading first the headlines, then the first paragraph,—often the whole gist of the article is in the first paragraph—that way a busy woman can count on keeping track at a time when every one of us ought to be on our toes to get what is happening every minute of time.

"The average woman today ought to read one paper that gives her point of view and two opposing points of view to draw her own conclusions. One's own prejudices and own ideas go into interpretation of public events. Women should train themselves to see both sides, then decide what they really think.

"Many people will never read editorials at all. It is grand to read editorials and opinion but not to accept without thought. All writing and all opinion is only good when you make it your own."

Source: Excerpted with permission from *The White House Press Conferences of Eleanor Roosevelt,* edited by Maurine Beasley. Copyright © 1983 by Garland Publishing, Inc.

July 6, 1933

TOPIC: National Woman's Party and the Equal Rights Amendment.
Mrs. Roosevelt: "I think the National Woman's Party ignores the fact that there is a fundamental difference between men and women. I don't mean by that women can't make as great a contribution, nor if they do the same work they not be paid the same wages. The mere fact that women basically are responsible for the future physical condition of the race means for many restrictions. It is a physical difference, not a mental.

"In my mail the most violent protestation against employment of married women comes from women themselves."

May 15, 1936

TOPIC: Garden party at the White House for inmates of the National Training School for Girls, a District of Columbia reformatory for Negroes. [Note by Strayer*] Mrs. Roosevelt went alone [on a visit to the reformatory] and told her press conference about it after her visit.
Mrs. Roosevelt: "I know of no place else where conditions exist like I found there. They have no psychiatrist. I think Dr. [Carrie] Smith [superintendent] said two girls were locked in cells when she came to the institution. I think she said 26 of the girls had syphilis and almost every girl had gonorrhea.

"There are no facilities to separate them from each other in cottages, each with one type of disease, but Dr. Smith separates them as far as possible. Every possible precaution is taken, but in those circumstances, what can you do? That is why Judge [Fay] Bentley [of the District of Columbia Juvenile Court] hasn't been willing to send any girls out there. She hasn't sent any girls there for a year.

"There was no teacher when Dr. Smith came. They now have one teacher that they are going to get a government appropriation for. Most of these girls are still school age. The youngest is 14. They go up to 21. Some of them have been there five years. The school has discarded library books that are falling to pieces.

"The girls have to be taken to Juvenile Court three times before they are committed out there. This is because of the physical conditions. The place has had no program to fit the girls to earn a living except doing the work of the institution, which, of course, is some preparation.

"They were making dresses to wear to the [White House] party when I was there the other day. They have always done the mending and sewing and made their own clothes because they always have to. They also were making gym suits of different colors for the different cottages. That, I thought, was beginning to give them a little more interest in life."

*Martha Strayer was one of the reporters.

June 16, 1938

TOPIC: Married women in the labor force.

. . . **Mrs. Weed:** "Do you think there is a greater moral obligation on women to give up their work, when they have other means of support, than there is on men in the same circumstances, married or single?"

Mrs. Roosevelt: "I think if the single woman has to support herself, the question does not arise if she is under more moral obligation than a man.

"So I think it boils down to a married woman, and then comes the question whether the man or woman should be the main support in a family. My own instinct is a feeling that most women, if it comes to a decision, have more ability to find employment for themselves than most men have. But that doesn't always hold true.

"I happen to know of a couple where the woman earns money and the man runs a farm. It's the kind of work which doesn't bring in a large amount of income but which makes living a very pleasant, happy thing, and he is happy and does the kind of thing he enjoys. It's a happy family. My instinct is to say that, as a rule, a woman is more adjustable."

May [Craig?]: "What is a woman's duty? Her first duty is to stay home and take care of her family, and the other is to take a job in the economic situation when jobs are scarce."

Mrs. Roosevelt: "Who is going to be the person to decide whether it is a woman's duty to stay at home and take care of her family?

"Second, who should say that where the skills of the woman were such that she could do that particular job better than anybody else, better than she could do any other, probably it would be economically sound as well as spiritually a good thing? On the other hand, there may be a great many people for whom it would neither be spiritually or economically the best thing for their children or for that individual."

---

4   As the transcripts of her White House press conferences reveal, ER was interested in the condition of African Americans. What does this speech to the National Urban League reveal about her racial views? Were they conservative or progressive?

"The Negro and Social Change" (1936)

Much that I am going to say tonight would apply with equal force to any of us living in this country. But our particular concern tonight is with one of the largest race groups in the country—the Negro race.

We have a great responsibility here in the United States because we offer

Source: Eleanor Roosevelt, "The Negro and Social Change," *Opportunity,* January 1936. Reprinted by permission of the Eleanor Roosevelt Literary Estate.

the best example that exists perhaps today throughout the world, of the fact that if different races know each other they may live peacefully together. On the whole, we in this country live peacefully together though we have many different races making up the citizenry of the United States. The fact that we have achieved as much as we have in understanding of each other is no reason for feeling that our situation and our relationship are so perfect that we need not concern ourselves about making them better. In fact we know that many grave injustices are done throughout our land to people who are citizens and who have an equal right under the laws of our country, but who are handicapped because of their race. I feel strongly that in order to wipe out these inequalities and injustices, we must all of us work together; but naturally those who suffer the injustices are most sensitive of them, and are therefore bearing the brunt of carrying through whatever plans are made to wipe out undesirable conditions.

Therefore in talking to you tonight, I would like to urge first of all that you concentrate your effort on obtaining better opportunities for education for the Negro people throughout the country. You *must* be able to understand the economic condition and the changes which are coming, not only in our own country, but throughout the world, and this, without better education than the great majority of Negro people have an *opportunity* to obtain today, is not possible. And without an improvement which will allow better work and better understanding, it will be difficult to remove the handicaps under which some of you suffer.

I marvel frequently at the patience with which those who work for the removal of bad conditions face their many disappointments. And I would like to pay tribute tonight to the many leaders amongst the colored people, whom I know and admire and respect. If they are apt at times to be discouraged and downhearted, I can only offer them as consolation, the knowledge that all of us who have worked in the past, and are still working for economic and social betterment, have been through and will continue to go through many periods of disappointment. But as we look back over the years, I have come to realize that what seemed to be slow and halting advances in the aggregate make quite a rapid march forward.

I believe, of course, that for our own good in this country, the Negro race as a whole must improve its standards of living, and become both economically and intellectually of higher calibre. The fact that the colored people, not only in the South, but in the North as well, have been economically at a low level has meant that they have also been physically and intellectually at a low level. Economic conditions are responsible for poor health in children. And the fact that tuberculosis and pneumonia and many other diseases have taken a heavier toll amongst our colored groups, can be attributed primarily to economic conditions. It is undoubtedly true that with an improvement in economic condition it will still be necessary not only to improve our educational conditions for children, but to pay special attention to adult education along the line of better living. For you cannot expect people to change overnight, when they have had poor conditions, and adjust themselves to all that we expect of people living as they *should* live today throughout our country. . . .

So that I think I am right when I say that it is not just enough to give people who have suffered a better house and better wages. You must give them education and understanding and training before you can expect them to take up their full responsibility.

I think that we realize the desirability today of many social changes; but we also must realize that in making these changes and bridging the gap between the old life and the new, we have to accept the responsibility and assume the necessary burden of giving assistance to the people who have not had their fair opportunity in the past.

One thing I want to speak about tonight because I have had a number of people tell me that they felt the Government in its new efforts and programs was not always fair to the Negro race. And I want to say quite often, it is not the intention of those at the top, and as far as possible I hope that we may work together to eliminate any real injustice.

No right-thinking person in this country today who picks up a paper and reads that in some part of the country the people have not been willing to wait for the due processes of law, but have gone back to the rule of force, blind and unjust as force and fear usually are, can help but be ashamed that we have shown such a lack of faith in our own institutions. It is a horrible thing which grows out of weakness and fear, and not out of strength and courage; and the sooner we as a nation unite to stamp out any such action, the sooner and the better will we be able to face the other nations of the world and to uphold our real ideals here and abroad.

We have long held in this country that ability should be the criterion on which all people are judged. It seems to me that we must come to recognize this criterion in dealing with all human beings, and not place any limitations upon their achievements except such as may be imposed by their own character and intelligence.

This is what we work for as an ideal for the relationship that must exist between all the citizens of our country. There is no reason why all of the races in this country should not live together each of them giving from their particular gift something to the other, and contributing an example to the world of "peace on earth, good will toward men."

5   Eleanor Roosevelt and Anna, her first child and only daughter, corresponded regularly. What does the letter on the following page reveal about the difficulties Eleanor had as First Lady?

Letter to Her Daughter (1937)

20 East 11th Street
New York City
March 3d [1937]

Darling,

. . . Pa is both nervous & tired. The court hue & cry [the Supreme Court packing controversy] has got under his skin. I thought stupidly his little outburst of boredom on meals was amusing & human & used it in my column & it was taken up by papers & radio & over the ticker & Steve [Early, press secretary] & Jimmy got hate letters & were much upset & Pa was furious with me. James came & reproved me & said I must distinguish between things which were personal & should not be said or none of them would dare to talk to me & he thought I should apologize to Father. I did before McDuffie [FDR's valet] Monday night before leaving as I couldn't see him alone & Pa answered irritably that it had been very hard on him & he would certainly say nothing more to me on any subject! So it has become a very serious subject & I am grieved at my poor judgment & only hope it won't be remembered long. Will I be glad when we leave the W.H. & I can be on my own!
    A world of love to you all & much to you darling.

Mother

Source: Bernard Asbell, ed., *Mother and Daughter: The Letters of Eleanor and Anna Roosevelt* (New York: Coward, McCann and Geoghegan, 1982), p. 79.

6   *This I Remember,* the second volume of Eleanor Roosevelt's autobiography, deals with her life from the early 1920s until her husband's death in 1945. In the following selections, she discusses the nature of her influence on FDR and her interest in several reforms. How much influence did Eleanor appear to have with FDR?

This I Remember (1949)

ELEANOR ROOSEVELT

Always, when my husband and I met after a trip that either of us had taken, we tried to arrange for an uninterrupted meal so that we could hear the

Source: Pages 177–179, 191–193 from *The Autobiography of Eleanor Roosevelt* by Eleanor Roosevelt. Copyright 1937, 1949, © 1958, 1961 by Anna Eleanor Roosevelt. Copyright © 1958 by Curtis Publishing Company. Reprinted by permission of HarperCollins Publishers, Inc.

whole story while it was fresh and not dulled by repetition. That I became, as the years went by, a better reporter and a better observer was largely owing to the fact that Franklin's questions covered such a wide range. I found myself obliged to notice everything. For instance, when I returned from a trip around the Gaspé, he wanted to know not only what kind of fishing and hunting was possible in that area but what the life of the fisherman was, what he had to eat, how he lived, what the farms were like, how the houses were built, what type of education was available, and whether it was completely church-controlled like the rest of the life in the village.

When I spoke of Maine, he wanted to know about everything I had seen on the farms I visited, the kinds of homes and the types of people, how the Indians seemed to be getting on and where they came from.

Franklin never told me I was a good reporter nor, in the early days, were any of my trips made at his request. I realized, however, that he would not question me so closely if he were not interested, and I decided this was the only way I could help him, outside of running the house, which was soon organized and running itself under Mrs. Nesbitt.

In the autumn I was invited by the Quakers to investigate the conditions that they were making an effort to remedy in the coal-mining areas of West Virginia. My husband agreed that it would be a good thing to do, so the visit was arranged. I had not been photographed often enough then to be recognized, so I was able to spend a whole day going about the area near Morgantown, West Virginia, without anyone's discovering who I was.

The conditions I saw convinced me that with a little leadership there could develop in the mining areas, if not a people's revolution, at least a people's party patterned after some of the previous parties born of bad economic conditions. There were men in that area who had been on relief for from three to five years and who had almost forgotten what it was like to have a job at which they could work for more than one or two days a week. There were children who did not know what it was to sit down at a table and eat a proper meal.

One story which I brought home from that trip I recounted at the dinner table one night. In a company house I visited, where the people had evidently seen better days, the man showed me his weekly pay slips. A small amount had been deducted toward his bill at the company store and for his rent and for oil for his mine lamp. These deductions left him less than a dollar in cash each week. There were six children in the family, and they acted as though they were afraid of strangers. I noticed a bowl on the table filled with scraps, the kind that you or I might give to a dog, and I saw children, evidently looking for their noonday meal, take a handful out of that bowl and go out munching. That was all they had to eat.

As I went out, two of the children had gathered enough courage to stand by the door, the little boy holding a white rabbit in his arms. It was evident that it was a most cherished pet. The little girl was thin and scrawny, and had a gleam in her eyes as she looked at her brother. She said, "He thinks we are not going to eat it, but we are," and at that the small boy fled down the road clutching the rabbit closer than ever.

It happened that [Assistant Secretary of State] William C. Bullitt was at dinner that night and I have always been grateful to him for the check he sent me the next day, saying he hoped it might help to keep the rabbit alive.

This trip to the mining areas was my first contact with the work being done by the Quakers. I liked the theory of trying to put people to work to help themselves. The men were started on projects and taught to use their abilities to develop new skills. The women were encouraged to revive any household arts they might once have known but which they had neglected in the drab life of the mining village.

This was only the first of many trips into the mining districts but it was the one that started the homestead idea. . . . It was all experimental work, but it was designed to get people off relief, to put them to work building their own homes and to give them enough land to start growing food.

It was hoped that business would help by starting on each of these projects an industry in which some of the people could find regular work. A few small industries were started but they were not often successful. Only a few of the resettlement projects had any measure of success; nevertheless, I have always felt that the good they did was incalculable. Conditions were so nearly the kind that breed revolution that the men and women needed to be made to feel their government's interest and concern. . . .

Franklin did not talk a great deal about the work he was doing, either at meals or in private family conversations. Most of us felt that when he was with his family he should have a respite from the concerns of his office.

When an administration bill was up before Congress, we often found that the number of Congressmen coming to his study in the evenings increased. I learned that I must make an evaluation of the bills on which he had to get support. He calculated votes closely on what was known as the administration policy, and considered "must" legislation.

Only bills that were "must" legislation got full administration support. In the first years these were largely economic measures; later on, they were measures for defense. While I often felt strongly on various subjects, Franklin frequently refrained from supporting causes in which he believed, because of political realities. There were times when this annoyed me very much.

I also remember wanting to get all-out support for the anti-lynching bill and the removal of the poll tax, but though Franklin was in favor of both measures, they never became "must" legislation. When I would protest, he would simply say: "First things first. I can't alienate certain votes I need for measures that are more important at the moment by pushing any measure that would entail a fight." And as the situation in Europe grew worse, preparations for war had to take precedence over everything else. That was always "must" legislation, and Franklin knew it would not pass if there was a party split.

Often people came to me to enlist his support for an idea. Although I might present the situation to him, I never urged on him a specific course of action, no matter how strongly I felt, because I realized that he knew of factors in the picture as a whole of which I might be ignorant.

One of the ideas I agreed to present to Franklin was that of setting up a national youth administration. Harry Hopkins, then head of the WPA, and Aubrey Williams, his deputy administrator and later head of the National Youth Administration, knew how deeply troubled I had been from the beginning about the plight of the country's young people. One day they said: "We have come to you about this because we do not feel we should talk to the President about it as yet. There may be many people against the establishment of such an agency in the government and there may be bad political repercussions. We do not know that the country will accept it. We do not even like to ask the President, because we do not think he should be put in a position where he has to say officially 'yes' or 'no' now."

I agreed to try to find out what Franklin's feelings were and to put before him their opinions and fears. I waited until my usual time for discussing questions with him and went into his room just before he went to sleep. I described the whole idea, which he already knew something of, and then told him of the fears that Harry Hopkins and Aubrey Williams had about such an agency. He looked at me and asked: "Do they think it is right to do this?" I said they thought it might be a great help to the young people, but they did not want him to forget that it might be unwise politically. They felt that a great many people who were worried by the fact that Germany had regimented its youth might feel we were trying to do the same thing in this country. Then Franklin said: "If it is the right thing to do for the young people, then it should be done. I guess we can stand the criticism, and I doubt if our youth can be regimented in this way or in any other way."

I went back to Harry Hopkins and Aubrey Williams the next day with Franklin's message. Shortly after, the NYA came into being and undoubtedly benefited many young people. It offered projects to help high school and college youngsters to finish school, and provided training in both resident and nonresident projects, supplementing the work of the Civilian Conservation Corps in such a way as to aid all youth.

It was one of the occasions on which I was proud that the right thing was done regardless of political considerations. As a matter of fact, however, it turned out to be politically popular and strengthened the administration greatly.

Attacks on Eleanor Roosevelt

As Eleanor Roosevelt began to champion a variety of reforms, she was assaulted by critics. What do their attacks reveal about the constraints on her?

Barry Bingham was the son of Robert W. Bingham, the publisher of the Louisville *Courier-Journal* and FDR's ambassador to Great Britain; McIntyre was FDR's appointments secretary.

Letter from Barry Bingham to Marvin McIntyre (1934)

The old propaganda story is being passed around in Louisville to the effect that Mrs. Roosevelt has made herself offensive to Southerners by a too great affection for Negroes. The tale is that she was visiting in South Carolina recently, and was scheduled to make a speech in one of the larger towns. She is said to have ridden to the auditorium, through the streets of the town, in an open car in which she sat next to a Negro woman, with whom she conversed sociably all the way.

Source: Eleanor and Franklin by Joseph P. Lash. Copyright © 1971 by Joseph P. Lash. Used by permission of W. W. Norton & Company, Inc.

 ## Excerpts from Letters to Franklin Roosevelt (1935)

From Fort Wayne, Indiana

[The First Lady] "would be rendering her country a far greater service if she would but uphold the dignity of the White House," . . .

From a New York woman

". . . is it not humanely [*sic*] possible to muzzle that female creature, known to the world as your wife?"

From a Philadelphia man

Mrs. Roosevelt should cease "gadding about the country and butting into matters that are no concern of hers. . . . My God, what a woman!"

Source: James R. Kearney, *Anna Eleanor Roosevelt: The Evolution of a Reformer* (Boston: Houghton Mifflin Company, 1968), pp. 228–229; originally from "President's Personal File #2," Box 1, Franklin D. Roosevelt Library.

Eleanor Roosevelt on Feminism

Eleanor Roosevelt was frequently asked about her stands on equality for women and the proposed equal rights amendment, which the National Woman's Party lobbied Congress to pass every year starting in 1923. What are her positions on these issues? Do these sources reveal contradictions in her views about female equality? Do they reveal attitudes shaped by class as well as gender?

Eleanor Roosevelt addressed this advice book to women coping with the Depression.

It's Up to the Women (1933)

If a woman does her own work, the vital thing for her to do is to organize it so well that when her husband returns home she is not an exhausted human being, but can still meet him with a smile and enter into whatever interests he may wish to discuss with her.

If she has a domestic helper in her household, she must remember that she is dealing with a human being, and it is well for her to try everything herself before she lays down her rules for any one else. I have a theory that, under our modern system in which it is rare for any one to have more than one maid in the house, if a young woman will systematize her own work, she can greatly assist whoever is working for her. For instance, if when she gets up she immediately puts her bedclothes to air, it will save either her or her maid the necessity of coming up to do it later on, or of making up the bed without airing. Habits of neatness can be formed by the mistress so that she keeps her own part of the house tidy, and when she enters the kitchen to give an order, or to do some piece of work, she does not leave behind her a trail of work for somebody else to do. Then the household will run smoothly, the maid will come to her for advice and she will soon find if she does her own part of the work, that there is no shirking on the part of those who work with her. . . .

. . . I have often thought that it sounded so well to talk about women being on an equal footing with men and sometimes when I have listened to the arguments of the National Woman's Party and they have complained that they could not compete in the labor market because restrictions were laid upon women's work which were not laid upon men's, I have been almost inclined to agree with them that such restrictions were unjust, until I came to realize that when all is said and done, women are different from men. They are equals in many ways, but they cannot refuse to acknowledge their differences. Not to acknowledge them weakens the case. Their physical functions in life are different and perhaps in the same way the contributions which they are to bring to the spiritual side of life are different. It may be that certain questions are waiting to be solved until women can bring their views to bear upon those questions. . . .

Source: Eleanor Roosevelt, *It's Up to the Women,* Frederick A. Stokes Company, 1933, pp. 25–26, 201–202.

News Item, "Definition of Feminism" (1935)

SPECIAL TO THE NEW YORK TIMES

Washington, May 7.—Mrs. Roosevelt gave today "by request" her definition of feminism as follows:

"Fundamentally, the purpose of feminism is that a woman should have an equal opportunity and equal rights with any other citizen of the country.

"I believe the desire of women for equality of opportunity and of recognition is just as alive, certainly in this country, and in fact more so, than it was ten years ago," she told her press conference.

"I may be wrong," she added. "I am conscious that I know very little, and I don't want to argue with anybody."

Source: The New York Times, May 8, 1935. Copyright © 1935 by The New York Times Co. Reprinted with permission.

 ## News Item, "Opposes Amendment" (1938)

SPECIAL TO THE NEW YORK TIMES

Washington, Feb. 7.—Opposition to the proposed equal-rights amendment and the tipping system, and approval of special laws for women in industry, were reiterated today by Mrs. Roosevelt.

"There is no question that professional people and people who work with their heads should be on the same basis, regardless of sex," she said.

"But I still believe in protective legislation for women in industrial groups and shall continue to believe in it until the whole situation in industry changes."

In regard to tipping, a live issue here in a controversy on whether tips should be included in estimating the minimum wage to be fixed for waitresses, Mrs. Roosevelt said she "disliked the whole idea of tipping," regarding it as an outgrowth of a less-than-living wage.

"However," she said, "if tips must be relied on for part of the income of waiters, then I think they might better be included in the bill and the total pooled and distributed among the employes on payday."

Source: The New York Times, February 8, 1938. Copyright © 1938 by The New York Times Co. Reprinted with permission.

CONCLUSION

Few students would disagree with one historian's claim that "the behavior of . . . individuals is more interesting . . . than their behavior as groups or classes."[11] Maybe that is why the biographical approach to history remains popular, even though historians today reject the idea that history is merely the biography of great people. Yet Eleanor Roosevelt's life demonstrates that biography does more than create an enjoyable path to the past. Rather, it shows the power of individuals to move at great odds against impersonal forces. As First Lady, Eleanor struggled against the social and economic forces that shaped the lives of people who had no biographers. As she sought her own "salvation," she also struggled with the cultural forces influencing her own life. Her successes and failures as a reformer thus reveal as much about her times as they do about her life.

Still, neither Eleanor Roosevelt's background nor her public activities made her typical. Few girls had the opportunity to grow up in late-nineteenth-century high society. Far fewer had the opportunity to become First Lady. In the past, that did not matter to most historians, who were more interested in people at the top of society than at the bottom. Today, however, many historians are interested in the lives of ordinary people. By writing history "from the bottom up," they reveal the historical significance of people who traditionally have lacked distinct voices. So in the next chapter, we turn to people whose lives were a world removed from Eleanor Roosevelt's.

FURTHER READING

Blanche Wiesen Cook, *Eleanor Roosevelt, 1884–1933* (New York: Viking, 1992).
———, *Eleanor Roosevelt, 1933–1938* (New York: Viking, 1999).
Tamara K. Hareven, *Eleanor Roosevelt: An American Conscience* (Chicago: Quadrangle Books, 1968).
Stella K. Hershan, *The Candles She Lit: The Legacy of Eleanor Roosevelt* (Westport, Conn.: Praeger Publishers, 1993).
Joseph P. Lash, *Eleanor and Franklin: The Story of Their Relationship, Based on Eleanor's Private Papers* (New York: W. W. Norton and Company, 1971).
Eleanor Roosevelt, *The Autobiography of Eleanor Roosevelt* (New York: Harper and Brothers, 1961).

NOTES

1. Eleanor Roosevelt, *This I Remember* (New York: Harper and Brothers, 1949), p. 113.
2. Doris Kearns Goodwin, "The Home Front," *The New Yorker,* August 15, 1994, p. 51.

3. Nelson W. Aldrich, *Old Money: The Mythology of America's Upper Class* (New York: Vintage Books, 1989), p. 212.

4. Quoted in William H. Chafe, "Biographical Sketch," in Joan Hoff-Wilson and Marjorie Lightman, eds., *Without Precedent: The Life and Career of Eleanor Roosevelt* (Bloomington: Indiana University Press, 1984), p. 4.

5. Eleanor Roosevelt, *This Is My Story* (New York: Harper and Brothers, 1937), p. 24.

6. Quoted in William H. Chafe, "Biographical Sketch," in Hoff-Wilson and Lightman, *Without Precedent,* p. 5.

7. Quoted in Lois Scharf, *Eleanor Roosevelt: First Lady of American Liberalism* (Boston: Twayne, 1987), p. 28.

8. Eleanor Roosevelt, *This Is My Story,* p. 40.

9. Quoted in Joseph P. Lash, *Eleanor and Franklin: The Story of Their Relationship, Based on Eleanor Roosevelt's Private Papers* (New York: W. W. Norton, 1971), p. 220.

10. Quoted in ibid., p. 355.

11. Quoted in Edward H. Carr, *What Is History?* (New York: Alfred A. Knopf, 1962), p. 56.

Chapter
8

History "From the Bottom Up": The Detroit Race Riot of 1943

The documents in this chapter offer facts and theories about the participants of the Detroit race riot of 1943.

Secondary Source

1. The Detroit Rioters of 1943 (1991), DOMINIC J. CAPECI, JR., and MARTHA WILKERSON

Primary Sources

2. A Handbill for White Resistance (1942)
3. Black Employment in Selected Detroit Companies, 1941
4. An Explanation for Strikes (1943)
5. Black Workers Protest Against Chrysler (1943)
6. A Complaint About the Police (1939)
7. Changes in White and Black Death Rates, 1910–1940
8. A Profile of the Detroit Rioters

*A*t 6:30 P.M. Monday, June 21, 1943, Moses Kiska, a 58-year-old African American, waited for a streetcar at Mack Avenue and Chene Street in Detroit. Kiska may have noticed a car drive by him and then turn around. Inside the car were four white youths, aged 16 to 20. Earlier, they had been looking for something to do and decided to drive around to see the fighting between blacks and whites that was turning Detroit into a bloody racial battleground. Late the night before, black and white youths had clashed on Belle Isle, a public park in the Detroit River. Less than a day later, rampaging African American and white mobs were assaulting one another, beating innocent motorists, pedestrians, and streetcar passengers, burning cars, destroying storefronts, and looting businesses.

As the four white youths drove around, one of them said, "Let's go out and kill us a nigger."[1] They continued to drive, but they couldn't find a target. They saw a lot of blacks, but they were in groups. They wanted someone by himself. Then on Mack Avenue they saw what they were looking for. The driver of the car grabbed his companion's gun, turned the car around, pulled up to the lone man, and pulled the trigger. As Moses Kiska fell to the ground, the car carrying the four boys sped off. "We didn't know him," one of the youths later testified. "He wasn't bothering us. But other people were fighting and killing and we felt like it, too."[2]

Moses Kiska was one of 34 people who lay dead after three days of rioting in Detroit. The riot was a brutal reminder to Americans in 1943 of deep racial divisions in their society. Today it reminds historians that they must know something about the lives of ordinary people in places like Detroit if they are to understand fully the impact of World War II on American society.

Before the mid-twentieth century, historians usually did not write such "grassroots" history. They relied mostly on written sources produced by an educated elite, and their histories were written without reference to the lives of people at society's bottom. When historians did examine ordinary people, it was usually within the context of movements or organizations. If they studied labor history, for instance, they focused on unions, not the lives of workers. Of course, there is much more to the lives of common people than their involvement in political or labor organizations. By the 1950s, such scholars as George Rudé, Eric Hobsbawm, and Christopher Hill began to explore "an unknown dimension of the past," that is, the lives of ordinary people.[3] These historians had been influenced by the Great Depression and World War II, powerful examples of the masses' involvement in history. They were often guided as well by the Marxist conviction that history was made in the peasant's hut as well as in the castle.

Unfortunately, these historians did not have a ready-made body of sources at hand. Since people at the bottom of society rarely leave written records to explain their lives, much of their history was initially restricted to riots and revolutions. Such events as European peasant revolts or the French and American revolutions brought to public notice many people who rarely attracted attention. These uprisings left historians with documentation of otherwise obscure lives.

Today, historians with tape recorders and computers can preserve the memories of ordinary people and analyze massive amounts of data from a census or legal documents. Such technology helps them explore "bottom up" history far removed from riots or revolutions. As a result, many scholars are now interested in the lives of everyone from seventeenth-century slaves to late twentieth-century migrant farm workers. At the same time, historians have not abandoned the study of civil disturbances such as the Detroit riot. Like other social upheavals, this riot thrust people at the bottom of the society into the public arena. For that reason it remains a good place to explore the lives of people mostly absent from the pages of history.

SETTING

In the months after Pearl Harbor, many observers saw trouble ahead on the home front. As black, white, and Hispanic workers converged on booming defense plants, racial and ethnic tensions began to rise. In 1943, more than 200 riots and racial conflicts had erupted across the country. In Los Angeles, a large war production center, sailors on leave attacked Mexican American youths who had embraced the zoot suit, a style characterized by baggy pants tied in at the ankle. The fighting lasted four days and ended only when military authorities intervened. In May, black and white workers clashed in a Mobile, Alabama, shipyard. Several weeks later, a white mob attacked the black section of Beaumont, Texas, leaving two dead. Then in August, a race riot in New York City resulted in five deaths and millions of dollars in property damage.

Before 1943, however, many observers had predicted that the greatest racial strife would be in Detroit. As automobile and other factories converted to defense production, thousands of Depression-ravaged people descended on the Motor City. Many were from the South, and most were poor. Eighteen months after Pearl Harbor, Detroit's population had surged by 350,000 people, 50,000 of them black. They joined the 160,000 African Americans already living in the city's slums. "Detroit," declared *Life* magazine, "is dynamite." The city, it predicted, "can either blow up Hitler or it can blow up the U.S."[4]

In June America's greatest "Arsenal of Democracy" exploded. After three days of rioting state and federal troops finally restored order. By then, property damage had run into the millions of dollars and war production had been halted for days. But the greatest toll was that suffered by African Americans. Twenty-five blacks had lost their lives, 17 of them killed by police. Blacks made up more than 75 percent of the approximately 600 injured people and 85 percent of the roughly 1,800 people arrested.

When the riot was over, Detroiters joined other Americans in the search for explanations. There were plenty of convenient targets: "thugs," Axis agents, the Ku Klux Klan, the police, Polish Americans, Italian Americans, Syrian Americans, and "hillbillies." One Mississippi newspaper even blamed Eleanor Roosevelt. The most popular scapegoat, however, was the African American. The lure of wartime jobs had drawn large numbers of southern blacks to northern cities like Detroit, where they were often scorned by longtime residents. Many observers thought that they were unable to adjust to northern life. Franklin Roosevelt's attorney general, for instance, recommended that the president limit the migration of blacks into cities that could not "absorb" them for "cultural" reasons. "It would seem pretty clear," he declared, "that no more Negroes should move to Detroit."[5]

After the riot, Detroit's white city leaders were also quick to point fingers. The mayor declared that the riots were started by young African American hoodlums. The Wayne County prosecutor charged that the leaders of the National Association for the Advancement of Colored People "were the biggest instigators of the race riot" and "would be the first indicted" if a grand jury were called.[6] A committee of city, county, and state law enforcement officials agreed with that assessment. It concluded that the "exhortation by many Negro leaders to be 'militant' in the struggle for racial equality played an important part in exciting the Negro people to violence."[7] Just as quickly, black leaders pointed to other causes: job discrimination in Detroit's booming defense plants, housing discrimination that forced blacks into expensive but run-down housing, police brutality, and the daily animosity of Detroit's white residents. Explanations of the riot revealed battle lines that were as clearly drawn as those in the riot itself.

INVESTIGATION

If Detroiters had ready answers to the causes of the riot, the sources in this chapter offer some as well. Your main assignment, therefore, is to determine who the Detroit rioters were and why they rioted. A good analysis of the riot should address the following questions:

1. **What is the explanation of historians Dominic Capeci and Martha Wilkerson for the Detroit riot?** Was the riot an irrational act or a form of protest?

2. **How would you characterize the rioters?** Do the characteristics of the rioters contradict contemporary observers' explanations for the riot?

3. **Was the Detroit riot for revenge or personal gain, or was it an ideological protest?** What is the authors' evidence for the motive of the rioters? Do the characteristics of the rioters reveal their motives?

4. **Do the primary sources support Capeci's and Wilkerson's conclusions?** Do these sources offer evidence that World War II changed the expectations of African Americans? What role should those expectations play in accounting for the riot?

SECONDARY SOURCE

1   In this essay, Dominic Capeci and Martha Wilkerson examine who rioted in Detroit and offer an explanation for their behavior. They rely on evidence from Detroit's criminal court records to study the background and assess the actions of some of the rioters. Their work reflects the challenge that historians often face when trying to establish the motives of people who leave few written records to explain their behavior. Your analysis of the Detroit riot should begin with a careful reading of the authors' argument. Pay particular attention to their explanation for the behavior of the rioters, and look for evidence for the motives of the rioters. Also note whether the authors offer evidence that World War II changed the attitudes of Detroit's black and white residents. Do you agree with the authors' characterization of rioters or with the assessment of Gustave Le Bon and other European scholars of collective violence?

The Detroit Rioters of 1943 (1991)

DOMINIC J. CAPECI, JR., AND MARTHA WILKERSON

To Charles "Little Willie" L.—and, no doubt, to many others who rose on Sunday morning to clear, sunny skies, summerlike temperatures, and a day free from monotonous work, the tension that made Detroit "dynamite" seemed ever-present. Twenty years old and single, L. lived with his brothers and sisters at 5815 Brush Street (see Detroit map). His apartment sat in the east side, black Detroit's oldest, most congested, run-down community, one extending from downtown Adams Street north to Leicester Court, bounded by Woodward Avenue on the east and St. Aubin Street on the west. His world, like that of most of the city's 185,000 black residents, consisted of dilapidated accommodations rendered "almost intolerable" by time and in-migration. Since his arrival from Brookhaven, Mississippi, five years earlier, Charles L. had witnessed an enormous influx of black newcomers, which had swelled to 2,100 per month since the previous year and increased the black population by 24 percent.

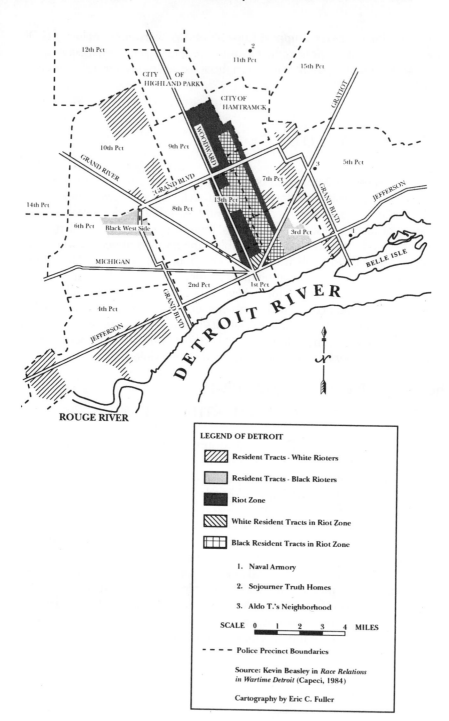

LEGEND OF DETROIT

Resident Tracts - White Rioters

Resident Tracts - Black Rioters

Riot Zone

White Resident Tracts in Riot Zone

Black Resident Tracts in Riot Zone

1. Naval Armory

2. Sojourner Truth Homes

3. Aldo T.'s Neighborhood

SCALE   0   1   2   3   4   MILES

- - - - Police Precinct Boundaries

Source: Kevin Beasley in *Race Relations in Wartime Detroit* (Capeci, 1984)

Cartography by Eric C. Fuller

Packed into a ghetto three-and-one-half miles square, which contained several viable institutions, diverse classes, and close-knit families, Charles L. and his neighbors found employment in the war-boom economy. He had worked as a laborer in grocery stores and factories for the past two years, no doubt denied access to well-paying defense jobs because of low skills, limited education, and "marked racial feelings." "Little Willie," who stood 5 feet 4 inches, weighed 140 pounds, and appeared dark-skinned, was considered "aggressive" and "antisocial"—perhaps the result of his diminutive size and ghetto experience. He seemed "criminalistic" to the Recorder's Court psychiatrist, although he boasted no arrest record. He knew discrimination firsthand, however, and had clashed recently with white youths and lawmen.

Seeking escape from the east side's confines, where the temperature broke 90 degrees on Sunday afternoon, Charles L. headed for Belle Isle. Perhaps he brooded along the way, angered by Detroit's inadequate recreation area and agitated by memories of Eastwood Park six days earlier. On Tuesday evening, he was one of fifty black teenagers and zoot suiters accosted by nearly 200 white high school students and servicemen at the privately owned amusement park in East Detroit. He lost the fight, as policemen arrested several whites and ejected all blacks. Charles L. had traveled over seven miles from his home to this amusement park, deep into lily-white territory. Consciously or otherwise, he also did so to protest the restrictive and humiliating conditions placed upon him—upon all black Detroiters. He embodied the "zoot effect," adopting expressive dress—broad shouldered, long-waisted coats, and bloused, pegged pants—behavior, and language that stroked his ego, parried racism, and affronted many of both races, who labeled such antics as abnormal, even gangsterlike, and mocked them in caricatures.

Small wonder that today Charles L. ventured more than three miles to Belle Isle—an island park in the Detroit River connected to the mainland by the Jefferson Avenue bridge—where 100,000 Detroiters converged to escape sultry weather and, ironically, wartime tensions. He arrived in midafternoon, one of many blacks who made up fully 80 percent of the crowd that jammed the isle's 985 acres of ball fields, beaches, and boardwalks, hiking trails and canoe livery, playgrounds and picnic areas. The large proportion of blacks present may have emboldened him, or the growing resentment of many whites, who objected to close racial associations, may have raised his own bitterness. In any event, around 3:30 P.M. he led a milling crowd of blacks in a series of altercations with whites, which officials said "fanned the flame of hatred" and led ultimately to the death of thirty-four persons.

Charles L. shot craps with several youths, both black and white, before a fight broke out over the question of crooked dice. The white cheaters fled the scene, and Charles L. and his friends were unable to catch them. Frustrated, he exhorted seven teenagers to avenge their humiliation in Eastwood Park and "take care of the Hunkies." Quickly he led them in a series of forays, assaulting whites, breaking up their picnics, and consuming their food. In thus evening the score, L. and his marauders reflected the racial tone of other confrontations that began to break out with increasing regularity (blacks and whites scuffling for pony rides or picnic grills). By 9:30 P.M. the exchange of blows and epithets escalated, recording the first hospital casualty—a white teenager assaulted three times within twenty minutes—and Charles L. surfaced again. At the playground, he and his pack attacked fourteen-year-old Gus Niarhos and stole his carfare. Failing to hail a homeward bus or chase down another white target, they headed across the crowded bridge to Detroit. It was now 10:45 P.M. Soon L. brushed against thirty-eight-year-old Joseph B. Joseph, called him a "white mother-fucking son of a bitch," and slammed him to the pavement, where other black youths kicked him and suggested hurling him into the river. As the victim struggled to his feet and raced into the path of two white sailors and their dates at the island end of the bridge, L. and his cohorts moved toward Jefferson Avenue.

Pushing and name calling—"black bitch," "white bastard"—turned to mayhem as one of the sailors blew his whistle and rallied some fifty bluejackets stationed at the armory on Jefferson Avenue. Fighting broke out all along the bridge and spilled onto the thoroughfare, where one of Charles L.'s gang unsuccessfully urged blacks to enter the fray, claiming, "a colored woman and her baby had been drowned." By 11:30, however, white numbers had soared and comprised most of the 5,000 persons in the area. Sailors, still smarting from a racial brawl the previous morning, bridge crossers, and nearby residents fought to reclaim the park and reestablish social distance: "We don't want any niggers on Belle Isle." They beat and chased blacks, spreading their vengeance one block either side of Jefferson Avenue and four blocks north on Grand Boulevard. During the next two and a half hours, the crowd dispersed as police officers flooded the intersection and took control without serious loss of life. They handled the disorder, said blacks, by "beating and arresting Negroes while using mere persuasion on whites."

Charles L. was neither among the twenty-eight blacks arrested nor the five injured. He made his way back to the east side and, along with several witnesses frightened by the crazed-looking white toughs, alerted others in the black community. He, or someone else, arrived at the east-side Forest Club at 12:30 A.M. and informed Leo T. of the fighting across-town on Jefferson Avenue.

Thirty-five-year-old T. lived with his wife at 976 Wilkins Street. A resident of Detroit since the age of three, he was familiar with past racial conflicts—the Ossian Sweet incident (1925), the Black Legion terrorism (1930s), and the Sojourner Truth housing disorder (1942). He had brushed with the law as a way of life: thirteen arrests for unarmed robbery, breaking and entering, disturbing the peace, frequenting a gambling place, destruction of property, and, as recently as May 1941, carrying concealed weapons; four convictions, two prison terms, and one probation violation. He had worked as a handy man at the Forest Club, a popular recreation center, since his last police encounter, operating a sound truck, selling dance tickets, and manning the coat room. Literate but crime-prone, he doubtlessly experienced alienation toward white society and especially its gendarmes. His victims, however, had hitherto been fellow blacks.

At the Forest Club that night, Leo T. made his way through the crowd of 700 dancers, climbed atop the bandstand, and stopped the music. Dressed in a dark suit and carrying a briefcase, he identified himself as Sergeant Fuller and announced that a riot was in progress on the island, where whites had thrown "a colored lady and her baby" off the bridge. Everyone "get your guns" and "go out there," he instructed; free transportation awaited outside. Then, having directed his anger against whites, he disappeared, and pandemonium broke out.

Leo T.'s shocking news stampeded Forest Club patrons into the street, but no vehicles idled at the curb for their convenience. Their numbers were unusually large because the night spot, which contained a bowling alley, dance floor, and skating rink, provided one of the few recreational outlets for blacks, and, on June 20, was holding a "big dance" that drew several hundred youths. Galvanized by the rumor of whites killing a black woman and child, which linked a specific violation of sacred mores with general hostile beliefs in white violence, dancers and pedestrians became vengeance-seeking mobs. They filled the intersection of Forest Avenue and Hastings Street, stoning white motorists and trolley passengers while taunting policemen who came to rescue them. One thousand persons of both sexes and various classes struck human targets and overwhelmed lawmen, whose depleted wartime ranks and Belle Isle emergency assignments made answering 500 east-side calls impossible. Unchecked, blacks beat, hit, and stabbed whites who crossed their path, sending one injured person every minute to Receiving Hospital.

Soon rioters roamed throughout "the colored district," flush with victory and, like counterparts of a later generation, "commonality of purpose." South of Canfield on Brush, they knocked unconscious a twenty-seven-year-old white man, who became the first fatality when crushed accidentally by a cab. North of Grand Boulevard on Holbrook, they fought fifty Chevrolet Gear and Axle shift workers, and created disturbances along Oakland Avenue at Owen and Westminster. In this section, a mile above the boulevard, black residents like John T. clashed with police and forced them to detour streetcars. Most in their early twenties, married, and employed as laborers—and well aware of the "hate strikes" that had rocked Detroit for the previous six months, denying promotion of blacks to more skilled, better paying jobs—they might have been pursuing white workers out of revenge.

As police sealed the ghetto and whites avoided it, rioters turned their attention to stores, and, sometime before dawn of June 21, began to loot them. In fact, within one hour of Leo T.'s announcement, they were smashing windows on Hastings Street. Their fury now spread out of control along all the major commercial streets: St. Antoine, Beaubien, Brush, and John R, east to

Hastings; Rivard, Russell, Riopelle, and Dequindre, west to St. Aubin. From Adams Street north to Grand Boulevard and ultimately beyond, residents shifted from an interracial or communal upheaval to a riot against property. Hemmed in by physical boundaries, they concentrated on symbols of white domination—lawmen, property, and goods—as white citizens, absentee land-lords, and shop owners slept beyond their reach. They confronted officers, injured several, and killed one, but drew deadly, often indiscriminate gun-fire, which would ultimately claim seventeen black lives. More often, rioters demolished store fronts and showcases, strewed mannequins and merchan-dise around the streets in the midst of broken glass, and left large segments of the business district looking as if it "had been bombed from the air with block busters." Looters, in turn, swept through drug and grocery stores, hab-erdasheries, pawnshops and taverns, confiscating everything from aspirin to liquor. Some stole alone, others in groups; some acted crazy, others deliber-ate; some targeted any store, but a great majority spared known "colored" es-tablishments or those later identified by hastily painted signs.

At 4:00 A.M., whites began to retaliate along Woodward Avenue, probably having heard of the upheaval from escaping passersby and laborers. Adoles-cents and young men gathered about the Roxy and Colonial theaters, stoning the cars of blacks that passed along the thoroughfare, which separated black ghetto and white west side, itself characterized by substandard dwellings and transient populations. They also assaulted black patrons exiting from the all-night cinemas and tried to push their way into the black community at Al-fred, but were driven back by police officers. In close residential proximity to east siders and competing with them for jobs and status, white assailants, like their predecessors in earlier interracial riots, sought to kick blacks back into their place. And, despite a lull in their activities around 6:30 A.M., they—again like earlier rioters—seemed proud of themselves and threatened fur-ther bloodshed. . . .

. . . White gangs controlled Woodward Avenue, halting traffic to drag blacks from trolleys and automobiles, beat them viciously, sometimes sense-less, overturn and incinerate their cars—all pay-back for east-side attacks. They roamed about, with little interference from bluecoats, whose numbers never exceeded 1,000, were divided between two war zones, and generally harbored racial prejudice. Inside the ghetto, where most officers found them-selves assigned, blacks continued to break into stores, forage for possessions, and run afoul of patrolmen. Looters represented older, more mature resi-dents, albeit no less resentful than the ruffians led by Charles L.

Rudolph M. certainly would have fought at Belle Isle. A twenty-three-year-old native of Louisiana, who had come to Detroit only thirteen months before the disturbance, he lived with his wife on Edmund Place, two blocks east of Woodward Avenue and midway between Forest Avenue and down-town. He worked in a store stocking shelves for wages far below those paid in the defense industry. Perhaps angered by his environment—slums largely built before 1915, often lacking indoor plumbing, and cruelly dubbed "Paradise Valley"—he turned his anger against absentee owners responsible for his plight. Rather than destroy his own dwelling, however, he selected a more practical target over a half mile from home: Paul's Drug Store at Hastings and Leland. He hurled first a brick and then, moments later, a bottle through the plate-glass window. He was only one of many in the missile-throwing crowd, but he alone drew the attention of police officers, who apprehended him after a short chase. He was found to be carrying a 7-inch butcher knife, a concealed weapon. Though he made no effort to slash his captors, his possession of the blade indicated fear and possibly Southern tradition. Significantly, his presence on the street and repeated attacks on the pharmacy revealed deep alienation and purposeful protest—the combination of ghetto isolation, oppression, numbers, and solidarity with wartime opportunities and anxieties.

Looters carried this racial complaint further. Their early morning plunder seemed symbolically defiant, and soon became wholesale theft by usually law-abiding citizens. Roy S., for instance, watched as several people tossed armfuls of merchandise out of a grocery store at 4717 St. Antoine, half a mile from his home on East Ferry. He and a companion were loading several pounds of pork loins, smoked ham, canned salmon, and cheese—then rare and rationed items—into their car, when police arrested them for larceny. Born in Gregory, Arkansas, but a Detroit resident for the past five years, S. lived with his wife and child and earned good money at Ford Motor Company. Approaching thirty years of age, seeming less disaffected and more established than window smashers like Rudolph M., he nonetheless helped himself to food thrown into the street. Possibly he considered such actions righteous redistribution and redefinition of property—as would some ghetto rioters a generation later. Yet S. never hinted at motivation; he told officers only that he had picked up the goods and indicated which store they came from. That a man like this should engage in behavior normally unlawful— but momentarily acceptable by many in the community—disclosed the drawing power and the grievance of mob activity; that he should collect mostly perishables that would have spoiled if left in the gutters and could have been purchased in the expensive but equitable rationing system, exhibited the ambivalence of moral standards and the anomie among oppressed people. Experiencing mixed emotions and motives in a wholly unregulated and opportunistic setting, Roy S. stole, but he did so for much more than "fun and profit."

Neither Rudolph M. nor Roy S. knew the proprietors of the stores they sacked, despite later contentions by observers that such actions manifested anti-Semitism. Living half a mile away and possessing little if any knowledge of which stores were Jewish-owned, they delivered symbolic attacks on "the white caste." They probably knew that German and, more recently, Russian Jews had occupied the east side before them and still controlled many of its apartments and businesses, yet the antagonisms that fueled the violence were customer-merchant rather than ethnic. They believed themselves exploited by all shopkeepers, not simply the white druggist and the Russian Jewish grocer. Certainly black anti-Semitism—growing out of socioeconomic competition and cultural conflict, which enjoyed a long tradition in the ghetto, and intensified in the face of Nazi propaganda—heightened tensions, but M. and S. reacted as opportunists seizing the moment rather than as ideologues punishing Semites. They struck at accessible, safe targets, emblems of white exploitation and black humility, and they struck as everyday residents, who had neither police records nor apparently political doctrines. . . .

. . . Concentrated in an enormous rectangle, stretching from downtown Detroit north to the city of Highland Park, running through the heart of the 1st, 13th, and 9th precincts and spilling over east and west into adjacent zones, upheaval also occurred in the black west side and above the Polish city of Hamtramck. Approximately three miles west of Woodward Avenue at Ironwood and Tireman, deep in the black middle-class community to which those who escaped the ghetto had moved, Thomas H. disturbed the peace. Like many living in this stable, upwardly mobile area of homeowners, he was married and employed in a skilled job; unlike most of those milling in the street, he had brushed with the police once before. He might have been displaying anger over reports of DPD brutality in the east side and indifference to white assaults downtown. At thirty-nine years of age, H. and his cohorts were older than most rioters elsewhere, possibly venting frustration over white society's disregard for their socioeconomic achievements and disdainful rejection of them as mere "niggers." . . .

The numbers and characteristics of those apprehended between June 21 and June 30 affected how the riot was interpreted by many people. Of nearly 2,000 arrestees, young, black males comprised the overwhelming majority, followed by far fewer white males and black and white females. These participants recorded a median age of twenty-five years; surprisingly few of the scores of juveniles seen at the riot were arrested. Regardless of age or gender, blacks filled the ranks of arrestees in greater proportions than their population in metropolitan Detroit. Their spokespersons attributed this gross imbalance to police bias, while bluecoat officials explained it in terms of black aggression. . . .

Those who witnessed or read about the rampage also blamed Southern newcomers. When [Mayor Edward] Jeffries stated that an influx of migrant workers contributed to the riot, he sparked the ire of editors like Ralph McGill of the *Atlanta Constitution*, who protested "the cheap and easy habit of blaming any and all racial troubles on the South." Such conflict grew out of civil injustices and economic inequities found in both Detroit and Dixie, lectured McGill, noting also that teenagers, not Southern laborers, had ignited the outburst. Despite McGill's logic, most Detroiters thought like their mayor. Popular *News* columnist W. K. Kelsey ascribed the disorder to scores of Southerners who encountered liberal conditions in the city, where blacks experiencing newfound freedom clashed with whites clinging to "Jim Crow notions." . . .

. . . Of course, more than black hooligans and Southern newcomers participated in the Detroit riot of 1943. Despite contemporary studies and public opinion, hoodlums and migrants shared the streets with lawful, longtime Detroiters. Rioters, in fact, included multitudes of ordinary men and women of both races. Their experiences, as well as those of teenagers, identify more completely those arrested for having been in the crowd. . . .

. . . The largest percentage of black men, slightly more than a quarter, fell between the ages of twenty-eight and thirty-seven, and the median age for all black male participants stood at twenty-seven years. Nearly 63 percent were married, and nearly 75 percent lived in Paradise Valley. Most were literate and employed, and over 85 percent had benefited from the war boom and worked as laborers; 9 percent of the black rioters worked as skilled and semiskilled operatives, suggesting even higher and more stable social standing. Significant also for understanding the spontaneous actions of normally upright residents, most black transgressors were arrested alone and for the first time in their lives. They rioted in their home precincts and within a half mile of their east side addresses.

Information from probation records indicated further social stability for black males. Overwhelmingly born and bred in Alabama, Georgia, and Mississippi, fully half of them had resided in Detroit for nine years or more—the median stay, just short of a decade. Most were married, nearly 40 percent were raising children, and over 50 percent had secured meaningful jobs within the past year; they represented working-class people hopeful of bright futures. Indeed, having endured the Great Depression and blatant racism, they must have sensed the potential for personal and racial advancement: Weekly wages of fifty dollars, median educations of eight years, and several successful protests over housing and employment had surely raised their expectations. . . .

In sum, usually law-abiding and hard-working men stood side-by-side with lawbreakers. No doubt many of both kinds were politically astute and racially proud. Black laborers and skilled workers, particularly those married, with children and education levels approaching that of whites, knew of—might even have participated in—recent DSR* incidents, housing controversies, or hate strikes that sharpened racial animus. Very likely their riot activity arose from the accumulation of blocked socioeconomic opportunities, which they attributed to white racists. They deemed the Belle Isle rampage and accompanying rumors as final provocation in a series of real and occasionally perceived wrongs. Fearful for their newfound prosperity and status, they struck as much to protect their stake in society as to destroy their

*Detroit Street Railway.

enemy, as much out of pride as anger. Black repeat offenders probably clashed with lawmen on familiar ground over perennial grudges. Slightly over 25 percent of all black male participants, however, exhibited calculated or mindless theft as they looted east-side stores, expressly those on Hastings Street. And a minute number of arrestees attacked white citizens or patrolmen, perhaps displaying a bloodlust that predated wartime frustrations. In essence, no single profile or motivation moved black males to action. Protestors and lawbreakers alike took part in several different kinds of riot for equally diverse reasons. . . .

Unsurprisingly, white male rioters were as diverse as their black counterparts. Nearly 65 percent of all white men were younger than twenty-three years old. Their ages extended from seventeen to fifty-four, the median age at twenty years—less extreme than the black range of fourteen to sixty-four and significantly younger than the black midpoint of twenty-seven. Consequently, over 70 percent of the white arrestees were single and over 55 percent worked as laborers, with 4 percent as clericals, 5 percent as semiskilled, 23 percent as skilled operatives, and the rest service employees or domestics. And, regardless of marital status or occupation, slightly more than 50 percent of all white participants lived relatively close to Belle Isle or on the fringes of Paradise Valley, and 40 percent more traveled over two miles to riot along its boundaries. Fully three quarters of all white offenders left their home precincts, determined to secure the perimeters of Detroit's color line against integrated housing and black upward mobility. Young adults, ordinarily law-abiding, mobilized to avenge past affronts aboard public conveyances, in municipal parks, and at downtown theaters, stores, and eateries.

Probation data reveals that almost all white arrestees were individuals with roots, on the make, and yet insecure. Most—53 percent—identified their home state as Michigan, and only one named the South as his origin; obviously far fewer white Southerners participated in the upheaval than was believed by officials, black leaders, and residents. Surprisingly, white in-migrants, Southern born or otherwise, stayed pretty clear of the disturbance. Neither Bedford B. nor Leonard O., placed on probation for carrying concealed weapons, qualified as "hillbillies"—those allegedly clannish, dirty, ignorant newcomers from Dixie. One came from a border state, the other from Michigan. Neither possessed police records, and both worked as machinists. They lived with their families, respectively, east of Cass in a neighborhood of white transients and north of Grand Boulevard in a mixed area rapidly becoming an extension of the black ghetto. Separated by nearly twenty years of life (forty-two versus twenty-three) and eight years of education (third grade versus eleventh), they shared little save their whiteness, offenses, and convictions. Both carried weapons, one a butcher knife, the other a nickel-plated revolver, and received sentences of short probation. Occasional drinking problems aside, both met the terms of probation. Having reported regularly, worked steadily, and provided a "suitable home," they were discharged with improvement. Their experiences belied the dominance of Southern or other groups of newcomers among white participants.

Despite . . . Southern cultural deprivation theories, over 80 percent of the white felons had resided in the city more than six years. In fact, 50 percent had lived as Detroiters for over seventeen years. Except for being significantly more single than black felons, they registered similar education levels, time of employment, and wages. They competed with blacks for jobs and status, which personalized and sharpened the racial rivalry. Most probably, they recalled the hardships of depression and, facing black competition on every front, feared slipping backward. . . .

Personal characteristics and riot activity also distinguished black female rioters from males of both races. (No data exist for white women, whose participation in the disturbances was completely ignored for the first two days out of the prejudice or chivalry of out-numbered, overtaxed lawmen.) Ranging from seventeen to forty-five years of age, black women tallied a median age of twenty-four and one-half years. Over 65 percent were single, yet almost half of those had been separated, divorced, or widowed. Regardless of marital status, 69 percent of all black females worked outside the home: 43 percent as domestics, cooks, or similar service workers, and 19 percent as common laborers. Their ages, marital statuses, employment rates, occupational categories, and police records identified most of them as predominantly older, mature, working class, and law-abiding. . . .

Prior to the 1960s, European scholars of collective violence in England and France followed the lead of Gustave Le Bon. They characterized early rioters as criminal, maladjusted, and riffraff, unstable persons fulfilling emotional needs and selfish, apolitical aims. Lacking quantifiable evidence and drawing on psychological interpretations, they posited breakdown and contagion theories: Urbanization and industrialization promoted antisocial behavior in some individuals, and these misfits exploded, drawing others into a "mental unity" of excitement, destruction, and anonymity.

Le Bon's theory is still quite popular with some officials and private citizens, but it began losing its credibility among scholars in the early 1960s. Some, like E. J. Hobsbawm and E. P. Thompson, resurrected and revised Karl Marx's solidarity theory, and interpreted collective violence as the struggle of working-class people for political power. Non-Marxist historians also explained riot as protest and participants as ordinary people seeking redress. Perhaps most influential is George Rudé's synthesis of preindustrial crowds, which posits violence as collective behavior evolving through a precise set of determinants. Rudé presented history from the bottom up and suggested similarities between food rioters and political rebels. He also encouraged further investigation of the mob in other eras and locales as a "living and many-sided historical phenomenon." Slightly more than a decade later, a comparative history of upheavals in England, France, and Germany between 1830 and 1930 by Charles Tilly, Louise Tilly, and Richard Tilly extended the revised history of collective violence into modern times and suggested parallels for the recent civil disorders in the United States. . . .

In fact, the Detroit rioters of 1943 provided the necessary example for understanding successive generations of white and black participants in riots dating back to the turn of the century and, particularly for blacks, forward to the 1960s. Taken together and allowing for distinctions of time, place, and riot patterns, . . . Detroit profiles have dashed officials' self-serving descriptions of earlier white rioters as riffraff and raised anew the possibility that rioters in other cities . . . represented several classes and ethnic groups. While additional research is needed of all those who erupted before World War II, Detroiters . . . came from the general populace and shared certain traits with them.

Indeed, participants in the 1943 Detroit outburst desired greater participation in society. White rioters felt threatened and their black counterparts resentful, for members of both races had made enough gains to want much more. Unlike more successful residents, they were too impatient to mark time amid democratic rhetoric and wartime change. Younger, more energized, and less influential than those who avoided violence, they sought redress in the streets; they rioted to improve rather than destroy the system. They came forth as neither mainstream nor misfit, but as desperate people seeking respectability through protest that shed blood and ironically reinforced their disrepute in the eyes of the public.

PRIMARY SOURCES

Most of the sources in this section reflect the social and economic conditions of Detroit's African American population and their view about those conditions. What, if anything, does this evidence reveal about the causes of the Detroit riot and the motives of the rioters?

2

In 1942, African Americans were accepted as tenants in the Sojourner Truth Homes, a public housing project located in a black–Polish neighborhood. When they arrived to move in, they were greeted by white mobs who beat them and stoned their cars.

A Handbill for White Resistance (1942)

Source: Archives of Labor and Urban Affairs, Wayne State University.

The Job Situation

What do the following sources reveal about job discrimination in Detroit during World War II?

Black Employment in Selected Detroit Companies, 1941

Aeronautical Products, Inc.	0.02 percent
Briggs Manufacturing Company	7.0 percent
Chrysler	2.5 percent*
Hudson Motor Company	1.8 percent
Murray Corporation of America	5.0 percent
Packard Corporation	11.0 percent*
Vicker, Inc.	3.0 percent*

*Most were foundry workers or janitors.

Source: Data from Richard W. Thomas, *Life for Us Is What We Make It* (Bloomington: Indiana University Press, 1992), p. 157.

In early 1943, blacks walked off their jobs at Chrysler and Ford plants to protest the working conditions they encountered. The *Michigan Chronicle,* a black newspaper, offered an explanation for the strikes at Ford.

An Explanation for Strikes (1943)

It is extremely significant that all of the so-called "Negro wild-cat strikes" in the local war plants have arisen in departments in which the Negro workers are jim-crowed and isolated because of their color. Rather than integrate the workers, the companies insist in most cases in creating separate racial gangs in the factory. They claim that this procedure eliminates trouble, yet the facts reveal that wherever workers are so segregated, the separate groups invariably pit themselves against each other and violence follows the slightest provocation. To the normal problem of general worker relations the companies add the second problem of racial relations.

Source: Reprinted from the *Michigan Chronicle,* [May 8, 1943 or March 27, 1943] by permission of the publisher.

In March 1943, 600 black male workers at the Chrysler Highland Park plant walked out to protest the working conditions of black women at the factory. Here two female workers offer their explanations for the protest.

Black Workers Protest Against Chrysler (1943)

We are not given the same opportunities for promotions that white women are given. In the first place, . . . the superintendent has stated that we have got to

Source: Reprinted from the *Michigan Chronicle,* [May 8, 1943 or March 27, 1943] by permission of the publisher.

do the hard work, such as pulling steel, running jitneys and heavy mopping. Many of us were hired as elevator operators but have never run an elevator at the plant because the men on the elevators refuse to transfer to work we are doing. They say the work is too hard for them. We have taken our complaints to the union—to the proper sources—but there has been no action. . . .

Many of us have trained for skilled jobs, hired as matrons but our jobs soon developed into common labor in the shop—labor for which the company is unable to hire men. White girls turn these jobs down and are given other work, but Negro women are told . . . they must do these jobs or ring their cards and go home. I was fired from my job because I wanted to change my clothes before going out to sweep around the building at 6 A.M. on a cold morning. I had been working in a hot place all night and would have been exposed to catching a severe cold. . . .

We are constantly being intimidated because we insist on eating in the regular places. When we first went to the plant they gave us separate toilets—far from our work—and we were told that we would have to eat our lunch in these restrooms. There is nothing but two benches and a low table in them. We don't know what they were used for before we were hired. Once when a colored girl changed her clothes in a white girl's restroom, she went back and found out that the buttons had been cut off her coat and her galoshes cut into shreds. We complained to the plant committeeman about this but have not heard anything from him.

 This editorial ran in the Detroit *Tribune,* a black newspaper, in 1939. Note black Detroiters' complaints about the police department.

A Complaint About the Police (1939)

The Detroit Police Department is apparently trying to establish a national record for brutality to Negro citizens. In spite of the many protests made to those in authority, the brutality continues. . . . Since January 1, this year, the number of Negroes slain in cold blood and savagely beaten and clubbed by local police officers has steadily mounted. . . . In addition to these and other murders by Detroit policemen in recent months, many other members of our race have been brutally clubbed and beaten by officers of the law, without just cause. . . . Policemen are paid by the taxpayers to preserve law and order and to protect human lives and public and private property, but they have no right to take the law into their own hands, as so many of them do. It is not their duty to act as judges, juries and executioners, in their dealings with Negroes. Policemen have no legal or moral right to let their racial or religious prejudices lead them to persecute members of our race or any other racial group, and when policemen . . . forget their duty as to indulge in such lawless acts of violence,

Source: Detroit *Tribune,* July 15, 1939.

they should be curbed, reprimanded, and in flagrant cases they should be dismissed from the Police Department and punished by the courts of justice.

Colored citizens of Detroit have been protesting for some time to those in local authority, and appealing to them to put a stop to this police brutality, but our protests thus far seem to have fallen on deaf ears.

---

7   Declining death rates are usually an indication of improving living conditions. Do these tables provide evidence about the expectations of blacks in Northern cities like Detroit? Do they reveal a difference between Detroit and the rest of the nation in that regard?

Changes in White and Black Death Rates, 1910–1940

Changes in White and Black Death Rates in Detroit, 1915–1940 (per 1,000)

Year	White Death Rate	Black Death Rate
1915	12.8	14.7
1920	12.8	24.0
1925	10.4	19.4
1930	8.7	15.6
1940	8.0	12.2

Changes in National Black and White Death Rates, 1910–1940 (per 1,000)

Year	White Death Rate	Black Death Rate
1910	14.5	21.7
1920	12.6	17.7
1930	10.8	15.6
1940	10.4	13.9

Source: Richard W. Thomas, *Life for Us Is What We Make It* (Bloomington: Indiana University Press, 1992), pp. 104, 105.

---

8   As you examine the table on the following pages, determine whether the data support or contradict the main essay's argument about the characteristics of the rioters. Do these statistics indicate significant differences between white and black rioters? More than 1,500 blacks and 250 whites were arrested; can historians draw valid generalizations about the Detroit rioters from such a sample?

A Profile of the Detroit Rioters

Characteristics	Black Males (N = 205)		White Males (N = 30)		Black Females (N = 11)		Total Sample (N = 246)	
	#	%	#	%	#	%	#	%
Black	205		—		11		216	87.7
Male	205		30		—		235	95.5
Median age	27 years		19 years		28 years		26 years	
Range of ages	16 to 64		17 to 41		17 to 38		16 to 64	
Married	129	62.9	11	36.7	4	36.4	144	58.5
Laborer	176	85.9	16	53.3	1	9.1	193	78.5
Employed	197	96.1	28	93.3	6	54.5	231	93.9
Resident precinct 3, 9, 13	150	73.2	10	33.3	10	90.0	170	69.1
Detroit resident	199	97.1	27	90.0	11	100.0	237	96.3
No previous arrest	124	60.5	21	70.0	11	100.0	156	63.4
Riot Behavior								
Felony	115	56.1	12	40.0	6	54.5	133	54.1
Misdemeanor	90	43.9	18	60.0	5	45.5	113	45.9
Weapon	59	28.8	13	43.3	1	9.1	73	29.7
Looting	55	26.8	1	0.03	7	63.6	63	25.6
Conduct	88	42.9	16	53.3	3	27.3	107	43.5
Arrested in home precinct	126	61.5	7	23.3	5	45.5	138	56.1
Arrested within mile of home	106	51.7	7	23.3	9	81.8	122	49.6
Arrested in precinct 1, 3, 9, 13	158	77.1	16	53.3	8	72.7	182	74.0

(cont. on next page)

Source: Excerpted from Dominic J. Capeci, Jr., and Martha Wilkerson, *Layered Violence: The Detroit Rioters of 1943*, p. 210. Copyright © 1991 by the University of Mississippi Press. Reprinted by permission of the University of Mississippi Press.

Additional Characteristics[1]	Black Males (N = 68)		White Males (N = 5)		Probation Records (N = 73)	
	#	%	#	%	#	%
Home state in South[2]	59	86.8	2	40.0	61	83.6
Acted alone	49	72.1	2	40.0	51	69.9
No children	41	60.3	2	40.0	43	58.9
Protestant	66	97.1	3	60.0	69	94.5
Median education	8 years		9 years		8 years	
Median length of residence	9.5 years		14 years		12 years	
Median length of present employment	1 year		1 year		1 year	
Median weekly salary	$50.00		$50.00		$50.00	

[1]These additional data are drawn from the probation records that could be located for male felons.

[2]South includes the lower South (South Carolina, Mississippi, Louisiana, Alabama, Georgia, Texas, and Florida), upper South (Tennessee, Virginia, Arkansas, and North Carolina), and border states (Kentucky and Missouri).

CONCLUSION

"There's a monotony about the injustices suffered by the poor . . ." the critic Dwight Macdonald once wrote. "Everything seems to go wrong with them. They never win. It's just boring."[8] Although there was nothing boring about the Detroit riot, Macdonald had a point. Unless an eruption had occurred there in 1943, Detroit's wartime slums would draw relatively little notice today. Macdonald's observation points to a problem facing historians looking at history "from the bottom up." The poor are not at the center of power. They normally do not make decisions affecting the lives of millions, and often their lives appear to change little until violence breaks the monotony. Historians would seem to find little worthy of study in them.

Yet wartime Detroit shows that historians must see beyond the "monotony" of everyday life. The city's slums reflected important changes in the lives of many Americans. Historians who wish to understand how World War II changed American society need to understand those who lived in the slums of cities like Detroit or New York. Because historians make generalizations about historical influences, they cannot lose sight of the people at society's bottom. Otherwise, they may explain less than they claim to. That is a good point to remember as we turn next to one historian's explanation regarding the influence of a single factor—anticommunism—on America's postwar culture.

FURTHER READING

Earl Brown, "The Detroit Race Riot of 1943," in *A Documentary History of the Negro People in the United States, 1933–1945,* ed. Herbert Aptheker (Secaucus, N.J.: Citadel Press, 1974).

A. Russell Buchanan, *Black Americans in World War II* (Santa Barbara, Calif.: Clio Books, 1977).

Alfred McClung Lee and Norman D. Humphrey, *Race Riot, Detroit 1943* (New York: Octagon Books, 1968).

Elaine Latzman Moon, *Untold Tales, Unsung Heroes: An Oral History of Detroit's African-American Community, 1918–1967* (Detroit: Wayne State University Press, 1994).

George Rudé, *The Crowd in History: A Study of Popular Disturbances in France and England, 1730–1848* (New York: John Wiley & Sons, 1964).

Richard W. Thomas, *Life for Us Is What We Make It* [A history of black Detroit] (Bloomington: Indiana University Press, 1992).

NOTES

1. Quoted in Alfred McClung Lee and Norman D. Humphrey, *Race Riot (Detroit, 1943)* (New York: Octagon Books, 1968), p. 38.

2. Ibid.

3. Eric J. Hobsbawm, "History from Below—Some Reflections," in *History from Below: Studies in Popular Protest and Popular Ideology in Honour of George Rudé,* ed. Frederick Krantz (Montreal: Concordia University, 1985), p. 65.

4. Quoted in Robert Conot, *American Odyssey: A Unique History of America Told Through the Life of a Great City* (New York: William Morrow, 1974), p. 379.

5. Quoted in Earl Brown, "The Detroit Race Riot of 1943," in *A Documentary History of the Negro in the United States, 1933–1945,* ed. Herbert Aptheker (New York: Citadel Press, 1969), p. 453.

6. Quoted in Conot, *American Odyssey,* p. 386.

7. Quoted in ibid.

8. Quoted in Michael Sragow, "The Individualist," *The New Yorker,* September 12, 1994, p. 90.

Chapter

9

Popular Culture as History: The Cold War Comes Home

The documents in this chapter deal with the anticommunist climate of the Cold War era.

Secondary Source

Primary Sources

*I*n March 1947 the House Un-American Activities Committee (HUAC) came to Hollywood to expose communist influence in the film industry. Ronald Reagan, Gary Cooper, Robert Taylor, Adolph Menjou, and other stars testified as "friendly" witnesses at HUAC's hearings. Menjou declared, "I am a witch hunter if the witches are Communists. . . . I would like to see them all back in Russia."[1] Other witnesses also shared evidence of subversion in Hollywood's studios. Animator Walt Disney told the committee of a communist plot to turn Mickey Mouse into a Marxist. Fervid anticommunist author Ayn Rand pointed to evidence of subversive influence in *Song of Russia* (1943), one of several pro-Soviet wartime films produced when the United States and the Soviet Union were allies in World War II. Rand declared that the movie made her "sick." It showed Russian schoolchildren smiling, and in Russia, Rand pointed out, children never smiled.

The committee, chaired by Representative Parnell Thomas, also heard from ten "unfriendly" witnesses. All of them refused to cooperate with HUAC, and Thomas had armed guards drag them from the hearing room. Later that year all were cited for contempt by the Congress and indicted by a grand jury. By 1950 the "Hollywood ten" were in prison. Two of the ten, screenwriters Ring Lardner, Jr., and Lester Cole, served time in the federal prison at Danbury, Connecticut. By the time they arrived, former HUAC chairman Thomas was already there, convicted in 1949 of padding his office payroll. One day Cole passed Thomas, who was in charge of the prison farm's chicken yard. "I see," Cole observed, "that you're still shoveling chicken shit."[2]

Cole and the other "Hollywood ten" did not get the last laugh with the communist hunters, however. By the time they were released from prison in 1951, anticommunist hysteria had only grown. That year HUAC returned to Hollywood to ferret out more communists and communist sympathizers. The committee obtained more than 300 names. By then, the major studios had begun blacklisting actors, screenwriters, and technicians, making it virtually impossible for them to find work. And the hunt for subversives had also spread well beyond Hollywood. The unexpected Soviet test of an atomic bomb, the conviction of the accused spy Alger Hiss in 1950, and the outbreak of the Korean War the same year had fed a growing fear of communism. So had Senator Joseph McCarthy's shocking accusations of a communist underground in the government. By 1950, the effort to root out alleged communist subversion had spread from Hollywood and the government to television, radio, and schools. When McCarthy was censured by the U.S. Senate four years later, McCarthyism had become a household word and thousands of lives and careers had been ruined.

The postwar anticommunist witch-hunt tarnished reputations, sent people to prison for their political convictions, and even led some to commit suicide. Because many of the accused were writers and performing artists, it also dramatically affected the postwar era's films, television programs, novels, and other expressions of popular culture. Producers of entertainment—and messages—

for mass consumption were visible targets of the communist hunters' investigations. Many were liberal, some were communists, and most had been enthusiastic supporters of America's alliance with the Soviet Union during World War II. It was not an accident that Hollywood was one of the first places to be searched for subversives, or that the search would quickly turn to television and radio networks and to other producers of popular entertainment.

Because of the vulnerability of writers, artists, and entertainers to anticommunist hysteria, popular culture is one of the best places to see the impact of the Cold War on American society. To understand the Cold War's impact on the popular messages in that era, historians must synthesize or combine evidence from such diverse sources as films, plays, songs, television programs, novels, and even comics. In this chapter, we piece together some of this evidence to create a picture of American popular culture in a period of anticommunist hysteria.

SETTING

As is true today, popular culture in the 1950s meant primarily movies, television programs, and recorded music as well as fiction, drama, and even fashion and comics. In the postwar years, however, spreading affluence, new technology, and growing numbers of children and teenagers made this culture more pervasive than ever. Its growing influence was evident in the new medium of television and in new forms of popular entertainment, from TV's situation comedies to rock 'n' roll. And many postwar commentators were appalled by what they saw and heard. Surveying postwar radio, television, movies, and novels, one critic declared popular culture to be "non-art."[3] Other observers lamented the homogenization of culture pitched to a mass audience.

Since the 1950s, scholars have continued to debate the limits and limitations of popular culture. Yet most of them would probably agree about its important characteristics. If "high" culture conforms to rigorous artistic standards, demands some effort to enjoy, and appeals to a limited audience, popular culture adheres to no fixed rules, requires no effort to enjoy and little training to understand, and thus appeals to a broad audience. At the same time, popular culture differs from folk culture: stories, songs, dances, and other forms of artistic expression usually created by a society's illiterate, lower classes. Folk culture is preserved in memory and is passed down orally, often over centuries. By contrast, popular culture is created and marketed by an entertainment industry and transmitted through channels of mass communication, both of which are dominated by large corporations. In other words, it is a commodity to be bought and sold for profit in the marketplace. Like other marketable commodities, it has a short "shelf life." Popular culture, then, travels instantly and disappears quickly, but often not before it has touched all levels of society.

Today, historians who study postwar popular culture are less interested in judging people's tastes than in understanding what its messages reveal about the period. They also see much more variety in the popular culture of the 1950s than did contemporary critics, who often focused on the burgeoning white, middle-class suburbs. Historians also recognize numerous influences on post-war popular culture: growing middle-class affluence, the spread of suburbia, the increasing importance of the automobile, the "baby boom," and the Cold War. Thus their task is to understand popular culture's messages and determine the role of varied influences in shaping them.

The glorification of mothers and homemakers, a dominant theme of postwar popular culture, illustrates the challenge. Undoubtedly, the baby boom and the growth of suburbs played a large role in fashioning this domestic ideal, which was broadcast widely in the movies, television, and magazines of the 1950s. Yet so may have other factors, including the Cold War. The domestic ideal was a comforting image and a useful tool in the battle against communism. The image of the suburban home with its contented homemaker seemed to be compelling evidence of American superiority in the Cold War. Thus when Richard Nixon engaged Soviet leader Nikita Khrushchev in their famous "kitchen debate" at an exhibition of American goods in Moscow in 1959, the vice president praised the American way of life because it had eased the domestic burden of women. Standing in front of a washing machine, Nixon told Khrushchev, "What we want is to make easier the life of our housewives."[4]

The postwar domestic ideal illustrates that popular culture's influence can run in many, often unexpected, directions. It also demonstrates that popular culture can be shaped by numerous influences. To understand its many messages, historians must draw from myriad, often unrelated, sources. And, as with any historical analysis, they must be careful not to attribute too much influence to a single cause.

INVESTIGATION

In the movie *Blackboard Jungle* (1955), an idealistic teacher played by Glenn Ford tells a high school class filled with rebellious students, "All your lives you're gonna hear stories—what some guy tells you, what you see in books and magazines—but you gotta examine these stories, look for the real meaning, and most of all . . . you gotta think for yourselves."[5] It was easy for postwar Americans to enjoy their favorite television programs, movies, music, or popular fiction without thinking much about them. Few perceived in them a common frame of reference. Now, with the advantage of hindsight, historians can synthesize a variety of sources into a coherent picture. In this chapter, we examine a wide array of cultural artifacts to determine the messages, assumptions, and values they reveal. The main problem is to determine what impact the fear of communism had on postwar American popular culture. Your analysis of the culture of the Cold War should address the following questions:

Who was censoring the media? The government or independent groups?
Was this censorship effective?
—not individually, but collectively it was

1. **Did the Cold War narrow postwar popular culture?** How did it "distort and enfeeble" cultural expression, according to historian Stephen Whitfield? How did it undermine challenges to the status quo?

2. **Did the Cold War affect various forms of popular culture the same way?** Do the sources reveal that some types of popular expression were blander than others? Were some more susceptible to outside pressures? What clues do the sources offer about why?

3. **Is Whitfield's argument in Source 1 about the impact of anticommunism on postwar popular culture supported or contradicted by the primary sources?** Do the sources reflect a cultural consensus, or do they demonstrate a clash of discordant messages and resistance to dominant standards? Is popular culture an influential force in American society, or is it merely a commodity that is influenced by other developments?

Before you begin, read the section in your textbook about the Cold War, especially its impact on American society in the 1950s. It will provide background that will help you analyze this chapter's sources. What is its view about the Cold War's impact on cultural expression?

SECONDARY SOURCE

1

In this selection, Stephen Whitfield explores the impact of anticommunism on various forms of popular culture. Pay particular attention to his argument about the main messages conveyed by postwar popular culture. What is the most important evidence that anticommunist hysteria influenced popular culture? Are Whitfield's examples representative?

The Culture of the Cold War (1991)

STEPHEN J. WHITFIELD

In 1951, one of the prisoners in a New York jail awaiting sentencing under the Smith Act for conspiring to advocate the violent overthrow of the American government was George Charney. The chairman of the state's Communist party and a member of the national committee, he became acquainted with an Italian-American hoodlum named Bob Raymondi, who since his teens in Brooklyn had associated with Murder, Inc., and was a veteran of seventeen years as an inmate of Dannemora. While dominating the prison population,

Source: Whitfield, Stephen J., *The Culture of the Cold War,* pp. 1, 2, 10, 11, 12, 34, 35, 37, 53, 71, 127, 131, 132, 133, 144, 200, 201, 202, 203. © 1996 The Johns Hopkins University Press. Reprinted with permission of The Johns Hopkins University Press.

Raymondi also sought to compensate for his poor formal education by chatting with the Marxist-Leninists who had been inserted among the other prisoners. One Saturday, Raymondi's sister visited him and was startled to learn how close he had gotten with Charney and others convicted under the Smith Act. "My God, Bob," she warned. "You'll get into trouble."

In this era, a specter was haunting America—the specter of Communism. Trying to exorcise it were legislators and judges, union officials and movie studio bosses, policemen and generals, university presidents and corporation executives, clergymen and journalists, Republicans and Democrats, conservatives and liberals. The specter that, a century earlier, Marx and Engels had described as stalking the continent of Europe was extending itself to the United States. . . . By introducing ideological politics, Communism became more loathed than organized crime, exacerbating fears that were to distort and enfeeble American culture throughout the late 1940s and the 1950s. . . .

. . . Censors endorsed the boycott of films that they had not seen; vigilantes favored the removal from library shelves of books that they had not read.

The confusion of the public and private realms was also characteristic of the era. Thus, the Federal Bureau of Investigation compiled dossiers on novelists who seemed unduly critical of their native land, and the bureau got into the movie business by secretly filming the patrons of a left-wing bookstore, Four Continents, in New York. At the same time, some representatives of Hollywood presented themselves to Congress as authorities on the theory and tactics of Marxism-Leninism. An awed member of the House Committee on Un-American Activities (HUAC) hailed even the mother of musical star Ginger Rogers as "one of the outstanding experts on communism in the United States," for example. While legislators were interrogating musicians and actors about their beliefs, university administrators were using political instead of academic criteria to evaluate the fitness of teachers. Even as some clergymen were advocating ferocious military measures to defeat an enemy that was constantly described as "atheistic," government officials were themselves asserting that the fundamental problem presented by Communism was not political but spiritual. . . .

. . . [T]he effect was . . . the suffocation of liberty and the debasement of culture itself. Even by the narrowest chauvinistic criteria of the Cold War, the United States thus diminished its ability in the global struggle to be seen as an attractive and just society. The politicization of culture might win the allegiance of those who cherished authority, but not of those who valued autonomy. The politicization of culture might appeal to reactionaries abroad, but not to foreigners who appreciated creativity or critical thought.

And though the state was intimately involved in restricting liberty, it acted with popular approval and acquiescence; the will of the majority was not thwarted. In effect, Americans imposed a starchy repression upon themselves. . . .

. . . One response can be explored at the murkier edges of popular sensibility, the locale of novelist Mickey Spillane. . . .

On the top ten fictional bestsellers of the decade of the 1950s, Spillane wrote an astounding six of them: number three, *The Big Kill* (1951); number five, *My Gun Is Quick* (1950); number six, *One Lonely Night* (1951); number seven, *The Long Wait* (1951); number eight, *Vengeance Is Mine* (1950); and number nine, *Kiss Me, Deadly* (1952). This catalogue does not count his most popular novel, *I, the Jury,* which had been published prior to the decade. By 1953, the New American Library had sold seventeen million paperbacks of his first six novels, which meant that having Spillane on the firm's list of authors was like a license to print money.

I, the Jury (1947) introduced a private investigator named Mike Hammer, a World War II veteran of such magnanimity that he harbors no hostility toward Nazis. Though he chose not to become a cop because a "pansy" bureaucracy was emasculating policemen with its rules and regulations, his real contempt is reserved for the professional and intellectual classes, for homosexuals, and above all for swarthy criminals like "the Mafia. The stinking slimy Mafia. An oversized mob of ignorant, lunk-headed jerks who ruled with fear and got away with it because they had the money to back themselves up."

The detective's hairy-chested heroics would have made such novels enormously popular even if they had been devoid of any explicit politics, but the overt anti-Communism of Spillane's fiction engraved it with the signature of the period. Two decades earlier, Hammer might have combated only organized criminals spawned in the lower depths; two decades later, the adversaries would have been a cabal of Third World terrorists. In the early 1950s, however, the Red Scare required his special skills. For the comrades and conspirators in *One Lonely Night,* Hammer has reserved kicks that can shatter bone on impact, bursts of lead from his .45, and the sadistic pleasures of strangulation.

In that novel, which sold more than 3 million copies, the detective seduces a millionaire's estranged granddaughter, whom boredom has driven to Communism. At first Hammer cannot fathom why Ethel Brighton, despite her early exposure to the attractions of capitalism, can embrace the twisted creed of Bolshevism. He suspects that she needs only the substitute of *his* embrace. Confident that his virility can transform her politics, he has her spend one night in his apartment, and concludes, "Now that she had a taste of life[,] maybe she'd go out and seek some different company for a change." He is wrong— or at least seems to be, and realizes that Ethel Brighton has continued to associate with the scum and perverts who comprise the Communist movement. So he strips and whips her. Eventually Hammer poses as a member of the Soviet intelligence apparatus; since no one in this supposedly very clandestine organization thinks of challenging his credentials, he considers these conspirators as "dumb as horse manure." These malignant dreamers of world conquest "had a jackal look of discontent and cowardice." When they are not merely credulous cretins, they are either vicious hypocrites or else clinically insane. The supreme villain in *One Lonely Night* is Oscar Deamer, who is both a Communist and a psychopath. Hammer tells this master criminal, just before choking him to death: "You were a Commie, Oscar, because you were batty. It was the only philosophy that would appeal to your crazy mind. It justified everything you did and you saw a chance of getting back at the world." The explanation for the appeal of Communism is, apparently, insanity.

In destroying such motiveless, psychopathic malevolence, Hammer personifies the rejection of liberalism. The cure for the plague of Communism cannot be the diffusion of New Deal programs to relieve economic misery, or the extension of the Four Freedoms to amplify the meaning of an open society, or more resonant calls to lighten the burden of social injustice. The solution, the creator of Hammer seems to fantasize, is violent prophylaxis. After the detective has saved his naked fiancée from hysterical Bolshevik flagellants, he murders them all, ... "I killed more people tonight than I have fingers on my hands," he later boasts. "I shot them in cold blood and enjoyed every minute of it. . . . They were Commies. . . . They were red sons-of-bitches who should have died long ago. . . . They never thought that there were people like us in this country. They figured us all to be soft as horse manure and just as stupid." . . .

To appraise the literary significance of such fiction would be utterly irrelevant, to sermonize against such appalling crudeness equally pointless. What needs underscoring is that, at least in the night battles of the Cold War for which Spillane recruited more Americans than any other author, the procedural rules and legal guarantees that helped make a civil society worth defending were treated with savage contempt. Justice was imagined as coming from the barrel of a pistol, and cruelty was not confined to Party headquarters but was exalted in the exploits of Mike Hammer. Because of the official limitations under which formal authority chafed, vigilante ruthlessness was the only effective antidote to unmitigated evil. . . .

The search to define and affirm a way of life, the need to express and celebrate the meaning of "Americanism," was the flip side of stigmatizing Communism; to decipher the culture of the 1950s requires tracing the formulation of this national ideology. It was not invented but inherited, and some of its components were intensified under the political pressures of the era. The belief system that most middle-class Americans considered their birthright—the traditional commitment to competitive individualism in social life, to the liberal stress on rights in political life, and to private enterprise in economic life—was adapted to the crisis of the Cold War. . . .

. . . [By the 1950s] the bounties pouring forth from American factories and laboratories, made available in such profusion in stores and markets, had become perhaps the chief ideological prop—the most palpable vindication—of "the American way of life." Success and virtue were so easily equated that, after *Life* magazine published *The Old Man and the Sea* (1952), the industrialist who became Eisenhower's secretary of the treasury was puzzled by the popular fascination with Hemingway's story. "Why would anybody be interested in some old man who was a failure," George M. Humphrey wondered, "and never amounted to anything anyway?"

Such assumptions help account for Barbie (b. 1958), the most popular doll in history. With her own national fan club, she received five hundred letters a week. Eleven and one-half inches tall, this late adolescent was endowed with a three-and-one-quarter-inch bust that smashed an anatomical taboo in the toy market. But what made her something of an icon of the Cold War were the fantasies of consumption that she evoked. Barbie came cheap: three dollars. But her full wardrobe cost more than one hundred dollars, and her appetite for more was insatiable: party dresses and casual attire, prom gowns and eventually a wedding ensemble (her boyfriend's name was Ken), outdoor outfits, professional uniforms. Barbie lived in a split-level house, patronized a beauty parlor, drove a Corvette. She "seemed to be only a product," one scholar concluded, "but she turned out to be a way of life," an affirmation of national supremacy. The capitalist "fetishism of commodities" that Marx found so repellent had advanced to the first line of defense....

... The movie industry was conscripted into the Cold War in 1947 when HUAC was invited to Los Angeles. The committee's host was the Motion Picture Alliance for the Preservation of American Ideals, an organization that struck a typical postwar stance in asserting that "co-existence is a myth and neutrality is impossible ... anyone who is not FIGHTING Communism is HELPING Communism." About fifteen hundred members of the film community had founded the alliance three years earlier; they included John Wayne, Gary Cooper, Walt Disney, Adolphe Menjou, and Cecil B. De Mille. Its first president was director Sam Wood, who felt so strongly about the subject that his will imposed as a condition of inheritance that his relatives (other than his wife) file affidavits in court that they "are not now, nor have they ever been, Communists." ...

... [By the 1950s] it was safer to produce films without any political or economic themes or implications at all. Although *Broken Arrow* (1950) had presented Cochise sympathetically as a peace-loving Apache, Monogram Studios abandoned its plans for a movie on Hiawatha, whose efforts to achieve peace among the Iroquois nations might be interpreted as a boost to Communist peace propaganda. Because novelist Theodore Dreiser had formally converted to Communism shortly before his death in 1945, Paramount got the jitters in adapting his classic of a generation earlier, *An American Tragedy*. So director George Stevens toned down the social analysis and highlighted the romance in *A Place in the Sun* (1951). Stevens's protagonist (Montgomery Clift) is no longer a victim of certain class relationships that Dreiser had shown motivating Clyde Griffiths toward homicide. Then even the inflated love story posed a problem when supporting actress Anne Revere took the Fifth Amendment, so Paramount cut out most of her major scenes....

... [I]t was prudent to avoid overtly political films. Consider, for instance, the fate of Universal's *The Senator Was Indiscreet* (1947), a satire about a bumbling Senator (William Powell) who does not realize that a new income tax bill applies to him as well. He runs for the presidency on a platform that includes adding his relatives to the payroll and giving every citizen the right to attend Harvard. The movie also dares to suggest that White House aspirants can be packaged with images that can maximize their appeal to the electorate. *The Senator Was Indiscreet* was written by Charles MacArthur, was rewritten and produced by Nunnally Johnson, and was the only movie that George S. Kaufman ever directed. None of the three was a political activist. All were renowned for their wit, which was lost on Congresswoman Clare Boothe Luce (R-Conn.) when it was screened for her. "Was this picture made by an American?" she demanded to know. *Life,* which her husband published, retracted its own favorable review of the film in a column called "On Second Thought." Editorials in other forums, plus the American Legion, also attacked the un-American propaganda of *The Senator Was Indiscreet.* Having approved the script, the Motion Picture Association of America had somehow missed its incendiary implications, leaving the trade organization with only the option of prohibiting the showing of *The Senator Was Indiscreet* overseas, which it did.

Partly as a result, the few dozen political films that were released in the postwar era bristled with titles like *The Iron Curtain* (1948), *The Red Menace* (1949), *The Red Danube* (1949), *Red Snow* (1952), and *The Steel Fist* (1952). The election year of 1952 was the peak, when twelve explicitly anti-Communist films were produced. Though Elizabeth Taylor and Robert Taylor were featured in *Conspirator* (1950) and John Wayne glamorized HUAC in *Big Jim McLain,* very few of these movies had large budgets or major stars. They were shot on the cheap and usually ended up as the second features on double bills. Because strongly ideological films were considered unlikely to attract the masses anyway, the studios apparently reasoned that anti-Communist pictures might mollify the American Legion and right-wingers in Congress without losing too much money. And although Menjou had predicted to HUAC that such movies "would be an incredible success," the studios' apprehensions proved correct: most of them bombed at the box office.

How was domestic Communism depicted in the films of the Cold War? Its adherents show no respect for national sanctums and symbols, which Party members traduce. They treat the Stars and Stripes with contempt. They conspire to meet one another by carrying an edition of *Reader's Digest* or a TWA flight bag and by picking such agreeable settings as the Boston Public Garden amid the swan boats. Communists are rude, humorless, and "cruel to animals," Nora Sayre noticed. "But we don't know how they treat children, since they never have any." Women in the Party are either disturbingly unfeminine, downright unattractive, or nearly nymphomaniacs. Bereft of the experience of "normal" love, they use sex for political seduction. A Party target in Republic Pictures' *The Red Menace* tells a blonde *femme fatale:* "I always thought the Commies peddled bunk. I didn't know they came as cute as you." After the comely comrade lets the dupe kiss her, she teasingly withdraws, then gives him a copy of *Das Kapital. . . .*

. . . When one independent, left-wing film was produced in 1954, it was unclear what was more impressive—the fact that in so politically parched an atmosphere *Salt of the Earth* could be made at all, or the fact that it faced so many barriers imposed by those who believed that liberty was an ornament of American life.

The movie was based on a 1951–52 strike by Mexican-American zinc miners, who demanded better safety regulations as well as equal treatment with Anglo employees. The strike was conducted by the International Union of Mine, Mill, and Smelter Workers, which the CIO had expelled in 1950 because it was Communist-controlled. Since no Hollywood studio would have touched such a subject in the 1950s, *Salt of the Earth* was a venture of the blacklisted. Director Herbert Biberman was a member of the Hollywood Ten, scenarist Michael Wilson took the Fifth Amendment before HUAC in 1951, and producer Paul Jarrico had co-written *Song of Russia*. . . .

. . . The fragility of the left-wing popular culture that faced extinction during the Cold War was symbolized by an encounter in 1956 in a New Jersey hospital. Harold Leventhal, a Communist who once plugged songs for Irving Berlin, went to Greystone Park to visit one of the inmates. A psychiatrist rummaged through the files on his desk, then exclaimed: "Guthrie, Guthrie, ah, Guthrie! A very sick man. Very sick. Delusional! He says he has written more than a thousand songs! And a novel too. And he says he has made records for the Library of Congress." Leventhal's reply was terse: "He has." . . .

. . . Born in 1912, Woody Guthrie had proudly cultivated an ardent pro-Communism by the late 1930s and did not waver thereafter. . . . A drifter and a loner, Guthrie was even jailed and given a six-month sentence in 1948 for writing obscene letters to a Los Angeles woman. His drinking and self-destructive rages were awful preludes to the congenital disease called Huntington's chorea that would eventually deprive him of control of mind and body. The atrophy would gradually worsen until he would quiver into horrifying disintegration, his brain utterly depleted.

Guthrie was functioning well enough to attend a major concert held in New York in 1956 to honor his work. Over a thousand people filled Pythian Hall, and at the end of the program the entire cast sang "This Land Is Your Land." Guthrie sat in the balcony, and the audience cheered him when it too joined in "This Land Is Your Land." Within a few months of that consolidation of the political culture to which Guthrie had contributed for two decades, he was committed to Greystone Park, and five years later to Brooklyn State Hospital. One pilgrim who came east to visit the hospitalized Guthrie early in 1961 would quickly become his most dazzling successor, taking audiences far beyond the "progressive" confines within which Guthrie had operated. Bob Dylan idolized Guthrie, sang and dressed like him, concocted a similar past, and recorded a "Song to Woody" on his first album in 1962. Born in 1941, the University of Minnesota dropout was immune to Guthrie's pro-Soviet politics. But Dylan transmitted an outrage against social injustice and war in such early songs as "Blowin' in the Wind" and "A Hard Rain's Gonna

Fall" that outstripped the appeal of Guthrie's music a generation earlier, though the successor himself soon abandoned the leftist orientation to which Guthrie himself had been so faithful. . . .

In the 1950s, when dissent was too easily equated with disloyalty, the influence of such figures sharply diminished. As a result, talents were thwarted, creative possibilities were stifled, and the development of a more vital and various national culture was unrealized.

PRIMARY SOURCES

This section contains a variety of sources, from movie advertisements to popular songs, reflecting postwar popular culture. Together, the primary sources offer important clues about the impact of anticommunism on the popular culture of the period. All of them may not support the same conclusion.

Movie Advertising and the Anticommunist Hysteria

After Germany invaded the Soviet Union in 1941, Hollywood movie studios produced numerous pro-Soviet films. Warner Brothers' *Mission to Moscow* (1943), based on former United States Ambassador Joseph Davies' memoir, was a good example. In the movie, Davies (Walter Huston) tells Stalin, "I believe, sir, that history will record you as a great benefactor of mankind."[6] By 1947, the Soviet Union was no longer an ally in the battle against Nazism and the HUAC was investigating alleged communist subversion in Hollywood. Studios were under intense pressure to demonstrate their anticommunist credentials. One result was the blacklisting of actors and other studio personnel. Another was a stream of B-grade movies exposing the dangerous menace of communist subversion. Although never big hits at the box office, these films showed that Hollywood took seriously the growing fear of domestic subversion. As you examine material produced to market several of these movies, determine what messages they give. Think about their impact on the public. Are these movies evidence of Hollywood's influence, or of its vulnerability to outside influences?

2   In 1935, United Artists released the movie *Red Salute,* starring Barbara Stanwyck and Robert Young. When a rich college girl becomes too friendly with a campus radical, her father sends her off to Mexico. There she meets a handsome border patrolman. The all-American patrolman quickly wins the girl's heart and the young student radical is sent packing by the patrolman and the student body. In 1953, *Red Salute* was re-released under the title *Runaway Daughter.*

Advertisement for *Runaway Daughter* (1953)

Source: RKO Radio Pictures, Copyright © 1953. Reprinted in Michael Barson, *"Better Red Than Dead!"* (New York: Hyperion, 1992), no page.

3   In this movie from Columbia Pictures, the FBI battles a vast communist spy network in Boston, where spies hope to steal the results of "an extraordinary scientific experiment" involving a new computer. The movie opens with the narrator praising the FBI for "protecting" Americans and then shows FBI agents opening other people's mail.

Promotional Material for *Walk East on Beacon* (1952)

Source: Walk East on Beacon. Copyright © 1952, renewed 1980 RD.DR Corporation. All rights reserved. Courtesy of Columbia TriStar Motion Picture Group.

4   Mark Goodson was a producer of television game shows, including *What's My Line, I've Got a Secret, Password,* and *Family Feud.* Before he died in 1992, Goodson was the subject of an oral history, a tape-recorded interview designed to preserve an individual's experiences and to share them with a broader audience. What does this portion of Goodson's oral history reveal about the forces that made television particularly vulnerable to the communist hysteria?

A Game Show Producer Remembers the Red Scare (1995)

I'm not sure when it began, but I believe it was early 1950. At that point, I had no connection with the blacklisting that was going on, although I had heard

Source: Red Scare: Memories of the American Inquisition, An Oral History by Griffin Fariello. Copyright © 1995 by Griffin Fariello. Used by permission of W. W. Norton & Company, Inc.

about it in the motion picture business and heard rumors about things that had happened on other shows, like *The Aldrich Family.* My first experience really was when we settled into a fairly regular panel on *What's My Line?* in mid-1950. The panel consisted of the poet Louis Untermeyer, Dorothy Kilgallen, Arlene Francis, and Hal Block, a comedy writer. Our sponsor was Stopette, a deodorant.

A few months into the show, I began getting mail on [left-wing poet] Louis Untermeyer. He had been listed in *Red Channels.** He was one of those folks who had supported the left-wing forces against Franco in Spain. I know that he also had allowed his name to be affiliated with the Joint Anti-Fascist Refugee Committee and had been a sponsor of the 1948 May Day parade. Back in the early 1920s, he had written articles for *The Masses.* But he was certainly not an active political person, at least as far as I knew.

CBS and Stopette also began receiving letters of protest. First, it was just a few postcards. Then it grew. Members of the Catholic War Veterans put stickers on drugstore windows, red, white, and blue stickers, warning "Stop Stopette Until Stopette stops Untermeyer."

We didn't pay too much attention until we got the call from CBS. Untermeyer and I were summoned to Ralph Colin's office, who was the general counsel for CBS at the time. Louis and Colin knew each other. Ralph asked him why he lent his name to the group. "I thought it was a good cause," Untermeyer said. "Louis, you're being very naive. These are very difficult times and you've put us in a bad spot. We're going to have to drop you." Untermeyer was very apologetic, but the decision had been made. He was let go.

I remember leaving that office feeling embarrassed. Untermeyer was in his sixties, a man of considerable dignity. He was a good American poet and I liked him; he was funny and articulate on the show. What's more, I had no political ax to grind.

That was the last of that kind of meeting. Soon afterwards, CBS installed a clearance division. There wasn't any discussion. We would just get the word—"Drop that person"—and that was supposed to be it. Whenever we booked a guest or a panelist on *What's My Line?* or *I've Got a Secret,* one of our assistants would phone up and say, "We're going to use so-and-so." We'd either get the okay, or they'd call back and say, "Not clear," or "Sorry, can't use them." Even advertising agencies—big ones, like Young & Ribicam and BBD&O—had their own clearance departments. They would never come out and say it. They would just write off somebody by saying, "He's a bad actor." You were never supposed to tell the person what it was about; you'd just unbook them. They never admitted there was a blacklist. It just wasn't done.

*Red Channels: The Report of Communist Influence in Radio and Television was a private publication that listed names of people affiliated with communist "causes." After it appeared in June 1950, it quickly became known as "the Bible of Madison Avenue." Advertising agencies, the television networks, and sponsors used it to remove "subversives" from the airwaves.

Some fairly substantial names were off-limits—big stars like Leonard Bernstein, Harry Belafonte, Abe Burrows, Gypsy Rose Lee, Judy Holliday, Jack Gilford, Uta Hagen, and Hazel Scott. Everyone, from the stars to the bit-part actors, was checked. We once did a show in California called *The Rebel*, and we used wranglers to take care of the horses—we had to clear all of their names. CBS, in particular, asked for loyalty oaths to be signed by everybody, making sure that you were not un-American. So far as I know, no one ever refused.

In 1952, *I've Got a Secret* got a new sponsor, R. J. Reynolds Tobacco Company, with its advertising agency, William Este. When they came aboard, someone from the agency called me and said, "Please get rid of Henry Morgan," one of the regular panelists on the show. Morgan had been named in *Red Channels*. I had known Henry for a long time; he was one of those young curmudgeons who was acidic at times, but he was by no means a Communist. His wife was involved with radical politics, but they were getting a divorce, and to some extent his name was just smeared.

I went to the agency and told them that they were crazy to try and get rid of Henry Morgan. They agreed that the charge in *Red Channels* was absurd, but they said they couldn't take the risk. That was the main thing—mail accusing them of being pro-Communist was not going to sell cigarettes. They gave me an ultimatum: dump Morgan or face the show's cancellation.

So I went to Garry Moore, the MC of the show and an established comedian. He was a conservative, a Republican from Maryland. I know that he liked Morgan. I said that if he'd be willing to back me up, I'd tell the agency I'd do the show without a sponsor. He agreed without hesitation. I phoned up William Este and said, "We're not going to do the show without Henry." The people at the agency were flabbergasted. It was virtually unheard-of to have this kind of confrontation. They told me they'd think about it, and in the end, they actually backed down. The show was not canceled, and some weeks later Morgan's name simply vanished from *Red Channels*.

Morgan never even knew. When I wrote the article about my experience, Henry called me. "I did not know that I was about to be dropped," he said. "I knew I was in *Red Channels* and I was outraged about that, but I didn't know I was about to be dropped." It was a revelation for him.

The Morgan episode was my first act of resistance. It was not something my lawyers ever encouraged. The watchword in the business is "Don't make waves."

The studios and the advertising agencies didn't have to subscribe to *Red Channels*. It was one of about a dozen publications. There were several private lists, and the major agencies and networks exchanged lists, most of which had several names each. I'd help you out by giving you my list and you'd help me out by giving me your list. There was a big interchange of listings. A fellow called Danny O'Shea was in charge of the listings at CBS, an ex-FBI man. *Red Channels* would maybe have a couple of hundred names, but there might be on the other list at CBS several hundred more. Anybody could show up on a list, stars, technicians, cowboys.

5　　Arthur Miller, author of *Death of a Salesman* (1949), *The Crucible* (1953), and other plays, discusses anticommunist pressures on Broadway in this oral history. In 1956, Miller appeared before HUAC. Refusing to testify, he was convicted for contempt of Congress, a decision later overturned by a higher court. Note Miller's explanation for Broadway's relative immunity from the anticommunist hysteria. Do the previous sources reflect his point about the difference between Broadway, on the one hand, and Hollywood and the broadcasting industry, on the other?

A Playwright Recalls the Red Scare (1995)

I drew some attention when I became involved with the Conference for Peace at the Waldorf in 1949. That was a kind of crossroads, I guess, at the time: when the Russians were—in fact, up to that moment almost—our allies and then suddenly they were turned into our enemy, and that conference was very important from that point of view.

At the time I was not working in films or for any broadcasting companies, or advertisers, so the effect on me was more obscure. It was simply that I would be attacked in the press from time to time. But I had no job to lose, so it was quite a bit different than it was for a lot of other writers who had either actual jobs that they would be thrown out of, or contracts with publishers that would have been affected. I didn't have anything like that, and obviously the Broadway situation was quite different, because we didn't have any big corporations investing in Broadway, there were just a lot of small investors who threw in their money to put a play on. So they were not so easily tampered with as the big companies were in Hollywood or the broadcasting industry. They could maintain more independence.

They had blacklists of writers, and as it later turned out, practically every American writer was on it. But not all of them were out front the way I found myself, because they weren't putting plays on, especially not in the Middle West. So the impact was greater on me than it would have been on, let's say, Steinbeck or somebody else.

We had a road company of *Death of a Salesman* in the Middle West that we finally had to close down. The American Legion especially, and I think the Catholic War Veterans, picketed it so heavily everywhere that people were

Source: Red Scare: Memories of the American Inquisition, An Oral History by Griffin Fariello. Copyright © 1995 by Griffin Fariello. Used by permission of W. W. Norton & Company, Inc.

intimidated and they didn't come. So there wasn't much business. They were attacking the play and me as being an anti-American.

Death of a Salesman questioned the ethos of the business civilization, which the play intimates has no real respect for individual human beings, whereas the going mythology was quite the opposite: in that nobody of any competence ever fails and that everything was pretty sound and terrific for everybody. So to put a play on where somebody who believes in the system, as Willy Loman does to his dying minute, ends up a suicide, it was rather a shock.

In fact, when they made the film they made Willy appear crazy. That was the whole drift of the film; that's why it was such a bad film in my opinion. They made him into a lunatic, and consequently you could observe him with the same distance you observe any crazy person, you don't really identify with him. In my opinion that was to make the play politically more palatable, but there were other artistic problems with that production which I disagreed with, but certainly this was the major one.

Columbia Studios actually made a short, cost them a couple of hundred thousand dollars, which they wanted to run before each showing of the film in the movie theaters. The short was shot at City College in New York City and was basically a very boring set of lectures by business administration professors who made it clear that Willy Loman represented nobody and that the play was really quite absurd and that the system was altogether different than as it was portrayed in the play and that the salesman's job was one of the best imaginable careers that a person could have and indeed that the system was based on salesmanship. When they got finished with this kind of analysis you wondered why they had produced the play at all as a film. I managed to make an empty threat that I would sue them if they did this, but in fact I think they themselves saw that the absurdity of the whole thing was even too much for them. They may have shown it, somebody told me that he had seen it once in some theater, but I don't think it was very widespread.

---

6   Lee Hayes and Pete Seeger were leaders in People's Artists, a left-wing music organization founded in 1949. People's Artists emphasized peace, civil rights, and the protection of civil liberties. From the beginning, its messages were not well received. Vigilantes in Peekskill, New York, broke up the organization's first concert. When it was rescheduled, mobs stoned the cars of concert-goers and more than 150 people were hospitalized. In 1950, People's Artists began publishing *Sing Out!*, a song magazine that helped to promote the folk music revival early in the decade. Its title was taken from *The Hammer Song,* which was featured on the cover of the first issue. After the magazine's release, one subscriber cancelled his subscription, protesting that "all you left out of that song was the sickle."[7] In the early 1960s, however, folk trio Peter, Paul, and Mary would turn *If I Had a Hammer* into a huge hit record. What does this song and its history say about the relationship between the Cold War and cultural expression?

The Hammer Song (1949)

LEE HAYES AND PETE SEEGER

Source: Copyright © Sing Out Corporation, reprinted with permission.

7 Ronnie Gilbert was the only female member of The Weavers, a popular folk music quartet whose hit *Goodnight Irene* sold two million records in the early 1950s. As you read this excerpt from Gilbert's oral history, note what effect the anticommunist crusade had on the group. Was popular music more or less susceptible to blacklisting than Hollywood, television, or Broadway?

A Folk Singer Remembers the Early 'Fifties (1995)

My interest in the Weavers was political as well as musical. We sang for unions. We sang for the Henry Wallace campaign.* I was all of eighteen or nineteen at the time. My background was political. My mother was a rank-and-file unionist, belonged to the International Ladies Garment Workers Union, and she was a singer. She taught me all the songs. So I come from a very proud, political union background. That was part of my nature and my life, you know. I still sing political songs. There's a different style and shape, I'm not so much a "folksinger" as I was then. I sing a wide variety of musical styles. But the lyrics that attract me are lyrics about something.

We incubated most of our material at the Village Vanguard. We were there for six months. It was a small club in New York that did all kinds of stuff, radical stuff, nonradical stuff, jazz. . . .

We sang everything that we sang later on. But we were very aware that we were entertainers. We would never even think of singing a song that wasn't good fun to do. Sure, we sang Spanish Civil War songs, one or two of them, 'cause they were musically exciting. And we would refer to them and say that this was a song that was written during the Spanish Civil War, and that perhaps if Hitler had been turned back during that war, we would never have had World War Two. We said really "subversive" things like that. And every now and then we'd sing something that related to a union. Very subversive, you know. You bet, that's the kind of thing we did. But when we appeared on television, we knew that we were singing for a very broad audience that wouldn't sit still for the explanation of a song. The song had to be directly of interest to them, and we sang what we thought was best in American folk music, and that was what we represented.

The Weavers were headline-makers. We were the hottest thing to come along in a long time in the music industry. . . . Had we not made "Goodnight Irene," had we not become hot performing artists, it's very possible that we would never have been caught up in the blacklist, because we wouldn't have been worth anything to anybody.

I mean, why are entertainers picked up in a blacklist like that? 'Cause they made headlines for the committee. The headlines you see in these old movies from the thirties—the Criminal or the Hunted Person comes into a hotel lobby, and everybody's reading the papers: "So-and-So Wanted," you know? Well, that actually happened to us. We were playing a nightclub engagement in Springfield, Illinois. And we came into the hotel lobby, and there were

*FDR's vice president and Progressive Party candidate for president in 1948.

Source: *Red Scare: Memories of the American Inquisition, An Oral History* by Griffin Fariello. Copyright © 1995 by Griffin Fariello. Used by permission of W. W. Norton & Company, Inc.

people reading the newspaper, and it said "Weavers Named Reds!" [Laughs.] And there we were! . . .

We were being followed all the time. I remember walking down the street in some place in Ohio, it might have been Akron, with these two guys following us behind. I was terrified. By that time it was very scary, because it involved groups like the American Legion, the Catholic War Veterans, and a very patriotic kind of macho. I was present at Peekskill, at the Paul Robeson concert, where people were badly injured by rock-throwing goons, with the police standing by doing absolutely nothing. So I knew that kind of thing could happen very easily. These guys followed us a long ways. I stopped and turned around and confronted them. One of them seemed very surprised, and he said, "Well, do you want your subpoena here, or in the club, while you're performing?" I said, "I'll take it now!" [Laughs.] . . .

I never did get subpoenaed again. Very quickly our work came down to nothing, there was no work to be had. We stuck together as long as we possibly could, and then it was pointless. Decca was not going to do any more recording. Decca was in the red when we recorded for them and we pulled them right out. It didn't help. It didn't make them loyal to us. [Laughs.] The music industry is the music industry. The Weavers were merchandise. Our songs were merchandise, just the way people are now.

| 8 | In his popular animal comic strip, Walt Kelly often targeted political figures. In the strip below, Kelly introduces a lynx named Simple J. Malarkey, who bears a striking resemblance to Joseph McCarthy. |

Malarkey takes over the Okefenokke Swamp's Bird Watching Club. Note Kelly's message about Malarkey's methods. Why was Kelly able to get away with such criticism while other popular artists and entertainers were not?

Pogo (1952)

WALT KELLY

Source: Copyright © Estate of Walt Kelly. Reprinted with Permission. From *The Pogo Papers,* 1952.

9   Jack Kerouac was a college dropout and leading figure in the Beats, a movement of poets and writers that rejected both literary and middle-class conventions. *On the Road,* which sold a half million copies, was Kerouac's semi-autobiographical novel about the travels of Sal Paradise and Dean Moriarty, characters based on Kerouac and fellow Beat Neil Cassady. Accompanied by plenty of sex and drug and alcohol use, their spontaneous trips around the country reflected a distinct lack of purpose. Is there a political message in Kerouac's work or does its message reside in its very lack of political content? Does this excerpt from *On the Road* provide evidence of the constriction of popular culture in the 1950s?

On the Road (1957)

JACK KEROUAC

It was drizzling and mysterious at the beginning of our journey. I could see that it was all going to be one big saga of the mist. "Whooee!" yelled Dean. "Here we go!" And he hunched over the wheel and gunned her; he was back in his element, everybody could see that. We were all delighted, we all realized we were leaving confusion and nonsense behind and performing our one and noble function of the time, *move.* And we moved! We flashed past the mysterious white signs in the night somewhere in New Jersey that say SOUTH (with an arrow) and WEST (with an arrow) and took the south one. New Orleans! It burned in our brains. From the dirty snows of "frosty fagtown New York," as Dean called it, all the way to the greeneries and river smells of old New Orleans at the washed-out bottom of America; then west. Ed was in the back seat; Marylou and Dean and I sat in front and had the warmest talk about the goodness and joy of life. Dean suddenly became tender. "Now dammit, look here, all of you, we all must admit that everything is fine and there's no need in the world to worry, and in fact we should realize what it would mean to us to UNDERSTAND that we're not REALLY worried about ANYTHING. Am I right?" We all agreed. "Here we go, we're all together . . . What did we do in New York? Let's forgive." We all had our spats back there. "That's behind us, merely by miles and inclinations. Now we're heading down to New Orleans to dig Old Bull Lee and ain't that going to be kicks and listen will you to this old tenorman blow his top"—he shot up the radio volume till the car shuddered—"and listen to him tell the story and put down true relaxation and knowledge." . . .

We arrived in Washington at dawn. It was the day of Harry Truman's inauguration for his second term. Great displays of war might were lined along Pennsylvania Avenue as we rolled by in our battered boat. There were B-29s,

PT boats, artillery, all kinds of war material that looked murderous in the snowy grass; the last thing was a regular small ordinary lifeboat that looked pitiful and foolish. Dean slowed down to took at it. He kept shaking his head in awe. "What are these people up to? Harry's sleeping somewhere in this town. . . . Good old Harry. . . . Man from Missouri, as I am. . . . That must be his own boat."

Dean went to sleep in the back seat and Dunkel drove. We gave him specific instructions to take it easy. No sooner were we snoring than he gunned the car up to eighty, bad bearings and all, and not only that but he made a triple pass at a spot where a cop was arguing with a motorist—he was in the fourth lane of a four-lane highway, going the wrong way. Naturally the cop took after us with his siren whining. We were stopped. He told us to follow him to the station house. There was a mean cop in there who took an immediate dislike to Dean; he could smell jail all over him. He sent his cohort outdoors to question Marylou and me privately. They wanted to know how old Marylou was, they were trying to whip up a Mann Act* idea. But she had her marriage certificate. Then they took me aside alone and wanted to know who was sleeping with Marylou. "Her husband," I said quite simply. They were curious. Something was fishy. They tried some amateur Sherlocking by asking the same questions twice, expecting us to make a slip. I said, "Those two fellows are going back to work on the railroad in California, this is the short one's wife, and I'm a friend on a two-week vacation from college."

The cop smiled and said, "Yeah? Is this really your own wallet?"

Finally the mean one inside fined Dean twenty-five dollars. We told them we only had forty to go all the way to the Coast; they said that made no difference to them. When Dean protested, the mean cop threatened to take him back to Pennsylvania and slap a special charge on him.

"What charge?"

"Never mind what charge. Don't worry about *that*, wise guy."

We had to give them the twenty-five. But first Ed Dunkel, that culprit, offered to go to jail. Dean considered it. The cop was infuriated; he said, "If you let your partner go to jail I'm taking you back to Pennsylvania right now. You hear that?" All we wanted to do was go. "Another speeding ticket in Virginia and you lose your car," said the mean cop as a parting volley. Dean was red in the face. We drove off silently. It was just like an invitation to steal to take our trip-money away from us. They knew we were broke and had no relatives on the road or to wire to for money. The American police are involved in psychological warfare against those Americans who don't frighten them with imposing papers and threats. It's a Victorian police force; it peers out of musty windows and wants to inquire about everything, and can make crimes if the crimes don't exist to its satisfaction.

---

*The Mann Act, passed in 1910, prohibited the transportation of women across state lines for immoral purposes.

CONCLUSION

Before historians can judge the importance of historical developments, they need to determine their influence. As this chapter makes clear, to do that they must often examine a wide variety of historical artifacts and evidence. Thus, to understand the impact of anticommunist hysteria on American popular culture after World War II, historians must consider everything from images in comic books to trends in popular music. Indeed, one of the biggest challenges confronting historians is to make sense of such seemingly unrelated evidence. To do this, they must synthesize, or combine various parts into a whole. Historical synthesis, in turn, depends on skills emphasized in earlier chapters: the ability to evaluate evidence carefully, to detect causal influences, to understand the role of ideology in history, and to examine the past from many perspectives. In the case of the postwar period, this ability to synthesize allows us to reconstruct what one historian called the "mentality of the fifties" and to understand its impact on American society. This skill, however, can be applied to any historical problem. As we shall see in the next chapter on the civil rights movement, for instance, historians must often reconstruct events primarily from the memories of individuals who took part in them. As we shall also see, synthesizing such evidence into a coherent and meaningful story often leads to new insights into the past.

FURTHER READING

David Caute, *The Great Fear: The Anti-Communist Purge Under Truman and Eisenhower* (New York: Simon and Schuster, 1978).

Griffin Fariello, *Red Scare: Memories of the American Inquisition: An Oral History* (New York: W. W. Norton and Company, 1995).

Cyndy Hendershot, *Anti-Communism and Popular Culture in Mid-Century America* (Jefferson, N.C.: McFarland and Company, Inc., 2003).

Richard Pells, *The Liberal Mind in a Conservative Age: American Intellectuals in the 1940s and 1950s* (New York: Harper and Row, 1985).

Edward Pessen, *Losing Our Souls: The American Experience in the Cold War* (Chicago: Ivan R. Dee, 1993).

Nora Sayre, *Running Time: Films of the Cold War* (New York: Dial Press, 1982).

NOTES

1. Quoted in David Caute, *The Great Fear: The Anti-Communist Purge Under Truman and Eisenhower* (New York: Simon and Schuster, 1978), p. 493.

2. Quoted in Griffin Fariello, *Red Scare: Memories of the American Inquisition: An Oral History* (New York: W. W. Norton, 1995), p. 263.
3. Dwight Macdonald, *Against the American Grain: Essays on the Effects of Mass Culture* (New York: Vintage Books, 1952), p. 4.
4. Quoted in Elaine Tyler May, *Homeward Bound: American Families in the Cold War Era* (New York: Basic Books, 1988), p. 16.
5. Quoted in Peter Biskind, *Seeing Is Believing: How Hollywood Taught Us to Stop Worrying and Love the Fifties* (New York: Pantheon Books, 1983), p. 6.
6. Quoted in Nora Sayre, *Running Time: Films of the Cold War* (New York: Dial Press, 1982), p. 61.
7. Peter Seeger Oral History in Griffin Fariello, *Red Scare: Memories of the American Inquisition: An Oral History* (New York: W. W. Norton, 1995), p. 364.
8. Quoted in Arnold Shaw, *The Rockin' '50s* (New York: Hawthorn Books, 1974), p. 146.

Chapter
10
History and Popular Memory: The Civil Rights Movement

The documents in this chapter relate to civil rights activity in Mississippi in the early 1960s and provide perspective on contemporary popular images of the civil rights movement.

Secondary Source

Primary Sources

*O*n August 28, 1963, Martin Luther King, Jr., approached the podium on the steps of the Lincoln Memorial. Before him lay a vast human sea. Perhaps a quarter of a million people, mostly black, sprawled around the Capitol Mall's reflecting pool. The massive assembly had gathered to pressure Congress into passing a civil rights bill that President John Kennedy had proposed earlier that summer. By now, their march on Washington had become, in the words of its organizer A. Philip Randolph, "the largest demonstration in the history of the nation."[1] As he stepped to the microphone, even King was amazed at the size of the crowd.

The civil rights leader was determined not to give Congress any excuse for not passing Kennedy's bill. Thus, his speech was designed to move the throng without sparking civil unrest. He also wanted it to be short, a "sort of Gettysburg Address." Both summoning and echoing Lincoln, King began: "Five score years ago, a great American, in whose symbolic shadows we stand today, signed the Emancipation Proclamation."[2] Like Lincoln's famous battlefield address a hundred years before, King's speech was carefully crafted, but hardly moved his audience. Then the voice of gospel singer Mahalia Jackson called out from behind him: "Tell them about your dream, Martin! Tell them about your dream!"[3] King began again, this time extemporaneously. When he was finished, he had shared his dream for America with his listeners and had given the nation another Gettysburg Address.

King's delivery of his "I Have a Dream" speech remains nearly four decades later one of the most vivid images to emerge from the 1960s. It has become emblematic not only of the march on Washington in 1963, but of the civil rights movement itself. Just as this protest in the summer of 1963 is today associated in the public mind with one man, so increasingly is the entire movement of which King and the Washington march were a part. Yet, as King's popular image has sharpened, other images surrounding the fight for black equality in the 1950s and 1960s have dulled. In other words, the popular memory of the struggle for civil rights has become highly selective. In this chapter, therefore, we examine the struggle for civil rights, how it is remembered today, and the accuracy of our collective memories about it.

SETTING

As the civil rights movement recedes into the past, public interest in it grows. Today, Martin Luther King Day provides Americans an annual reminder about the black fight for equality. Responding to rising popular interest, Hollywood has produced several hit movies in the last two decades about the black struggle in the 1960s. Meanwhile, students of the civil rights movement have written numerous academic and popular accounts since the late 1960s. Historians' views regarding the movement have not remained static, though, and many of them now question the contemporary popular views of it.

In the last three decades or so, most popular and many scholarly examinations of the civil rights movement have focused mainly on its leaders, especially Martin Luther King, Jr. In these accounts, the movement's main goal was to secure federal action in the area of civil rights and the primary initiative for black rights came from a few men—civil rights leaders and, sometimes, even white politicians. It was directed, furthermore, by the leaders of such national organizations as the National Association for the Advancement of Colored People (NAACP), the Congress of Racial Equality (CORE), and the Southern Christian Leadership Conference (SCLC), a view supported by the prominent role that these groups played in some important events in the struggle for black rights. Since its founding by W. E. B. Du Bois and others in 1909, the NAACP had engaged in a long series of legal battles against racial discrimination, including the one that led to the landmark public school desegregation ruling in *Brown* v. *Board of Education* in 1954. Founded in 1942, CORE began a battle for integration during World War II using nonviolent protests to desegregate public facilities. By 1962, the Chicago-based organization had launched the Freedom Rides, during which black and white riders attempting to desegregate the South's interstate bus systems were met with mob violence. The SCLC, founded by King and other black activists in the wake of the Montgomery bus boycott of 1956, had deep roots in Southern black churches. By the early 1960s, the Atlanta-based and King-led organization was engaged with other groups in nonviolent direct action to promote desegregation, most noticeably in Albany, Georgia, in 1961 and 1962 and in Birmingham, Alabama, in 1963.

Prominent though these groups were in a number of civil rights battles, some historians in the 1980s began to challenge the view that the movement could be understood primarily as the work of a few national organizations or their leaders. Without denying the important—even heroic—role played by King, they criticized accounts of the civil rights movement that presented him as its creator and leader. They also charged that these accounts too often concentrated on such big events as the Montgomery bus boycott, the Birmingham marches, and the march on Washington, and thus overlooked the deep roots of the movement in the community-organizing efforts of determined activists as early as the 1930s. In fact, historians' complaints often echoed those voiced by many former civil rights activists, who charged that a complex and multifaceted struggle was frequently oversimplified and distorted in history books and in the news media. As a result, they said, the concerns and contributions of thousands of men and women who participated in the black struggle were ignored. Some critics were especially disturbed by popular accounts that portrayed the federal government—even the Federal Bureau of Investigation—as collaborators of the movement, as did *Mississippi Burning,* the 1989 movie about the murder of three civil rights workers in 1964. As one civil rights activist (and wife of another) expressed it in 1988, "I have three children, and I have read interpretations that make me cry, to think that my boys would be left with such ridiculous explanations of what their mother and father were doing in those days . . . ."[4]

Sharing these concerns, some scholars began to take a closer look at the civil rights movement at the local level. The leaders of national civil rights organizations, they concluded, did not initiate some of the well-publicized demonstrations—or countless other protests in communities throughout the South. Nor did King and other leaders control the men and women who *did*. Rather, there was frequent tension between local and national leaders over tactics, goals, and ideology. Local leaders were not that interested in launching protests to gain national attention and spur the passage of civil rights legislation in Congress. Instead, they were often more concerned with empowering blacks in their own communities, building local institutions, and—in the words of historian Clayborne Carson—creating "new social identities for participants and for all Afro-Americans."[5] In fact, as they studied these local struggles, some scholars began to question the appropriateness of the very term "civil rights movement" to describe these broader goals. More accurate, suggested Carson, is the term "black freedom struggle."[6]

Increased interest in the local roots of the civil rights struggle naturally led historians to look more closely at such organizations as the Student Nonviolent Coordinating Committee (SNCC—pronounced "Snick"), which launched numerous grassroots organizing efforts across the South in the early 1960s. Founded by students who sat in the "whites only" sections of North Carolina lunch counters and waited to be assaulted and arrested, SNCC quickly moved from sit-ins to a broad challenge to the racial status quo. It is perhaps best known for its efforts to register black voters in Mississippi. There, SNCC activists worked with CORE and the NAACP to set up the Council of Federated Organizations (COFO) in 1962 to engage in a Voter Education Project. The COFO had registered more than a half million black voters in the South by 1964, but it had made little headway in Mississippi, where fewer than 4,000 voters had been registered and SNCC organizers had become the victims of vigilante and police attacks. Attempting to turn the tide in 1964, SNCC launched the Mississippi Freedom Summer Project, which brought nine hundred college students into the state. The students assisted with voter registration and enlisted support for the Mississippi Freedom Democratic Party, established to challenge the state's white Democratic party. By one tally, Freedom Summer was marked by a thousand arrests, thirty bombings, eighty beatings, and at least six murders of civil rights workers, including those of COFO local organizers Michael Schwerner and James Chaney and summer volunteer James Goodman. By that fall, about 17,000 blacks had filled out registration forms, but only 1,600 had been allowed to register. Nonetheless, the involvement of affluent white college students in Freedom Summer had focused national attention on conditions in Mississippi. By then, SNCC's efforts in Mississippi had brought other changes as well. Listening to the people involved in them, many historians argue, provides a different view of the civil rights struggle than traditionally presented in history books—or on Martin Luther King Day.

INVESTIGATION

Because the postwar black struggle for civil rights spanned many years, encompassed a variety of concerns, and involved numerous organizations and literally hundreds of thousands of participants, it is not surprising that scholars' assessments of it differ. Nor is it surprising that they have often looked primarily at Martin Luther King, Jr., and other leaders who operated on a broad stage and eventually captured national attention. This chapter, however, focuses on lesser-known participants operating in a narrower place and time—Mississippi in the early 1960s. More specifically, it considers the activities of the Student Nonviolent Coordinating Committee and its efforts to register voters and mobilize blacks in other ways. Much of the history presented here is based on the recollections of individuals who helped to make it. As you evaluate these sources, keep in mind that historians must treat such first-hand accounts with the same care that they exercise with any historical evidence. As we saw in earlier chapters, primary sources often reflect the biases or point of view of those who created them. Furthermore, many of these sources are recollections of events years after they occurred, and, as we all know, time often changes our perspective on events. Nonetheless, the participants in the civil rights movement have valuable experiences and memories that can help us evaluate *popular* memories of it. Your main job, then, is twofold. You must first determine what a grassroots view reveals about the origins of the civil rights struggle, its goals, and impact. Then you can assess the concerns raised by one historian about Americans' collective memories about it. Addressing the following questions will assist your investigation:

1. **According to historian Charles Payne in Source 1, how have many popular and scholarly accounts distorted our understanding of the civil rights movement?** According to Payne, how does an understanding of grassroots civil rights organizing efforts in Mississippi offer a more accurate view of the movement than focusing on such leaders as Martin Luther King, Jr.?

2. **What do Payne's essay and the primary sources reveal about the goals of the civil rights movement?** To what extent were the goals of those involved in the civil rights organizing efforts in Mississippi in the early 1960s achieved?

3. **What do these sources reveal about the most important obstacles confronting the civil rights movement?** What do they reveal about the divisions within it?

4. **How does a "bottom-up" approach offer a different view of the black struggle from one that focuses on the movement's leaders?** How did the sources in this chapter alter *your* views about the civil rights movement?

Before you begin, read your textbook's discussion of the civil rights movement. Pay particular attention to its treatment of Martin Luther King, Jr., and other leaders of the movement. Note what it says about the Student Nonviolent Coordinating Committee and about grassroots organizing of blacks in the South. In your textbook's account, does the impetus for the civil rights struggle come from above or below, that is, from leaders of civil rights organizations or from the efforts of many less prominent African Americans to change the racial status quo?

SECONDARY SOURCE

1   In this selection, historian Charles Payne examines the organizing efforts of SNCC activists who participated in the Council of Federated Organizations' Voter Education Project in Mississippi, which began in 1962. This excerpt from his study of SNCC's grassroots organizing in Mississippi focuses on the work that led up to Freedom Summer in 1964 and some of the accomplishments of the organizers there. In it, Payne discusses the activities of such COFO organizers as SNCC's Robert Moses, a Harvard University graduate student and director of the Voter Education Project, Dave Dennis of CORE, who served as Moses's assistant, and COFO president Aaron Henry of the Mississippi NAACP. Payne's account also includes many other people: SNCC staff member Fannie Lou Hamer, a sharecropper's daughter who had been shot at and beaten for her attempts to register to vote; Ella Jo Baker, a founder of SNCC and organizer of the North Carolina student sit-ins in 1960; and other less prominent SNCC workers. As you read this discussion, determine what Payne sees as the most important effects—and lessons—of the SNCC/COFO Mississippi organizing activity. What role do Martin Luther King, Jr., and other civil rights leaders play in these efforts? What are the main goals of the Mississippi organizers? What accounts for the distortions in the popular and media accounts of the civil rights movement, according to Payne?

I've Got the Light of Freedom (1995)
CHARLES M. PAYNE

As late as 1960, fewer than two percent of Mississippi's Black adults were registered to vote. During the early summer of 1962, a handful of youthful organizers fanned out across the state to stimulate voter-registration drives. Seldom more than two or three to a county at first, they went into towns that few Americans had ever heard of—Greenwood, Hattiesburg, Holly Springs, Ruleville, Greenville. The organizers represented a coalition of civil rights groups, but most owed their primary allegiance to the Student Nonviolent Coordinating Committee, . . . the organization that had, under the watchful eye of Ella Baker, grown out of the sit-ins of 1960.

Wherever they were sent, the civil rights activists found that their initial reception by local Blacks was less than enthusiastic. The movement was generally dismissed as "dat mess." Reprisals were virtually certain. Those who were even thought to be interested in the movement might lose their jobs. Those who did join could expect to be shot at and to have their churches bombed and their homes targeted by arsonists. People who were able to survive the winter months only because of surplus commodities from the federal government could expect to lose them. Farmers who needed loans to get their crops started in the spring could expect their credit to be withdrawn. People who needed medical care could expect it to be refused. As one white landowner said, with completely unintended irony, to a Black family as he kicked them off his land, "Your food, your work and your very lives depend on good-hearted white people."

Nonetheless, a significant number of the Black residents in towns across the state eventually chose to cast their lot with the movement. The first organizers to come to Greenwood, near the heart of the Mississippi Delta, had to sleep catch-as catch can. Within a year, the level of movement activity was sufficient to bring the normal functioning of the city to a virtual standstill. Within two years, Black Greenwood was so much behind the movement that it could have slept a small army of civil rights workers (and did). It was one of the decade's earliest successful campaigns in the rural South. . . .

. . . The forty-one workers [of the Mississippi field staff] comprised about one-third of the total SNCC staff in the Deep South. Thirty-five of them were Black. Two of the six whites and twenty-five of the Blacks came from the Deep South. The white youngsters and most of the northern Blacks came from middle-class homes; their fathers were ministers or teachers or civil-service workers. All of the southern workers came from homes where the mothers had been maids or domestic workers, and most of the fathers had been farmers, factory workers, truck drivers, and construction workers. The ages ran from fifteen to over fifty, but most were in their late teens or early twenties. The staff, then, was mostly Black, mostly southern, mostly from working-class backgrounds. . . .

. . . By July [1963], thirteen hundred county residents had attempted to register, unsuccessfully, of course, in all but a few cases. COFO found an alternative way of encouraging political participation. Some volunteer law students found a Reconstruction era law that allowed unregistered citizens to vote provided they submitted an affidavit asserting they were qualified to vote. On that basis, COFO decided to participate in the gubernatorial primary scheduled for August 6.

The idea was to encourage as many people as possible to vote by affidavit. COFO people would serve as poll watchers. People reluctant to go to the polls could cast a freedom ballot that would be collected and disposed of by COFO. For six weeks, they explained the idea through canvassing and mass meetings, teaching people to prepare sample affidavits, how to find polling places, and the like. Response was good. During the week before the primary mass meetings were held nightly with an average attendance of two hundred. . . .

The night of the election, SCLC's Andy Young and SNCC chairman John Lewis spoke at [a] mass meeting that reflected the celebratory air of the day. "Difficult to capture," SNCC's Mike Miller wrote, "is the mood of the day—the air of jubilation at going to vote, and the infusion of this spirit in the Greenwood staff." . . .

. . . Encouraged by the participation in the primary, COFO decided to take part in the election that fall by holding its own registration and running its own candidates. The Freedom Vote was intended, first, to show that the masses of Negroes did in fact want to vote. (Polls at the time showed that forty percent of white southerners did not think Negroes really wanted to vote.) Second, it was intended to mock the legitimacy of the regular election by making the point that the candidates elected did not represent hundreds of thousands of Negroes. Aaron Henry ran for governor, with Ed King, a white native Mississippian and chaplain at Tougaloo, as his running mate. If Henry had suffered less than other leaders from repression in the 1950s, he made up for it in the sixties. He was arrested for leading a boycott of Clarksdale stores, his wife lost her job, he was arrested on allegations of child molestation, his home had been either firebombed or hit by lightning, and in July 1963 he spent a week on the chain gang, for parading without a permit.

Those who were registered—fewer than twenty-five thousand Negroes statewide—were encouraged to vote in the regular election and write in the names of the Freedom candidates. Everyone else was encouraged to vote in COFO's mock election, allowing them to register their opinions without exposing themselves to much danger.

There was nothing mock about the way COFO approached the election. They set up an elaborate statewide campaign organization, took out newspaper and television ads, and held rallies across the state. By October, Aaron Henry was making a speech a night. In mid-month, the campaign received some extra manpower. Eighty to ninety college students recruited by Allard Lowenstein from Stanford and Yale took two weeks off to help with the campaign. . . .

The vote was a great success across the state. Perhaps eighty thousand Freedom ballots were cast in COFO's first statewide organizing campaign, less than half of what COFO had hoped for but enough to make the point. National media coverage was considerable, due in no small part to the media's considerable interest in the white students from Yale and Stanford. Given that, why not bring an even larger number of students into the state for the following summer? The idea was first fully broached at a meeting in Greenville in November 1963. More media attention could lead to a greater degree of protection for civil rights workers. Most COFO staff . . . opposed the idea. Even before the idea was raised, there had been some discomfort among veteran staff about the slowly growing role of whites in the movement. It contradicted the principle of developing organizers where they found them. Given their education, whites coming into the movement were going to gravitate to leadership positions, supplanting local people, who were beginning to take on more leadership responsibility. If lives were at risk, it was largely the lives of COFO organizers, and most COFO staff preferred continuing running that risk to risking the long-term viability of their community-building efforts. Tactical issues aside, there were some who just plain didn't want to be bothered with a bunch of white folks on a daily basis. For that matter, the idea of bringing in outsiders, had that been Black staff from the Atlanta office, didn't sit well with some veteran staff members, mostly southern Blacks, who had done the most and risked the most to build a viable movement.

Bob Moses, Lawrence Guyot, Mrs. [Fannie Lou] Hamer, and CORE's Dave Dennis were among the proponents. Mrs. Hamer told opponents, "If we're trying to break down segregation, we can't segregate ourselves." Other proponents saw real risks in the idea but thought that the potential benefits outweighed them and that some way had to be found to offer some protection to the local people with whom they were working. Older local leaders were generally very much in favor of bringing the students in. The debate, in SNCC style, went on over the course of that winter.

SNCC's initial community-organizing venture in the state had been brought to a halt by the murder of Herbert Lee.* Another series of killings in the same part of the state, the Southwest, ultimately ended the arguments over Freedom Summer. . . .

. . . They had watched Herbert Lee get gunned down and couldn't do anything about it. Now at least they were in a position to force some national attention onto Mississippi, thereby putting pressure on the federal government to protect Black life in the state. It was self-consciously an attempt to use the nation's racism, its tendency to react only when white life was endangered, as a point of leverage. Moses and Dave Dennis put all of their authority behind the Summer Project. . . .

Since the summer involved large numbers of white people, we have a great deal of literature on it, far more than on the three years of organizing that preceded it. [One aspect] of that period [is] especially interesting here: Freedom Schools. . . . When Ella Baker first went to New York in 1927 she organized a Negro history club for youngsters at the Harlem Y. This may have

---

*Herbert Lee, who assisted Robert Moses in voter registration, was killed in September 1961 by a Mississippi state legislator, who was acquitted by a coroner's jury.

been her first "political" act in the city. No doubt, she saw it as a way to raise consciousness, to help people develop themselves. The Freedom Schools in Mississippi were an experiment in the same tradition. By late 1963, strategic thinking in SNCC was increasingly concerned with "parallel institutions."

If existing institutions did not meet the needs of Black Mississippians, what kinds of institutions would? Freedom Schools were one reflection of that thinking, but they also exemplified a much older tendency within the community-organizing tradition. During one of the early planning sessions for the summer, Charlie Cobb, the Howard University student who had first come to the Delta in the fall of 1962, proposed a summer Freedom School program "to fill an intellectual and creative vacuum in the lives of young Negro Mississippians, and to get them to articulate their own desires, demands and questions . . . to stand up in classrooms around the state and ask their teachers a real question." The schools were expected to be "an educational experience for students which will make it possible for them to challenge the myths of our society, to perceive more clearly its realities and to find alternatives and ultimately, new directions for action." Cobb envisioned the schools handling perhaps a thousand students of high school age. In fact, somewhere between twenty-five hundred and three thousand students actually showed up, and their ages ranged from seven to seventy. Cobb's original idea of having one teacher for every four or five kids had to be dropped, and the number of schools was increased from twenty-five to forty-one.

Part of the classwork consisted of traditional academic subjects. In Mississippi, though, traditional subjects were often not available in Black schools. Publicly supported Black schools tended not to offer typing, foreign languages, art, drama, or college-preparatory mathematics. Apart from whatever intrinsic interest they held, these subjects were popular with students partly because they symbolized equality. It was the Citizenship Curriculum that made the schools distinctive. It was built around a set of core questions, including:

1. What does the majority culture have that we want?
2. What does the majority culture have that we don't want?
3. What do we have that we want to keep?

One unit of the curriculum asked students to compare their social reality with that of others in terms of education, housing, and employment; one section called for them to compare the adjustment of Negroes to Mississippi with the adjustment of Jews to Nazi Germany. Another unit was intended to convince students that "running away" to the North wasn't going to solve anything. The "Introducing the Power Structure" unit tried "to create an awareness that some people profit by the pain of others or by misleading them." The unit on poor whites tried to help students understand how the power structure manipulated the fears of poor whites. "Material Things and Soul Things" was a critique of materialism. The last area of the curriculum was a study of the movement itself. The section on nonviolence made sure to present it as something beyond a mere refraining from doing anyone physical harm; students were admonished to practice nonviolence of speech and thought as well. The curriculum reflects how far discussion within SNCC had progressed beyond a narrow concern with civil rights. . . .

. . . The questions SNCC was raising about the nature of leadership and how leadership potential might be developed, the sheer persistence of organizers, the continuity of 1960s organizing with that done in earlier years, the questioning of the basic premises of American society—none of these were likely to become a key part of the story as framed by the press, and partly for that reason they never became a part of collective consciousness about the movement in the way that the "Big Events" did. . . .

. . . Much of SNCC's organizing was a response to their assumption that national institutions, including the press, were more interested in what happened to whites than to Blacks. The press had shown little interest in the mock elections that SNCC was running in Mississippi in the fall of 1963, but when white volunteers—the students from Yale and Stanford—came, the elections became a "story." Freedom Summer, of course, was predicated on the idea that privileged white volunteers would bring the concern of the nation with them. The unprecedented media coverage of the summer concentrated not on local Blacks or experienced organizers but on the volunteers. That surprised no one in SNCC, but it was nonetheless embittering. . . .

The undervaluation of the leadership role played by ordinary people corresponded to an overconcentration on the role of national leaders, Dr. King in particular. In 1963, when SCLC was about to announce the accords that had been reached with the power structure in Birmingham, it was decided that Fred Shuttlesworth, by far the most important local leader, should speak first at the press conference. The national press corps had hardly assembled to hear Fred Shuttlesworth. "Although Shuttlesworth announced the terms of the settlement, the reporters would not be satisfied until they heard it from King himself, as most of their readers knew nothing of Shuttlesworth." . . . In deciding that Shuttlesworth was not a part of the story, the press missed an opportunity to learn something about the historical depth of the struggle and the variety of leadership styles that sustained it. . . .

Scholarly and popular histories of the movement have traditionally reflected the same underlying analytical frames as did contemporaneous media. That has begun to change within the last decade, encouraged by a chorus of complaints from movement participants that they could not recognize their own movement in most histories. Even taking recent improvements into account, we are far short of what we might hope for. The issues that are invisible to the media and to the current generation of Black activists are still almost as invisible to scholars. . . .

As academic histories come to reflect a greater variety of social perspectives, it is not clear how popular culture will be affected. It may be that the top-down . . . conception of the movement is so deeply ingrained in popular culture, so constantly reinforced and so consistent with our national vanities, that new scholarship will be unable to dent it. We are likely to soon see a wave of scholarship that paints a more careful conception of Martin Luther King's role, but nonetheless, every January, the airwaves will be filled with "I Have a Dream."

Most of us who study the movement want to believe that our work can have some impact. Addressing an audience of scholars and movement activists, CORE's James Farmer said:

> I think that knowledge of the past is vital but historical knowledge is not an end in itself. The more we learn about the past, the more we must recognize that we learn about it in order to bring a more humane society into being in this country. Otherwise, historical knowledge is meaningless.

None of us understands fully how to use what we know of the past to shape a more just present, but we can be sure that social analysis which does not somehow make it clear that ordinary, flawed, everyday sorts of human beings frequently manage to make extraordinary contributions to social change, social analysis which does not make it easier for people to see in themselves and in those around them the potential for controlling their own lives takes us in the wrong direction. . . . Alice Walker has written that if the movement has done nothing else it has given Blacks a history of men (and women) better than presidents. Perhaps not. Even at this late date, at the level of popular culture the history has been largely homogenized, the men and women better than presidents largely forgotten, which may make it more difficult to produce any more like them.

PRIMARY SOURCES

Most of the sources in this section deal with the grassroots organizing efforts in Mississippi before and during Freedom Summer in 1964. Many of the sources are from the memoirs or oral histories of the participants in this activity. In other words, they reflect the *personal* memories of those involved in the civil rights struggle. As you read them, keep in mind whether they support Charles Payne's argument in Source 1 that journalists and historians have distorted our *collective* memory of the black struggle for equality by focusing too narrowly on civil rights leaders.

SNCC and the Early Efforts to Organize Mississippi

The sources in this section deal with SNCC's roots in the student sit-ins and with the attempts of civil rights activists to organize Mississippi in the years before the Freedom Summer in 1964. As you read these sources consider what they reveal about the differences between SNCC and other civil rights organizations. What do they demonstrate about the obstacles confronting those who challenged the racial status quo? What impact did this early organizing have? Why was SNCC more effective at grassroots organizing than other civil rights organizations, according to these participants in early civil rights activity?

2   Ella Jo Baker called the conference that led to the founding of SNCC and exercised a strong influence on it in its early years. In an oral history conducted by a Harvard University graduate student in 1966, Baker discussed the organization's move from the sit-ins to other activities, its goals, and its differences from other civil rights organizations.

A SNCC Founder Discusses Its Goals (1966)

Q. What is the basic goal of SNCC?

A. To change society so that the have-nots can share in it. . . .

Q. Could you discuss in detail SNCC's move from the sit-ins to other things?

A. In the early days, there was little communication, except on a highly personal basis, as between friends and relatives, in the sit-in movement. I had originally thought of pulling together 120–125 sit-in leaders for a leadership training conference—but the rate of spread of the sit-ins was so rapid and the response so electrifying, both North and South, that the meeting ended up with 300 people. Many colleges sent representatives; there was a great thrust of human desire and effort. The first sit-in took place February 1, 1960; the meeting in Raleigh was around April 17, 1960, for three days. Nineteen colleges above the Mason-Dixon Line sent representatives, most of them white. There were so many Northerners that at the meeting it was decided that Northerners could not participate in decision-making. This decision was made sort of by mutual agreement after discussion, because the Northerners recognized that the thrust of the action came from the South. They had been drawn magnetically to the

Source: Reprinted with the permission of the publisher from Emily Stoper, *The Student Nonviolent Coordinating Committee: The Growth of Radicalism in a Civil Rights Organization* (Brooklyn, N.Y.: Carlson Publishing Inc., 1989), pp. 265–266, 267–268.

movement because of their great admiration for the wonderful, brave Southerners. The Southerners wanted it that way, at that meeting, because of the divergent levels of political thinking both within the Northern group and between
the North and the politically unsophisticated Deep South. (There were many
representatives from Georgia, Louisiana, Alabama, although only token representation from Mississippi.) There was an outstanding leadership group from
Nashville. It was a basic insecurity that caused the South to keep the North out
of decision-making. The North and South used different terminology, had trouble communicating. This has cropped up again in SNCC. It became more subdued in the summer of '64 when there was a real program to be carried out. . . .

Moreover, some of those who took part (I realize in retrospect) saw a basic
difference in the role of leadership in [SCLC and SNCC]. In SCLC, the organization revolved around King; in SNCC, the leadership was group-centered (although I may have had some influence). Southern members of the movement
were somewhat in awe of each other. There was a feeling that it was the "dawn
of a new era," that something new and great was happening and that only they
could chart the course of history. A strong equalitarian philosophy prevailed.
There was a belief you could just go into an area and organize if you had had
no leadership experience. SNCC rejected the idea of a God-sent leader. A basic
goal was to make it unnecessary for the people to depend on a leader, for them
to be strong themselves. SNCC hoped to spread into a big movement, to develop leadership from among the people. At first it had a rotating chairman-
ship, for periods of about two months. Marion Barry was the first chairman.
He was selected at the Raleigh meeting as temporary chairman with no opposition. This was in deference to the role of the Nashville movement, of which
he was a leader. (Nashville had already had mass arrests after which the
demonstrators had decided to stay in jail.) Marion had already demonstrated
his capacity both to suffer and to confront the white man. He was seen as a real
martyr. The Nashville group brought with it the influence of the Reverend
James Lawson, who believed in nonviolence as a religious principle. . . .

Q. What is SNCC's basic goal, that makes it unique?

A. The NAACP, Urban League, etc., do not *change* society, they want to get in.
It's a combination of concern with the black goal for itself and, beyond that,
with the whole society, because this is the acid test of whether the outs can
get in and share in equality and worth. By worth, I mean creativity, a contribution to society. SNCC defines itself in terms of the blacks but is concerned
with all excluded people.

Q. Has there been a change in SNCC's goal over time?

A. During the sit-in movement, we were concerned with segregation of public accommodations. But even then we recognized that that was only a sur-

face goal. These obvious "irritants" had to be removed first; this was natural. Some people probably thought this in itself would change race relations; others saw deeper. . . .

Q. Would you tell in detail how SNCC's policy changed after the sit-ins?

A. From the start, there were those who knew sitting-in would not bring basic changes. Youngsters who had not thought it through had not bargained with the intractable resistance of the power structure. The notion of "appeals to the conscience" assumed that there is a conscience, and after a while the question began to be raised, *is* there a conscience? Students, because they were most out front in the movement, began to see this and its political connotations. People began asking who *really* controlled things.

---

3   Amzie Moore was a World War II veteran and an early leader in the black struggle in Mississippi. In this oral history conducted by a white Southern journalist in the mid-1970s, Moore recalled his early involvement with the NAACP and later with SNCC. (Those parts of the interview that are indented and set off with a line in the left margin are out of sequence. They were transposed by the original author for greater clarity.)

[A Mississippi Civil Rights Pioneer Bids] Farewell to the "N-Double-A" (ca. 1975)

AMZIE MOORE

When did you get involved in the NAACP?

Well, I came out of the Army in nineteen hundred and forty-six, and in nineteen hundred and fifty-one, somebody held a meeting in a church and elected me president of the NAACP, and I'd never been [to a meeting]. Well, I think at that time they were just passing the buck, getting rid of it as a hot potato. And I decided maybe I wasn't going to serve, and then finally it was kinda forced upon me, and I just went on.

Forced upon you in what way?

Well, by people I suppose. I clearly understood that the individuals who met and had me elected were people who just really didn't wanna fool with it, 'cause they weren't gonna fall out with their white friends on account of it.

Source: My Soul Is Rested by Howell Raines, copyright © 1977 by Howell Raines. Used by permission of G. P. Putnam's Sons, a division of Penguin Group (USA) Inc., pp. 234–237.

So they just said, "Well, here's what we'll do. We'll just move it off to him. He's young and able to take it." I think that's how I became involved. Finally enrolled about six hundred members, became vice president-at-large of the state conference of the NAACP branches, and up until SNCC came in, it was a matter of legal maneuvering. Nobody dared move a peg without some lawyer advisin' him.

Were you able to really accomplish much in the Delta through that sort of . . .

I don't think so really, because, you see, the base of operations was too far away. We met in Jackson. That's a hundred and thirty sumpin' miles from here. We had a nice crowd, but we didn't know about methods and procedures for demanding things. . . .

Anyway, in nineteen hundred and fifty-five, Emmett Till was found dead in the Tallahatchie River, and they had newspapers from all over the continent North America, some from India, and it was the best advertised lynching that I had ever heard. Personally, I think this was the beginning of the Civil Rights Movement in Mississippi in the twentieth century. . . . From that point on, Mississippi began to move.

Following the Freedom Bus Ride in nineteen hundred and sixty-one, I was invited to Atlanta by Bob Moses.

How did you meet him?

He came down and spent a while and invited me to the meeting in Atlanta. It must have been the spring before I went over the following fall.

Why did he come to you?

Now, that's the sixty-four-thousand-dollar question, and I don't know until yet why Bob came to me, but he found me and spent most of the time that summer at my house. In the fall of that year, I went to Atlanta to the meeting of the Student Nonviolent Coordinating Committee and invited them to come to Mississippi. So they came, set up their first office in Jackson, Mississippi, and then kind of spread it out all over the state. Activities were going on in McComb, Jackson, Indianola, Cleveland, Ruleville. . . . They had more courage than any group of people I've ever met. . . .

In that initial meeting that you had with Moses, did y'all discuss voter-registration tactics?

Well . . . Moses and I talked about it when he was here visiting me in the summer. The first thing we had to try to figure out: How can we expose the conditions in Mississippi with reference to people voting? How can we uncover what is covered? So then we got together, we went into homes, we persuaded people to go up and register. We had cameras from everywhere, television, the newspapers, and the whole thing was brought out. . . .

You knew they would be turned away?

Oh, we were well aware of that. . . .

Was it generally known that you were working with SNCC?

I think so. Of course, there was a little jealousy at that time between the N-Double-A-C-P and SNCC. The N-Double-A-C-P at that time seemed to have been a legal organization that required going to court and this type thing.

SNCC was an organization of strong, intelligent, young people who had no fear of death and certainly did not hesitate to get about the business for which they came here. It wasn't a matter of meeting in the Masonic Order or office or at a church to do this. They met anywhere, at any time. One great thing I think was introduced in the South with reference to SNCC's tactics was the business of organizing leadership. If 'leven people went to jail this evening who the power structure considered leaders, tomorrow morning you had 'leven more out there. [Laughs] And the next morning 'leven more.

I found that SNCC was for business, live or die, sink or swim, survive or perish. They were moving, and nobody seemed to worry about whether he was gonna live or die. [Laughs]

. . . Are you gonna sit here and tell me that didn't cross your mind?

Sho' I was scared to death. Now don't misunderstand me. [Laughs] Yeah. . . . It came across my mind because I was constantly threatened. I was called at night and told, "In five minutes, your house gon' blow up." If I'd run out, I coulda been shot, and if I had stayed in, I coulda been blown to pieces. So then, here I am between two opinions. I've got to decide to stay in the house or run out. I mean, What's "safe" . . . ?

Did you get any adverse reaction from your N-Double-A-C-P associates when you . . .

[Laughs] When I went over to SNCC? Well, naturally.

What form did it take?

Well . . . it was like, "Maybe these kids don't know what they're doing. . . . It could get a lotta people hurt." I think what I really did was stayed away from N-Double-A-C-P meetings for years. Now, I didn't join an organization with SNCC. I just worked with 'em. That's more or less how it was. Now, the NAACP certainly has done a lot of great things. Don't misunderstand me. . . . Mr. Wilkins, he's a fine man. He'd fly down and hold our conferences and hold our annual "days" and raise our freedom money and be advised by different people outa New York office. And that was it. . . .

> But when an individual stood at a courthouse like the courthouse in Greenwood and in Greenville and watched tiny figures [of the SNCC workers] standing against a huge column . . . [against white] triggermen and drivers and lookout men riding in automobiles with automatic guns . . . *how they stood* . . . how gladly they got in the front of that line, those leaders, and went to jail! It didn't seem to bother 'em. It was an awakening for me. . . .

Why did SCLC never create the kind of impact on Mississippi that it did in other Southern states?

Well, SCLC had a group of preachers following it. Now don't misunderstand me, I think the world and all of ministers. I don't have anything against ministers, but their outlook was entirely different from SNCC's young people. Kids wore blue jeans, and I used to have sleeping in my house six and eight and ten, twelve, who had come. I bought a lots of cheese, and always we'd eat cheese and peaches, and sometimes we would get spaghetti and ground chuck or ground beef and make a huge tub of meatballs and spaghetti to fill everybody up. And this is how we were, and everybody knew they were there, wasn't any secret. They'd eat that without complaining. . . . You *know* they're being really persecuted and pushed to the wall, and they always had a smile and was always ready to try to do something. . . . To me, it was just a new leader. . . .

4   SNCC's civil rights organizing drew a quick response from many white Mississippians, as this record indicates.

Chronology of Violence, 1961 (1963)

AUGUST 15, AMITE COUNTY: Robert Moses, Student Nonviolent Coordinating Committee (SNCC) registration worker, and three Negroes who had tried

Source: Papers of the Highlander Education and Research Center, State Historical Society of Wisconsin. Reprinted by permission.

unsuccessfully to register in Liberty, were driving toward McComb when a county officer stopped them. He asked if Moses was the man ". . . who's been trying to register our niggers." All were taken to court and Moses was arrested for "impeding an officer in the discharge of his duties," fined $50 and spent two days in jail.

AUGUST 22, AMITE COUNTY: Robert Moses went to Liberty with three Negroes, who made an unsuccessful attempt to register. A block from the courthouse, Moses was attacked and beaten by Billy Jack Caston, the sheriff's first cousin. Eight stitches were required to close a wound in Moses' head. Caston was acquitted of assault charges by an all-white jury before a justice of the peace.

AUGUST 26, MC COMB, PIKE COUNTY: Hollis Watkins, 20, and Elmer Hayes, 20, SNCC workers, were arrested while staging a sit-in at the F. W. Woolworth store and charged with breach of the peace. They spent 36 days in jail.

AUGUST 27 AND 29, MC COMB, PIKE COUNTY: Five Negro students from a local high school were convicted of breach of the peace following a sit-in at a variety store and bus terminal. They were sentenced to a $400 fine each and eight months in jail. One of these students, a girl of 15, was turned over to juvenile authorities, released, subsequently rearrested, and sentenced to 12 months in a state school for delinquents.

AUGUST 29, MC COMB, PIKE COUNTY: Two Negro leaders were arrested in McComb as an aftermath of the sit-in protest march on city hall, charged with contributing to the delinquency of minors. They were Curtis C. Bryant of McComb, an official of the NAACP, and Cordelle Reagan, of SNCC. Each arrest was made on an affidavit signed by Police Chief George Guy, who said he had information that the two ". . . were behind some of this racial trouble."

AUGUST 30, MC COMB, PIKE COUNTY: SNCC workers Brenda Travis, 16, Robert Talbert, 19, and Isaac Lewis, 20, staged a sit-in in the McComb terminal of the Greyhound bus lines. They were arrested on charges of breach of the peace and failure to obey a policeman's order to move on. They spent 30 days in jail.

SEPTEMBER 5, LIBERTY, AMITE COUNTY: Travis Britt, SNCC registration worker, was attacked and beaten by whites on the courthouse lawn. Britt was accompanied at the time by Robert Moses. Britt said one man hit him more than 20 times. The attackers drove away in a truck.

SEPTEMBER 7, TYLERTOWN, WALTHALL COUNTY: John Hardy, SNCC registration worker, took two Negroes to the county courthouse to register. The registrar told them he ". . . wasn't registering voters" that day. When the three turned to leave, Registrar John Q. Wood took a pistol from his desk and struck Hardy over the head from behind. Hardy was arrested and charged with disturbing the peace.

SEPTEMBER 13, JACKSON, HINDS COUNTY: Fifteen Episcopal ministers (among them three Negroes) were arrested for asking to be served at the lunch counter of the Greyhound bus terminal. They were charged with inviting a breach of the peace. They were found not guilty of the charge on May 21, 1962, by County judge Russell Moore.

SEPTEMBER 25, LIBERTY, AMITE COUNTY: Herbert Lee, a Negro who had been active in voter registration, was shot and killed by white state representative E. H. Hurst in downtown Liberty. No prosecution was undertaken, the authorities explaining that the representative had shot in self-defense.

OCTOBER 4, MC COMB, PIKE COUNTY: The five students who were arrested as a result of the August 29 sit-in in McComb returned to school, but were refused admittance. At that, 116 students walked out and paraded downtown to the city hall in protest. Police arrested the entire crowd, but later released all but 19, all of whom were 18 years old or older. They were charged with breach of the peace and contributing to the delinquency of minors and allowed to go free on bail totalling $3,700. At the trial on October 31, Judge Brumfield, finding the students guilty, and sentencing each to a $500 fine and six months in jail, said: "Some of you are local residents, some of you are outsiders. Those of you who are local residents are like sheep being led to the slaughter. If you continue to follow the advise [sic] of outside agitators, you will be like sheep and be slaughtered."

---

5 Fannie Lou Hamer, one of twenty children of a sharecropper, was typical of the poor, black Mississippians targeted by SNCC. She also came to epitomize the political commitment that organizers hoped to see develop in them. (The part of the interview that is indented and set off with a line in the left margin is out of sequence. It was transposed by the original author for greater clarity.)

[A Sharecropper's Daughter Responds to the Voter Registration Campaign (ca. 1975)]

FANNIE LOU HAMER

Well, we were living on a plantation about four and a half miles east of here. . . . Pap had been out there thirty years, and I had been out there eighteen years, 'cause we had been married at that time eighteen years. And you know, things were just rough. . . . I don't think that I ever remember working for as much as four dollars a day. Yes, one year I remember working for four dollars a day, and I was gettin' as much as the men, 'cause I kept up with the time. . . . But anyway, I just knowed things wasn't right.

So then that was in 1962 when the civil rights workers came into this county. Now, I didn't know anything about voter registration or nothin' like

Source: My Soul Is Rested by Howell Raines, copyright © 1977 by Howell Raines. Used by permission of G. P. Putnam's Sons, a division of Penguin Group (USA) Inc., pp. 249–252.

that, 'cause people had never been told that they could register to vote. And livin' out in the country, if you had a little radio, by the time you got in at night, you'd be too tired to listen at what was goin' on. . . . So they had a rally. I had gone to church that Sunday, and the minister announced that they were gon' have a mass meeting that Monday night. Well, I didn't know what a mass meeting was, and I was just curious to go to a mass meeting. So I did . . . and they was talkin' about how blacks had a right to register and how they had a right to *vote*. . . . Just listenin' at 'em, I could just see myself votin' people outa office that I know was wrong and didn't do nothin' to help the poor. I said, you know, that's sumpin' I really wanna be involved in, and finally at the end of that rally, I had made up my mind that I was gonna come out there when they said you could go down that Friday to try to register.

She remembers the date precisely: August 31, 1962. She and seventeen others climbed aboard an old bus owned by a black man from neighboring Bolivar County. SNCC had chartered it for the thirty-mile ride to the county seat in Indianola. Once there, she was the first into the registrar's office.

. . . He brought a big old book out there, and he gave me the sixteenth section of the Constitution of Mississippi, and that was dealing with de facto laws, and I didn't know nothin' about no de facto laws, didn't know nothin' about any of 'em. I could copy it like it was in the book . . . but after I got through copying it, he told me to give a reasonable interpretation and tell the meaning of that section that I had copied. Well, I flunked out. . . .

So then we started back to Ruleville and on our way back to Ruleville, this same highway patrolman that I had seen steady cruisin' around this bus stopped us. We had crossed that bridge, coming over from Indianola. They got out the cars, flagged the bus down. When they flagged the bus down, they told all of us to get off of the bus. So at this time, we just started singing "Have a Little Talk with Jesus," and we got off the bus, and all they wanted then was for us to get back on the bus. They arrested Bob [Moses] and told the bus driver he was under arrest. So we went back then to Indianola. The bus driver was fined one hundred dollars for driving a bus with too much yellow in it. Now ain't that ridiculous?

For what?

Too much yellow. Said the bus looked too much like a school bus. That's funny, but it's the truth. But you see, it was to frighten us to death. This same bus had been used year after year hauling cotton choppers and cotton pickers to Florida to try to make a livin' that winter, and he had never been arrested before. But the day he tried . . . to carry us to Indianola, they fined him a hundred dollars, and I guess it was so ridiculous that they finally cut the fine down to thirty dollars, and all of us *together*—not one, but all us together—had enough to pay the fine. So we paid the fine, and then we got back on the bus and come on to Ruleville.

So Rev. Jeff Summers, who live on Charles Street, just the next street over, he carried me out there on the Marlowe Plantation where I had worked for eighteen years. And when I got out there, my little girl—she's dead now, Dorothy—she met me and one of Pap's cousins, and said that man [who owned the plantation] had been raising a lot of Cain ever since we left, that he had been in the field more times than he usually come a day, because I had gone to the courthouse. See, the people at the courthouse would call and tell it. So they was kinda scared, and quite natural I began to feel nervous, but I knowed I hadn't done nothin' wrong. So after my little girl told me, wasn't too long 'fore Pap got off, and he was tellin' me the same thing that the other kids had told me.

I went on in the house, and I sat down on a little old bed that belonged to the little girl, and when I sat down on the bed, this man [who owned the plantation] he come up and he asked Pap, "Did you tell Fannie Lou what I said?" And Pap said, "Yessir, I sho' did." And I got up and walked to the door, and then he asked me, "Did Pap tell you what I said?" I said, "He told me." And he said, "I mean that. You'll have to go back to Indianola and withdraw, or you have to leave this place." So I said, "Mr. Dee, I didn't go down there to register for you. I went down there to register for myself." And that made him madder, you know.

So he told me, "I want your answer now, yea or nay." And he said, 'They gon'"—now, I don't know who the *they* were, whether it was the white Citizens Council or the Ku Klux Klan, 'cause I don't think one is no worse than the other—"they gon' worry me tonight. They gon' worry the hell outa me, and I'm gon' worry hell outa you. You got 'til in the mornin' to tell me. But if you don't go back there and withdraw, you got to leave the plantation."

So I knowed I wasn't goin' back to withdraw, so wasn't nothin' for me to do but leave the plantation. So Pap brought me out that same night and I come to Mrs. Tucker's, a lady live over on Byron Street. I went to her house, and I stayed, and Pap began to feel nervous when he went to the [plantation maintenance] shop and saw some buckshot shells. And they don't have buckshot shells to *play* with in August and September, because you ain't huntin' or nothin' like that.

On September tenth—again she recalls the date precisely—came the nightrider attack. . . . The riders shot into the McDonald home, where the SNCC workers were staying, and into the Tucker home, where Mrs. Hamer had been given shelter. "They shot in that house sixteen times, tryin' to kill me," she remembers. She fled to the home of a niece in Tallahatchie County when the nighttime terrorism continued on into the fall.

I stayed away, 'cause things then—you could see 'em at night. They would have fires in the middle of the road. . . . You wouldn't see no Klan signs, but just make a fire in the middle of the road. And it was *so dangerous,* I stayed in Tallahatchie County all of September and then October, and then November I come back to Ruleville. I was comin', I didn't know why I was comin', but I was just sick of runnin' and hadn't done nothin'. . . . I started tryin' to find a place to stay, 'cause we didn't have nothin'.

The woman who had been her sixth-grade school teacher put her in touch with a black woman who had a three-room house for rent "for eighteen dollars a month and that was a lotta money." She and her family moved in on December 3.

That was on a Sunday, and that Monday, the fourth of December, I went back to Indianola to the circuit clerk's office and I told him who I was and I was there to take that literacy test again.

I said, "Now, you cain't have me fired 'cause I'm already fired, and I won't have to move now, because I'm not livin' in no white man's house." I said, "I'll be here every thirty days until I become a registered voter." 'Cause that's what you would have to do: go every thirty days and see had you passed the literacy test. . . . I went back then the tenth of January in 1963, and I had become registered. . . . I passed the second one, because at the second time I went back, I had been studying sections of the Mississippi Constitution, so I would know if I got one that was simple enough that I might could pass it.

I passed that second test, but it made us become like criminals. We would have to have our lights out before dark. It was cars passing that house all times of the night, driving real slow with guns, and pickups with white mens in it, and they'd pass that house just as slow as they could pass it . . . three guns lined up in the back. All of that. This was the kind of stuff. Pap couldn't get nothin' to do. . . .

So I started teachin' citizenship class, and I became the supervisor of the citizenship class in this county.* So I moved around the county to do citizenship education, and later on I become a field secretary for SNCC—I guess being about one of the oldest people at that time that was a field secretary, 'cause they was real young.

*Hamer taught in a SCLC voter-education program.

Freedom Summer

In 1964, COFO organizers decided to bring hundreds of mostly white, affluent, Northern college students to Mississippi to participate in the Mississippi Freedom Summer Project, whose main goal was black voter registration. What do these sources reveal about the reasons for the Freedom Summer, the broader goals of its organizers, and the dangers and obstacles confronting the participants?

---

6   In the spring of 1964, CORE's Dave Dennis and SNCC's Robert Moses discussed the wisdom of bringing white college students to Mississippi to register black voters. Their decision, as recalled here by Dennis in a later oral history, led to Freedom Summer.

[A Black Activist Endorses White Participation (ca. 1975)]
DAVE DENNIS

We knew that if we had brought in a thousand blacks, the country would have watched them slaughtered without doing anything about it. Bring a thousand whites and the country is going to react to that in two ways. First of all is to protect. We made sure that we had the children, sons and daughters, of some very powerful people in this country over there, including Jerry Brown, who's now governor of California, for instance . . . we made sure of that. . . . The idea was not only to begin to organize for the Democratic Convention, but also to get the country to begin to respond to what was going on there. They were not gonna respond to a thousand blacks working in that area. They would respond to a thousand young white college students, and white college females who were down there. All right? And that's the reason why, and if there were gonna take some deaths to do it, the death of a white college student would bring on more attention to what was going on than for a black college student getting it. That's cold, but that was also in another sense speaking the language of this country. What we were trying to do was get a message over to the country, so we spoke their language. And that had more to do with that decision to bring 'em in by the two of us at the top than anything else.

You [and Bob Moses] discussed it that clearly?

Uh-mm, the two of us did. The two of us discussed it. That was not opened up to the staff and everything else in the meetings, because the fact is that we didn't know who was working for the press or whatever, and most things that happened in staff meetings always got out. And that's something we didn't want to. Now I guess it can be told. . . . We didn't plan anything that happened, for it to happen. That's what the Klan and the rest of 'em did, you know. We didn't plan any of the violence. [Pauses] But we just wanted the country to respond to what was going on.

Source: My Soul Is Rested by Howell Raines, copyright © 1977 by Howell Raines. Used by permission of G. P. Putnam's Sons, a division of Penguin Group (USA) Inc., p. 274.

What sorts of problems, if any, did that decision cause you and Moses?

Well, I can't speak for Bob. It caused problems—I mean, psychologically—for me in terms of the fact that you felt responsible for what happened to people, you know, and I still do. I mean, it's the price that I had to pay and the price that I still pay for the decision. [Pauses] But it was something that had to be done. You see, one of the things is that we were in a war, and it wasn't very romantic for those people involved in it.

---

7 SNCC's Lawrence Guyot, a member of the COFO staff, recalled in an oral history the violence dealt civil rights workers during Freedom Summer and the federal government's response to it. Note what Guyot saw as the only protection from white violence. (The part of the interview that is indented and set off with a line in the left margin is out of sequence. It was transposed by the original author for greater clarity.)

[A SNCC Organizer Recalls Federal Intervention (ca. 1975)]
LAWRENCE GUYOT

Oh, man, look . . . [claps his hands for emphasis] . . . we were an open book. The phones were tapped, people knew where we were going, people knew where we bought our gas, where we lived . . . you name it. Fortunately, we didn't operate internally as though we had something to hide. I mean, our protection was the black community. We never doubted that and we knew it and we acted like it. I have no doubt that the twenty-five [black] people who really made decisions in that state politically at that time could have been wiped out in a day—*and would have been.* I mean, what's to prevent it?

I don't know, you may think I'm overstating my case, because I was individually involved, but I have no doubt about it. Logically that's the way the state deals with that kinda situation; that's the way it woulda been dealt with. But the national attention, the involvement of the President, the concern of the CIA. Allen Dulles came to Mississippi.* The FBI then began its infiltrating of the Klan and the Civil Rights Movement. I'm sure this was when the surveillance and tapping of King was stepped up.

The only time that I really have opposition to the role of the federal government in Mississippi was when Allen Dulles came to Mississippi and

---

*Allen Dulles, former director of the Central Intelligence Agency, came to Mississippi as a special representative of President Lyndon Johnson.

Source: My Soul Is Rested by Howell Raines, copyright © 1977 by Howell Raines. Used by permission of G. P. Putnam's Sons, a division of Penguin Group (USA) Inc., pp. 288–289.

met with myself, Aaron Henry, Bob Moses, Dave Dennis, a couple of other people, and said, "Look, I'm going to meet with the governor in an hour"—this was when they were looking for the bodies of Schwerner, Chaney, and Goodman—"and we want this mess cleaned up."

And Aaron Henry stood up and said, "What do you mean?"

Dulles said, "Well, these civil rights demonstrations are causin' this kind of friction, and we're just not gonna have it, even if we have to bring troops in here."

Fortunately, Aaron Henry took the right position, 'cause he said, "You talkin' to the wrong people. . . . Everything we're trying to do is constitutionally protected and we oughta be having more help from the federal government rather than you, as an agent of the federal government, come and tell us to be quiet." *Now that happened.*

---

8 In letters to friends and family members back home, the college students involved in Freedom Summer often discussed their experiences in Mississippi. As you read this letter, consider what it demonstrates about the civil rights workers' goals—and obstacles they confronted.

A Letter from a Freedom Summer Volunteer (1964)

Dear folks,   Mileston, August 18

One can't move onto a plantation cold; or canvas a plantation in the same manner as the Negro ghetto in town. It's far too dangerous. Many plantations—homes included—are posted, meaning that no trespassing is permitted, and the owner feels that he has the prerogative to shoot us on sight when we are in the house of one of *his* Negroes.

Before we canvas a plantation, our preparation includes finding out whether the houses are posted, driving through or around the plantation without stopping, meanwhile making a detailed map of the plantation.

We're especially concerned with the number of roads in and out of the plantation. For instance, some houses could be too dangerous to canvas because of their location near the boss man's house and on a dead end road. In addition to mapping, we attempt to talk to some of the tenants when they are off the plantation, and ask them about conditions. The kids often have contacts, and can get on the plantation unnoticed by the boss man, with the pretense of just visiting friends.

Source: Reprinted with the permission of the publisher from "A Letter from a Freedom Summer Volunteer" (1964), from Leon Friedman, ed., *The Civil Rights Reader: Basic Documents of the Civil Rights Movement* (New York: Walker & Company, 1967).

Our canvassing includes not only voter registration, but also extensive reports on conditions—wages, treatment by the boss man, condition of the houses, number of acres of cotton, etc. Much more such work needs to be done. The plantation system is crucial in Delta politics and economics, and the plantation system must be brought to an end if democracy is to be brought to the Delta. . . .

Love, Joel

9   Besides voter registration, one of the major activities of Freedom Summer participants was organizing and teaching in the Mississippi Freedom Schools. Directed by Staughton Lynd, a white history professor at Spelman College, the Freedom Schools were established to teach black students in such basic skills as reading, writing, and arithmetic. They also had another purpose, though, as revealed in an article written by a Freedom School organizer shortly after Freedom Summer.

"Deeper Than Politics: The Mississippi Freedom Schools" (1964)

The original plan for Freedom Schools developed from Charles Cobb's dream that what could be done in Mississippi could be deeper, more fundamental, more far-reaching, more revolutionary than voter registration alone: more personal, and in a sense more transforming, than a political program. The validity of the dream is evidenced by the fact that people trying desperately to keep alive while working on voter registration could take seriously the idea that Mississippi needs more than for Negroes to have the right to vote.

The decision to have Freedom Schools in Mississippi seems to have been a decision, then, to enter into every phase of the lives of the people of Mississippi. It seems to have been a decision to set the people free for politics in the only way that people can become live and that is totally. It was an important decision for the staff to be making, and so it is not surprising that the curriculum for the proposed schools became everyone's concern. They worked and argued about what should be taught, about what the realities of Mississippi are, and how these realities affect the kids, and how to get the kids to discover themselves. And then, Staughton Lynd, the director, came in to impose a kind of beautiful order on the torment that the curriculum was becoming— torment because it was not just curriculum: it was each person on the staff painfully analyzing what the realities of the world were, and asking . . . what

Source: Peter B. Levy, ed., *Documentary History of the Modern Civil Rights Movement* (New York: Greenwood Press, 1992), pp. 142–144; originally from Liz Fusco, "Deeper Than Politics: The Mississippi Freedom Schools," *Liberation* (November 1964), pp. 17–19.

right he had to keep it from them until now. And because of these sessions, the whole concept of what could be done in Mississippi changed. It was because the people trying to change Mississippi were asking themselves the real questions about what is wrong with Mississippi that the summer project in effect touched every aspect of the lives of Negroes in Mississippi, and started to touch the lives of the whites as well. . . .

The so-called "Citizenship Curriculum" set up two sets of questions. The "primary" set was: (1) Why are we (teachers and students) in Freedom Schools? (2) What is the Freedom Movement? (3) What alternative does the Freedom Movement offer us? The "secondary" set of questions (which seemed to me more important because more personal) was: (1) What does the majority culture have that we want? (2) What does the majority culture have that we don't want? (3) What do we have that we want to keep?

The continual raising of these questions in many contexts may be said to be what the Freedom Schools were about. This was so because in order to answer them it was necessary for the students to confront other questions of who he is, what his world is like, and how he fits into or is alienated from it. . . .

. . . The kids began to see two things at once: that the North was no real escape, and that the South was not some vague white monster doomed irrationally to crush them. Simultaneously, they began to discover that they themselves could take action against injustices which have kept them unhappy and impotent.

Through the study of Negro history they began to have a true sense of themselves as a people who could produce heroes. . . . Beginning to sense the real potency of organized Negroes in Mississippi, the kids in the Freedom Schools found an immediate area of concern in the Negro schools they attended or had dropped out of: the so-called "public" schools. They had grievances, but until drawn into the question-asking, had only been able to whine, accept passively, or lash out by dropping out of school or getting expelled. By comparing the Freedom Schools with the regular schools, they began to become articulate about what was wrong in the regular schools and the way things should be instead. "Why don't they do this at our school?" was the first question asked; and then there began to be answers which led to further questions, such as "Why don't our teachers register to vote, if they presume to teach us about citizenship?" "Why can't our principal make his own decisions instead of having to follow the order of the white superintendent?" "Why do we have no student government?" or "Why doesn't the administration take the existing student government seriously?"

Always in the end, the main question was why are we not taken seriously— which came also out of why there are no art classes, no language classes, why there is no equipment in the science labs, why the library is inadequate, the classes overcrowded. This is of course the question that the adults were asking about the city, county, and state, and the question that the Freedom Democratic Party asked—at the Democratic National Convention. . . .

10 In 1965, SNCC and COFO organizers compiled poems written by Freedom School students and published them as a book. As you read these selections, consider to what extent the schools seemed to have fulfilled their goals.

Freedom School Poetry (1965)

"Fight on Little Children," Edith Moore, age 15, McComb.

Fight on little children, fight on
You know what you're doing is right.
Don't stop, keep straight ahead
You're just bound to win the fight.

Many hardships there will be;
Many trials you'll have to face.
But go on children, keep fighting
Soon freedom will take hardship's place.
Sometimes it's going to be hard;
Sometimes the light will look dim.
But keep it up, don't get discouraged
Keep fighting, though chances seem slim.
In the end you and I know
That one day the fact they'll face.
And realize we're human too
That freedom's taken slavery's place.

"Freedom in Mississippi," David March, age 16, Indianola.

In the middle of the night,
a stressive bell of Hope is ringing
Everyone is on the eve of fear and success
is not yet come
Until Everyone Wakes up and Speaks out
in an overcoming voice, the slums will Remain.
Let Not the pulling out of a few
go down the whole crowd.
If this remains we will forever be
under bowed.

Source: Peter B. Levy, ed., *Documentary History of the Modern Civil Rights Movement* (New York: Greenwood Press, 1992), pp. 144–146.

"Mine," Alice Jackson, age 17, Jackson.

I want to walk the streets of town
Turn into any restaurant and sit down
And be served the food of my choice,
And not be met by a hostile voice.
I want to live in the best hotel for a week,
Or go for a swim at a public beach.
I want to go to the best University
and not be met with violence or uncertainty.
I want the things my ancestors
thought we'd never have.
They are mine as a Negro, an American;
I shall have them or be dead.

SNCC and Political Change

As a result of SNCC's and the COFO's organizing efforts in Mississippi, the Mississippi Freedom Democratic Party sent 68 delegates to the Democratic National Convention in Atlantic City in August 1964. At the convention, the delegates challenged the legitimacy of Mississippi's regular Democratic delegates, whose party had excluded blacks from the polls and office holding. Although Fannie Lou Hamer and other delegates were able to advance their case at nationally televised hearings conducted by the Democratic convention's credentials committee, their hopes for acceptance by the convention were soon dashed. Lyndon Johnson, fearful of losing the Democratic South to his Republican opponent, intentionally preempted Hamer's moving testimony before the credentials committee by suddenly appearing on television himself. Later, under orders from Johnson, the convention offered only two at-large seats to the Freedom party delegation. Summing up the Freedom party delegates' reaction, Hamer declared that they "didn't come all this way for no two seats!"[7] The Freedom party's experience at the Democratic convention proved a bitter experience for many involved in SNCC/COFO organizing in Mississippi. As you read the sources below, consider what they reveal about the tensions created by Freedom Summer and the lessons some black activists drew from this experience. What do they reveal about the reasons that such SNCC activists as Stokely Carmichael became advocates of "black power" later in the 1960s? Did such a position represent a radical change for SNCC?

Jane Stembridge, a student at the Union Theological Seminary, worked as the "office secretary" for the SNCC executive committee starting in 1960. In that capacity, she was privy to many discussions held by the organization's leaders. Stembridge was interviewed by Emily Stoper, a graduate student at Harvard University, in 1966.

An "Insider" Recalls the Divisions in SNCC (1966)

JS: I don't think SNCC people, even in the early days, were interested in brotherhood, in reconciliation, in integration. SNCC has not changed radically, taking the position of Black Power. I think SNCC wanted desegregation, they wanted Negro rights, they wanted to go to Woolworth's and eat, but they simply didn't say the same things that Dr. King has said and I don't think they wanted the same things that he seems to want. They also were in a bigger hurry than SCLC. They were also alienated by SCLC's big office and office staff and all the red tape and the same old kind of organization, bureaucracy thing, that stayed in Atlanta and really didn't have much contact with the grass roots, or so it seemed then and still does, really. That this is just another Negro organization, is what they would say. Very cynical about it and just really didn't want to have anything to do with it. . . .

ES: What effect did the summer of '64 have on SNCC?

JS: Well, it did focus some attention on the state of Mississippi. People did get killed. It did reinforce the old ideas. It did put the cap on the development of local leadership to some extent. This varied from project to project, depending on what kind of white kids had come in there and what kind of local people were there to begin with. Most of the white kids tried to be sensitive to this kind of thing; some of them were not sensitive to it. But it did impede that. I think the biggest lesson SNCC learned from it was that you can't bring in white kids to help develop Negro leadership. It's an impossibility. I think that's true, too. And it was after the summer project that I learned that I could not help develop Negro leadership because I was white. . . .

ES: Was their presence one of the reasons that other people were upset? . . .

JS: Well, their presence made some of the Negro people angry. I mean there were some Southern Negro kids who were on the SNCC staff who were just as insecure as local Negroes and the fact that a white kid came in and could do this or that, the other, made them mad as hell. Again, you talk about black power and black this and black the other, which is not what Stokely's saying or why Stokely's saying what he's saying, but there was some personal antagonism towards them. The more whites that came in, the greater this antagonism. "This is our organization. This is our identity. Why the hell does

Source: Reprinted with the permission of the publisher from Emily Stoper, *The Student Nonviolent Coordinating Committee: The Growth of Radicalism in a Civil Rights Organization* (Brooklyn: Carlson Publishing Inc., 1989).

this kid have to come and join it," kind of thing. The more that came in, naturally, the madder they got.

In her autobiography, Fannie Lou Hamer discussed what she learned from her experiences at the Democratic National Convention in 1964.

Fannie Lou Hamer on the Lessons of 1964 (1967)

In 1964 we registered 63,000 black people from Mississippi into the Freedom Democratic Party. We formed our own party because the whites wouldn't even let us register. We decided to challenge the white Mississippi Democratic Party at the National Convention. We followed all the laws that the white people themselves made. We tried to attend the precinct meetings and they locked the doors on us or moved the meetings and that's against the laws they made for their ownselves. So we were the ones that held the real precinct meetings. At all these meetings across the state we elected our representatives to go to the National Democratic Convention in Atlantic City. But we learned the hard way that even though we had all the law and all the righteousness on our side—that white man is not going to give up his power to us.

We have to build our own power. We have to win every single political office we can, where we have a majority of black people. . . .

. . . The question for black people is not, when is the white man going to give us our rights, or when is he going to give us good education for our children, or when is he going to give us jobs—if the white man gives you anything—just remember when he gets ready he will take it right back. We have to take for ourselves.

Source: Clayborne Carson et al., *The Eyes on the Prize Civil Rights Reader: Documents, Speeches, and Firsthand Accounts from the Black Freedom Struggle, 1954–1990,* Viking Press, © 1991, pp. 282–284, 285–286; originally from Stokely Carmichael, "What We Want," *New York Review of Books,* September 22, 1996.

Elected chairman of SNCC in 1966, Stokely Carmichael was a leading advocate for "black power." In an essay published in the same year, he explained what he meant by this slogan that many whites found threatening.

Source: Clayborne Carson et al., *The Eyes on the Prize Civil Rights Reader: Documents, Speeches, and Firsthand Accounts from the Black Freedom Struggle, 1954–1990,* Viking Press, © 1991, pp. 282–284, 285–286; originally from Stokely Carmichael, "What We Want," *New York Review of Books,* September 22, 1996.

"What We Want" (1966)

One of the tragedies of the struggle against racism is that up to now there has been no national organization which could speak to the growing militancy of young black people in the urban ghetto. There has been only a civil rights movement, whose tone of voice was adapted to an audience of liberal whites. It served as a sort of buffer zone between them and angry young blacks. None of its so-called leaders could go into a rioting community and be listened to. In a sense, I blame ourselves—together with the mass media—for what has happened in Watts, Harlem, Chicago, Cleveland, Omaha. Each time the people in those cities saw Martin Luther King get slapped, they became angry; when they saw four little black girls bombed to death, they were angrier; and when nothing happened, they were steaming. We had nothing to offer that they could see, except to go out and be beaten again. We helped to build their frustration. . . .

An organization which claims to be working for the needs of a community—as SNCC does—must work to provide that community with a position of strength from which to make its voice heard. This is the significance of black power beyond the slogan.

Black power can be clearly defined for those who do not attach the fears of white America to their questions about it. We should begin with the basic fact that black Americans have two problems: they are poor and they are black. All other problems arise from this two-sided reality: lack of education, the so-called apathy of black men. Any program to end racism must address itself to that double reality. . . .

The concept of "black power" is not a recent or isolated phenomenon: It has grown out of the ferment of agitation and activity by different people and organizations in many black communities over the years. Our last year of work in Alabama added a new concrete possibility. In Lowndes County, for example, black power will mean that if a Negro is elected sheriff, he can end police brutality. If a black man is elected tax assessor, he can collect and channel funds for the building of better roads and schools serving black people—thus advancing the move from political power into the economic arena. In such areas as Lowndes, where black men have a majority, they will attempt to use it to exercise control. This is what they seek: control. Where Negroes lack a majority, black power means proper representation and sharing of control. It means the creation of power bases from which black people can work to change statewide or nationwide patterns of oppression through pressure from strength—instead of weakness. Politically, black power means what it has always meant to SNCC: the coming-together of black people to elect representatives and *to force those representatives to speak to their needs.* It does not mean merely putting black faces into office. A man or woman who is black and from the slums cannot be automatically expected to speak to the needs of black people. Most of the black politicians we see around the country today are not what SNCC means by black power. The power must be that of a community, and emanate from there. . . .

Ultimately, the economic foundations of this country must be shaken if black people are to control their lives. The colonies of the United States—and this includes the black ghettoes within its borders, north and south—must be liberated. For a century, this nation has been like an octopus of exploitation, its tentacles stretching from Mississippi and Harlem to South America, the Middle East, southern Africa, and Vietnam; the form of exploitation varies from area to area but the essential result has been the same—a powerful few have been maintained and enriched at the expense of the poor and voiceless colored masses. This pattern must be broken. As its grip loosens here and there around the world, the hopes of black Americans become more realistic. For racism to die, a totally different America must be born. . . .

But our vision is not merely of a society in which all black men have enough to buy the good things of life. When we urge that black money go into black pockets, we mean the communal pocket. We want to see money go back into the community and used to benefit it. We want to see the cooperative concept applied in business and banking. We want to see black ghetto residents demand that an exploiting store keeper sell them, at minimal cost, a building or a shop that they will own and improve cooperatively; they can back their demand with a rent strike, or a boycott, and a community so unified behind them that no one else will move into the building or buy at the store. The society we seek to build among black people, then, is not a capitalist one. It is a society in which the spirit of community and humanistic love prevail. . . .

CONCLUSION

As we saw in the previous chapter, even popular culture in the postwar era was not immune from the influences of anticommunist hysteria. This chapter reminds us that our view of the past is not immune from the influence of popular culture itself. Few episodes in recent American history illustrate better than the civil rights struggle how perceptions of the past have been shaped by images embedded in our culture. Because this struggle ultimately received extensive media coverage, popular memories of it have been shaped, as historian Charles Payne pointed out, by a few "Big Events" highlighted by the media. Payne's point reminds us once again that the way we frame our view of the past—the process by which events are selected, emphasized, and presented—is never objective. Because these "Big Events" often put a handful of prominent leaders in the spotlight, Payne's point also illustrates the lessons of Chapters 7 and 8, that is, whether we choose to look at history from the "top down" or the "bottom up" will determine the past that we see. Finally, examining the civil rights struggle also reminds us that such questions matter. As Payne observes—and as we shall see when we turn to the Vietnam War in the next chapter—the way we view the past determines the lessons that we draw from it.

FURTHER READING

Clayborne Carson, *In Struggle: SNCC and the Black Awakening of the 1960s* (Cambridge, Mass.: Harvard University Press, 1981).

James Forman, *The Making of Black Revolutionaries* (New York: The Macmillan Company, 1972).

Cheryl Lynn Greenberg, ed., *A Circle of Trust: Remembering SNCC* (New Brunswick, N.J.: Rutgers University Press, 1998).

Henry Hampton and Steve Fayer, eds., *Voices of Freedom: An Oral History of the Civil Rights Movement from the 1950s through the 1980s* (New York: Bantam Books, 1990).

Doug McAdam, *Freedom Summer* (New York: Oxford University Press, 1988).

Nicholaus Mills, *Like a Holy Crusade: Mississippi 1964—The Turning of the Civil Rights Movement in America* (Chicago: Ivan R. Dee, 1992).

Robert Weisbrot, *Freedom Bound: A History of America's Civil Rights Movement* (New York: W. W. Norton & Company, 1990).

NOTES

1. Quoted in Nicholaus Mills, *Like a Holy Crusade: Mississippi 1964—The Turning of the Civil Rights Movement in America* (Chicago: Ivan R. Dee, 1992), p. 28.
2. Quoted in ibid., pp. 28, 29.
3. Quoted in Robert Weisbrot, *Freedom Bound: A History of America's Civil Rights Movement* (New York: W. W. Norton & Company, 1990), p. 82.
4. Quoted in Fred Powledge, *Free at Last? The Civil Rights Movement and the People Who Made It* (Boston: Little, Brown and Company, 1990), p. xix.
5. Clayborne Carson, "Civil Rights Reform and the Black Freedom Struggle," in Charles W. Eagles, ed., *The Civil Rights Movement in America* (Jackson: University Press of Mississippi, 1986), p. 27.
6. Ibid., p. 23.
7. Quoted in Weisbrot, *Freedom Bound,* p. 122.

Chapter

11

Causation and the Lessons of History: Explaining America's Longest War

This chapter presents two secondary sources and several primary sources dealing with America's involvement in the Vietnam War.

Secondary Sources

Primary Sources

*T*he end of the Vietnam War came suddenly in 1975. For eighteen hours on April 29, marine and air force helicopters hovered over landing pads on the roofs of a few of Saigon's tallest buildings. As the Viet Cong and North Vietnamese troops advanced on the capital, the helicopters lifted more than 1,000 Americans and 5,000 South Vietnamese to waiting ships in the South China Sea. Meanwhile, the U.S. embassy was a scene of confusion. Thousands of South Vietnamese desperately looking for a way out of their country had come to the compound. When they tried to scale the walls, marine guards used their boots and rifle butts to force them back. One North Vietnamese commander said they were "fighting their way in, smashing doors, climbing walls, climbing each other's backs, tussling, brawling, and trampling each other as they sought to flee."[1]

At 5:00 the next morning the American ambassador, under orders from President Ford to get out "without a moment's delay," boarded a CH-46 helicopter. Then nine more CH-46s landed and took off with the remaining marines, who had to spray Mace to fend off the Vietnamese still trying to break into the compound. When the last helicopter lifted off, three years after the last American combat troops had gone home, American involvement in Vietnam was finally over. Within hours, so was the war that the United States had officially abandoned two years before. By the afternoon, communist troops rolled into the heart of Saigon, smashed their way into the presidential palace, and raised their single-starred flag in triumph.

The United States expended an estimated $600 billion to defend South Vietnam. American planes dropped more than 10 million tons of bombs on the Southeast Asian country. About 2.7 million American soldiers fought there. Approximately 300,000 of them were wounded, and nearly 58,000 lost their lives. All of it had been done to prevent what happened in Saigon on April 30. Confronting failure, many Americans could only wonder what the effort had been for. "Now it's all gone down the drain and it hurts," said one Pennsylvanian who had lost a son in Vietnam. "What did he die for?"[2] In the three decades since the fall of South Vietnam, the sense of failure and personal loss has gradually lessened. Now many historians study the Vietnam War to discover why the United States fought this war as it did. They also want to know why it turned out as it did and what it would have taken for it to end differently. In this chapter we turn to those questions about America's longest war and its biggest military loss.

SETTING

Four years before the fall of South Vietnam, Lyndon Johnson predicted that the debate about Vietnam would continue for a long time as historians made "judgments on the decisions made and the actions taken."[3] In fact, the historical debate about Vietnam started even before LBJ left the presidency. With the war still raging, many historians wanted to know how the United States had come to be involved in Vietnam in the first place. Contemporary answers to that question varied. Such radical historians as Patrick J. Hearden and Gabriel Kolko saw the war as the result of a rational assessment by American policymakers concerned about a capitalist economy's need for markets and resources. Other students of the war, including Arthur Schlesinger and David Halberstam, argued that successive administrations made a series of mistakes that gradually and unthinkingly led the United States into a quagmire. Still others disputed the notion that the United States ended up in Vietnam by accident. Daniel Ellsberg, the Defense Department analyst who leaked *The Pentagon Papers*—a secret history of the war—to the *New York Times,* argued that presidents from Truman to LBJ were concerned about losing Vietnam to communism. These presidents, Ellsberg argued, made clear-sighted decisions and had no illusions about the chances of long-run success. Other scholars have also argued against the unthinking nature of America's commitment to Vietnam. In a study of the foreign policy elite, for instance, John Donovan argued that American policymakers were guided by a belief in containing communist expansion and simply misapplied the policy to Vietnam.

After the fall of South Vietnam, the debates shifted focus. They now reflected the failure of America's commitment and an increasingly conservative national mood. By the late 1970s, such revisionists as Harry G. Summers, Jr., and Norman Podhoretz began to treat the American effort in Vietnam more sympathetically. Instead of asking why the United States fought there, they inquired how the war was fought and how it could have turned out differently. Their guiding assumption was that the United States could have won. Rejecting earlier assessments that saw Vietnam as a mistake, they also drew a different lesson from America's military experience there. Rather than accept the conclusion that the United States should "never again" become involved militarily in distant lands, revisionists pointed to the dangers of isolationism and "appeasement."

More recently, Loren Baritz, Gary Hess, Larry Berman, and other scholars have taken on the revisionists. These postrevisionists are critical of American intervention in Vietnam and argue that the United States could not have won the war for many reasons, including the American ignorance about Vietnamese culture and society. Some of them are also more sympathetic to Lyndon Johnson, who was responsible for the rapid American military escalation in the late 1960s. Far from the blundering and thoughtless hawk of many earlier accounts, they view LBJ as a cautious leader who understood the difficulty of military success in Vietnam and actually expressed doubts about escalation. Many postrevisionists argue that the way America fought the war was determined by domestic political considerations. LBJ chose to escalate the war in a limited way to save his Great Society domestic program. A masterful politician, Johnson simply miscalculated when it came to the war. Ironically, while pointing to LBJ's flawed judgment, these postrevisionists also demonstrate that he got one thing right about Vietnam: It will be a long time before this war loses its power to elicit deeply felt debate.

INVESTIGATION

In this chapter you have the opportunity to compare two historians' assessments of the war in Vietnam. Their discussions focus on the policies and conduct of the war by the Johnson administration. Your primary job is to compare and evaluate these two historians' conclusions about the reason for the American failure in Vietnam and about the lessons that they draw from it. Your analysis should address the following main questions:

1. **What assumptions guided the escalation of the war in Vietnam, according to historians George Herring and Loren Baritz in Source 1 and Source 2?** Why do the authors think these assumptions were flawed? How do the authors respond to the argument that the war could have turned out differently?

2. **What role do Herring and Baritz assign to Lyndon Johnson in explaining the American failure in Vietnam?** Do the authors agree about the role of Johnson's personality and beliefs in determining American war policy?

3. **Are the historians' arguments in the essays supported by the evidence in the primary sources?** Do the primary sources suggest that the main reason for the American failure in Vietnam was the inherent difficulty of fighting a limited war, false assumptions rooted in American culture, or some other factor?

Before you begin, read the sections about Vietnam in your textbook, especially those dealing with the escalation of the war during the Johnson administration.

SECONDARY SOURCES

1   In this selection, historian George Herring offers an explanation for the way the United States fought in Vietnam. It focuses on the Johnson administration's decision to fight a limited war: one that would not arouse the passions of Americans, but rather could be fought in "cold blood." Note Herring's explanation for the American leaders' lack of an overall strategy for fighting the war and the extent to which Johnson's personality shaped American war policy. Does Herring explain why the Johnson administration failed to wage limited war successfully?

Fighting in "Cold Blood": LBJ's Conduct of Limited War in Vietnam (1994)

GEORGE HERRING

Of the two great questions concerning involvement in Vietnam—why did the United States intervene and why did it fail—the latter has provoked the most emotional controversy. Historically, as a nation, America has been uniquely successful, so much so that its people have come to take success for granted. When failure occurs, scapegoats are sought and myths concocted to explain what is otherwise inexplicable. In the case of Vietnam, many critics of America's conduct of the war have thus insisted that a different approach would have produced the "proper" results. Such arguments can never be proven, of course, and they are suspect in method. As Wayne Cole observed many years ago of a strikingly similar debate in the aftermath of World War II, the "most heated controversies . . . do not center on those matters for which the facts and truth can be determined with greatest certainty. The interpretive controversies, on the contrary, rage over questions about which the historian is least able to determine the truth." . . .

The most glaring deficiency is that in an extraordinarily complex war there was no real strategy. President Johnson and Secretary of Defense Robert S. McNamara provided no firm strategic guidance to those military and civilian advisers who were running programs in the field. They set no clearcut limits on what could be done, what resources might be employed, and what funds expended. Without direction from the top, each service or agency did its own thing. Strategy emerged from the field on an improvised basis without careful calculation of the ends to be sought and the means used to attain them.

Perhaps equally important and less generally recognized, despite widespread and steadily growing dissatisfaction among the president's top advisers with the way the war was being fought and the results that were being obtained, there was no change of strategy or even systematic discussion of such a change. Not until the shock of the 1968 Tet offensive compelled it were the basic issues of how the war was being fought even raised. Even then, they were quickly dropped and left largely unresolved. Despite talk among the president's top advisers of borrowing a page from the communists' book and fighting while negotiating, the administration after Tet replaced one makeshift strategy with another, perpetuating and in some ways exacerbating the problems that had afflicted its management of the war from the beginning.

Closely related to and to some extent deriving from the absence of strategy was the lack of coordination of the numerous elements of what had become by 1966 a sprawling, multifarious war effort. Johnson steadfastly

Source: LBJ and Vietnam: A Different Kind of War by George C. Herring. Copyright © 1994. By permission of the author and the University of Texas Press.

refused to assume overall direction of the war, and he would not create special machinery or designate someone else to run it. In Vietnam, therefore, each service or agency tended to go about its own business without much awareness of the impact of its actions in other areas or on other programs. The air war against North Vietnam operated separately from the ground war in South Vietnam (and the air war in Laos was run separately from both). . . .

It is more difficult to determine why these problems existed. In part, no doubt, institutional imperatives were at fault. The rule in bureaucracy . . . is that when an organization does not know what to do—or is not told what to do—it does what it knows how to do. Thus, in the absence of strong leadership from the top, the various services and agencies acted on the basis of their own standard operating procedures whether or not they were appropriate or compatible. CIA operative William Colby recalls warning McGeorge Bundy during the U.S. buildup in 1965 that the growing militarization of the war was diverting attention from the more urgent problems in the villages of South Vietnam. He pleaded with the presidential adviser to refocus the administration's attention toward the proper area. "You may be right, Bill," Colby remembered Bundy answering, "but the structure of the American government won't permit it." "What he meant," Colby concluded, "was that the Pentagon had to fight the only war it knew how to fight, and there was no American organization that could fight any other." This was most true of the army, air force, and navy, but it was also true of the civilian agencies.

Limited war theory also significantly influenced the way the war was fought. Korea and especially the Truman-MacArthur controversy stimulated a veritable cult of limited war in the 1950s and 1960s, the major conclusion of which was that in a nuclear age where total war was unthinkable limited war was essential. McNamara, William and McGeorge Bundy, Rusk,* and indeed Lyndon Johnson were deeply imbued with limited war theory, and it determined in many crucial ways their handling of Vietnam. Coming of age in World War II, they were convinced of the essentiality of deterring aggression to avoid a major war. Veterans of the Cuban missile crisis, they lived with the awesome responsibility of preventing nuclear conflagration and they were thus committed to fighting in "cold blood" and maintaining tight operational control over the military. They also operated under the mistaken assumption that limited war was more an exercise in crisis management than the application of strategy, and they were thus persuaded that gradual escalation would achieve their limited goals without provoking the larger war they so feared. Many of their notions, of course, turned out to be badly flawed.

To an even greater extent, Lyndon Johnson's own highly personalized style indelibly marked the conduct of the war and contributed to its peculiar frustrations. LBJ was a "kind of whirlwind," David Lilienthal has observed,

---

*William Bundy was assistant secretary of state for eastern affairs; McGeorge Bundy was a national security advisor; Dean Rusk was secretary of state.

a man of seemingly boundless energy who attempted to put his personal brand on everything he dealt with. He dominated the presidency as few others have. He sought to run the war as he ran his household and ranch, his office and *his* government, with scrupulous attention to the most minute detail. As with every other personal and political crisis he faced he worked tirelessly at the job of commander in chief of a nation at war. His approach was best typified by his oft-quoted and characteristically hyperbolic boast that U.S. airmen could not bomb an outhouse in North Vietnam without his approval. In the case of Vietnam, however, the result was the worst of both worlds, a strategic vacuum and massive intrusion at the tactical level, micromanagement without real control. Whether he would admit it or not, moreover, LBJ quickly found in Vietnam a situation that eluded his grasp and dissipated even *his* seemingly inexhaustible storehouse of energy.

In so many ways, the conduct of the war reflected Johnson's modus operandi. The reluctance to provide precise direction and define a mission and explicit limits, the highly politicized, for Johnson characteristically middle-of-the-road approach that gave everybody something and nobody what they wanted, that emphasized consensus and internal harmony over results on the battlefield or at the negotiating table, all these were products of a thoroughly political and profoundly insecure man, a man especially ill at ease among military issues and military people.

Johnson's intolerance for any form of intragovernmental dissent and his unwillingness to permit, much less order, a much-needed debate on strategic issues deserve special note. It was not, as his most severe critics have argued, the result of his determination to impose a hermetically sealed system or his preference for working with sycophants, the so-called Caligula syndrome. LBJ was a domineering individual, to be sure, and he did have a strong distaste for conflict in his official family. As David Barrett and others have pointed out, however, he eagerly sought out and indeed opened himself to a wide diversity of viewpoints. Whatever their faults, the people that worked with him were anything but sycophants.

The problem went much deeper than that. In part, it reflected the peculiar mix of personalities involved, the rigorous standards of loyalty of a Rusk or McNamara, Harriman's determination to retain influence at the cost of principle and candor. From Johnson's standpoint, it was largely a matter of control. "He wanted to control everything," Joe Califano* recalled. "His greatest outbursts of anger were triggered by people or situations that escaped his control." He therefore discouraged the sort of open exchange of ideas, freewheeling discussion of alternatives, or ranging policy reviews that might in any way threaten his control. His admonition to McGeorge Bundy that his advisers must not "gang up" on him reflected his reluctance to permit them to engage in discussions except under his watchful eye. . . .

*W. Averell Harriman was an ambassador-at-large; Joseph Califano was a presidential aide.

It would be a serious mistake to attribute America's failure in Vietnam solely or even largely to bureaucratic imperatives, the false dogmas of limited war theory, or the eccentricities of Johnson leadership style. Had the United States looked all over the world in 1965 it might not have been able to find a more difficult place to fight. The climate and terrain were singularly inhospitable. More important, perhaps, was the formless, yet lethal, nature of warfare in Vietnam, a conflict without distinct battlelines or fixed objectives where traditional concepts of victory and defeat were blurred. And from the outset, the balance of forces was stacked against the United States in the form of a weak, divided, and far too dependent client lacking in political legitimacy and a fanatically determined and resilient enemy that early on seized and refused to relinquish the banner of Vietnamese nationalism.

American military leaders have left ample testimony of the complex and often baffling challenge they faced in Vietnam and on the home front. Speaking of the "fog of war" in December 1967, [General Earle] Wheeler observed that Vietnam was the "foggiest war" in his memory and the first where the fog was "thicker away from the scene of the conflict than on the battlefield." Marine Gen. Lewis Walt concurred. "Soon after I arrived in Vietnam," he later admitted, "it became obvious to me that I had neither a real understanding of the nature of the war nor any clear idea how to win it." Abysmal ignorance of Vietnam and the Vietnamese on the part of Lyndon Johnson, his advisers, and the nation as a whole thickened the fog of war, contributing to a mistaken decision to intervene, mismanagement of the conflict, and ultimate failure.

A considerable part of the problem also lay in the inherent difficulty of waging limited war. Limited wars, as Stephen Peter Rosen has noted, are by their very nature "*strange* wars." They combine political, military, and diplomatic dimensions in the most complicated way. Conducting them effectively requires rare intellectual ability, political acumen, and moral courage.

Johnson and his advisers went into the conflict confident—probably overconfident—that they knew how to wage limited war, and only when the strategy of escalation proved bankrupt and the American people unwilling or unable to fight in cold blood did they confront their tragic and costly failure. . . .

Nor is there any obvious solution to the dilemma of domestic opinion. Vietnam exposed the enormous difficulties of fighting in cold blood. Without arousing popular emotions and especially without measurable success on the battlefield it was impossible over a long period of time to sustain popular support. Frederick the Great's dictum that war could only be successful when people did not know about it could not possibly work in the age of instant communications and mass media, especially when, as in the case of Vietnam, the size of the U.S. commitment quickly outgrew the presumed parameters of limited war. On the other hand, trying to play down the war also caused major problems. The Johnson and Nixon administrations both went to considerable lengths to maintain the semblance of normality at home. Thus, as D. Michael Shafer has observed, "those fighting [in Vietnam] faced the bitter irony that back in 'The World' life went on as normal while they risked their lives in a war their government did not acknowledge and many fellow citizens considered unnecessary or even immoral."

Johnson's inability to wage war in cold blood produced what appears on the surface a great anomaly—one of the shrewdest politicians of the twentieth century committing a form of political suicide by taking the nation into a war he would have preferred not to fight. To some extent, of course, LBJ was the victim of his considerable political acumen. He took the nation to war so quietly, with such consummate skill (and without getting a popular mandate) that when things turned sour the anger was inevitably directed at him. His inability to manage effectively the war he got [in] so skillfully is typical of his leadership record. He was also much more effective in getting domestic programs through Congress than in managing them once enacted. In the final analysis, however, Johnson's failure reflects more than anything else the enormity of the problem and the inadequacy of the means chosen to address it.

Partial mobilization or a declaration of war provides at best debatable alternatives. George Bush's apparent success in mobilizing support for the Persian Gulf War in 1991 confirmed in the eyes of some critics the deficiencies of Johnson's leadership in Vietnam. In fact, the remarkable popular support for the Gulf War and especially for the troops was in a very real sense an expiation of lingering guilt for nonsupport in Vietnam. It also owed a great deal to perceptions of military success and the rapidity with which the war ended. In any event, Johnson's and Rusk's reservations about the dangers of a declaration of war in the Cold War international system were well taken, and congressional sanction in the War of 1812 and the Mexican War did nothing to stop rampant and at times crippling domestic opposition.

However much we might deplore the limitations of Johnson's leadership and the folly of limited war theory, they alone are not responsible for America's failure in Vietnam. That conflict posed uniquely complex challenges for U.S. war managers both in terms of the conditions within Vietnam itself and the international context in which it was fought. American policymakers thus took on in Vietnam a problem that was in all likelihood beyond their control.

In the new world order of the post–Cold War era, the conditions that appeared to make limited war essential and that made the Vietnam War especially difficult to fight will probably not be replicated, and the "lessons" of Vietnam will have at best limited relevance. There are many different kinds of limited war, however. Korea, Vietnam, the Persian Gulf War (which was, after all, limited in both ends and means) were as different from each other as each was from World War II. What they shared was the complexity in establishing ends and formulating means that is inherent in the institution of limited war itself. Even in this new era, therefore, it would be well for us to remember Vietnam and to recall Lady Bird Johnson's 1967 lament: "It is unbearably hard to fight a limited war."

2   In his study of the Vietnam War, historian Loren Baritz argues that American culture not only led the United States into Vietnam but also determined the way Americans fought the war. Note how Baritz explains the American failure in Vietnam and how the cause of failure manifested itself in the actions of the Johnson administration and American military personnel. How does Baritz account for the American determination to fight in "cold blood" and for the failure of the Johnson administration to formulate a war strategy? How does his explanation for failure in Vietnam differ from Herring's?

God's Country and American Know-How (1986)
LOREN BARITZ

America was involved in Vietnam for thirty years, but never understood the Vietnamese. We were frustrated by the incomprehensible behavior of our Vietnamese enemies and bewildered by the inexplicable behavior of our Vietnamese friends. For us, this corner of Asia was inscrutable. These Asians successfully masked their intentions in smiles, formal courtesies, and exotic rituals. The organic nature of Vietnamese society, the significance of village life, the meaning of ancestors, the relationship of the family to the state, the subordinate role of the individual, and the eternal quest for universal agreement, not consensus or majorities, were easily lost on the Americans.

Most of the Vietnamese were so poor, American GIs said that they lived like animals. Some said they were animals. They did not bathe, had no toilets, and ate food whose smell made some young Americans vomit. There was something about the very great age of Vietnamese culture that seemed to resist our best efforts to understand. . . . They were not part of our century and not part of our world.

When we did try to impose changes, for the better of course, the resistance of the people could seem like ingratitude or stupidity, as it did to a young GI, Steve Harper. The Vietnamese enraged him. "We were there to help but Vietnamese are so stupid they can't understand that a great people want to help a weak people." He said that "somebody had to show poor people better ways of livin', like sewer disposal and sanitation and things like that." He once watched an American team enter a village to teach the peasants sanitation while members of South Vietnam's army stood around laughing because they thought it was a pointless waste of energy. His worst experience was his R&R tour in Tokyo, "the greatest sin city":

Source: Loren Baritz, *Backfire: A History of How American Culture Led Us into Vietnam and Made Us Fight the Way We Did.* Copyright 1985 by Loren Baritz. Originally published by William Morrow & Company, New York. Reprinted with the permission of Gerald McCauley Agency, Inc.

I would walk down the Ginza, their main street, and look at all the slant eyes and I swear I'd start to get sick. I was even tempted by some of the prostitutes but one look at their faces and I'd walk away in disgust. . . . I began to get angry at Asians and at my own country. Why couldn't they take care of their own problems?

Americans who were most responsible for our Vietnam policies often complained about how little they knew about the Vietnamese. They mistakenly thought they were especially uninformed about the northerners. For example, General Maxwell Taylor, America's ambassador to Saigon, admitted that "we knew very little about the Hanoi leaders . . . and virtually nothing about their individual or collective intentions." . . .

Our difficulties were not with the strangeness of the land or the inscrutability of its people. Modern, secular, well-educated people, such as we are, such as General Taylor and Dr. Kissinger* were, can learn about exotic people in distant places. Our difficulty was not with the peculiarities of the Vietnamese. The problem was us, not them. Our difficulty was that the foot soldier slogging through a rice paddy, the general in his Saigon office planning great troop movements, the official in the Pentagon, and the Presidents who made the war were all Americans. Peer de Silva, a CIA chief of station in Saigon, said, "The American official posted in Asia very often finds himself, whether he realizes it or not, standing solemnly before the Asians, his finger pointed skyward and the word 'repent' on his lips." We wanted the Vietnamese to repent for being Vietnamese. There was something about the condition of being an American that prevented us from understanding the "little people in black pajamas" who beat the strongest military force in the world.

In common with most Asians, the Vietnamese had one custom that American soldiers could not tolerate. The people of Vietnam hold hands with their friends. Two Vietnamese soldiers would walk down the street holding hands. An American marine from south Boston noticed this custom: "They all hold hands, see. I fucking hated that." The intensity of this marine's reaction was characteristic of America's fighting men. The custom proved to the GIs that South Vietnamese men were homosexuals, and this diagnosis explained why the Vietnamese were incompetent warriors, raising the question about why Americans had to die in defense of perverts. . . .

This could all be dismissed as just another example of American cultural ignorance except that it occasionally had hideous consequences. A marine's truck was stopped by South Vietnamese soldiers who wanted the Americans to take a wounded South Vietnamese soldier to a hospital. His leg had been shot off. One of the marines said, "Fuck him. Let him hop." But the commander of the truck told the wounded man to climb in. "The fucking little slope grabbed my leg." The truck commander said that he had been in Vietnam long enough "to know that most of them are queer. They hold hands and stuff." One of the Americans "whacked" the wounded soldier and told

*Henry Kissinger was a national security advisor and, later, secretary of state.

the driver to get going. They threw the wounded man out of the moving truck: "The poor fucking bastard was screaming and crying and begging us. 'Fuck you, you slope. Out you go.'"

The Americans did not see guerrillas or North Vietnamese strolling hand in hand down the street, or if they did they did not realize they were North Vietnamese. It was usual for grunts to respect the enemy more than the ally. As GIs watched our gunships pulverize an area, one said, "You couldn't believe that anyone would have the courage to deal with that night after night . . . and you cultivated a respect for the Viet Cong and NVA [North Vietnamese army] . . . ." He also told of a lone sniper firing at a marine base from his hole in the ground. The marines fired everything they had at him, but he always reappeared to fire another round. Finally, napalm was dropped on his position and the entire area was burned to the ground. "When all of it cleared, the sniper popped up and fired off a single round, and the Marines in the trenches cheered. They called him Luke the Gook, and after that no one wanted anything to happen to him."

Thomas Bailey, an interrogation officer stationed in Saigon in the early seventies, believed that Americans did not understand themselves well enough to understand the Vietnamese. He became frustrated because "their civilization was so much older than ours, although we would characterize them as being uncivilized. I would have a difficult time defining the way in which they were more civilized than we were, but they were. It's my gut feeling." It was difficult for the young Americans who were sent to save the South Vietnamese both from themselves and from North Vietnam to encounter people who did not want to be saved in the way we intended. "Government is not important," a villager said, "rice is important." America corrupted the urban elites of South Vietnam by dangling riches in front of them. But it was the city dwellers, especially the Buddhists, who struggled hardest against the other corruption, the cultural pride and myopia of the Americans. They were as proud of their traditions and culture as we were of ours. . . .

Americans were ignorant about the Vietnamese not because we were stupid, but because we believe certain things about ourselves. Those things necessarily distorted our vision and confused our minds in ways that made learning extraordinarily difficult. To understand our failure we must think about what it means to be an American.

The necessary text for understanding the condition of being an American is a single sentence written by Herman Melville in his novel *White Jacket*: "And we Americans are the peculiar, chosen people—the Israel of our time; we bear the ark of the liberties of the world." This was not the last time this idea was expressed by Americans. It was at the center of thought of the men who brought us the Vietnam War. It was at the center of the most characteristic American myth. . . .

In countless ways Americans know in their gut—the only place myths can live—that we have been Chosen to lead the world in public morality and to instruct it in political virtue. We believe that our own domestic goodness results in strength adequate to destroy our opponents who, by definition, are enemies of virtue, freedom, and God. Over and over, the founding Puritans described their new settlement as a beacon in the darkness, a light whose radiance could keep Christian voyagers from crashing on the rocks, a light that could brighten the world. In his inaugural address John Kennedy said, "The energy, the faith, the devotion which we bring to this endeavor [defending freedom] will light our country and all who serve it—and the glow from that fire can truly light the world." . . .

In other words, we assumed that we had a superior moral claim to be in Vietnam, and because, despite their quite queer ways of doing things, the Vietnamese shared our values, they would applaud our intentions and embrace our physical presence. Thus, Vice-President Humphrey later acknowledged that all along we had been ignorant of Vietnam. He said that "to LBJ, the Mekong and the Pedernales were not that far apart." Our claim to virtue was based on the often announced purity of our intentions. It was said, perhaps thousands of times, that all we wanted was freedom for other people, not land, not resources, and not domination. . . .

Joining the American sense of its moral superiority with its technological superiority was a marriage made in heaven, at least for American nationalists. We told ourselves that each advantage explained the other, that the success of our standard of living was a result of our virtue, and our virtue was a result of our wealth. Our riches, our technology, provided the strength that had earlier been missing, that once had forced us to rely only on our virtue. Now, as Hiroshima demonstrated conclusively, we could think of ourselves not only as morally superior, but as the most powerful nation in history. The inevitable offspring of this marriage of an idea with a weapon was the conviction that the United States could not be beaten in war—not by any nation, and not by any combination of nations. For that moment we thought that we could fight where, when, and how we wished, without risking failure. For that moment we thought that we could impose our will on the recalcitrant of the earth. . . .

In Vietnam we had to find a technology to win without broadening the war. The nuclear stalemate reemphasized our need to find a more limited ground, to find, so to speak, a way to fight a domesticated war. We had to find a technology that would prevail locally, but not explode internationally. No assignment is too tough for the technological mentality. In fact, it was made to order for the technicians who were coming into their own throughout all of American life. This war gave them the opportunity to show what they could do. This was to be history's most technologically sophisticated war, most carefully analyzed and managed, using all of the latest wonders of managerial procedures and systems. It was made to order for bureaucracy. . . .

In summary, our national myth showed us that we were good, our technology made us strong, and our bureaucracy gave us standard operating procedures. It was not a winning combination. . . .

To make matters worse, President Johnson had a warm and giving nature. He genuinely believed that all the peoples of the earth were the same in their need for food, health, and education, as of course they are. He had no comprehension that different cultures search for the satisfaction of these essential needs in quite different ways. His understanding of the Vietnamese, North and South, was minimal. His textbook was his own experience in west Texas; his textbook was his own life. That is what Vice-President Humphrey meant when he said that for LBJ the Pedernales and the Mekong were not so far apart. That is why the President could even think of offering a massive flood-control project to the North Vietnamese if they would only please stop fighting. He could imagine trading an enormous TVA project in exchange for the ideology of the North. With typical enthusiasm, he said "We're going to turn the Mekong into a Tennessee Valley." North Vietnam responded that this was a "bribe." . . .

He believed that his was the voice of "the common people" because he thought he was one of them, and believed that he therefore understood their needs and dreams whether in America or Vietnam. While he was destroying the country with bombing, defoliation, and napalm, he could without cynicism speak of peace and progress. He believed that the destruction was unfortunately necessary before the construction could occur. That was Ho Chi Minh's fault. . . .

War is a product of culture. It is an expression of the way a culture thinks of itself and the world. Different cultures go to war for different reasons and fight in different ways. There is an American way of war. Our Vietnam War was started and fought in ways our culture required. . . .

American political culture—the self-righteousness of our nationalism—merged with the impulses of our technological culture—tell us what to do and we'll do it, no questions asked. President Kennedy's enthusiasm for counterinsurgency led the nation to assume that we could successfully intervene in Vietnamese politics in ways that were foreign to America's genius. Our managerial sophistication and technological superiority resulted in our trained incompetence in guerrilla warfare.

The conclusion is obvious: If this nation cannot use its managerial and technological strengths in international conflict, it would be wise to avoid engagement. If our expensive weapon systems will not contribute to victory, it would be wise not to pretend that we have other resources. . . .

The technician's mind is organized around the question *how*. He is motivated by a desire, sometimes a need, to solve problems. He is rational, practical, hardheaded, and believes that if an idea can be transformed into a solution that actually works, the idea was true. Most of the war's planners exhibited these traits. Three other attributes of the technological mentality had an even more direct impact on the war. The technician's language is amoral, dispassionate, and optimistic. For example, Secretary McNamara's perception of Vietnam as a limited war reveals all these habits of mind: "The greatest contribution Vietnam is making—right or wrong is beside the point—is that it is developing an ability in the United States to fight a limited war, to go to war without the necessity of arousing the public ire." . . .

North Vietnam finally won its war because it was willing to accept more death than we considered rational. That is why the bombing campaigns failed. It is not that our technology failed. Our cultural perceptions failed when so many intelligent men in high positions simply assumed that our enemy's culture was sufficiently like ours that he would quit at a point where we believed we would quit.

We lost the war because we were never clear about the guerrillas, their popular support, the North Vietnamese, or ourselves. Our marvelously clever technology did not help us to understand the war and, in fact, confused us even more because it created our unquestioning faith in our own power. Finally, the North's decision to continue fighting, and our decision to stop, were each consistent with the cultural imperatives of each nation. Because the army of South Vietnam was trained by us to fight in the American style, it was forever dependent on a supply of hardware and fuel. That army was incongruent with the culture it was trying to defend.

This is why the military's continuing claim that we could have won the war if it had been allowed to fight differently is pointless. We could not have fought it differently. The constraints on the tactics of the war, and the absence of a political goal to shape those tactics, were products of American culture at the time. It is meaningless to argue that "next time we'll do it differently and win." The only reasonable prediction about the cultural pressures surrounding a "next time" is that they will at least resemble those that existed in the 1960s and exist now.

PRIMARY SOURCES

The Vietnam War left historians with a wealth of primary sources. Many of them reveal the thinking of policymakers, including LBJ and his top advisers. Others reflect the experience of military personnel in Vietnam. Some of the primary sources in this chapter document the concerns of policymakers in the Johnson administration as they considered military options. Others demonstrate the nature of the Vietnam War, the consequences of the administration's war policies, and the attitudes of Americans about Vietnam. Together such sources can help historians understand, perhaps better than many of the participants themselves, why the United States fought the war the way it did and why the war ended as it did.

3   One month before Lyndon Johnson decided to send an additional 125,000 American combat troops to Vietnam, he told Secretary of Defense Robert McNamara what he foresaw there. Do the doubts LBJ expresses here help to explain the Johnson administration's later conduct of the war?

LBJ Expresses Doubts About Vietnam (1965)

I think that in time . . . it's going to be difficult for us to very long prosecute effectively a war that far away from home with the divisions that we have here and particularly the potential divisions. And it's really had me concerned for a month and I'm very depressed about it because I see no program from either Defense or State that gives me much hope of doing anything except just praying and grasping to hold on during [the] monsoon [season] and hope they'll quit. And I don't believe they're ever goin' to quit. And I don't see . . . that we have any . . . plan for victory militarily or diplomatically. . . . Russell* thinks we ought to take one of these [regime] changes to get out of there. I do not think we can get out of there with our treaty like it is and with what all we've said and I think it would just lose us face in the world and I just shudder to think what all of 'em would say.

*Richard B. Russell (D-Ga.), Johnson's old Senate mentor and powerful chairman of the Senate Armed Services Committee.

Source: In Retrospect: The Tragedy and Lessons of Vietnam by Robert S. McNamara, pp. 190–191. Copyright © 1995 by Random House, Inc.; originally from June 21, 1965, 12:15 p.m., Tape 6506.04, Program Number 18, Presidential Recordings, Lyndon Baines Johnson Library.

4   Because they are often written to justify past actions and policies, memoirs must be evaluated very carefully, particularly when such sources deal with such a controversial subject as Vietnam. In his memoir, Johnson defended his decision to seek a middle course in Vietnam. Note how he justifies his decision in this excerpt. Were his assumptions well founded? How does this statement compare to that in Source 3?

LBJ Recalls His Decision to Escalate (1971)

We continued our review of the military situation and the requirement for additional forces. Our military commanders had refined their estimates and indicated they could meet the immediate demand with 50,000 men. I called a meeting of the National Security Council two days later, on July 27. I asked McNamara at that time to summarize again the current need as he saw it.

Source: Lyndon Johnson, *The Vantage Point: Perspectives of the Presidency, 1963–1969* (New York: Holt, Rinehart and Winston, 1971), pp. 148–149.

McNamara noted that the Viet Cong had increased in size through local recruitment and replacements from the North. Regular North Vietnamese army units had increased in number and strength. Communist control of the countryside was growing. A dozen provincial capitals were virtually isolated from surrounding rural areas. The South Vietnamese army was growing, but not nearly fast enough to keep pace with the expanding enemy forces. Without additional armed strength, South Vietnam would inevitably fall to Hanoi. I told the NSC there were five possible choices available to us.

"We can bring the enemy to his knees by using our Strategic Air Command," I said, describing our first option. "Another group thinks we ought to pack up and go home."

"Third, we could stay there as we are—and suffer the consequences, continue to lose territory and take casualties. You wouldn't want your own boy to be out there crying for help and not get it."

"Then, we could go to Congress and ask for great sums of money; we could call up the reserves and increase the draft; go on a war footing; declare a state of emergency. There is a good deal of feeling that ought to be done. We have considered this. But if we go into that kind of land war, then North Vietnam would go to its friends, China and Russia, and ask them to give help. They would be forced into increasing aid. For that reason I don't want to be overly dramatic and cause tensions. I think we can get our people to support us without having to be too provocative and warlike.

"Finally, we can give our commanders in the field the men and supplies they say they need."

I had concluded that the last course was the right one. I had listened to and weighed all the arguments and counterarguments for each of the possible lines of action. I believed that we should do what was necessary to resist aggression but that we should not be provoked into a major war. We would get the required appropriation in the new budget, and we would not boast about what we were doing. We would not make threatening noises to the Chinese or the Russians by calling up reserves in large numbers. At the same time, we would press hard on the diplomatic front to try to find some path to a peaceful settlement.

I asked if anyone objected to the course of action I had spelled out. I questioned each man in turn. Did he agree? Each nodded his approval or said "yes."

---

5 In 1965, the Johnson administration initiated Rolling Thunder, a bombing campaign against North Vietnam. As you read this assessment, note the CIA's conclusion about the effects of that campaign and what this report reveals about the problems the United States confronted in waging a war in Vietnam using sophisticated technology.

The Central Intelligence Agency Reports on the War (1967)

Through the end of April 1967 the US air campaign against North Vietnam—Rolling Thunder—had significantly eroded the capacities of North Vietnam's limited industrial and military base. These losses, however, have not meaningfully degraded North Vietnam's material ability to continue the war in South Vietnam.

Total damage through April 1967 was over $233 million, of which 70 percent was accounted for by damage to economic targets. The greatest amount of damage was inflicted on the so-called logistics target system—transport equipment and lines of communication.

By the end of April 1967 the US air campaign had attacked 173 fixed targets, over 70 percent of the targets on the JCS [Joint Chiefs of Staff] list. This campaign included extensive attacks on almost every major target system in the country. The physical results have varied widely. . . .

North Vietnam's ability to recuperate from the air attacks has been of a high order. The major exception has been the electric power industry. . . .

The recuperability problem is not significant for the other target systems. The destroyed petroleum storage system has been replaced by an effective system of dispersed storage and distribution. The damaged military target systems—particularly barracks and storage depots—have simply been abandoned, and supplies and troops dispersed throughout the country. The inventories of transport and military equipment have been replaced by large infusions of military and economic aid from the USSR and Communist China. Damage to bridges and lines of communications is frequently repaired within a matter of days, if not hours, or the effects are countered by an elaborate system of multiple bypasses or pre-positioned spans.

Source: CIA Intelligence Memo, May 12, 1967, declassified document reprinted in Gareth Porter, ed., *Vietnam: The Definitive Documentation of Human Decisions* (Stanfordville, N.Y.: Earle M. Coleman, 1979), II: pp. 470–472.

6   Twenty years after the fall of South Vietnam, Robert McNamara published his memoir. In this excerpt, he discusses LBJ's decision to commit combat troops to Vietnam. Note McNamara's explanation for LBJ's determination to downplay the escalation of the war and how his recollection of this decision differs from Johnson's. What accounts for the difference?

McNamara Recalls the Decision to Escalate (1995)

On January 27, 1965—just one week after the inauguration—Mac* and I gave President Johnson a short but explosive memorandum. Mac and I believed events were at a critical juncture. We told LBJ:

> The worst course of action is to continue in this essentially passive role which can only lead to eventual defeat and an invitation to get out in humiliating circumstances. We see two alternatives. The first is to use our military power in the Far East and to force a change in Communist policy. The second is to deploy all our resources along a track of negotiation, aimed at salvaging what little can be preserved with no major addition to our present military risks. [We] tend to favor the first course, but we believe that both should be carefully studied.

After months of uncertainty and indecision, we had reached the fork in the road.

The first six months of 1965 that followed our memo marked the most crucial phase of America's thirty-year involvement in Indochina. Between January 28 and July 28, 1965, President Johnson made the fateful choices that locked the United States onto a path of massive military intervention in Vietnam, an intervention that ultimately destroyed his presidency and polarized America like nothing since the Civil War.

During this fateful period, Johnson initiated bombing of North Vietnam and committed U.S. ground forces, raising the total U.S. troop strength from 23,000 to 175,000—with the likelihood of another 100,000 in 1966 and perhaps even more later. All of this occurred without adequate public disclosure or debate, planting the seeds of an eventually debilitating credibility gap. . . .

Why did President Johnson refuse to take the American people into his confidence? Some point to his innate secretiveness, but the answer is far more complex. One factor was his obsession with securing Congress's approval and financing of his Great Society agenda; he wanted nothing to divert attention and resources from his cherished domestic reforms. The other was his equally strong fear of hard-line pressure (from conservatives in both parties) for greater—and far riskier—military action that might trigger responses, especially nuclear, by China and/or the Soviet Union. The president coped with his dilemma by obscuring it—an unwise and ultimately self-defeating course. . . .

From the beginning of our involvement in Vietnam, the South Vietnamese forces had been giving us poor intelligence and inaccurate reports. Sometimes these inaccuracies were conscious attempts to mislead; at other times they were the product of too much optimism. And sometimes the inaccuracies merely reflected the difficulty of gauging progress accurately.

But I insisted we try to measure progress. Since my years at Harvard, I had

*National Security Advisor McGeorge Bundy.

Source: In Retrospect: The Tragedy and Lessons of Vietnam by Robert S. McNamara. Copyright © 1995 by Random House, Inc.

gone by the rule that it is not enough to conceive of an objective and a plan to carry it out; you must monitor the plan to determine whether you are achieving the objective. If you discover you are not, you either revise the plan or change the objective. I was convinced that, while we might not be able to track a front line, we could find variables that would indicate our success or failure. So we measured the targets destroyed in the North, the traffic down the Ho Chi Minh Trail, the number of captives, the weapons seized, the enemy body count, and so on.

The body count was a measurement of the adversary's manpower losses; we undertook it because one of Westy's* objectives was to reach a so-called crossover point, at which the Vietcong and North Vietnamese casualties would be greater than they could sustain. Critics point to use of the body count as an example of my obsession with numbers. "This guy McNamara," they said, "he tries to quantify everything." Obviously, there are things you cannot quantify; honor and beauty, for example. But things you can count, you ought to count. Loss of life is one, when you are fighting a war of attrition. We tried to use body counts as a measurement to help us figure out what we should be doing in Vietnam to win the war while putting our troops at the least risk.

*General William Westmoreland.

American Personnel in Vietnam

Americans fought against the Vietnamese and alongside them in an unconventional war waged by an often unseen enemy. In oral histories, memoirs, and interviews, many of the soldiers expressed their thoughts about the war, the South Vietnamese, and the enemy. What do these sources reveal about American attitudes toward the Vietnamese and about the problems Americans encountered as they fought an unconventional war? What do they reveal about policymakers' assumptions regarding the war?

Philip Caputo was a marine lieutenant in Vietnam in 1965. His memoir, *A Rumor of War,* describes his experiences there.

Fighting a Technological War of Attrition (1977)

Everything rotted and corroded quickly over there: bodies, boot leather, canvas, metal, morals. Scorched by the sun, wracked by the wind and rain of the monsoon, fighting in alien swamps and jungles, our humanity rubbed off of

Source: Excerpts from *A Rumor of War* by Philip Caputo. By permission of The Aaron Priest Literary Agency.

us as the protective bluing rubbed off the barrels of our rifles. We were fighting in the cruelest kind of conflict, a people's war. It was no orderly campaign, as in Europe, but a war for survival waged in a wilderness without rules or laws; a war in which each soldier fought for his own life and the lives of the men beside him, not caring who he killed in that personal cause or how many or in what manner and feeling only contempt for those who sought to impose on his savage struggle the mincing distinctions of civilized warfare—that code of battlefield ethics that attempted to humanize an essentially inhuman war. According to those "rules of engagement," it was morally right to shoot an unarmed Vietnamese who was running, but wrong to shoot one who was standing or walking; it was wrong to shoot an enemy prisoner at close range, but right for a sniper at long range to kill an enemy soldier who was no more able than a prisoner to defend himself; it was wrong for infantrymen to destroy a village with white-phosphorus grenades, but right for a fighter pilot to drop napalm on it. Ethics seemed to be a matter of distance and technology. You could never go wrong if you killed people at long range with sophisticated weapons. And then there was that inspiring order issued by General Greene: kill VC. In the patriotic fever of the Kennedy years, we had asked, "What can we do for our country?" and our country answered, "Kill VC." That was the strategy, the best our best military minds could come up with: organized butchery. But organized or not, butchery was butchery, so who was to speak of rules and ethics in a war that had none?

---

8 Medic David Ross, who served in Vietnam from 1965 until 1967, provided an oral history of his experience.

A Medical Corpsman Recalls the Vietnamese People (1981)

When Americans are talking about Vietnamese or people in India or somewhere similar, it's not like we're looking at them like they're our next-door neighbors. If someone came to our neighborhood and burned all of our houses and most of our possessions and put us in flying saucers which we'd never seen before and zipped us across the universe, setting us down somewhere in tent city in the middle of a sandbox with wire all around us, I guess we might not be too excited about it. Most of us were never able to see the Vietnamese as real people. I remember President Johnson in one of the psyop [psychological warfare] flicks we saw saying that the communists weren't like us—they didn't have feelings. But I always remembered that old woman or remembered after a B-52 strike going into this area where there was a little girl with her leg . . . traumatic amputation . . . and . . . still alive. Her mother

Source: Everything We Had by Al Santoli. Copyright © 1981 by Albert Santoli and Vietnam Veterans of America. Used by permission of Random House, Inc.

dead. The whole place turned upside down, a few people still screaming, some people wandering around with the look of the dead, a totally shocked daze. I wondered how people would feel in Pittsburgh if the Vietnamese came over in B-52s and bombed them. And while I feel some real sympathy for the POWs who were airmen, I pick Pittsburgh simply because it's a steel city and it has the image of the real hard-working honest American man. I'm trying to imagine a bunch of steelworkers after their wives, children, fiancées, parents, grandparents, have been blown up or are running around screaming in agony and some Vietnamese pilot comes swooping down in a parachute. I don't imagine they'd give him a very friendly reception. . . .

There was another thing I remember, too. We were going through a rice-paddy area in armored personnel carriers, and of course track vehicles going through a rice paddy isn't . . . The amount of labor they put into maintaining the rice and the paddy berms and the irrigation system and everything—it's all by hand. They don't have the equipment. It's all built a basket of dirt at a time and things have built up over generations. We're just ripping through there on the tracks, tearing the whole damn thing apart. This farmer out there is stomping on his hat and beating his hand against his head. I guess, really, the bottom line is that all his stocks and bonds and his future and his Mercedes and his dreams he hoped for his kids, we just drove through there and in three or four minutes made a helluva mess of it.

For eight months starting in the fall of 1968, Bobby Muller was in Vietnam as a Marine lieutenant. Paralyzed by a bullet through his spine, Muller later founded the Vietnam Veterans of America.

A Marine Remembers His Shock (1987)

Probably the first two months I was there, I spent out in the bush. Out there the war was easy in a way because there was no ambiguity. Anybody you met out there was hard core NVA* regular. No "good guy, bad guy" problem. Later, when we came back to work the coastal area where there were villages and refugees, that's when things started to go "wait a second." Cam Lo, which is one I remember very well, was a refugee village where people had been taken from another place called Gio Linh, ten or fifteen miles away. I didn't understand it then, but for Vietnamese, villagers, their rice paddy and their little ancestral burial ground defines their universe. You take them away as we did and you've totally disrupted what they relate to. And in Cam Lo what I experienced was just hatred in the eyes of people.

*North Vietnamese Army.

Source: "American Views of the Vietnamese," from *The Bad War* edited by Kim Willenson, copyright © 1987 by Newsweek, Inc. Used by permission of Dutton Signet, a division of Penguin Group (USA) Inc.

The Vietnamese did not like us and I remember I was shocked. I still naively thought of myself as a hero, as a liberator. And to see the Vietnamese look upon us with fear or hatred visible in their eyes was a shock. The only thing we were good for is to sell us something. And frankly every time we operated around Cam Lo we got fucked with. Any patrol, any operation, any convoy passing by would get a smack. So the people that I thought would regard us as heroes were the very people that we were fighting, and all of a sudden my black-and-white image of the world became real gray and confused.

Then I came into contact with the ARVN* and that was all the more absurd. First there were some joint operations and then I went with MACV† as an advisor and worked with three different ARVN battalions and that's when everything just went screwy in my head. Every night I slept with the battalion commander. We had personal bodyguards and the reason was that a good percentage of the guys in the ranks were VC‡ or even North Vietnamese. The bodyguards were to protect us against getting blown away by the guys we were fighting with. We went out into the A Shau valley for what was supposed to be a ten-day operation and it wound up being ten weeks, and we lost a good number of guys not because of firefights but because they took as much rice as they could carry and they split. The A Shau was badlands. It was not a friendly place. And when you leave your unit out in the A Shau you ain't leaving to go bring in the crops back at the farm. You're leaving because you're joining the other side.

It was a joke. The enemy was a tough, hard, dedicated fucking guy, and the ARVN didn't want to hear about fighting. It was LaLa Land. Every, every, every, *every* firefight that we got into, the ARVN broke, the ARVN fucking ran. I was with three different battalions and the story never changed. I almost fell over laughing once. I had an Australian I was working with, and this NVA unit had just ambushed us. We had two companies of ARVN, and finally they got on line to counterattack, and the company commanders give the order to move and nobody moves. And they have to run up and down line with little sticks, beating these guys and kicking them in the fucking rear end to get them up out of their holes. And the Aussie and I look at each other, and we know then and there that this ain't going to work.

*Army of the Republic of Vietnam (South Vietnam).
†Military Assistance Command, Vietnam.
‡Viet Cong.

Gary Larsen was a foreign service officer in Vietnam from 1969 to 1973.

A Foreign Service Officer Acknowledges American Ignorance (1987)

The thing I remember most vividly is how little we knew about Vietnam. It was as though the people, their culture, their country existed in another dimension which [only] obliquely intersected with ours. To be sure, we made the obligatory gestures. We had our linguists, our culture specialists, our orientation studies. Yet for the vast majority of Americans the Vietnamese were puppets and their country a stage on which we pulled the strings and rearranged the props at our whim.

This is not surprising when you consider that we had no consideration of Vietnam as an ancient civilization. What was surprising was that our efforts to learn were so meager and so late. Very few people ever realized, for example, that the streets of Saigon were largely named for kings, heroes, and poets rather than for trees, flowers, and places. Or that Vietnam had a flourishing civilization when Washington, D.C., was only a swamp. Ironically, Vietnam's literary masterpiece, Kim Van Kieu, which occupies a place in Vietnam analogous to that held in the West by the masterpieces of Chaucer and Dante, never appeared in this country until 1973, the year we finally declared peace and withdrew.

Our ignorance was reinforced by our inability to communicate. There were, of course, some people who spoke the language, read the literature, and invested the time to pierce the veil. Unfortunately, they rarely made the decisions, and when their comments were at odds with accepted policy, they were dismissed as having "poor attitudes," or as having "gone native." In the absence of English-speaking counterparts, the only people [most of us] felt comfortable talking to were our interpreters, who often unknown to us, seized control of the dialogue and while our interest waned, put forth their own ideas—or ours as they understood them—and in the process promoted themselves.

We compounded this infidelity to competence by vacations, short tours, and our own enclaves. In fact life in Saigon was so complete, and the circle of office, PX, and clubs so secure, that one could go for extended periods of time meeting only Vietnamese who served as drivers, secretaries, maids, and bartenders. And when the occasional ceremony or meeting brought us into contact with other Vietnamese, we retreated into small talk, cliches, and drink, which isolated us from any deep awareness of where we were or what we were doing.

This ignorance nourished our arrogance. For if we were not aware of the

Source: "American Views of the Vietnamese," from *The Bad War* edited by Kim Willenson, copyright © 1987 by Newsweek, Inc. Used by permission of Dutton Signet, a division of Penguin Group (USA) Inc.

consequences of our presence, we could proceed blissfully with actions based on our own one-dimensional view of the country and the people. And proceed we did, getting no smarter but simply overwhelmed. As somebody once said, "We did not have twenty years of experience. We had one year twenty times." In the end we made peace and withdrew with the same arrogant disregard for the people and their country which had characterized our whole involvement. And the lessons were buried under self-praise for a noble effort and guilt-expiating succor for tens of thousands of refugees. Fortunately, there is ample blame for all involved.

CONCLUSION

History is the collective memory that we use to guide us in the present. However, sometimes its lessons are not clear. Few wars have been more carefully scrutinized as the Vietnam War, but historians disagree about the lessons it yields. They have different explanations for the way Americans fought it and thus for the way it turned out.

Some historians locate the cause of America's defeat in its leaders' decisions about how to fight the war. These decisions, in turn, reflected such forces as personality or bureaucratic mentality. For these historians, the lesson of Vietnam is to avoid similar decisions in the future. Other historians see a deeper cause for defeat in certain American assumptions that made military disaster a virtual certainty. For these historians America's failure in Vietnam can be traced to a single powerful force: American culture.

Yet Vietnam may hold a lesson that has nothing to do with avoiding future military disasters. It involves the unintended consequences that wars have on societies fighting them. As we saw by examining nativism in Chapter 6 and the Cold War in Chapter 9, cultural assumptions can have powerful consequences. Yet culture is not static, as Vietnam's impact on Americans makes clear. The disillusionment fostered by this war helped crack a powerful Cold War culture. Ideas about gender made up one prominent strand woven into that culture. As we will see next, changing ideas about gender contributed to its unraveling in the 1960s and 1970s.

FURTHER READING

Larry Berman, *Lyndon Johnson's War: The Road to Stalemate in Vietnam* (New York: W. W. Norton and Company, 1989).
Frances FitzGerald, *Fire in the Lake: The Vietnamese and the Americans in Vietnam* (Boston: Little, Brown, 1972).

George Herring, *America's Longest War: The United States in Vietnam, 1950–1975,* rev. ed. (New York: McGraw-Hill, Inc., 1986).

David Levy, *The Debate over Vietnam* (Baltimore: Johns Hopkins University Press, 1991).

Norman Podhoretz, *Why We Were in Vietnam* (New York: Simon and Schuster, 1982).

Al Santoli, *Everything We Had: An Oral History of the Vietnam War by Thirty-three American Soldiers Who Fought It* (New York: Ballantine Books, 1981).

NOTES

1. Quoted in "A North Vietnamese Commander Celebrates the 'Great Spring Victory,'" in *Major Problems in the History of the Vietnam War,* ed. Robert J. McMahon, 2nd ed. (Lexington, Mass.: D. C. Heath, 1995), p. 578.

2. Quoted in George C. Herring, *America's Longest War: The United States in Vietnam, 1950–1975* (New York: John Wiley, 1979), p. 264.

3. Lyndon B. Johnson, *The Vantage Point: Perspectives of the Presidency, 1963–1969* (New York: Holt Rinehart and Winston, 1971), p. x.

Chapter

12

Gender, Ideology, and Historical Change: Explaining the Women's Movement

The sources in this chapter relate to the rise of the women's movement in the 1960s and 1970s.

Secondary Sources

1. Cold War Ideology and the Rise of Feminism (1988),
   ELAINE TYLER MAY

2. Women's Liberation and Sixties Radicalism (2002), ALICE ECHOLS

Primary Sources

3. The Problem That Has No Name (1963), BETTY FRIEDAN

4. Civil Rights and the Rise of Feminism (1987), MARY KING

5. NOW's Statement of Purpose (1966)

6. Redstockings Manifesto (1969)

7. "What's Wrong with 'Equal Rights' for Women?" (1972),
   PHYLLIS SCHLAFLY

8. On Women and Sex (1972), JOYCE MAYNARD

9. Our Bodies, Ourselves (1973)

10. The Politics of Housework (ca. 1970), PAT MAINARDI

11. Sex Ratios of High School and College Graduates in the United States, 1940–1980

12. Women's Labor Force Participation, by Marital Status, 1940–1987

13. Median Earnings of Year-round, Full-time Workers, by Sex, 1955–1985

*E*vidence of coming turmoil was everywhere in 1965. In the first week of June, *Newsweek* detailed several scenarios for the growing war in Vietnam. One of them read that the United States "steadily enlarges its ground combat commitment but its hopes are frustrated; there is no conclusion to the war in sight."[1] The same week, *U.S. News & World Report* covered an "uproar" in Chicago over segregated public schools, yet another sign that the civil rights movement had moved north by the mid-1960s. In the same issue, *U.S. News* reported on the growing campus demonstrations against U.S. foreign policy: "Speakers draw cheers with demands for American withdrawal from the war against the Communists in Vietnam."[2]

Far less obvious was the hint of looming trouble in *Time*'s cover story the following week on the best-selling poet Phyllis McGinley, a suburban Connecticut housewife. McGinley proclaimed that women exercise their greatest influence in the home. She "finds herself the sturdiest exponent of the glory of housewifery," *Time* observed, "standing almost alone against a rising chorus of voices summoning women away from the hearth." The loudest voice in the chorus, the story also noted, belonged to Betty Friedan, whose best-selling "broadside," *The Feminine Mystique* (1963), proclaimed "that the college-educated woman who seeks fulfillment in domesticity will never find it . . . ." Given McGinley's nine books of poetry, two volumes of essays, fifteen children's books, and one Pulitzer Prize, *Time* could only conclude that Friedan's attitude was "tinged with envy."[3]

Values are often defended only when they are no longer taken for granted. *Time*'s profile of McGinley exposed growing doubts by 1965 that women could find happiness only at home. Indeed, in the coming years the rejection of domesticity fed a powerful women's movement that transformed the way homes, workplaces, churches, and the halls of government looked and functioned. Three decades after a suburban housewife like Phyllis McGinley could become a controversial figure, historians ask what gave rise to a women's movement that caught most Americans off guard in the 1960s. In this chapter, we consider some of their answers.

SETTING

By 1970, the growing women's protest had a name: the "women's liberation movement." Journalists, commentators, and women activists themselves had other labels for it as well. Some called it the "women's rights movement." Others labeled it "feminist protest," and later many settled on "the women's movement." The failure to pin one name on the women's revolt of the 1960s and 1970s reveals something about it. First, it was a movement only in the loosest sense. As *Newsweek* put it in 1970, "the women's liberation movement [is] a very loose designation for a multiplicity of small groups led by a multiplicity of women."[4] All of the participants might agree that women were subject to sexism and sexual discrimination and thus did not enjoy full equality in American society. Yet not all women activists shared the same analysis of their problems. Nor did they agree on what to do about them. Liberation, they discovered, could mean many things.

Women's diverse backgrounds influenced their analysis of the gender problem. Social class, education, occupation, marital status, and even sexual orientation influenced women's views of equality. Thus the women's movement had little appeal for many black, Hispanic, and working-class women, who often saw their inequality in economic or racial terms. On the other hand, it attracted many educated, middle-class women, for whom *The Feminine Mystique* struck a responsive chord. Friedan had asserted that education and employment outside the home was the solution for women's unhappiness and lack of self-esteem. When the National Organization for Women (NOW) was formed in 1966 with Friedan as its first president, its ranks were filled with professional women who faced discrimination in the job market and felt bridled by traditional attitudes about women's domestic duties. NOW denied hostility toward men, however. Rather, it called for "a fully equal partnership of the sexes," and pressed for an end to sexual discrimination through such measures as the Equal Rights Amendment.

By the late 1960s, younger women began to challenge NOW with different analyses of women's oppression and alternative responses to it. Often veterans of the civil rights and antiwar movements or New Left political organizations, these radical feminists dismissed NOW's efforts to end sexual discrimination through political action as "bourgeois" and insufficient. They also pointed out that gaining equality in the workplace, the political arena, the media, and elsewhere in the "public" sphere was not enough. With no equality in the "private" sphere of domestic relations, women would be expected to "do it all."

For radical feminists, NOW's legislative solutions were too narrow, and women could not be truly liberated without a radical restructuring of society. Some insisted that women's liberation could only be achieved with the rejection of capitalism. Yet most radical feminists advanced cultural rather than economic radicalism. They divided with moderates not on questions about the economic order but on the matters of marriage and family. Radicals like Kate Millett and Susan Brownmiller, for instance, argued that women could liberate themselves through communal living arrangements and even by ending women's function as childbearers. Others, such as the Radicalesbians, insisted that the problem lay in heterosexual relations. Rather than point to the barriers to access, radical feminists emphasized the oppressive nature of a male-dominated society and the need to view all relations between men and women in political terms.

The difference, said some feminists, was between the moderates' "egalitarian ethic" and the radicals' "liberation ethic." Yet it was not quite that simple. Friedan and other moderates had advocated the liberation of women from an ideology of domesticity, and radicals were guided by the ideal of gender equality. In addition, both moderates and radicals proclaimed opposition to sexism. Moreover, by the mid-1970s there were thousands of feminist groups raising numerous issues supported by both sides, including legal abortion, domestic violence, women's health, and child care. Maybe the most accurate assessment of the growth of women's groups was offered by one feminist writer, who proclaimed, "It's not a movement, it's a State of Mind."[5]

By 1975, that "state of mind" had influenced public consciousness. The protests and lobbying of women's groups and a flood of books and articles by such feminists as Kate Millett, Gloria Steinem, and Robin Morgan had raised awareness of women's issues. Feminism had gained legitimacy, although not in the radical sense of eliminating gender differences. By the end of the 1970s, laws and court decisions embodied many demands of the women's movement. Although factionalized and under a conservative counterattack, women had succeeded in altering their status as a group and changing the lives of countless women and men.

INVESTIGATION

Like the antebellum women's rights movement, the feminist revolt of the 1960s and 1970s was led mostly by middle-class women. Also like the earlier movement, it rebelled against an ideology at the same time that it was divided by ideology. And like the pre–Civil War women's protest, it arose at a time of widespread unrest. To understand the rise of feminist protest in the 1960s and 1970s, historians must therefore study a number of influences on women. They must also consider the power of ideology to stimulate and define the limits of reform.

This chapter examines what led many women to become women's rights advocates seeking legal equality and equal treatment in the workplace, or even to become feminists seeking to completely redefine the meaning of gender. It presents two historians' contrasting views about the changes responsible for the rise of the women's movement. Your main assignment is to evaluate these arguments and develop an explanation for the rise of the women's movement in the 1960s and 1970s. Your analysis should explain the impact of economic, social, political, and cultural changes on women's views about their status. It should also address the following main questions:

1. **How do the explanations of historians Elaine Tyler May and Alice Echols for the rise of the women's movement differ?** Which one better explains its rise? Why? Are their explanations mutually exclusive?

2. **What do the primary sources reveal about the experiences that led many**

women to change their views about their status? What did major cultural, political, and economic trends, including the civil rights and antiwar movements and the sexual revolution, have to do with the rise of the women's movement?

3. **What do the sources reveal about the major goals of the women's movement and the most important factors limiting their attainment?** How do May's and Echols's explanations for the limits of the women's movement differ?

Before you begin, read the sections in your textbook on the status of women in postwar society and on the women's movement of the 1960s and 1970s. Note how your text accounts for the rise of this movement.

SECONDARY SOURCES

1   In this selection, historian Elaine Tyler May examines the impact of political changes on American families, specifically the relationship between the demise of a Cold War ideology and the ideal of domesticity in the 1960s. Pay attention to May's argument about the way a Cold War ideology "contained" women. Does she make a convincing case that a domestic ideology and Cold War militance rose and fell together? Do you think the postwar marriage and baby booms were the result of Cold War ideology or of other factors, such as the return of peace and prosperity? Also think about whether the idea of containment can be applied to family relations and if May shows that containment cut off pre–Cold War changes within families.

Cold War Ideology and the Rise of Feminism (1988)
ELAINE TYLER MAY

The politics of the cold war and the ideology and public policies that it spawned were crucial in shaping postwar family life and gender roles. . . .

With security as the common thread, the cold war ideology and the domestic revival reinforced each other. The powerful political consensus that supported cold war policies abroad and anticommunism at home fueled conformity to the suburban family ideal. In turn, the domestic ideology encouraged private solutions to social problems and further weakened the potential for challenges to the cold war consensus. Personal adaptation, rather than political resistance, characterized the era. But postwar domesticity never fully delivered on its promises. The baby-boom children who grew up in suburban homes abandoned the containment ethos when they came of age.

Source: Homeward Bound by Elaine Tyler May. Copyright © 1988 by Elaine Tyler May. Reprinted by permission of Basic Books, a member of Perseus Books, L.L.C.

As young adults in the 1960s, they challenged both the imperatives of the cold war and the domestic ideology that came with it. At the same time, they forged new paths to pursue the unfulfilled dreams of their parents. . . .

. . . Among the first to criticize the status quo were postwar parents themselves. In 1963, Betty Friedan published her exposé of domesticity, *The Feminine Mystique*. Friedan gave a name to the "problem that has no name" for career homemakers. A postwar wife and mother herself, Friedan spoke directly to women . . . who had lived according to the domestic containment ideology. She urged them to break away from their domestic confines, go back to school, pursue careers, and revive the vision of female independence that had been alive before World War II. *The Feminine Mystique* became an immediate best-seller and created a national sensation. The book enabled discontented women across the country to find their voices. It was as if someone was finally willing to say that the emperor had no clothes; soon a chorus joined in support. Hundreds of readers wrote to Friedan, telling their stories. These personal testimonies reveal the stated and unstated messages that this generation of parents gave their children.

The letters to Friedan reveal widespread disenchantment among women who had struggled to conform to the prevailing familial norm. Some of the writers were children of activist parents who had fought for equal rights in the early part of the century. Nearly all expressed the hope that their children would avoid the domestic trap in which they found themselves. . . .

A Mount Holyoke graduate who joined the "stampede back to the nest" described her path into domesticity: "I entered graduate school at Yale, met a man, left school, and married in 1951. I have since then moved thirteen times, lived in eight states, had four miscarriages and produced two children." But she also struggled at home and alone to become a painter. So "finally, when I fill out the income tax now, it is occupation: Painter, not housewife. . . .

Friedan's book sparked readers to comment not only on the connection between women's and men's fate, but between domesticity and cold war politics. One woman believed that political activism was the only way to bring women out of "their cozy cocoons in America," but she also perceived that challenges to women's roles would be seen as un-American. Women would need to "make determined efforts to free themselves," she noted, "and they may expect hostility from conservative elements politically as well as from their fellow timid sisters and timid men. I am not advocating that women become Communist sympathizers, but I am expecting that progressive women will be so labelled." . . .

Many of the women who wrote to Friedan were those who could respond to her call for self-realization through education and careers. They were affluent. If married, they had husbands who provided an income that was adequate enough to allow them to develop outside interests for self-fulfillment. But there were others who found Friedan's message troubling. It was fine to have ambitions, but it was another matter to work out of necessity, face a sex-segregated job market, and do double duty at home as well.

One woman expressed her irritation at "the false emphasis that is placed on the entire matter of women fulfilling themselves through a career. The vast majority of working women don't have careers. We have jobs, just like men. We work for money to buy things that our families need. If we're lucky, we like our jobs, and find some satisfaction in doing them well, but it is hard to hold a commercial job, raise a family and keep a house." . . .

As these letters indicate, domestic containment was not going to die a quick or natural death. Yet it was clearly doomed from its own internal contradictions. Betty Friedan spoke for a generation whose children would later be credited with initiating a decade of political and social upheaval, but many of their parents had paved the way. Even those who thought that it was too late to change their own ways and routines knew it was not too late for their children. They encouraged their children—implicitly if not explicitly—to follow new paths. Frustrated women and exhausted men provided ambiguous role models for children hoping to avoid the discontent of their mothers and the pressure and ill health the stresses of the work place had inflicted on their fathers.

Still, change came slowly. In the early 1960s, it was not immediately obvious that a unique historical era was coming to an end. Signs that the postwar consensus was beginning to crack were hardly more visible than they had been in the fifties: a few voices of dissent from the intelligentsia, the growing popularity of counterculture heroes such as Elvis Presley and James Dean, and the spread of the civil rights movement from black activists in the South to northern whites. Oral contraceptives first became available in 1960, but they did not immediately bring about a change in behavior, even though years later, many would credit (or blame) "The Pill" for the "sexual revolution." Most cultural signs still pointed toward the cold war consensus at home and abroad, and the ideology of domesticity was still alive and well. . . .

On November 1, 1961, 50,000 American housewives walked out of their homes and jobs in a massive protest, "Women Strike for Peace." These activists were among the first postwar middle-class whites to organize against the social and political status quo. Several of the leaders of the strike were part of a small group of feminists who had worked on behalf of women's rights throughout the forties and the fifties. According to *Newsweek*, the strikers "were perfectly ordinary looking women. . . . They looked like the women you would see driving ranch wagons, or shopping at the village market, or attending PTA meetings . . . many [were] wheeling baby buggies or strollers." Within a year their numbers grew to several hundred thousand.

Anticommunists worried that Women Strike for Peace signaled that "the pro-Reds have moved in on our mothers and are using them for their own purposes," and the Federal Bureau of Investigation kept the group under surveillance from its inception in 1961. The following year, the leaders of Women Strike for Peace were called before the House Un-American Activities Committee. Under questioning, these women spoke as mothers, claiming that saving American children from nuclear extinction was the essence of "Americanism," thereby turning the ideology of domesticity against the assumptions of the cold war. These women carried the banner of motherhood into politics, much like their reformist Victorian sisters in the last century. But their ability to attack the cold war with domesticity as their tool and make a mockery of the congressional hearings indicates that the familial–cold war consensus was beginning to lose its grip.

Increasing political pressure resulted in several important new public policies that challenged the status quo. In 1961, President Kennedy established the President's Commission on the Status of Women, chaired appropriately by an activist from the 1930s, Eleanor Roosevelt. Within the next three years, Congress passed the Equal Pay Act and Title VII of the Civil Rights Act (which prohibited discrimination on the basis of sex, as well as race, color, religion, and national origin), and the United States and the Soviet Union signed the first treaty banning the atmospheric testing of nuclear weapons.

While these policies were taking shape, Students for a Democratic Society (SDS), inspired largely by the civil rights movement, gained thousands of members in chapters across the country. Out of the student movement came the antiwar movement and the new feminism. By the late sixties, hundreds of thousands of young activists mobilized against the gender assumptions as well as the cold war policies that had prevailed since World War II.

The simultaneous attack on domestic containment and the cold war ideology also found expression in the popular culture. Within a few months of the publication of *The Feminine Mystique* came Stanley Kubrick's film, *Dr. Strangelove: Or, How I Learned to Stop Worrying and Love the Bomb,* a biting satire that equated the madness of the cold war with Americans' unresolved sexual neuroses. Such attacks against the sanctity of the postwar domestic ideology and the politics of the cold war would have been risky endeavors ten years earlier. The film probably would have been suppressed and its creators called before the House Un-American Activities Committee. By the early sixties, however, although the cold war was still in full force, and some viewers found the film offensive and un-American, critics as well as audiences were, for the most part, wildly enthusiastic.

By the end of the decade, the new feminist movement had pushed beyond Betty Friedan's call for self-realization into a full-fledged assault on sexism in all its forms, organized by younger women who emerged from their activism in the civil rights movement and the New Left with newly discovered skills and strengths. The new feminists demanded access to professional occupations and skilled jobs, protested low wages, and worked for pay equity. They formed consciousness-raising groups all over the country, challenged the gender division of labor in the home, and railed against the sexual double standard. In a 1970 survey of women entering an open-admission, tuition-free public university, most saw their future role as "married career woman with children"—a vast change from the 1950s when most women of all classes saw their future career as homemaker. . . .

Married or divorced, professional as well as nonprofessional wage-earning women continued to face inequalities at work and at home. Nevertheless, political activism opened up new opportunities for women to achieve autonomy that had been unavailable to their mothers. Women of the fifties, constrained by tremendous cultural and economic pressures to conform to domestic containment, gave up their independence and personal ambitions. Once they made the choice to embrace domesticity, they did their best to thrive within it and claimed that their sacrifices were ultimately worthwhile. Many of their daughters abandoned security and material comfort to follow a more autonomous path that brought them face to face with economic hardship and pervasive discrimination. Yet, like their mothers, many would say that the struggles were worth it. Their mothers paid a price for security and dependence; the daughters paid a price for autonomy and independence. In both cases, the lack of equal opportunity for women limited their options. Yet there is no question that the daughters had more opportunities than their mothers as a result of the hard-won political achievements of the sixties and seventies: they were no longer bound to the home.

Political goals were only partially achieved, however. Even before the end of the 1960s, the "silent majority" rose up against the noisy, youthful minority. In 1968, the quintessential fifties politician, Richard Nixon, was back in the White House, this time as president. The ideology of the cold war, although dealt a serious blow by the disastrous war in Vietnam, remained a powerful force in national politics—and it continued to be tied to the ideology of domesticity. Those who claimed that South Vietnam fell as a result of softness against communism also blamed feminism for what they perceived as the destruction of the family.

It is no accident that in the wake of feminism, the sexual revolution, and the peace movement of the 1960s, the New Right emerged in the 1970s and 1980s as a powerful political force with the dual aims of reviving the cold war and reasserting the ideology of domesticity. It should not be surprising that the most vigorous opponent of the Equal Rights Amendment, Phyllis Schlafly, began her career as an avid Cold Warrior. Proponents of the New Right gained strength by calling for militance in foreign policy, opposing the Equal Rights Amendment, and condemning student radicalism, the counterculture, feminism, and the sexual revolution. They went on to triumph in 1980, with the election of Ronald Reagan to the presidency.

Reagan, like Nixon, received his political groundings in the late 1940s and 1950s as an anticommunist crusader in California. Appropriately, his media image was that of the family man par excellence, as he promoted home-centered consumerism as host of the General Electric Theater. The all-electric home that Reagan advertised (and also inhabited) was virtually identical to the

"model home" Nixon praised in Moscow in 1959. In the 1960s, Reagan carried his image into California politics, where he promised to crack down on
student protestors. With Reagan in the White House in the 1980s, the rhetoric of containment returned, with its support for cold-war militance and calls
for a strengthened "traditional" family. . . .

It is clear that in recent decades, the domestic ideology and cold war militance have risen and fallen together. Immediately after World War II, stable
family life seemed necessary for national security, civil defense, and the
struggle for supremacy over the Soviet Union. For a generation of young
adults who grew up amid depression and war, domestic containment was a
logical response to specific historical circumstances. It allowed them to pursue, in the midst of a tense and precarious world situation, the quest for a
sexually fulfilling, consumer-oriented personal life that was free from hardship. But the circumstances were different for their children, who broke the
consensus surrounding the cold war and domestic containment. Whether the
baby-boom children will ultimately be more successful than their parents in
achieving fulfilling lives and a more just and tolerant world remains to be
seen. But one thing is certain: gender, family, and national politics are still in-
tertwined in the ongoing saga of postwar cultural change.

2   In this selection, Alice Echols relates the rise of feminist consciousness in
the 1960s to numerous changes in American society, especially the rise
of other protest movements. What connection does she see between
the women's liberation movement and the civil rights, antiwar, and student
movements? Does Echols explain the rise of a women's rights movement, as
symbolized by the National Organization for Women? How would you compare Echols's conclusion about the impact of the women's liberation movement
to Elaine Tyler May's conclusion in Source 1 about the limited success of the
women's movement?

Women's Liberation and Sixties Radicalism (2002)
ALICE ECHOLS

On September 7, 1968, the sixties came to that most apple-pie of American institutions, the Miss America Pageant. One hundred women's liberation activists descended upon Atlantic City to protest the pageant's promotion of
physical attractiveness as the primary measure of women's worth. Carrying
signs that read, "Miss America Is a Big Falsie," "Miss America Sells It,"

Source: Shaky Ground: The '60s and its Aftershocks (Paper) by Echols, Alice/. Copyright 2002 by
Columbia Univ Press. Reproduced with permission of Columbia Univ Press in the format Textbook
via the Copyright Clearance Center.

and "Up Against the Wall, Miss America," they formed a picket line on the boardwalk, sang anti-Miss America songs in three-part harmony, and performed guerrilla theater. Later that day, they crowned a live sheep Miss America and paraded it on the boardwalk to parody the way the contestants, and, by extension, all women, "are appraised and judged like animals at a county fair." They tried to convince women in the crowd that the tyranny of beauty was but one of the many ways that women's bodies were colonized. By announcing beforehand that they would not speak to male reporters (or to any man for that matter), the demonstrators challenged the sexual division of labor that consigned female reporters to the "soft" stories while reserving for male reporters the coveted "hard" news stories. Newspaper editors who wanted to cover the protest were thus forced to pull their women reporters from the society pages.

The protesters set up a "Freedom Trash Can" and filled it with various "instruments of torture"—high-heeled shoes, bras, girdles, hair curlers, false eyelashes, typing books, and representative copies of *Cosmopolitan, Playboy,* and *Ladies Home Journal.* They had wanted to burn the contents of the Freedom Trash Can, but they were thwarted by a city ordinance prohibiting bonfires on the boardwalk. However, word had been leaked to the press that the protest would include a symbolic bra-burning, and, as a consequence, reporters were everywhere. Although they burned no bras that day on the boardwalk, the image of the bra-burning, militant feminist remains part of our popular mythology about the women's liberation movement. . . .

In its wit, passion, and irreverence, not to mention its expansive formulation of politics (to include the politics of beauty, no less!), the Miss America protest resembled other sixties demonstrations. . . . Judging from their response, this new thing, "women's liberation," was about as popular as the antiwar movement. The protesters were jeered, harassed, and called "man-haters" and "commies." One man suggested that "it would be a lot more useful" if the demonstrators threw themselves, and not their bras, girdles, and make-up, into the trash can.

But nothing—not even the verbal abuse they encountered on the boardwalk—could diminish the euphoria women's liberationists felt as they started to mobilize around their own, rather than other people's, oppression. Ann Snitow speaks for many when she recalls that in contrast to her experience in the larger, male-dominated protest Movement,* where she had felt sort of "blank and peripheral," women's liberation was like "an ecstasy of discussion." Precisely because it was about one's own life, there was, she says, "nothing distant about it." Robin Morgan has claimed that the Miss America protest "announced our existence to the world." That is only a slight exaggeration, for as a consequence of the protest, women's liberation achieved

---

*Echols uses the term "Movement" to refer primarily to the black, student, and antiwar protest movements of the 1960s. She refers to the women's liberation movement as the "movement."

the status of a movement both to its participants and to the media; as such, the Miss America demonstration represents an important moment in the history of the sixties.

Although the women's liberation movement only began to take shape toward the end of the decade, it was a quintessentially sixties movement. It is not just that many early women's liberation activists had prior involvements in other sixties movements, although that was certainly true, as has been ably documented by Sara Evans. And it is not just that, of all the sixties movements, the women's liberation movement alone carried on and extended into the 1970s that decade's political radicalism and rethinking of fundamental social organization. Although that is true as well. Rather, it is that the larger, male-dominated protest Movement, despite its considerable sexism, provided much of the intellectual foundation and cultural orientation for the women's liberation movement, many of whose ideas and approaches—especially its concern with revitalizing democratic process and reformulating "politics" to include the personal—were refined and recast versions of those already present in the New Left and the black freedom movement. . . .

Women's discontent with their place in America in the 1960s was, of course, produced by a broad range of causes. Crucial in reigniting feminist consciousness in the 1960s was the unprecedented number of women (especially married white women) being drawn into the paid labor force, as the service sector of the economy expanded and rising consumer aspirations fueled the desire of many families for a second income. As Alice Kessler-Harris has pointed out, "homes and cars, refrigerators and washing machines, telephones and multiple televisions required higher incomes." So did providing a college education for one's children. These new patterns of consumption were made possible in large part through the emergence of the two-income family as wives increasingly "sought to aid their husbands in the quest for the good life." By 1960, 30.5 percent of all wives worked for wages. Women's growing labor force participation also reflected larger structural shifts in the U.S. economy. Sara Evans has argued that the "reestablishment of labor force segregation following World War II ironically reserved for women a large proportion of the new jobs created in the fifties due to the fact that the fastest growing sector of the economy was no longer industry but services." Women's increasing labor force participation was facilitated as well by the growing number of women graduating from college and the introduction of the birth control pill in 1960.

Despite the fact that women's "place" was increasingly in the paid work force (or perhaps because of it), ideas about women's proper role in American society were quite conventional throughout the fifties and the early sixties, held there by a resurgent ideology of domesticity—what Betty Friedan coined the "feminine mystique." But, as Jane De Hart-Mathews has observed, "the bad fit was there: the unfairness of unequal pay for the same work, the low value placed on jobs women performed, the double burden of housework and wage work." By the mid-sixties at least some American women felt that the contradiction between the realities of paid work and higher education on the one hand, and the still pervasive ideology of domesticity on the other hand, had become irreconcilable.

However, without the presence of other oppositional movements the women's liberation movement might not have developed at all as an organized force for social change. It certainly would have developed along vastly different lines. The climate of protest encouraged women, even those not directly involved in the black movement and the New Left, to question conventional gender arrangements. Moreover, as already noted, many of the women who helped form the women's liberation movement had been involved as well in the male-dominated Movement. If the larger Movement was typically indifferent, or worse, hostile, to women's liberation, it was nonetheless through their experiences in that Movement that the young and predominately white and middle-class women who initially formed the women's liberation movement became politicized. The relationship between women's liberation and the larger Movement was at its core paradoxical. The Movement was a site of sexism, but it also provided white women a space in which they could develop political skills and self-confidence, a space in which they could violate the injunction against female self-assertion. Most important, it gave them no small part of the intellectual ammunition—the language and the ideas—with which to fight their own oppression. . . .

. . . Women's liberationists shared new leftists' and black radicals' rejection of liberalism, and, as a consequence, they often went to great lengths to distinguish themselves from the liberal feminists of the National Organization for Women (NOW). (In fact, their disillusionment with liberalism was more thorough during the early stages of their movement-building than had been the case for either new leftists or civil rights activists because they had lived through the earlier betrayals around the War and civil rights. Male radicals' frequent denunciations of feminism as "bourgeois" also encouraged women's liberationists to distance themselves from NOW.) NOW had been formed in 1966 to push the federal government to enforce the provisions of the 1964 Civil Rights Act outlawing sex discrimination—a paradigmatic liberal agenda focused on public access and the prohibition of employment discrimination. To women's liberationists, NOW's integrationist, access-oriented approach ignored the racial and class inequalities that were the very foundation of the "mainstream" that the feminists of NOW were dedicated to integrating. In the introduction to the 1970 bestseller she edited, *Sisterhood Is Powerful*, Robin Morgan declared that "NOW is essentially an organization that wants reforms [in the] second-class citizenship of women—and this is where it differs drastically from the rest of the Women's Liberation Movement." In *The Dialectic of Sex* Shulamith Firestone described NOW's political stance as "untenable even in terms of immediate political gains" and deemed it "more a leftover of the old feminism rather than a model of the new." Radical feminist Ti-Grace Atkinson went even further, characterizing many in NOW as only wanting "women to have the same opportunity to be oppressors too."

Women's liberationists also took issue with liberal feminists' formulation of women's problem as their exclusion from the public sphere. Younger activists argued instead that women's exclusion from public life was inextricable from their subordination in the family, and would persist until this larger problem was addressed. For instance, Firestone claimed the solution to women's oppression wasn't inclusion in the mainstream, but the eradication of the biological family, which she argued was the "tapeworm of exploitation."

Of course, younger activists' alienation from NOW was often more than matched by NOW members' annoyance with them. Many liberal feminists were appalled (at least initially) by women's liberationists' politicization of personal life. NOW founder Betty Friedan frequently railed against women's liberationists for waging a "bedroom war" that diverted women from the real struggle of integrating the public sphere.

Women's liberationists believed that they had embarked upon a much more ambitious project—the virtual remaking of the world. Nothing short of radically transforming society was sufficient to deal with what they were discovering: that gender inequality was thoroughly embedded in everyday life. As Shulamith Firestone put it, "sex-class is so deep as to be invisible." The pervasiveness of sexism and gender's status as a naturalized category demonstrated to women's liberationists the inadequacy, the shallowness, of NOW's legislative and judicial remedies and the necessity of thoroughgoing social transformation. Thus, whereas liberal feminists talked of ending sex discrimination, women's liberationists called for nothing less than the destruction of patriarchy and capitalism. As defined by feminists, patriarchy, in contrast to sex discrimination, defied reform. . . .

The totalism of their vision would have been difficult to translate into a concrete reform package, even had they been interested in doing so. But electoral politics and the legislative and judicial reforms that engaged the energies of liberal feminists did little to animate most women's liberationists. Like other sixties radicals, they were instead taken with the idea of developing forms that would prefigure the utopian community of the imagined future. . . .

Sixties radicalism proved compelling to many precisely because it promised to transform life. Politics was not about the subordination of self to a larger political cause; instead it was the path to self-fulfillment. This ultimately was the power of sixties radicalism. . . . Thus the idea that "politics is how you live your life, not who you vote for," as Yippie leader Jerry Rubin put it, could and did lead to a subordination of politics to lifestyle. But if the idea led some to confuse personal liberation for political struggle, it led others to embrace an asceticism that sacrificed personal needs and desires to political imperatives. Some women's liberation activists followed this course, interpreting the idea that the personal is political to mean that one's personal life should conform to some abstract standard of political correctness. At first this tendency was mitigated by the founders' insistence that there were no personal solutions, only collective solutions, to women's oppression. However, over time one's self-presentation, marital status, and sexual preference frequently came to determine one's standing or ranking in the movement. The most notorious example of this involved the New York radical group, The Feminists, who established a quota to limit the number of married women in the group. Policies such as these prompted Barbara Ehrenreich to question "a feminism which talks about universal sisterhood, but is horrified by women who wear spiked heels or call their friends 'girls.'" At the same time, what was personally satisfying was sometimes upheld as politically correct. In the end, both the women's liberation movement and the larger protest Movement suffered, as the idea that the personal is political was often interpreted in ways that made questions of lifestyle absolutely central. . . .

To engender this sense of sisterhood or "we-ness," women's liberationists developed consciousness-raising, a practice involving "the political reinterpretation of personal life." According to its principal architects, its purpose was to "awaken the latent consciousness that . . . all women have about our oppression." In talking about their personal experiences, it was argued, women would come to understand that what they had believed were personal problems were, in fact, "social problems that must become social issues and fought together rather than with personal solutions."

New York women's liberationist Kathie Sarachild was reportedly the person who coined the term consciousness-raising. However, the technique originated in other social movements. As Sarachild noted in 1973, those who promoted consciousness-raising "were applying to women and to ourselves as women's liberation organizers the practice a number of us had learned in the civil rights movement in the South in the early 1960s." There they had seen that the sharing of personal problems, grievances, and aspirations— "telling it like it is"—could be a radicalizing experience. Moreover, for some women's liberationists consciousness-raising was a way to avoid the tendency of some in the movement to try to fit women into existing (and often Marxist) theoretical paradigms. By circumventing the "experts" on women and going to women themselves, they would be able not only to construct a theory of women's oppression but to formulate strategy as well. Thus women's liberationists struggled to find the commonalities in women's experiences in order to generate generalizations about women's oppression.

Consciousness-raising was enormously successful in exposing the insidiousness of sexism and in engendering a sense of identity and solidarity among the largely white, middle-class women who participated in "c-r" groups. By the early seventies even NOW, whose founder Betty Friedan had initially derided consciousness-raising as so much "navel-gazing," began sponsoring c-r groups. But the effort to transcend the particular was both the strength and weakness of consciousness-raising. If it encouraged women to locate the common denominators in their lives, it inhibited discussion of women's considerable differences. Despite the particularities of white, middle-class women's experiences, theirs became the basis for feminist theorizing about women's oppression. . . .

Accounts of sixties radicalism usually cite its role in bringing about the dismantling of Jim Crow and disfranchisement, the withdrawal of U.S. troops from Vietnam, and greater gender equality. However, equally impor-tant, if less frequently noted, was its challenge to politics as usual. Sixties rad-icals succeeded both in reformulating politics, even mainstream politics, to include personal life, and in challenging the notion that elites alone have the wisdom and expertise to control the political process. For a moment, people who by virtue of their color, age, and gender were far from the sites of formal power became politically engaged, became agents of change.

Given the internal contradictions and shortcomings of sixties radicalism, the repressiveness of the federal government in the late sixties and early sev-enties, and changing economic conditions in the United States, it is not sur-prising that the movements built by radicals in the sixties either no longer exist or do so only in attenuated form. Activists in the women's liberation movement, however, helped to bring about a fundamental realignment of gender roles in this country through outrageous protests, tough-minded polemics, and an "ecstasy of discussion." Indeed, those of us who came of age in the days before the resurgence of feminism know that the world today, while hardly a feminist utopia, is nonetheless a far different, and in many re-spects a far fairer, world than what we confronted in 1967.

PRIMARY SOURCES

The sources in this section will help you further analyze the two essays and thus formulate answers to the main questions in the Investigation section. These sources reflect a number of economic, cultural, political, and demographic in-fluences on the women's movement. They also illustrate the varied ways women attempted to achieve equality and some of the obstacles they confronted.

3   Betty Friedan attacked the postwar domestic ideal in her best-selling book, *The Feminine Mystique*. As you read this excerpt, note what prob-lem accompanied the widespread acceptance of the domestic ideal, according to Friedan. Why was the feminine mystique so powerful in the 1960s? Did its hold have more to do with demographic or with political factors?

The Problem That Has No Name (1963)

BETTY FRIEDAN

The problem lay buried, unspoken, for many years in the minds of American women. It was a strange stirring, a sense of dissatisfaction, a yearning that women suffered in the middle of the twentieth century in the United States. Each suburban wife struggled with it alone. As she made the beds, shopped for groceries, matched slipcover material, ate peanut butter sandwiches with her children, chauffeured Cub Scouts and Brownies, lay beside her husband at night—she was afraid to ask even of herself the silent question—"Is this all?"

For over fifteen years there was no word of this yearning in the millions of words written about women, for women, in all the columns, books and articles by experts telling women their role was to seek fulfillment as wives and mothers. Over and over women heard in voices of tradition and of Freudian sophistication that they could desire no greater destiny than to glory in their own femininity. Experts told them how to catch a man and keep him, how to breastfeed children and handle their toilet training, how to cope with sibling rivalry and adolescent rebellion; how to buy a dishwasher, bake bread, cook gourmet meals, and building a swimming pool with their own hands; how to dress, look, and act more feminine and make marriage more exciting; how to keep their husbands from dying young and their sons from growing into delinquents. They were taught to pity the neurotic, unfeminine, unhappy women who wanted to be poets or physicists or presidents. They learned that truly feminine women do not want careers, higher education, political rights—the independence and the opportunities that the old-fashioned feminists fought for. Some women, in their forties and fifties, still remembered painfully giving up those dreams, but most of the younger women no longer even thought about them. A thousand expert voices applauded their femininity, their adjustment, their new maturity. All they had to do was devote their lives from earliest girlhood to finding a husband and bearing children. . . .

The suburban housewife—she was the dream image of the young American women and the envy, it was said, of women all over the world. The American housewife—freed by science and labor-saving appliances from the drudgery, the dangers of childbirth and the illnesses of her grandmother. She was healthy, beautiful, educated, concerned only about her husband, her children, her home. She had found true feminine fulfillment. As a housewife and mother, she was respected as a full and equal partner to man in his world. She was free to choose automobiles, clothes, appliances, supermarkets; she had everything that women ever dreamed of.

In the fifteen years after World War II, this mystique of feminine fulfillment became the cherished and self-perpetuating core of contemporary American culture. Millions of women lived their lives in the image of those pretty pictures of the American suburban housewife, kissing their husbands goodbye in front of the picture window, depositing their station-wagonsful of children at school, and smiling as they ran the new electric waxer over the spotless kitchen floor. They baked their own bread, sewed their own and their children's clothes, kept their new washing machines and dryers running all day. They changed the sheets on the beds twice a week instead of once, took the rug-hooking class in adult education, and pitied their poor frustrated mothers, who had dreamed of having a career. Their only dream was to be perfect wives and mothers; their highest ambition to have five children and a beautiful house, their only fight to get and keep their husbands. They had no thought for the unfeminine problems of the world outside the home; they wanted the men to make the major decisions. They gloried in their role as women, and wrote proudly on the census blank "Occupation: housewife." . . .

If a woman had a problem in the 1950's and 1960's, she knew that something must be wrong with her marriage, or with herself. Other women were satisfied with their lives, she thought. What kind of a woman was she if she did not feel this mysterious fulfillment waxing the kitchen floor? She was so ashamed to admit her dissatisfaction that she never knew how many other women shared it. If she tried to tell her husband, he didn't understand what she was talking about. She did not really understand it herself. For over fifteen years women in America found it harder to talk about this problem than about sex.

4   Like pre–Civil War women's rights activists, many modern feminists were first involved in other reforms or protests before becoming committed to feminism. Mary King, the author of this selection, was a white civil rights worker involved in the Student Nonviolent Coordinating Committee, a civil rights organization founded in 1960 to coordinate efforts to desegregate the South. Many black and white college students were members of SNCC. What effect did involvement in the civil rights movement have on King as a woman?

Civil Rights and the Rise of Feminism (1987)
MARY KING

1. Staff was involved in crucial constitutional revisions at the Atlanta staff meeting in October. A large committee was appointed to present revisions to the staff. The committee was all men.
2. Two organizers were working together to form a farmers league. Without

Source: Mary E. King, *Freedom Song.* Copyright 1987 by Mary Elizabeth King. Originally published by William Morrow & Company, New York. Reprinted with the permission of Gerard McCauley Agency, Inc.

asking any questions, the male organizer immediately assigned the clerical work to the female organizer although both had had equal experience in organizing campaigns.

3. Although there are women in Mississippi project who have been working as long as some of the men, the leadership group in COFO is all men.

4. A woman in a field office wondered why she was held responsible for day to day decisions, only to find out later that she had been appointed project director but not told.

5. A fall 1964 personnel and resources report on Mississippi projects lists the number of people in each project. The section on Laurel however, lists not the number of persons, but "three girls."

6. One of SNCC's main administrative officers apologizes for appointment of a woman as interim project director in a key Mississippi project area.

7. A veteran of two years work for SNCC in two states spends her day typing and doing clerical work for other people in her project. . . .

Undoubtedly this list will seem strange to some, petty to others, laughable to most. The list could continue as far as there are women in the movement. Except that most women don't talk about these kinds of incidents, because the whole subject is not discussable—strange to some, petty to others, laughable to most. The average white person finds it difficult to understand why the Negro resents being called "boy," or being thought of as "musical" and "athletic," because the average white person doesn't realize that he assumes he is superior. And naturally he doesn't understand the problem of paternalism. So too the average SNCC worker finds it difficult to discuss the woman problem because of the assumption of male superiority. Assumptions of male superiority are as widespread and deep rooted and every much as crippling to the woman as the assumptions of white supremacy are to the Negro. Consider why it is in SNCC that women who are competent, qualified and experienced, are automatically assigned to the "female" kinds of jobs such as typing, desk work, telephone work, filing, library work, cooking and the assistant kind of administrative work but rarely the "executive" kind.

The woman in SNCC is often in the same position as that token Negro hired in a corporation. The management thinks that it has done its bit. Yet every day the Negro bears an atmosphere, attitudes and actions which are tinged with condescension and paternalism, the most telling of which are when he is not promoted as the equally or less skilled whites are. . . .

---

5 The National Organization for Women proclaimed its premises and goals at its first meeting in 1966. Note what NOW saw as the principal problems confronting women. Did its proposals to achieve equality pertain to the "public" or the "private" sphere? How does this statement reflect the influence of other developments in American society by the 1960s?

NOW's Statement of Purpose (1966)

We, men and women who hereby constitute ourselves as the National Organization for Women, believe that the time has come for a new movement toward true equality for all women in America, and toward a fully equal partnership of the sexes, as part of the world-wide revolution of human rights now taking place within and beyond our national borders.

The purpose of NOW is to take action to bring women into full participation in the mainstream of American society now, exercising all the privileges and responsibilities thereof in truly equal partnership with men.

We believe the time has come to move beyond the abstract argument, discussion and symposia over the status and special nature of women which has raged in America in recent years: the time has come to confront, with concrete action, the conditions that now prevent women from enjoying the equality of opportunity and freedom of choice which is their right as individual Americans, and as human beings.

NOW is dedicated to the proposition that women first and foremost are human beings, who, like all other people in our society, must have the chance to develop their fullest human potential. We believe that women can achieve such equality only by accepting to the full the challenges and responsibilities they share with all other people in our society, as part of the decision-making mainstream of American political, economic and social life.

We organize to initiate or support action, nationally or in any part of this nation, by individuals or organizations, to break through the silken curtain of prejudice and discrimination against women in government, industry, the professions, the churches, the political parties, the judiciary, the labor unions, in education, science, medicine, law, religion and every other field of importance in American society. . . .

There is no civil rights movement to speak for women, as there has been for Negroes and other victims of discrimination. The National Organization for Women must therefore begin to speak.

WE BELIEVE that the power of American law, and the protection guaranteed by the U.S. Constitution to the civil rights of all individuals, must be effectively applied and enforced to isolate and remove patterns of sex discrimination, to ensure equality of opportunity in employment and education, and equality of civil and political rights and responsibilities on behalf of women, as well as for Negroes and other deprived groups. . . .

WE DO NOT ACCEPT the token appointment of a few women to high-level positions in government and industry as a substitute for a serious continuing effort to recruit and advance women according to their individual abilities. To this end, we urge American government and industry to mobilize the same resources of ingenuity and command with which they have solved problems of far greater difficulty than those now impeding the progress of women.

WE BELIEVE that this nation has a capacity at least as great as other nations, to innovate new social institutions which will enable women to enjoy true equality of opportunity and responsibility in society, without conflict with their responsibilities as mothers and homemakers. In such innovations, America does not lead the Western world, but lags by decades behind many European countries. We do not accept the traditional assumption that a woman has to choose between marriage and motherhood, on the one hand, and serious participation in industry or the professions on the other. We question the present expectation that all normal women will retire from job or profession for ten or fifteen years, to devote their full time to raising children, only to reenter the job market at a relatively minor level. . . .

WE REJECT the current assumptions that a man must carry the sole burden of supporting himself, his wife, and family, and that a woman is automatically entitled to lifelong support by a man upon her marriage, or that marriage, home and family are primarily woman's world and responsibility—hers, to dominate, his to support. We believe that a true partnership between the sexes demands a different concept of marriage, an equitable sharing of the responsibilities of home and children and of the economic burdens of their support. We believe that proper recognition should be given to the economic and social value of homemaking and child care. To these ends, we will seek to open a reexamination of laws and mores governing marriage and divorce, for we believe that the current state of "half-equality" between the sexes discriminates against both men and women, and is the cause of much unnecessary hostility between the sexes.

---

6   Redstockings was one of many radical feminist organizations that had sprung up by the late 1960s. How does this analysis of women's inequality differ from NOW's? Do Redstockings's analysis and rhetoric reveal the influence of other protest movements in the 1960s?

Redstockings Manifesto (1969)

I.   After centuries of individual and preliminary political struggle, women are uniting to achieve their final liberation from male supremacy. Redstockings is dedicated to building this unity and winning our freedom.

II.   Women are an oppressed class. Our oppression is total, affecting every

Source: Mary Beth Norton, *Major Problems in American Women's History* (Lexington, Mass.: D. C. Heath and Company, 1989), p. 400.

facet of our lives. We are exploited as sex objects, breeders, domestic servants, and cheap labor. We are considered inferior beings, whose only purpose is to enhance men's lives. Our humanity is denied. Our prescribed behavior is enforced by the threat of physical violence.

Because we have lived so intimately with our oppressors, in isolation from each other, we have been kept from seeing our personal suffering as a political condition. This creates the illusion that a woman's relationship with her man is a matter of interplay between two unique personalities, and can be worked out individually. In reality, every such relationship is a *class* relationship, and the conflicts between individual men and women are *political* conflicts that can only be solved collectively.

III.   We identify the agents of our oppression as men. Male supremacy is the oldest, most basic form of domination. All other forms of exploitation and oppression (racism, capitalism, imperialism, etc.) are extensions of male supremacy: men dominate women, a few men dominate the rest. All power structures throughout history have been male-dominated and male-oriented. Men have controlled all political, economic and cultural institutions and backed up this control with physical force. They have used their power to keep women in an inferior position. *All men* receive economic, sexual, and psychological benefits from male supremacy. *All men* have oppressed women.

---

7   Phyllis Schlafly, the chairwoman of STOP ERA, was a leading critic of the Equal Rights Amendment. On what grounds does she argue against equal rights for women? What does this source reveal about important factors limiting the success of the women's movement?

"What's Wrong with 'Equal Rights' for Women?" (1972)
PHYLLIS SCHLAFLY

Of all the classes of people who ever lived, the American woman is the most privileged. We have the most rights and rewards, and the fewest duties. Our unique status is the result of a fortunate combination of circumstances.

1. We have the immense good fortune to live in a civilization which respects the family as the basic unit of society. This respect is part and parcel of our laws and our customs. It is based on the fact of life—which no legislation or agitation can erase—that women have babies and men don't.

If you don't like this fundamental difference, you will have to take up your complaint with God because He created us this way. The fact that women,

Source: Reprinted with permission from The Phyllis Schlafly Report, February 1972.

not men, have babies is not the fault of selfish and domineering men, or of the establishment, or of any clique of conspirators who want to oppress women. It's simply the way God made us.

Our Judeo-Christian civilization has developed the law and custom that, since women must bear the physical consequences of the sex act, men must be required to bear the other consequences and pay in other ways. These laws and customs decree that a man must carry his share by physical protection and financial support of his children and of the woman who bears his children, and also by a code of behavior which benefits and protects both the woman and the children.

The Greatest Achievement of Women's Rights

This is accomplished by the institution of the family. Our respect for the family as the basic unit of society, which is ingrained in the laws and customs of our Judeo-Christian civilization, is the greatest single achievement in the entire history of women's rights. It assures a woman the most precious and important right of all—the right to keep her own baby and to be supported and protected in the enjoyment of watching her baby grow and develop.

The institution of the family is advantageous for women for many reasons. After all, what do we want out of life? To love and be loved? Mankind has not discovered a better nest for a lifetime of reciprocal love. A sense of achievement? A man may search 30 to 40 years for accomplishment in his profession. A woman can enjoy real achievement when she is young—by having a baby. She can have the satisfaction of doing a job well—and being recognized for it.

Do we want financial security? We are fortunate to have the great legacy of Moses, the Ten Commandments, especially this one: "Honor thy father and thy mother that thy days may be long upon the land." Children are a woman's best social security—her best guarantee of social benefits such as old age, pension, unemployment compensation, workman's compensation, and sick leave. The family gives a woman the physical, financial and emotional security of the home—for all her life.

The Financial Benefits of Chivalry

2. The second reason why American women are a privileged group is that we are the beneficiaries of a tradition of special respect for women which dates from the Christian Age of Chivalry. The honor and respect paid to Mary the Mother of Christ, resulted in all women, in effect, being put on a pedestal.

This respect for women is not just the lip service that politicians pay to "God, Motherhood, and the Flag." It is not—as some youthful agitators seem to think—just a matter of opening doors for women, seeing that they are seated first, carrying their bundles, and helping them in and out of automobiles. Such good manners are merely the superficial evidences of a total attitude toward women which expresses itself in many more tangible ways, such as money. . . .

The Real Liberation of Women

3. The third reason why American women are so well off is that the great American free enterprise system has produced remarkable inventors who have lifted the backbreaking women's work from our shoulders.

In other countries and in other eras, it was truly said that "Man may work from sun to sun, but woman's work is never done." Other women have labored every waking hour—preparing food on wood burning stoves, making flour, baking bread in stone ovens, spinning yarn, making clothes, making soap, doing the laundry by hand, heating irons, making candles for light and fires for warmth, and trying to nurse their babies through illnesses without medical care.

The real liberation of women from the backbreaking drudgery of centuries is the American free enterprise system which stimulated inventive geniuses to pursue their talents—and we all reap the profits. The great heroes of women's liberation are not the straggly-haired women on television talk shows and picket lines, but Thomas Edison who brought the miracle of electricity to our homes to give light and to run all those labor-saving devices—the equivalent, perhaps, of a half dozen household servants for every middle-class American woman. Or Elias Howe who gave us the sewing machine which resulted in such an abundance of ready made clothing. Or Clarence Birdseye who invented the process for freezing foods. Or Henry Ford, who mass-produced the automobile so that it is within the price-range of every American, man or woman. . . .

The Fraud of the Equal Rights Amendment

In the last couple of years, a noisy movement has sprung up agitating for "women's rights." Suddenly everywhere we are afflicted with aggressive females on television talk shows yapping about how mistreated American women are, suggesting that marriage has put us in some kind of "slavery," that housework is menial and degrading, and—perish the thought—that women are discriminated against. New "women's liberation" organizations are popping up, agitating and demonstrating, serving demands on public officials, getting wide press coverage always, and purporting to speak for some 100,000,000 American women.

It's time to set the record straight. The claim that American women are downtrodden and unfairly treated is the fraud of the century. The truth is that American women never had it so good. Why should we lower ourselves to "equal rights" when we already have the status of special privilege?

The proposed Equal Rights Amendment states: "Equality of rights under the law shall not be denied or abridged by the United States or by any state on account of sex." So what's wrong with that? Well, here are a few examples of what's wrong with it.

This amendment will absolutely and positively make women subject to the draft. Why any woman would support such a ridiculous and un-American proposal as this is beyond comprehension. Why any Congressman who had any regard for his wife, sister or daughter would support such a proposition is just as hard to understand. Foxholes are bad enough for men, but they certainly are not the place for women—and we should reject any proposal which would put them there in the name of equal rights. . . .

Another bad effect of the Equal Rights Amendment is that it will abolish women's right to child support and alimony, and substitute what the women's libbers think is a more "equal" policy, that "such decisions should be within the discretion of the court and should be made on the economic situation and need of the parties in the case."

Under present American laws, the man is *always* required to support his wife and each child he caused to be brought into the world. Why should women abandon these good laws—by trading them for something so nebulous and uncertain as the "discretion of the Court"? . . .

Women's Libbers Do NOT Speak for Us

The "women's lib" movement is not an honest effort to secure better jobs for women who want or need to work outside the home. This is just the superficial sweet-talk to win broad support for a radical "movement." "Women's lib" is a total assault on the role of the American woman as wife and mother, and on the family as the basic unit of society.

Women's libbers are trying to make wives and mothers unhappy with their career, make them feel that they are "second class citizens" and "abject slaves." Women's libbers are promoting free sex instead of the "slavery" of marriage. They are promoting "Federal" day care-centers for babies instead of homes. They are promoting abortions instead of families.

Why should we trade in our special privileges and honored status for the alleged advantage of working in an office or assembly line? Most women would rather cuddle a baby than a typewriter or factory machine. Most women find that it is easier to get along with a husband than a foreman or office manager. Offices and factories require many more menial and repetitious chores than washing dishes and ironing shirts.

Women's libbers do *not* speak for the majority of American women. American women do *not* want to be liberated from husbands and children. We do *not* want to trade our birthright of the special privilege of American women—for the mess of pottage called the Equal Rights Amendment. . . .

The Sexual Revolution and the Women's Movement

The civil rights and antiwar movements brought important changes to American society in the 1960s. So, too, did a sexual revolution. As you read these selections, think about the relationship between a sexual revolution in the 1960s and the rise of the women's movement. How did a more liberated social climate bring both liberation and tyranny for women?

 In this selection a writer looks at the effects of the sexual revolution.

On Women and Sex (1972)
JOYCE MAYNARD

For about three weeks of my freshman year at college I had two roommates instead of one—the girl in the bottom bunk and her friend, who made our quarters especially cramped because, in addition to being six feet tall with lots of luggage, he was male. We slept in shifts—they together, until I came back to the room at night, then he outside in the living room on the couch, until she got up, then he in her bed and I in mine, or I in hers and he in mine, because it was easier for me to get out from the bottom without waking him, and he needed his sleep. . . . We never made it a threesome, but the awkwardness was always there (those squeaking bedsprings . . .), as it was for many girls I knew, and many boys. Coming back to the room and announcing my presence loudly with a well-directed, well-projected cough or a casual murmur, "Hmmmm—I think I'll go to my room now," it occurred to me that it wasn't my roommate but I—the one who slept alone, the one whose only pills were vitamins and aspirin—I was the embarrassed one. How has it happened, what have we come to, that the scarlet letter these days isn't A, but V? . . .

The sexual revolution. It's a cliché, but it exists all right, and its pressures are everywhere. All the old excuses ("I might get pregnant," "I'm not that kind of girl") are gone. Safe and increasingly available contraceptives (for anyone brave and premeditative enough to get them) make premarital sex possible; changing moral standards, an increased naturalness, make it commonplace; elegant models of sexual freedom—Julie Christie, Catherine Deneuve—have made it fashionable. Consider a virgin in the movies. Is there a single pretty young heroine who doesn't hop unself-consciously into bed? (Who is there left for her to identify with—Doris Day?) Then there are magazines, filled with discussions of intricate sexual problems (the timing of orgasms . . . do I get one? do I give one?) while the virgin remains on a whole other level—her fears compounded. (Our old, junior high notion of sex was that it got done to you; the girl with the purple eyeshadow just let it happen. Today all kinds of problems in technique make the issue much more complicated for an inexperienced, media-blitzed girl: not just *will I* but *can I*.) The people who've been making

Source: Reprinted by permission of the author from *Looking Back* by Joyce Maynard (New York: Doubleday, 1973).

nice, simple love for years now, while the virgin became more and more unique, have, quite understandably, gone on to other things. There is foreplay and afterplay and the 999 positions of the *Kamasutra* . . . The train has left the station before the virgin's bought her ticket or even, maybe, packed her bags. . . .

 This source is an excerpt from the preface to the first edition of a book that has had a long history and a wide influence.

Our Bodies, Ourselves (1973)

The history of this book, *Our Bodies, Ourselves,* is lengthy and satisfying.

It began in a small discussion group on "women and their bodies" which was part of a women's conference held in Boston in the spring of 1969, one of the first gatherings of women meeting specifically to talk with other women. For many of us it was the very first time we had joined together with other women to talk and think about our lives and what we could do about them. Before the conference was over, some of us decided to keep on meeting as a group to continue the discussion, and so we did.

In the beginning we called ourselves "the doctors group." We had all experienced similar feelings of frustration and anger toward specific doctors and the medical maze in general, and initially we wanted to do something about those doctors who were condescending, paternalistic, judgmental and noninformative. As we talked and shared our experiences with one another, we realized just how much we had to learn about our bodies. So we decided on a summer project—to research those topics which we felt were particularly pertinent to learning about our bodies, to discuss in the group what we had learned, then to write papers individually or in groups of two or three, and finally to present the results in the fall as a course for women on women and their bodies.

As we developed the course we realized more and more that we really *were* capable of collecting, understanding, and evaluating medical information. Together we evaluated our reading of books and journals, our talks with doctors and friends who were medical students. We found we could discuss, question and argue with each other in a new spirit of cooperation rather than competition. We were equally struck by how important it was for us to be able to open up with one another and share our feelings about our bodies. The process of talking was as crucial as the facts themselves. Over time the facts and feelings melted together in ways that touched us very deeply, and that is reflected in the changing titles of the course and then the book—from *Women and Their Bodies* to *Women and Our Bodies* to, finally, *Our Bodies, Ourselves.* . . .

Many, many other women have worked with us on the book. A group of gay women got together specifically to do the chapter on lesbianism. Other chapters were done still differently. For instance, the mother of one woman in the group volunteered to work on menopause with some of us who have not gone through that experience ourselves. . . .

From the very beginning of working together, first on the course that led to this book and then on the book itself, we have felt exhilarated and energized by our new knowledge. Finding out about our bodies and our bodies' needs, starting to take control over that area of our lives, has released for us an energy that has overflowed into our work, our friendships, our relationships with men and women, and for some of us, our marriages and our parenthood. . . .

A second important result of this kind of learning is that we are better prepared to evaluate the institutions that are supposed to meet our health needs—the hospitals, clinics, doctors, medical schools, nursing schools, public health departments, Medicaid bureaucracies and so on. For some of us it was the first time we had looked critically, and with strength, at the existing institutions serving us. The experience of learning just how little control we had over our lives and bodies, the coming together out of isolation to learn from each other in order to define what we needed, and the experience of supporting one another in demanding the changes that grew out of our developing critique—all were crucial and formative political experiences for us. We have felt our potential power as a force for political and social change.

The learning we have done while working on *Our Bodies, Ourselves* has been a good basis for growth in other areas of life for still another reason. For women throughout the centuries, ignorance about our bodies has had one major consequence—pregnancy. Until very recently pregnancies were all but inevitable, biology *was* our destiny—that is, because our bodies are designed to get pregnant and give birth and lactate that is what all or most of us did. . . . It was not until we researched carefully and learned more about birth-control methods and abortion, about laws governing birth control and abortion, and not until we put all this information together with what it meant to us to be female, that we began to feel we could truly set out to control whether and when we would have babies.

This knowledge has freed us to a certain extent from the constant, energy-draining anxiety about becoming pregnant. It has made our pregnancies better because they no longer happen to us, but we actively choose them and enthusiastically participate in them. It has made our parenthood better because it is our choice rather than our destiny. . . . This is why people in the women's movement have been so active in fighting against the inhumane legal restrictions, the imperfections of available contraceptives, the poor sex education, the highly priced and poorly administered health care that keep too many women from having this crucial control over their bodies.

There is a fourth reason why knowledge about our bodies has generated so much new energy. For us, body education is core education. Our bodies are the physical bases from which we move out into the world; ignorance, uncertainty—even, at worst, shame—about our physical selves create in us an alienation from ourselves that keeps us from being the whole people that we could be. Picture a woman trying to do work and to enter into equal and satisfying relationships with other people—when she feels physically weak because she has never tried to be strong; when she drains her energy trying to change her face, her figure, her hair, her smells, to match some ideal norm set by magazines, movies and TV; when she feels confused and ashamed of the menstrual blood that every month appears from some dark place in her body; when her internal body processes are a mystery to her and surface only to cause her trouble (an unplanned pregnancy, or cervical cancer); when she does not understand or enjoy sex and concentrates her sexual drives into aimless romantic fantasies, perverting and misusing a potential energy be-cause she had been brought up to deny it. Learning to understand, accept, and be responsible for our physical selves, we are freed of some of these pre-occupations and can start to use our untapped energies. Our image of our-selves is on a firmer base, we can be better friends and better lovers, better *people*, more self-confident, more autonomous, stronger and more whole.

---

10   *The Feminine Mystique* proclaimed that women would find fulfillment through work outside the home. Note how this essay illustrates some of the problems women faced as they began to reject domesticity. Does it help to explain why feminists began to put increasing emphasis on reform within the "private" sphere?

The Politics of Housework (ca. 1970)

PAT MAINARDI

Liberated women—very different from Women's Liberation! The first signals all kinds of goodies, to warm the hearts (not to mention other parts) of the most radical men. The other signals—HOUSEWORK. The first brings sex without marriage, sex before marriage, cozy housekeeping arrangements ("I'm living with this chick") and the self-content of knowing that you're not the kind of man who wants a doormat instead of a woman. That will come later. After all, who wants that old commodity anymore, the Standard Amer-ican Housewife, all husband, home and kids. The New Commodity, the Lib-erated Woman, has sex a lot and has a Career, preferably something that can be fitted in with the household chores—like dancing, pottery, or painting.

Source: Mary C. Lynn, ed., *Women's Liberation in the 20th Century,* pp. 104–108, 109–110. Copy-right © 1975 by John Wiley & Sons, Inc. This material is used by permission of John Wiley & Sons, Inc.

On the other hand is Women's Liberation—and housework. What? You say this is all trivial? Wonderful! That's what I thought. It seemed perfectly reasonable. We both had careers, both had to work a couple of days a week to earn enough to live on, so why shouldn't we share the housework? So I suggested it to my mate and he agreed—most men are too hip to turn you down flat. You're right, he said. It's only fair.

Then an interesting thing happened. I can only explain it by stating that we women have been brainwashed more than even we can imagine. Probably too many years of seeing television women in ecstasy over their shiny waxed floors or breaking down over their dirty shirt collars. Men have no such conditioning. They recognize the essential fact of housework right from the very beginning. Which is that it stinks.

Here's my list of dirty chores: buying groceries, carting them home and putting them away; cooking meals and washing dishes and pots; doing the laundry; digging out the place when things get out of control; washing floors. The list could go on but the sheer necessities are bad enough. All of us have to do these things, or get someone else to do them for us. The longer my husband contemplated these chores, the more repulsed he became, and so proceeded the change from the normally sweet considerate Dr. Jekyll into the crafty Mr. Hyde who would stop at nothing to avoid the horrors of—housework. As he felt himself backed into a corner laden with dirty dishes, brooms, mops and reeking garbage, his front teeth grew longer and pointier, his fingernails haggled and his eyes grew wild. Housework trivial? Not on your life! Just try to share the burden. . . .

Participatory democracy begins at home. If you are planning to implement your politics, there are certain things to remember:

1. He *is* feeling it more than you. He's losing some leisure and you're gaining it. The measure of your oppression is his resistance.
2. A great many American men are not accustomed to doing monotonous repetitive work which never issues in any lasting, let alone important, achievement. This is why they would rather repair a cabinet than wash dishes. If human endeavors are like a pyramid with man's highest achievements at the top, then keeping oneself alive is at the bottom. Men have always had servants (us) to take care of this bottom strata of life while they have confined their efforts to the rarefied upper regions. It is thus ironic when they ask of women—where are your great painters, statesmen, etc. Mme Matisse ran a millinery shop so he could paint. Mrs. Martin Luther King kept his house and raised his babies.
3. It is a traumatizing experience for someone who has always thought of himself as being against any oppression or exploitation of one human being by another to realize that in his daily life he has been accepting and implementing (and benefiting from) this exploitation; that his rationalization is little different from that of the racist who says "Black people don't feel

pain" (women don't mind doing the shitwork); and that the oldest form of oppression in history has been the oppression of 50% of the population by the other 50%. . . .

I was just finishing this when my husband came in and asked what I was doing. Writing a paper on housework. Housework? he said, *Housework?* Oh my god how trivial can you get. A paper on housework.

Women's Changing Education and Employment Experience

As it can for other population groups, statistical information can reveal important changes in women's lives. As you examine these charts, consider whether they reveal reasons why many women in the 1960s rejected domesticity and joined the women's movement. Do they also provide evidence for the impact of that movement?

Sex Ratios of High School and College Graduates in the United States, 1940–1980

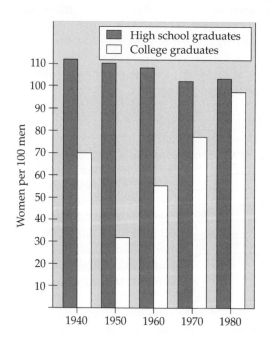

Source: U.S. Bureau of the Census, *Historical Statistics of the United States, Colonial Times to 1970* (Washington, D.C.: GPO, 1975), pp. 379, 385–86; U.S. Bureau of the Census, *Statistical Abstract of the United States: 1988* (Washington, D.C.: GPO, 1987, 108th ed.), p. 140.

12 Women's Labor Force Participation, by Marital Status, 1940–1987

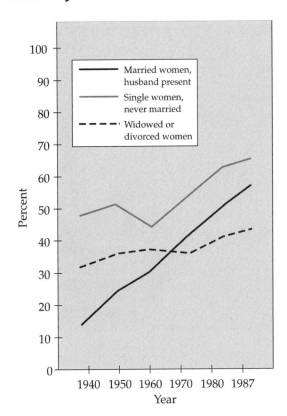

Source: U.S. Bureau of the Census, *Historical Statistics of the United States, Colonial Times to 1970* (Washington, D.C.: GPO, 1975), p. 133; U.S. Bureau of the Census, *Statistical Abstract of the United States: 1988* (Washington, D.C.: GPO, 1987, 108th ed.), p. 373.

13   Median Earnings of Year-round, Full-time Workers, by Sex, 1955–1985

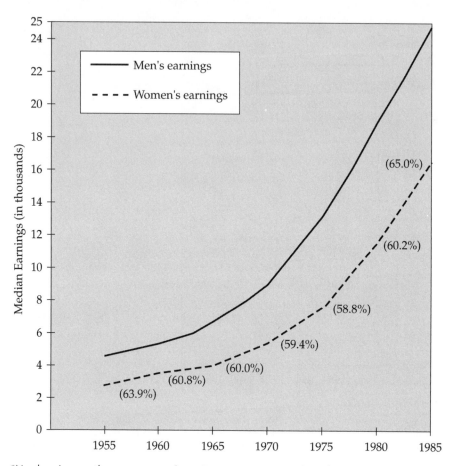

*Numbers in parentheses are women's earnings as a percentage of men's.

Source: U.S. Department of Labor, Women's Bureau, Bulletin 298, *Time of Change: 1983 Handbook on Women Workers* (Washington, D.C.: GPO, 1983), p. 82; U.S. Bureau of the Census, *Money Income of Households, Families and Persons in the United States: 1986.* Current Population Reports, Series P-60, no. 159, 100–101.

CONCLUSION

One month before *Time* magazine proclaimed 1975 "The Year of the Women" and a decade after it put Phyllis McGinley on its cover, *Newsweek* magazine ran a story on the exploding field of women's history. The timing of the stories was no coincidence. One of the most important consequences of the women's movement was the interest it stimulated in uncovering women's past. As we have already seen in this volume, our view of the past is shaped by the way people think about the present—and vice versa. As women began to think in new ways about their status in contemporary society, they also began to think differently about their place in the past. They found women mostly excluded from the pages of history, a reflection of their subordinate position in American society. Like African Americans, women began to recapture their past when they began to fight for equality.

The women's movement, which greatly stimulated the study of women's history, is now history itself. As this chapter's secondary sources demonstrate, women's historians do not write about it only to "raise consciousness," to prove past oppression, or to recount women's past contributions. More important, they are interested in placing women in the mainstream of the American past. They seek to understand the way women's experience influenced and in turn was influenced by American society and culture. Thus they illustrate important points about historical inquiry that we have seen repeatedly in this volume. For instance, to understand the rise of the women's movement, historians must consider the effects of many causal influences. To understand the motivations of feminists, moreover, those influences can rarely be considered apart from ideology. The study of the contemporary women's movement also reminds us that history happens to elites and non-elites alike. In fact, it is a double reminder of that message, because the voices of women in general and non-elite women in particular have usually not been heard in the past. By making connections between the "private" sphere of family life and the "public" sphere, the women's movement demonstrates why historians must be interested in more than the activities of statesmen and generals.

Finally, the modern women's movement illustrates the importance of historians' motivations. As we have seen in this chapter, historians are guided by contemporary concerns even as they seek to understand the past on its own terms. Although they may write history that serves to defend or attack contemporary policies, historians do not turn to the past merely to do that. That is a good lesson to keep in mind as we turn in the next chapter to the issue of multicultural education.

FURTHER READING

Lois Banner, *Women in Modern America: A Brief History* (San Diego: Harcourt Brace Jovanovich, 1984).

Nancy Cott, *The Grounding of Modern Feminism* (New Haven, Conn.: Yale University Press, 1987).

Sara Evans, *Personal Politics: The Roots of Women's Liberation in the Civil Rights Movement and the New Left* (New York: Vintage Books, 1979).

Betty Friedan, *The Feminine Mystique* (New York: W. W. Norton and Company, 1963).

Mary Thom, ed., *Letters to Ms., 1972–1987* (New York: Henry Holt and Company, 1987).

Winifred Wandersee, *On the Move: American Women in the 1970s* (Boston: Twayne Publishers, 1988).

NOTES

1. *Newsweek,* June 7, 1965, p. 55.
2. *U.S. News & World Report,* June 7, 1965, pp. 12, 53.
3. *Time,* June 18, 1965, pp. 75, 78.
4. *Newsweek,* March 23, 1970, pp. 71–72.
5. Quoted in Nancy Woloch, *Women and the American Experience* (New York: McGraw-Hill, 1984), p. 518.

Chapter

13

Why Historical Interpretation Matters: The Battle Over Multicultural Education

The sources in this chapter provide various perspectives on the impact of multi-culturalism in education in the 1990s.

Secondary Sources

1. Multiculturalism and Disunity (1991), ARTHUR SCHLESINGER, JR.
2. Empire, Racism, and Multiculturalism (2000), JUAN GONZALEZ

Primary Sources

3. "The Visigoths in Tweed" (1991), DINESH D'SOUZA
4. Stereotypes and Multicultural Education (1991), SHAWN WONG
5. "The Danger in Multiple Perspectives" (1991), ALBERT SHANKER
6. "In Defense of Multiculturalism" (1991), NATHAN GLAZER
7. Building Bridges or Burning Them? (1992)
8. Musical Instruments in a Multicultural Textbook (1994)
9. Proposition 227 Arguments (1998)
10. The Lessons of Bilingual Education (1998)

*I*n 1980, historian Stephen Thernstrom of Harvard compared America's "ethnic revival" to jogging. Both, he declared, were "fashionable at the moment." Yet the editor of a then-newly-released encyclopedia of ethnic groups in the United States doubted that Americans' renewed interest in ethnicity would persist. This revival, Thernstrom observed in an interview with a major newsmagazine, does not "run very deep."[1] A decade later, however, it was still going strong. Americans would fight numerous battles related to the nation's increasing racial and ethnic diversity through the 1990s. From affirmative action to benefits for illegal immigrants, the conflicts raged over a wide terrain.

Some of the biggest battles related to ethnicity were fought over multicultural curriculum and bilingual education in the schools. Thanks to a heightened awareness of ethnicity, American education became the focus of a heated debate that moved well beyond school board meetings. Questions about what and how American students learned, from kindergarten through college, became hot topics in the last decade of the century on the nation's radio talk shows and the front pages of its newspapers. To many Americans, the nation's students had been subjected to a dangerous and divisive "cult of ethnicity." To others, the efforts of schools to acknowledge and accommodate the country's diverse ethnic makeup represented its best hope for realizing the American ideal of equality.

Historians found themselves and their discipline at the center of an acrimonious debate over school curriculum. This occurred for two reasons that they could easily appreciate. First, school administrators, school boards, parents, and others realized that *what* and *whose* history students learned in school were not merely "academic" questions, but held important implications for contemporary society. Second, both sides in this battle made arguments for or against changes in school curriculum, including even bilingual education, based on their own reading of the past. In other words, they turned to history as a guide. In fact, nowhere has a widespread acknowledgment of history's relevance been more evident recently than in the debates over multiculturalism. This chapter, then, explores the role of history and historical interpretation in the curriculum debates related to America's great "ethnic revival" at the end of the twentieth century.

SETTING

Like any widely used term, multiculturalism means different things to different people. Culture, of course, is usually associated with a common language, history, religion, customs, and even geographical origin. These elements of cultural inheritance often contribute to a sense of group identity. Multiculturalism recognizes such group identities in varying degrees and validates, in the words of one recent study, "affirmation of ethnic distinctiveness."[2] Some advocates of multiculturalism concluded that school curricula must acknowledge multiple perspectives simply because people from different cultures naturally view many things differently. Others went further. They insisted that the traditional curriculum reflected a long history of racism and oppression of minorities. Changing it, they argued, would help overcome the effects of this oppression. Whatever multiculturalism came to mean in the minds of advocates or opponents, the heated debates surrounding it in the 1990s usually related to one question: whether affirmations of group identity undermined a sense of national identity or actually contributed to social harmony.

Even as historians and their discipline were drawn into this debate, they also sought to explain the heightened sense of ethnic identity in the last decades of the twentieth century. Most historians agree on the important role played by two factors in stimulating a late-twentieth-century "ethnic revival": the end of the Cold War and increasing globalization. With the collapse of the Soviet bloc in Eastern Europe and then of the Soviet Union itself in 1991, the ideological division between communist and western, free-market nations disappeared. The long Cold War struggle had suppressed deep-seated ethnic rivalries in many lands. In the 1990s, those rivalries resurfaced in Kosovo, Bosnia, Chechnia, and elsewhere, often with much bloodshed. Meanwhile, advances in communications and transportation resulted in the easier movement of goods—and people—across national boundaries. As technology, in effect, shrank the globe in the late twentieth century, millions of workers and immigrants moved to distant countries with different cultures. By the end of the decade, for instance, more than two million people of Turkish descent lived in Germany. At the same time, the population of minority ethnic groups in Great Britain totaled approximately four million, due mainly to immigration from Asian and African nations that were once part of Britain's overseas empire. As the growing links between advanced and developing economies uprooted millions of people from different cultures, a heightened awareness of ethnic differences and the need to accommodate them was one inevitable result.

Nowhere was that need to accommodate ethnic differences more apparent than in the United States. Many historians point to a massive wave of immigrants in the late twentieth century as one obvious explanation. This immigration was boosted by the economic and technological changes associated with globalization. Even more important, though, were changes in the nation's immigration laws. In 1965, Congress passed the Immigration and Naturalization Act, replacing the national quota system, which had been in effect since the 1920s and had favored immigrants from northern Europe. (See Chapter 6.) The new law gave preference to family reunification and skills of immigrants, especially in occupations facing labor shortages. At the same time, it led to a dramatic increase in the number of immigrants entering the United States in the last decades of the twentieth century. By the 1980s, more than 800,000 legal immigrants entered the country every year, a number that jumped to more than one million a year in the 1990s. The new law also resulted in sweeping changes in the makeup of the nation's immigrant population. The "new" immigrants of the late twentieth century were overwhelmingly from Latin America, Asia, and Africa. Between 1965 and the turn of the century, according to one estimate, twenty million immigrants arrived from Latin America, Asia, and the Caribbean. In the same years, more immigrants arrived from Africa than had come as involuntary immigrants during slavery.

Besides immigration, many historians also emphasize the role played by the civil rights, women's, Native-American, and "Chicano-power" movements of the 1960s and 1970s in heightening Americans' ethnic consciousness. These movements, they point out, naturally fostered the idea of "group rights"—a notion further reinforced by federal affirmative action policies. First created in the late 1960s to implement the civil rights legislation passed earlier in the decade, affirmative action guidelines were intended to help African Americans overcome the continuing inequities related to a long history of discrimination. Gradually, though, the guidelines began to be applied to other groups. By 1970, four groups— "Negro, Oriental, American Indian, and Spanish Surnamed Americans"—had been included in the federal government's affirmative action guidelines. In coming years, an increasing number of federal benefits would be tied to such ethnic designations. In 1977, for instance, Hispanics, Native Americans, Asian Americans, Pacific Islanders, and Alaskan Natives, as well as blacks, became eligible for preferential treatment when Congress passed a little-noticed program for federal construction contracts. Later, federal entities from the Small Business Administration to the Civil Rights Office of the Labor Department expanded affirmative action programs. The number of "disadvantaged" groups covered by their guidelines also expanded to include immigrants from such countries as Vietnam, Korea, Laos, Cambodia, and Indonesia.

Sustained by these multiple influences, ethnic-group consciousness began to transform American education by the 1980s. Already in the 1970s, antiwar protests on college campuses had challenged authority and inspired demands for classes that examined the experiences of blacks, Hispanics, women, Native Americans, and other groups with histories of unequal treatment. During the 1980s, demands for multicultural curricula were further fueled by growing frustration with continuing racial inequalities in American society. By the 1980s, some black educators, dismayed by the stubborn academic achievement gap between many blacks and other students, called on predominately African American, urban schools to adopt an Afrocentric curriculum. Emphasizing Africa's cultural heritage in the schools, they argued, would enhance black students' self-esteem and academic performance. Perhaps the most powerful impetus for the adoption of multicultural curricula, however, arose from America's rapidly changing ethnic makeup. In the early 1980s, the spread of bilingual education programs, designed originally to provide equal opportunity to "Spanish-surnamed pupils," was one obvious example. Backed by federal mandates, the Office of Civil Rights had negotiated bilingual education agreements with more than four hundred school districts nationwide by 1980, mostly in states with large Hispanic-immigrant populations.

In later years, the impact of the nation's increasing diversity on schools became evident in other ways, though. In 1987, California—home to millions of new immigrants—endorsed new social studies and history curriculum guidelines for public schools that emphasized the role of immigrants in both the state and the nation. Two years later, New York—another state with a large immigrant and nonwhite student population—adopted an elementary social studies program entitled *Curriculum of Inclusion,* which declared that a multicultural education would leave "children from European cultures" with a "less arrogant perspective."[3] By the early 1990s, schools in many other states also adopted textbooks and curriculum guidelines emphasizing a multicultural approach. That was especially true after the development of the National History Standards, a federally backed effort by historians and educators to devise standards for teaching elementary and high school history. Begun in 1991 and completed in 1994, the history standards project emphasized cultural diversity in the study of both American history and western civilization. Meanwhile, many colleges undergoing dramatic changes in the ethnic makeup of their student bodies also started ethnic studies programs and revamped traditional courses. In 1987, for instance, Stanford University decided that its long-standing western civilization sequence should be broadened to include works from non-western cultures.

When *Time* magazine devoted an entire issue in 1993 to America's increasing ethnic diversity, multiculturalism had already become a household word. By then, it was also transforming the curriculum in many of the nation's schools. Yet it remained a controversial idea and would continue to elicit a powerful reaction in many Americans through the rest of the decade. A growing backlash against it was evident in the passage of English-only ballot initiatives in California and other states. It was equally apparent in the loud public debate about schools' growing commitments even to English-language multicultural curricula, such as that contained in the National History Standards guidelines. At the beginning of the new century, that debate goes on. The persistence of globalization, widespread ethnic conflict, immigration, and concern about inequalities in American society guarantee that it will remain an important and controversial issue well into the new century.

INVESTIGATION

In this chapter, you will have the opportunity to assess the battle over multicultural education in the 1990s and its implications for what and how students learn in school. In particular, you will be able to consider the impact of multiculturalism on the study of history in the schools. To do this, you will need to compare the conclusions of the two essays, both of which make historical arguments to support their conclusions. Then, with the aid of primary sources, you should be able to make a cogent argument about how and why it has affected school curriculum and why that matters. A good analysis will address the following questions:

1. **How would you compare the views of the American past presented in Source 1 and Source 2?** How does each author's view of the past support his conclusions about multiculturalism?

2. **What does the evidence in this chapter reveal about the reasons why demands for a multicultural approach to curriculum became so widespread by the 1990s?** What do the sources reveal about the factors that shape public school curricula?

3. **What does the evidence in this chapter suggest about the impact of multicultural education in the 1990s?** Is there evidence in the sources that heightened ethnic consciousness undermined a sense of unity among students or fostered greater understanding?

4. **What do you think is the most important lesson to be drawn from the battle over multiculturalism and bilingual education?** What evidence supports that lesson? Do the subjects or sources in previous chapters of this book shed light on it?

Before you begin, read the sections in your textbook on the important trends in American society in the last decades of the twentieth century. In particular, you will find it helpful to read about the major social, cultural, and political changes in this period. If your text mentions the conflicts related to multiculturalism, to what does it attribute them?

SECONDARY SOURCES

1 In this selection from his best-selling book *The Disuniting of America,* Pulitzer-prize-winning historian Arthur Schlesinger, Jr., sets forth his views about multicultural education, especially as it pertains to the treatment of history. Is Schlesinger a supporter of multicultural education? What does he see as its main consequences? How does he use history to support his conclusions?

Multiculturalism and Disunity (1991)

ARTHUR SCHLESINGER, JR.

The vision of America as melted into one people prevailed through most of the two centuries of the history of the United States. But the twentieth century has brought forth a new and opposing vision. One world war destroyed the old order of things and launched Woodrow Wilson's doctrine of the self-determination of peoples. Twenty years after, a second world war dissolved the western colonial empires and intensified ethnic and racial militancy around the planet. In the United States itself, new laws eased entry for immigrants from South America, Asia, and Africa and altered the composition of the American people. . . .

. . . A cult of ethnicity has arisen both among non-Anglo whites and among nonwhite minorities to denounce the idea of a melting pot, to challenge the concept of "one people," and to protect, promote, and perpetuate separate ethnic and racial communities.

The eruption of ethnicity had many good consequences. The American culture began at last to give shamefully overdue recognition to the achievements of minorities subordinated and spurned during the high noon of Anglo dominance. American education began at last to acknowledge the existence and significance of the great swirling world beyond Europe. All this was to the good. Of course history should be taught from a variety of perspectives. Let our children try to imagine the arrival of Columbus from the viewpoint of those who met him as well as from those who sent him. Living on a shrinking planet, aspiring to global leadership, Americans must learn much more about other races, other cultures, other continents. As they do, they acquire a more complex and invigorating sense of the world—and of themselves.

But pressed too far, the cult of ethnicity has had bad consequences too. The new ethnic gospel rejects the unifying vision of individuals from all nations melted into a new race. Its underlying philosophy is that America is not a nation of individuals at all but a nation of groups, that ethnicity is the defining experience for most Americans, that ethnic ties are permanent and indelible, and that division into ethnic communities establishes the basic structure of American society and the basic meaning of American history.

Implicit in this philosophy is the classification of all Americans according to ethnic and racial criteria. But while the ethnic interpretation of American history, like the economic interpretation, is valid and illuminating up to a point, it is fatally misleading and wrong when presented as the whole picture. The ethnic interpretation, moreover, reverses the historic theory of America as one people—the theory that has thus far managed to keep American society whole.

Instead of a transformative nation with an identity all its own, America in this new light is seen as preservative of diverse alien identities. Instead of a nation composed of individuals making their own unhampered choices, America increasingly sees itself as composed of groups more or less ineradicable in their ethnic character. The multiethnic dogma abandons historic purposes, replacing assimilation by fragmentation, integration by separatism. It belittles *unum* and glorifies *pluribus*.

The historic idea of a unifying American identity is now in peril in many arenas—in our politics, our voluntary organizations, our churches, our language. And in no arena is the rejection of an overriding national identity more crucial than in our system of education.

The schools and colleges of the republic train the citizens of the future. Our public schools in particular have been the great instrument of assimilation and the great means of forming an American identity. What students are taught in schools affects the way they will thereafter see and treat other Americans, the way they will thereafter conceive the purposes of the republic. The debate about the curriculum is a debate about what it means to be an American.

The militants of ethnicity now contend that a main objective of public education should be the protection, strengthening, celebration, and perpetuation of ethnic origins and identities. Separatism, however, nourishes prejudices, magnifies differences and stirs antagonisms. The consequent increase in ethnic and racial conflict lies behind the hullabaloo over "multiculturalism" and "political correctness," over the iniquities of the "Eurocentric" curriculum, and over the notion that history and literature should be taught not as intellectual disciplines but as therapies whose function is to raise minority self-esteem. . . .

. . . Immigrants, [nineteenth-century Frenchman Alexis de] Tocqueville said, become Americans through the exercise of the political rights and civic responsibilities bestowed on them by the Declaration of Independence and the Constitution. . . .

A century after Tocqueville, another foreign visitor, Gunnar Myrdal of Sweden, called the cluster of ideas, institutions, and habits "the American Creed." Americans "of all national origins, regions, creeds, and colors," Myrdal wrote in 1944, hold in common "the *most explicitly expressed* system of general ideals" of any country in the West: the ideals of the essential dignity and equality of all human beings, of inalienable rights to freedom, justice, and opportunity.

The schools teach the principles of the Creed, Myrdal said; the churches preach them; the courts hand down judgments in their terms. Myrdal saw the Creed as the bond that links all Americans, including nonwhite minorities, and as the spur forever goading Americans to live up to their principles.

"America," Myrdal said, "is continuously struggling for its soul." The American Creed had its antecedents, and these antecedents lay primarily in a British inheritance as recast by a century and a half of colonial experience. How really new then was the "new race"? Crèvecoeur's vision implied an equal blending of European stocks. . . . In fact, the majority of the population of the 13 colonies and the weight of its culture came from Great Britain.

Having cleared most of North America of their French, Spanish, and Dutch rivals, the British were free to set the mold. The language of the new nation, its laws, its institutions, its political ideas, its literature, its customs, its precepts, its prayers, primarily derived from Britain. Crèvecoeur himself wrote his book not in his native French but in his acquired English. The "curse of Babel," Melville said, had been revoked in America, "and the language they shall speak shall be the language of Britain."

The smelting pot thus had, unmistakably and inescapably, an Anglocentric flavor. For better or worse, the white Anglo-Saxon Protestant tradition was for two centuries—and in crucial respects still is—the dominant influence on American culture and society. This tradition provided the standard to which other immigrant nationalities were expected to conform, the matrix into which they would be assimilated. . . .

The Anglocentric domination of schoolbooks was based in part on unassailable facts. For better or for worse, American history has been shaped more than anything else by British tradition and culture. Like it or not, as Andrew Hacker, the Queens political scientist, puts it, "For almost all this nation's history, the major decisions have been made by white Christian men." To deny this perhaps lamentable but hardly disputable fact would be to falsify history. But history can also be falsified by suppression of uglier aspects of Anglo rule—callous discrimination against later immigrants, brutal racism against nonwhite minorities—and by the creation of filiopietistic myths. . . .

The belated recognition of the pluralistic character of American society has had a bracing impact on the teaching and writing of history. The women's-liberation movement, the civil rights movement, the ethnic upsurge, and other forms of group self-assertion forced historians to look at old times in new ways. Scholars now explore such long-neglected fields as the history of women, of immigration, of blacks, Indians, Hispanics, and other minorities. Voices long silent ring out of the darkness of history.

The result has been a reconstruction of American history partly on the merits and partly in response to ethnic pressures. In 1987 the two states with both the greatest and the most diversified populations—California and New York—adopted new curricula for grades one to 12. Both state curricula materially increased the time allotted to non-European cultures.

The New York curriculum went further in minimizing Western traditions. A two-year global-studies course divided the world into seven regions— Africa, South Asia, East Asia, Latin America, the Middle East, Western Europe, and Eastern Europe—with each region given equal time. The history of Western Europe was cut back from a full year to one quarter of the second year. American history was reduced to a section on the Constitution; then a leap across Jefferson, Jackson, the Civil War, and Reconstruction to 1877.

In spite of the multiculturalization of the New York state history curriculum in 1987—a revision approved by such scholars as Eric Foner of Columbia and Christopher Lasch of Rochester—a newly appointed commissioner of education yielded to pressures from minority interests to consider still further revision. In 1989, a Task Force on Minorities: Equity and Excellence (not one historian among its 17 members) brought in a report, its first sentence sounding the keynote:

> African-Americans, Asian-Americans, Puerto Ricans/Latinos and Native Americans have all been the victims of an intellectual and educational oppression that has characterized the culture and institutions of the United States and the European American world for centuries.

The "systematic bias toward European culture and its derivatives," the report asserts, has "a terribly damaging effect on the psyche of young people of African, Asian, Latino, and Native American descent." The dominance of "the European-American monocultural perspective" explains why "large numbers of children of non-European descent are not doing as well as expected." The 1987 curriculum revision, the report concedes, did include more material on minority groups, but "merely adding marginal examples of 'other' cultures to an assumed dominant culture" cannot counteract "deeply rooted racist traditions"; all it produces is "Eurocentric multiculturalism." . . .

Cultural pluralism is a necessity in an ethnically diversified society. But the motives behind curriculum reform sometimes go beyond the desire for a more honest representation of the past. "Multiculturalism" arises as a reaction against Anglo- or Eurocentrism; but at what point does it pass over into an ethnocentrism of its own? The very word, instead of referring as it should to all cultures, has come to refer only to non-Western, nonwhite cultures. The president of the Modern Language Association even wonders why "we cannot be students of Western culture and multiculturalism at the same time." Can any historian justify the proposition that the five ethnic communities into which the New York state task force wishes to divide the country had equal influence on the development of the United States? Is it a function of schools to teach ethnic and racial pride? When does obsession with differences begin to threaten the idea of an overarching American nationality? . . .

The use of history as therapy means the corruption of history as history. All major races, cultures, nations have committed crimes, atrocities, horrors at one time or another. Every civilization has skeletons in its closet. Honest history calls for the unexpurgated record. How much would a full account of African despotism, massacre, and slavery increase the self-esteem of black students? Yet what kind of history do you have if you leave out all the bad things?

Even if history is sanitized in order to make people feel good, there is no evidence that feel-good history promotes ethnic self-esteem and equips students to grapple with their lives. Afrocentric education, on the contrary, will make black children, as William Raspberry has written, "less competent in the culture in which they have to compete." After all, what good will it do young black Americans to take African names, wear African costumes, and replicate African rituals, to learn by music and mantras, rhythm, and rapping, to reject standard English, to hear that because their minds work differently a first-class education is not for them? Will such training help them to understand democracy better? Help them to fit better into American life? "General [Colin] Powell did not reach his present post," Jacques Barzun reminds us, "by believing that Black English was sufficient for the career he wanted to pursue." . . .

The separatist impulse is by no means confined to the black community. Another salient expression is the bilingualism movement, ostensibly conducted in the interests of all non-English speakers but particularly a Hispanic-American project. . . .

In recent years the combination of the ethnicity cult with a flood of immigration from Spanish-speaking countries has given bilingualism new impetus. The presumed purpose is transitional: to move non-English-speaking children as quickly as possible from bilingual into all-English classes. The Bilingual Education Act of 1968 supplies guidelines and funding; the 1974 Supreme Court decision in *Lau* v. *Nichols* (a Chinese-speaking case) requires school districts to provide special programs for children who do not know English.

Alas, bilingualism has not worked out as planned: rather the contrary. Testimony is mixed, but indications are that bilingual education retards rather than expedites the movement of Hispanic children into the English-speaking world and that it promotes segregation more than it does integration. Bilingualism shuts doors. It nourishes self-ghettoization, and ghettoization nourishes racial antagonism. Bilingualism "encourages concentrations of Hispanics to stay together and not be integrated," says Alfredo Matthew Jr., a Hispanic civic leader, and it may well foster "a type of apartheid that will generate animosities with others, such as Blacks, in the competition for scarce resources, and further alienate the Hispanic from the larger society."

Using some language other than English dooms people to second-class citizenship in American society. "Those who have the most to lose in a bilingual America," says the Mexican-American writer Richard Rodriguez, "are the foreign-speaking poor." Rodriguez recalls his own boyhood: "It would have pleased me to hear my teachers address me in Spanish. . . . But I would have delayed . . . having to learn the language of public society. . . . Only when I was able to think of myself as an American, no longer an alien in *gringo* society, could I seek the rights and opportunities necessary for full public individuality."

Monolingual education opens doors to the larger world. "I didn't speak

English until I was about 8 years of age," Governor Mario Cuomo recently recalled, "and there was a kind of traumatic entry into public school. It made an immense impression on me." Traumatic or not, public school taught Cuomo the most effective English among politicos of his generation.

Yet a professor at the University of Massachusetts told Rosalie Pedalino Porter, whose long experience in bilingual education led to her excellent book *Forked Tongue,* that teaching English to children reared in another language is a form of political oppression. Her rejoinder seems admirable: "When we succeed in helping our students use the majority language fluently . . . we are empowering our students rather than depriving them."

Panicky conservatives, fearful that the republic is over the hill, call for a constitutional amendment to make English the official language of the United States. Seventeen states already have such statutes. This is a poor idea. The English language does not need statutory reinforcement and the drive for an amendment will only increase racial discrimination and resentment.

Nonetheless, a common language is a necessary bond of national cohesion in so heterogeneous a nation as America. The bilingual campaign has created both an educational establishment with a vested interest in extending the bilingual empire and a political lobby with a vested interest in retaining a Hispanic constituency. Like Afrocentricity and the ethnicity cult, bilingualism is an elitist, not a popular, movement—"romantic ethnicity," as Myrdal called it; political ethnicity too. Still, institutionalized bilingualism remains another source of the fragmentation of America, another threat to the dream of "one people." . . .

---

2   In this selection, from a popular history of Latinos in America, Puerto Rican-born journalist Juan Gonzalez takes up the late-twentieth-century "discord over how we interpret and teach the American experience." In so doing, he makes clear his views about multicultural education. How does Gonzalez respond to Schlesinger? How does his view of history differ from Schlesinger's? How does he connect the issues of language and culture?

Empire, Racism, and Multiculturalism (2000)
JUAN GONZALEZ

In his 1991 polemic, *The Disuniting of America,* historian Arthur Schlesinger, Jr., rails against the rising "cult of ethnicity" or "compensatory history" by contemporary advocates of multiculturalism and bilingualism. In the process,

Schlesinger serves up his version of the creation story of America: "Having cleared most of North America of their French, Spanish, and Dutch rivals, the British were free to set the mold. The language of the new nation, its laws, its institutions, its political ideas, its literature, its customs, its precepts, its prayers, primarily derived from Britain."

Unfortunately, whether the mythmaking comes from Bible Belt conservatives like Judge [Samuel] Kiser* or eastern liberals like Schlesinger, it suffers from the same flaw—a failure to accept that the quest for empire, fueled by the racialist theory of Manifest Destiny, divided and deformed the course of ethnic relations from our nation's inception, fragmenting and subverting any quest for one "national language" and "national culture."

Few of us would disagree that English is the *common* language of the country. Yet the very process of territorial expansion—not just immigration—created repeated battles throughout U.S. history over whether English should be the only recognized tongue. A number of ethnic groups have attempted to preserve their native languages at the same time they adopted English, while our government, especially at the federal level, sought just as strenuously to suppress efforts at bilingualism.

Those language battles from prior eras do not all fall under one neat category—rather, a close examination of them reveals three main trends, and the qualitative differences between those trends gets lost in the rhetoric of the current debate. The first category includes the millions of immigrants who came here from Europe and Asia voluntarily seeking American citizenship, and who, by doing so, were cutting ties with their homelands, adopting the language of their new country and accepting a subsidiary status, if any, for their native tongues.

The second category was made up of the slaves from dozens of African nations who were brought here in chains, forced from the start to give up their various mother tongues, and not permitted even to acquire a reading or writing knowledge of English so that the slaveowners could more easily control and dominate them.

The third category, and the one least understood, encompasses those people who were already living in the New World when their lands were either conquered or acquired by the United States: the Native Americans, the French Creoles of Louisiana, the Mexicans, and the Puerto Ricans. These latter groups became American citizens by force. Congress declared them so without any vote or petition on their part; it did not care what language they spoke nor did it seek their public oath of allegiance.

Since a new sovereignty was imposed on them while they were still residing on their old lands, these "annexed" Americans could hardly consider themselves foreigners. This turned them into persistent defenders of the right

*A Texas judge who ordered a U.S. citizen of Mexican descent to speak English at home to her daughter.

to use their own language, and the new Anglo authorities who took over administration of the states or territories in which they resided occasionally understood that viewpoint and accommodated them. The federal government, on the other hand, reacted with hostility to any linguistic diversity.

Throughout the past two centuries, Anglo historians consistently relegated the languages of these conquered nationalities to the margins of the American experience, dismissing their cultures as either primitive or nonexistent. Despite that marginalization, Latinos in particular managed to preserve their language and traditions by fashioning a parallel subterranean storehouse of music, dance, theater, journalism, literature, and folklore—in English, as well as Spanish. Over time, the culture of Mexicans, Puerto Ricans, Cubans, and other Latinos who resided here gradually fused with one anothers', while continuing to borrow elements from their Latin American homelands. At the same time, this emerging U.S.-Latino culture combined with and reshaped aspects of African American and Euro-American music, dance, and theater, creating in the process a dazzling array of hybrid forms that are today uniquely American, and which are most evident in musical genres such as Tex-Mex, Cubop, Latin jazz, Latin rock, bugaloo, salsa, rap, and even country rock, but which have spread to other areas of the arts as well. Only in recent years, with the phenomenal growth of Latino immigration, has this underground cultural stream finally surfaced and begun to sweep away the melting-pot myth of the United States. Despite that resurgence, Latinos remain invisible to mainstream chronicles of American culture, and they are virtually absent from the culture's most influential contemporary media, Hollywood movies and television.

The Early Battles Over Language

From the very beginning, the thirteen colonies confronted a quandary over language. Before independence, German was virtually the only tongue spoken throughout fifteen thousand square miles of eastern Pennsylvania, while Dutch was widely used in the Hudson River Valley. Between 1732 and 1800, at least thirty-eight German-language newspapers were published in the Pennsylvania colony, and the University of Pennsylvania established a program in German bilingual education as early as 1780. So widespread was the use of German that the first U.S. Census reported 8.7 percent of Americans spoke it as their first language, almost identical to the proportion of Hispanics in our country in 1990.

The prevalence of a German linguistic minority continued into the twentieth century. By 1900, as many as 600,000 children in American public and parochial schools were being taught in German, nearly 4 percent of the country's school population. Only with the Americanization policy that accompanied World War I was German finally eliminated as a language of instruction.

The experience of European immigrants, however, is not as relevant to the modern-day language debate as that of the annexed nationalities. When Louisiana became a state in 1812, for instance, the majority of its residents spoke French. As a result, until the 1920s, all laws and public documents in the state were published in French and English. The courts, the public schools, even the state legislature operated in two languages. Louisiana's second governor, Jacques Villere, spoke no English and always addressed the legislature in French. As more settlers moved in, and English speakers became the majority during the 1840s, the use of French declined, but it did so through the evolution of the population, not through government fiat, and the rights of French-speaking children continued to be recognized in the public schools.

After the Treaty of Guadalupe Hidalgo imposed American citizenship on the Mexicans living in the annexed territories, Congress did not require its new subjects to swear allegiance to their new nation or adopt a new language. Those who did not want to become citizens had to publicly register their refusal but the lives of the *mexicanos* continued pretty much as before. As late as the 1870s, more than a quarter century after annexation, New Mexico's legislature operated mostly in Spanish. By then, only two of fourteen counties had switched to jury trials in English and most of the public schools conducted instruction either all in Spanish or bilingually. This did not mean that New Mexicans resisted learning English, only that their opportunities to learn the language were minimal in isolated rural communities where they composed the overwhelming majority. Because of that, New Mexico was one of the last territories to become a state, in 1913, but it boasted a *mexicano* majority until 1940. A similar process evolved in the Rio Grande Valley of Texas, only there *mexicanos* have remained the overwhelming majority for 250 years, with most residents still retaining the use of Spanish while also being fluent in English.

Then there is the language experience of some Native Americans. Oklahoma's Cherokees built a public school system in the 1850s in which 90 percent of the children were taught in their native language while also learning English. So successful was the effort that Cherokee children of that era registered higher levels of English literacy than white children in the neighboring states of Texas and Arkansas. But in the late 1800s, the federal government initiated a policy of Americanization. It forcibly removed thousands of Indian children from their families and shipped them to boarding schools to learn English. The disastrous result, as documented by repeated studies during the second half of the twentieth century, was that 40 percent of Cherokee children became *illiterate in any language* and 75 percent dropped out of school.

Finally, there is Puerto Rico's forgotten language saga. Shortly after the U.S. occupation of the island in 1898, Congress declared the territory officially bilingual, even though its population had spoken Spanish for four hundred years and almost no one spoke English. Military governor Guy Henry promptly ordered all public school teachers to become fluent in the language of their new country, and he instituted an English-proficiency test for high school graduation. Despite widespread resistance from island politicians, educators, and students, the territory's Anglo administrators proceeded to make English the language of instruction in all island schools. The result was a near-total breakdown of the education system as thousands of students stopped attending classes, and those who stayed struggled to learn academic subjects in a language they did not understand.

Efforts to force Puerto Ricans to learn English continued unsuccessfully for nearly half a century, with only a brief reversion to Spanish instruction in the 1930s when José Padin, the island's education commissioner, tried to reintroduce Spanish. But President Roosevelt promptly fired Padin on the advice of Secretary of the Interior Harold Ickes and brought back the English-only policy. Things remained that way until 1949, when the island's first native-born elected governor, Luis Muñoz Marín, finally ended the hated policy of language suppression. Even though Muñoz and the local legislature reinstituted Spanish as the language of instruction, they still required pupils to learn English as a second language. The Popular Democrats took their reforms one step further in 1965; they brought back Spanish as the official language of the island's local courts. Congress, however, insisted that English remain as the language of the federal courts on the island.

The mere existence of Puerto Rico—an entire U.S. territory whose residents speak Spanish—has created enormous problems for theorists of a monolingual U.S. nation. In 1917, the same year Congress established a literacy test for all foreigners applying for citizenship, it declared Puerto Ricans citizens without requiring them to demonstrate any English proficiency! Once Puerto Ricans began moving to the United States in big numbers after World War II, this contradiction of U.S. citizens who spoke no English was exacerbated. The situation produced such a dilemma that Congress had to include a special "Puerto Rican" provision in the Voting Rights Act of 1965. That law, which suspended literacy tests in southern states where they had been used to prevent blacks from voting, also had a part, Section 4(e), introduced by New York senator Robert Kennedy, that prohibited New York State, which had a sixth-grade education requirement for voters at the time, from denying the vote to any citizen whose education had been in an American-flag school where "predominant classroom instruction was other than English." Through that provision, Congress acknowledged that, at least in the case of Puerto Ricans, U.S. territorial expansion had created Spanish-speaking citizens with a claim to certain linguistic rights.

The Mexican, Puerto Rican, French Creole, and Native American language experiences, then, are markedly different from that of European immigrants, who, as Schlesinger notes, "stayed for a season with their old language" before the next generation adopted English. Spanish, Cajun, and the surviving Native American languages are not "foreign." They are the tongues of long-settled linguistic minorities who were absorbed by an expanding multinational state.

International law has long recognized that linguistic minorities within a multiethnic state like ours have a right to protection against discrimination. Article 53 of the United Nations Charter, for example, urges member states to promote "universal respect for and observance of human rights and fundamental freedom for all without distinction as to race, sex, *language* or religion" (my emphasis). Similar descriptions can be found in the UN Universal Declaration of Human Rights and in proclamations of the European and Inter-American states.

Those principles, however, are routinely violated in this country, where federal courts prohibit discrimination because of a person's race, religion, or national origin, but continue to permit language discrimination. A classic example occurred in Texas in 1975 in the case of *García* v. *Gloor.* Héctor García, the plaintiff in the case, was a twenty-four-year-old native-born Texan who attended public schools in Brownsville and who spoke both English and Spanish. His parents, however, were Mexican immigrants and the family always spoke Spanish at home, so he felt more comfortable in Spanish.

García was hired as a salesman by Gloor Lumber and Supply, Inc. specifically because he could speak Spanish to its customers, but the company had a policy that employees could not speak Spanish *to one another* on the job, though they were free to speak whatever language they wanted off the job. In June 1975, García was dismissed after violating the company rule several times, whereupon he filed a federal discrimination complaint. At the trial, the U.S. district court found that seven of the eight salesmen Gloor employed, and thirty-one of its thirty-nine employees, were Hispanic, that 75 percent of the customers in the Brownsville business area also were Hispanic, and that many of Gloor's customers wished to be waited on by salesmen who spoke Spanish. Alton Gloor, an officer and stockholder, testified that there were business reasons for the Spanish ban, among them: English-speaking customers objected to communications between employees that they could not understand; pamphlets and trade literature were only in English, so employees needed to improve their English skills; and supervisors who did not speak Spanish could better oversee their subordinates. The court ruled in Gloor's favor, finding no discrimination.

The case eventually went to the U.S. Court of Appeals for the Fifth Circuit, which agreed in a May 1980 decision that "Mr. Garcia's use of Spanish was a significant factor" in his firing. The court concluded, however, that García had not suffered national discrimination, even though he presented an expert witness who testified that the "Spanish language is the most important aspect of ethnic identification for Mexican Americans," and even though he was backed in his contention by the Equal Employment Opportunity Commission. The court's decision went on to say

> Mr. Garcia was fully bilingual. He chose deliberately to speak Spanish instead of English while actually at work. . . . Let us assume, as contended by Mr. Garcia, there was no genuine business need for the rule and that its adoption by Gloor was arbitrary. The EEO Act does not prohibit all arbitrary employment practices. . . . It is directed only at specific impermissible bases of discrimination, race, color, religion, sex, or national origin. National origin must not be confused with ethnic or sociocultural traits or an unrelated status, such as citizenship or alienage . . . a hiring policy that distinguishes on some other ground, such as grooming codes or how to run his business, is related more closely to the employer's choice of how to run his business than to equality of employment.

In other words, because García was bilingual, he had lost any right to speak his language—the language for which he was hired and the majority language in the community—at work. Spanish was a "preference" of his, the court said, and an employer could legally ban it just as he could ban "persons born under a certain sign of the zodiac or persons having long hair or short hair or no hair at all." The court thus performed a Solomon-like miracle—severing García's nationality from his language.

The language debate is a nagging reminder that conquering a territory by force does not guarantee the assimilation of that territory's original inhabitants, nor does the passing of a few generations assure the gradual disappearance of their culture. For if conquered people feel themselves systematically mistreated by their conquerors, they inevitably turn their language and culture into weapons of resistance, into tools with which they demand full equality within the conquering society. This is precisely what happened with Latinos in America toward the end of the twentieth century.

Unfortunately, even some of the best Anglo historians have misread that movement as one that is seeking separation rather than inclusion. Take Pulitzer prize-winner Arthur Schlesinger's response to the multicultural movement. "It may be too bad that dead white European males have played so large a role in shaping our culture," Schlesinger writes in *The Disuniting of America*, "But that's the way it is. One cannot erase history."

The alarmism of Schlesinger and others notwithstanding, no one in the multicultural movement except a few bizarre ethnocentrists ever sought to erase the historical role of "dead white European males" in American history. Rather, most exponents of that movement have endeavored to undo the damage created by several centuries of what Edward Said, one of America's most perceptive social critics, has properly called "cultural imperialism."

A culture's music, song, fiction, theater, and popular lore, Said notes, together with specialized disciplines, sociology, literary history, ethnography, and the like, comprise the narratives by which a people understand the best of themselves, their place in the world, their identity. But over the course of civilization, culture became attached to specific nations and states, and at least since the time of the Greeks, those attachments have led to classifications, often antagonistic notions of "us" and "them," of superior and inferior societies, thus turning culture into another weapon by which the strong dominate the weak. As Said notes,

> The main battle in imperialism is over land, of course; but when it came to who owned the land, who had the right to settle and work on it, who kept it going, who won it back, and who now plans its future—these issues were reflected, contested, and even for a time decided in narrative [culture]. . . . [T]he power to narrate, or to block other narratives from forming and emerging, is very important to culture and imperialism and constitutes one of the main connections between them.

In the United States, the link between culture and empire has been harder to grasp, partly because our heterogeneous immigrant society has made even the definition of a "dominant" culture more difficult to distill, but that link is just as strong as it was between the former European powers and their colonies, insists Said:

> Before we can agree what the American identity is made of, we have to concede that as an immigrant settler society superimposed on the ruins of considerable native presence, American identity is too varied to be a unitary and homogeneous thing; indeed the battle within it is between advocates of a unitary identity and those who see the whole as a complex but not reductively unified one. . . .
>
> Partly because of empire, all cultures are involved in one another; none is single and pure, all are hybrid, heterogeneous, extraordinarily differentiated, and un-monolithic. This, I believe, is as true of the contemporary United States as it is of the modern Arab world.

In his pioneering literary analysis, *Culture and Imperialism,* Said goes on to demonstrate how many of the West's greatest fiction writers, [Daniel] Defoe, [Joseph] Conrad, [Rudyard] Kipling, [Jane] Austen, [Andre] Malraux, T. E. Lawrence, [Herman] Melville, and [Albert] Camus, all unconsciously promoted in their works the imperial ambitions of their separate nations, while they ignored or overlooked the intrinsic value of the colonial cultures in which their novels were set.

Much the same has happened in this country with both classical and popular traditions and culture. During the nineteenth century, Anglo settlers in the Southwest readily adapted the Spanish hacienda styles of architecture, Spanish names for cities, rivers, and even states, Mexican food, the *vaquero* life of the Mexican *rancho*, or the hunting, camping, and solitary worship of nature so prevalent among Native Americans, while they refused to regard the Mexicans or Indians among them as equals.

PRIMARY SOURCES

This section contains sources related to the late-twentieth-century battles over multicultural education, especially its impact on the history taught in schools. These sources reflect a variety of viewpoints, including educators and students, and do not support a single conclusion. The first six sources deal with multicultural education, especially as it pertains to the teaching of history in the public schools; the last two deal with the related issue of bilingual education. In all these sources, look for evidence that supports Schlesinger's or Gonzalez's conclusions about the lessons to be drawn from the battles over multicultural education.

3   Dinesh D'Souza is the author of *Illiberal Education: The Politics of Race and Sex on Campus.* In this excerpt from an article originally published in *Forbes* magazine, D'Souza attacks multiculturalism on college campuses. On what grounds does he do so? How does he explain the push for multicultural education in colleges?

"The Visigoths in Tweed" (1991)

DINESH D'SOUZA

An academic and cultural revolution has overtaken most of our 3,535 colleges and universities. It's a revolution to which most Americans have paid little attention. It is a revolution imposed upon the students by a university elite, not one voted upon or even discussed by the society at large. It amounts, according to University of Wisconsin–Madison Chancellor Donna Shalala, to "a basic transformation of American higher education in the name of multiculturalism and diversity."

The central thrust of this "basic transformation" involves replacing traditional core curricula—consisting of the great works of Western culture—with curricula flavored by minority, female, and Third World authors.

Here's a sample of the viewpoint represented by the new curriculum. Becky Thompson, a sociology and women's studies professor, in a teaching manual distributed by the American Sociological Association, writes: "I begin my course with the basic feminist principle that in a racist, classist, and sexist society we have all swallowed oppressive ways of being, whether intentionally or not. Specifically, this means that it is not open to debate whether a white student is racist or a male student is sexist. He/she simply is."

Source: Dinesh D'Souza, "The Visigoths in Tweed," *Forbes*, April 1, 1991. Reprinted by Permission of Forbes Magazine © 2004 Forbes Inc.

Professors at several colleges who have resisted these regnant dogmas about race and gender have found themselves the object of denunciation and even university sanctions. Donald Kagan, dean of Yale College, says: "I was a student during the days of Joseph McCarthy, and there is less freedom now than there was then."

As in the McCarthy period, a particular group of activists has cowed the authorities and bent them to its will. After activists forcibly occupied his office, President Lattie Coor of the University of Vermont explained how he came to sign a sixteen-point agreement establishing, among other things, minority faculty hiring quotas. "When it became clear that the minority students with whom I had been discussing these issues wished to pursue negotiations in *the context of occupied offices* . . . I agreed to enter negotiations." As frequently happens in such cases, Coor's "negotiations" ended in a rapid capitulation by the university authorities.

At Harvard, historian Stephan Thernstrom was harangued by student activists and accused of insensitivity and bigotry. What was his crime? His course included a reading from the journals of slave owners, and his textbook gave a reasonable definition of affirmative action as "preferential treatment" for minorities. At the University of Michigan, renowned demographer Reynolds Farley was assailed in the college press for criticizing the excesses of Marcus Garvey and Malcolm X; yet the administration did not publicly come to his defense.

University leaders argue that the revolution suggested by these examples is necessary because young Americans must be taught to live in and govern a multiracial and multicultural society. Immigration from Asia and Latin America, combined with relatively high minority birth rates, is changing the complexion of America. Consequently, in the words of University of Michigan President James Duderstadt, universities must "create a model of how a more diverse and pluralistic community can work for our society."

No controversy, of course, about benign goals such as pluralism or diversity, but there is plenty of controversy about how these goals are being pursued. Although there is no longer a Western core curriculum at Mount Holyoke or Dartmouth, students at those schools must take a course in non-Western or Third World culture. Berkeley and the University of Wisconsin now insist that every undergraduate enroll in ethnic studies, making this virtually the only compulsory course at those schools.

If American students were truly exposed to the richest elements of other cultures, this could be a broadening and useful experience. A study of Chinese philosophers such as Confucius or Mencius would enrich students' understanding of how different peoples order their lives, thus giving a greater sense of purpose to their own. Most likely, a taste of Indian poetry such as Rabindranath Tagore's *Gitanjali* would increase the interest of materially minded young people in the domain of the spirit. An introduction to Middle Eastern history would prepare the leaders of tomorrow to deal with the mounting challenge of Islamic culture. It would profit students to study the rise of capitalism in the Far East.

But the claims of the academic multiculturalists are largely phony. They pay little attention to the Asian or Latin American classics. Rather, the non-Western or multicultural curriculum reflects a different agenda. At Stanford, for example, Homer, Plato, Dante, Machiavelli, and Locke are increasingly scarce. But often their replacements are not non-Western classics. Instead the students are offered exotic topics such as popular religion and healing in Peru, Rastafarian poetry, and Andean music.

What do students learn about the world from the books they are required to read under the new multicultural rubric? At Stanford one of the non-Western works assigned is *I, Rigoberta Menchú*, subtitled "An Indian Woman in Guatemala."

The book is hardly a non-Western classic. Published in 1983, *I, Rigoberta Menchú* is the story of a young woman who is said to be a representative voice of the indigenous peasantry. Representative of Guatemalan Indian culture? In fact, Rigoberta met the Venezuelan feminist to whom she narrates this story at a socialist conference in Paris, where, presumably, very few of the Third World's poor travel. Moreover, Rigoberta's political consciousness includes the adoption of such politically correct causes as feminism, homosexual rights, socialism, and Marxism. By the middle of the book she is discoursing on "bourgeois youths" and "Molotov cocktails," not the usual terminology of Indian peasants. One chapter is titled "Rigoberta Renounces Marriage and Motherhood," a norm that her tribe could not have adopted and survived.

If Rigoberta does not represent the convictions and aspirations of Guatemalan peasants, what is the source of her importance and appeal? The answer is that Rigoberta seems to provide independent Third World corroboration for Western left-wing passions and prejudices. She is a mouthpiece for a sophisticated neo-Marxist critique of Western society, all the more powerful because it seems to issue not from some embittered American academic but from a Third World native. For professors nourished on the political activism of the late 1960s and early 1970s, texts such as *I, Rigoberta Menchú* offer a welcome opportunity to attack capitalism and Western society in general in the name of teaching students about the developing world.

---

4   Shawn Wong, a professor of American Ethnic Studies at the University of Washington, points to his own experience as a child to defend multicultural education in this excerpt from an article originally published in the *Washington Post*.

Stereotypes and Multicultural Education (1991)
SHAWN WONG

I attended the second grade in Taiwan. Given my last name, this is perhaps not a startling revelation. What was startling about this experience was that I was born and raised in Berkeley, California. I spoke no Chinese. In Taiwan I was enrolled in an all-American, predominantly white U.S. Navy school. On the school bus that first day the children chanted, "No Chinese allowed!" I thought they were referring to my mother.

My elementary school education began in the fifties in Berkeley and was scattered all over the Pacific Islands and California—eleven schools from kindergarten through high school. My memories are predominantly of being the "new kid," the outsider, of having to answer the question "What are you?" I never thought I was much different from my classmates until that experience in Taiwan. The consistently monocultural education offered in the eleven public schools I attended spoke to our common backgrounds, made us a homogeneous school population, but did not inform us about the kid sitting next to us, let alone a global neighbor.

The irony today is that some school districts in California—for example, schools in Santa Clara County—predict not only that they will be predominantly "minority," but also that, specifically, they may be more than 50 percent Asian by 1994. The change in curriculum to meet the needs of our new American identity must begin not at the public school level but in the institutions of higher education that train our teachers. While the push in colleges and universities for American ethnic studies requirements is a minuscule step toward preparing students for a changing America, those steps are often met with great resistance.

Those who oppose transformation of the curriculum say they fear the "classics" of Western European culture or the traditional liberal arts education will be relegated to second place in academia's priorities. They fear the classical American university education is being threatened, in the name of cultural diversity, by a new educational activism that will take over the curriculum instead of buildings. The problem is that the monoculturalists and academic traditionalists want us to believe that the movement towards multiculturalism is a kind of reverse racism when, in fact, it is the monoculturalists who do not apprehend reality: the language and the images of our society have already changed.

America is already a multiracial and multicultural society, not, as some would have us believe, merely approaching this state. We are there. The nation has changed in numbers and in language. And what the naysayers fail to note is that many of the moves to change college and university curricula are student-initiated. Students know they will be unable to compete in twenty-first-century America with a monocultural, monolingual education.

Much of the scholarship surrounding Asian American history and culture is infested with stereotypes, both positive and negative, from the "model minority" myth to the image of the shrewd and ruthless gang member. To say that the economic shift to Asia doesn't affect the image of Asians in America is to ignore the rise in hate crimes against Asians in America. The racial fear of hordes of Asians immigrating to America in the nineteenth century has been replaced today with the fear of a horde of Toyotas contributing to the trade deficit. In the introduction to *Aiiieeeee! An Anthology of Asian American Writers* (1974), which I coedited with Frank Chin, Jeffrey Chan, and Lawson Inada, we say: "Before we can talk about our literature, we have to explain the sensibility. Before we can explain our sensibility we have to outline our histories. Before we can outline our history, we have to dispel the stereotypes.

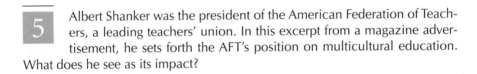

5   Albert Shanker was the president of the American Federation of Teachers, a leading teachers' union. In this excerpt from a magazine advertisement, he sets forth the AFT's position on multicultural education. What does he see as its impact?

"The Danger in Multiple Perspectives" (1991)

ALBERT SHANKER

We are in the midst of a revolution in the teaching of American history. Most people would agree it's long overdue. In the past, our history has been taught as a drama in which white men had all the good roles. It was a spectacular, flag-waving saga designed to create loyalty, patriotism and a sense of the rightness of everything the U.S. did—and it worked. But the picture was incomplete and it was not honest. It ignored the contributions of women, of African-Americans, of immigrants, of the labor movement and others; it ignored important occasions on which we betrayed our ideals. I don't know anyone today who would defend that kind of patriotic saga of progress or deny that an honest treatment of our history would naturally be multicultural.

But this isn't what some people mean by multiculturalism, and certain popular ideas about the subject are very troublesome. For example, the pro-

Source: Albert Shanker, "The Danger in Multiple Perspectives," advertisement in *The New Republic,* March 25, 1991, p. 47. Reprinted by permission of *The New Republic,* © 1991, The New Republic, LLC.

posal that the New York State Board of Regents recently accepted, "One Nation, Many Peoples: A Declaration of Cultural Interdependence," sounds reasonable—and certainly the racist language that characterized the "Curriculum of Inclusion," an earlier report to the Regents, has disappeared. But even the latest proposal will encourage intellectual dishonesty and promote divisiveness instead of healing it.

The main point of the report is that history and social studies should be taught from the point of view of "multiple perspectives," and that this should start in the earliest grades. Now, "multiple perspectives" is an excellent phrase. It sounds open-minded, which is what the pursuit of knowledge should be. But when you put the concept into the classroom, what does it mean?

For a teacher presenting a historical event to elementary school children, using multiple perspectives probably means that the teacher turns to each child and asks the child's point of view about the event. To an African-American child this would mean, "What is the African-American point of view?" To a Jewish child. "What is the Jewish point of view?" And to an Irish child, "What is the Irish point of view?"

This is racist because it assumes that a child's point of view is determined by the group he comes from. But is there a single African-American or Jewish or Irish point of view? A child may have a point of view based on the fact that he is rich or poor or that he has read extensively or that he comes from a family of conservative Republicans or Marxists. In a society like ours, we are often, and delightfully, surprised that people do not carry with them the views that stereotypes call for. Is it a teacher's job to tell children that they are entitled to only one point of view because of the racial, religious or ethnic group they come from? Should schools be in the business of promoting racial stereotypes and fostering differences where they may not exist? . . .

Schools have also, historically, been places where children of varying backgrounds learned to live together. Assigning kids different points of view based on their ethnic, racial or religious background will exacerbate conflict or even create it when none exists. Kids who are now happy to think of themselves primarily as Americans may learn to think of themselves primarily as Hispanics or African-Americans or Jews.

Throughout the world, countries made up of different peoples are coming apart. It would be tragic if here in the U.S., where almost all feel that they are first and foremost Americans, we adopted a curriculum that would pull us apart.

Nathan Glazer, a professor of sociology and education at Harvard University, was a member of the New York State education commission, which recommended in 1991 that the state's public schools adopt more multicultural social studies curricula. What does Glazer see as the most important impetus behind multicultural education? How does he defend multiculturalism's impact on the teaching of history?

"In Defense of Multiculturalism" (1991)

NATHAN GLAZER

Multiculturalism can mean many things, and no one argues with a curriculum that gives proper weight to the role of American Indians, blacks, Asians, and European immigrant and ethnic groups in American history. But as currently used, the word "multiculturalism" is something of a misnomer. It suggests a general desire or need for students to have something in the curriculum that relates to their own ethnic traits, if these exist, or to those of their parents or ancestors. I don't think this desire is particularly widespread among many ethnic groups. "We are all immigrants" is nice rhetoric, but in fact we are not all immigrants. Some of us came in the last decade, some of our parents came long before that, many millions of us have only the haziest idea of how many ancestors came from where. Since 1980 the census has included a new question. "What is your ancestry?" The great majority of respondents report two, three, or more ancestries. Tens of millions simply insist on being "American," and nothing else.

Nor does multiculturalism reflect the increased immigration of recent decades, particularly to some of our largest cities, such as New York, Los Angeles, San Francisco, and Miami. It is not the new immigrants who are arguing for multiculturalism. Most of them would be content with the education provided to the previous waves of European immigrants, which paid not a whit of attention to their ethnic or racial background, or to their distinct culture or language. A product of that kind of education, I was also quite content with it.

But if it is not the new immigration that is driving the multicultural demands, what is? Multiculturalism in its present form derives basically from black educators. It is one of the longest settled elements in the American population that makes the sharpest case for multiculturalism. Asians, who make up half of current immigrants, are not much concerned. Nor are Spanish-speaking immigrants from Central and South America. Puerto Ricans and Mexican-Americans do tend to support bilingual education and the maintenance of the Spanish language. But they are definitely junior partners in the fight for multiculturalism.

I'm convinced that were it not for the pattern of poor achievement among blacks in the schools, the multicultural movement would lose much of its

Source: Nathan Glazer, "In Defense of Multiculturalism," *The New Republic,* September 2, 1991, pp. 18–21. Reprinted by permission of *The New Republic,* © 1991, The New Republic, LLC.

force. Even taking into account recent progress among blacks, shown in NAEP (National Assessment of Educational Progress) scores, SAT scores, and high school graduation rates, blacks still regularly score below whites, often below Hispanics and Native Americans, and far below Asians. Multiculturalism, and one of its variants, Afrocentrism, is presented to us by black educators and leaders as one of the means whereby this deficiency may be overcome. . . .

. . . In the elementary and high schools, a properly nuanced historical truth based on the best available evidence has always been only one interest among many. History in the schools has always played a socializing, nationalizing function (sometimes a regional pride function, as in the Southern versions of some texts). That function was the inculcation of patriotism in immigrants, and their assimilation to a culture deriving from England, and the experience of English-speaking colonists.

Some recent trends, even without the pressure of multiculturalists, are already changing that pattern. The most important is the general challenge to an unquestioning, simple, and direct American patriotism.

What does one do in the face of these trends? One thing is to fight the errors, distortions, untruths, imbalances. Some of the comments attached to the report did that, and the report fortunately did not add further weight to the more extreme claims. But the sharper critics of the report, I believe, have failed to recognize that demographic and political pressures change the history that is to be taught. They direct us to look for things we could not have noticed before. Assertions that are at first glance fantastic may have to be given some modest acquiescence. Yes, it seems that there were some Egyptian pharaohs who were racially black. (What one makes of it is another matter.) Yes, it seems that some ancient Greeks believed that they got their gods, myths, mystical knowledge from ancient Egypt. Martin Bernal's *Black Athena* will eventually leave some deposit in textbook accounts. (It will be ironic if one consequence of Afrocentrism is that our students, who know nothing of ancient Greece and less of ancient Egypt, will now be forced to learn something in order to accommodate the argument of African influences!) Yes, there is another side to the story of the expansion of Europe and imperialism. Yes, it is possible that, as the economic historian Barbara Solow argues, the weight of slave-produced plantation products was much greater in shaping the economy of the American colonies than is generally understood. Yes, there is a Mexican perspective on the Mexican-American War, and when one deals with classes that are dominantly Latin American it would be best to know it.

---

7 This article from the *Los Angeles Times* discusses the implementation of multiculturalism in Los Angeles, which has one of the most ethnically diverse public school systems in the nation. What does it reveal about the impact of multicultural education on students?

Building Bridges or Burning Them? (1992)

Multiculturalism—the notion that ethnic and cultural groups in the United States should preserve their identities instead of fusing them in a melting pot—has become a byword in education in Los Angeles and other cities.

But now, the educators at the elementary, secondary and university levels are rethinking that idea—and worrying that past efforts to teach multiculturalism may have widened the ethnic divisions they were meant to close.

Fearing that the current approach—which relies largely on ethnic studies courses and the recognition of special holidays and heroes—may have unintentionally isolated students from each other, teachers and academics are gingerly beginning to question the way multiculturalism has been taught. . . .

Not that these educators have abandoned multiculturalism as a concept. Nor do they suggest schools are solely to blame for ethnic tensions in society and on campus. But, in growing numbers, they are struggling to better define multiculturalism's goals and ways to teach it.

At present, many courses either focus entirely on one ethnic population or teach a standard history and throw a few ethnic names into the mix. The new approach would teach events as they had happened—as interconnected and inclusive history that changed lives in every ethnic group, and was also changed by all of those groups.

The discussion is so new that it has barely begun to show up in the pages of education journals. But it is gaining speed among teachers, administrators and university professors, many who were surprised to discover that others are voicing the same concerns.

Even students, searching for reasons why violence erupted recently at North Hollywood High School and other campuses in the Los Angeles Unified School District, suggested that some youngsters have misunderstood lessons about ethnic pride, developing ethnic chauvinism instead.

"They teach you that you have to identify with your own group," said Karina Escalante, a senior at Cleveland High School in Reseda, where African-American and Latino students clashed last year.

She said students receive conflicting messages that teach them pride in their ethnic identities but not how those identities can and should mesh with others in society. "They tell you to keep with your own. Then they tell you to go out and mix. They should have a program that says, "'Yes, you should identify yourself but then you have to go out and mix.'"

Educators in the Los Angeles district say they are particularly troubled and point to the violence that broke out in October between African-American and Latino students at North Hollywood and Hamilton high schools.

Esther Taira, the resource teacher who in 1986 spearheaded the development of a multicultural curriculum for the district's high schools, said she would design her course very differently today.

"We do have ethnic-specific courses, but they do not create the bridges we need," said Taira, whose course is an elective offered only in some schools. "Even when we do talk about more than one group, we tend to focus on similarities, and that ignores the problems in the streets. It is the differences that are the issue."

Among youngsters, feelings of isolation can start early.

In Christine Toleson's fifth-grade and Marcia Klein's sixth-grade classes at Pacoima Elementary School, where the walls are festooned with posters in English and Spanish, students said they felt happy and proud when the school celebrated holidays or held "appreciation days" for their ethnic group. Most students said they remembered discussing their heritage in class.

But very few students raised their hands when asked whether they remembered discussing the culture of a different ethnic group.

"On Martin Luther King Day they were celebrating black people," said Gerardo Nunes, a Latino fifth-grader. "I went over there. Other people were not my color. I felt all alone." . . .

In the Los Angeles public schools, teachers at all levels are encouraged to talk about the different cultures represented by their students. Most schools conduct festivals or hold special assemblies or parties to celebrate such holidays as the birthday of Martin Luther King Jr. or Cinco de Mayo, which marks the day Mexico defeated French forces in the Battle of Puebla. . . .

. . . [E]ven the celebration of ethnic holidays has caused problems, with one group believing that another got more attention or boycotting another group's festivities, said Casey Browne, who heads the peer counseling program at North Hollywood High.

"To some extent I think we bring on racial tensions when we celebrate one holiday over another," Brown said. "Some schools do a better job on certain holidays then they do on others, and then the other kids feel left out."

Such problems have developed, said Bernadine Lyles, the school district's multicultural education unit adviser, because "the climate was not prepared" for students to want to celebrate the cultures of others.

She noted that a framework for multicultural education adopted by the school board last spring emphasizes "activities that would bring groups together, rather than those activities that might look like separation."

In the new course that Taira is developing, lessons are organized around historical themes instead of ethnicity.

If the subject is American agriculture, Taira said, the teacher might discuss how farming and ranching affected the lives of black American slaves, Chinese and Mexican immigrants and poor whites who worked as sharecroppers—all within broader contexts such as family farms or the plantation economy of the South.

"There has been a drawing back from the notion that we just have to add more African-Americans, or add more Latinos, as well as the notion that we have to focus on victims," Moore said. "People are in a complex relationship with each other. They may be victims in one set of relationships and served in others."

Students sum up the situation most poignantly—and appear to offer the most hope.

After last month's racial brawl at North Hollywood High, senior Pele Keith called out to a group of African-American and Latino students who were arguing about the events of that troubled day.

"They say brown pride, but look, I'm just as brown as she is," Pele, an African-American, said, placing her arm alongside the arm of a Latino friend, Patti Martinez.

"Look at that," Patti sang out in reply, "the same color."

---

8 The source below is from a fifth grade social studies textbook called *America Will Be,* which was developed to meet new multicultural guidelines for public schools in California in the late 1980s. Adopted for statewide use in California in 1991, it generated much controversy due to its multicultural emphasis. As one of the book's authors, University of California historian Gary Nash, declared in 1991, "We needed to break through the stereotype of American history as Pilgrims coming to this nation and spreading Anglo-American history across the continent."[4] The first lesson of the book, which focuses on New Orleans as a place where many cultures melded, introduces students to that multicultural focus. This source is from a feature called "A Closer Look," which is found in many of the book's other lessons and is designed to give the student an opportunity to use objects or pictures to "become a historical detective." Does this source better support the argument in Source 1 or Source 2? How so?

Musical Instruments in a Multicultural Textbook (1994)

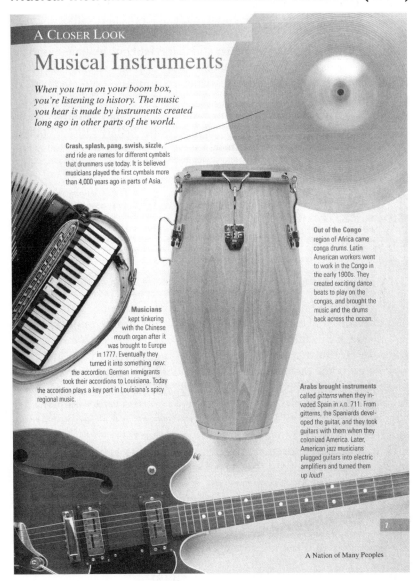

A CLOSER LOOK

Musical Instruments

When you turn on your boom box, you're listening to history. The music you hear is made by instruments created long ago in other parts of the world.

Crash, splash, pang, swish, sizzle, and ride are names for different cymbals that drummers use today. It is believed musicians played the first cymbals more than 4,000 years ago in parts of Asia.

Out of the Congo region of Africa came conga drums. Latin American workers went to work in the Congo in the early 1900s. They created exciting dance beats to play on the congas, and brought the music and the drums back across the ocean.

Musicians kept tinkering with the Chinese mouth organ after it was brought to Europe in 1777. Eventually they turned it into something new: the accordion. German immigrants took their accordions to Louisiana. Today the accordion plays a key part in Louisiana's spicy regional music.

Arabs brought instruments called *gitterns* when they invaded Spain in A.D. 711. From gitterns, the Spaniards developed the guitar, and they took guitars with them when they colonized America. Later, American jazz musicians plugged guitars into electric amplifiers and turned them up *loud!*

A Nation of Many Peoples

Source: Beverly J. Armento et al., *America Will Be* (Boston: Houghton Mifflin Company, 1994), p. 7. Photography by Ralph Brunke. Reprinted with permission.

9
In the 1980s and 1990s, by far the leading sources of immigrants were the nations of Latin America, especially Mexico. They were often associated with a growing debate about bilingual education, although dual-language programs would also be extended to other non-English-speaking students. By the 1990s, the issue of bilingual education had become an important part of the debate over multicultural education. Opponents of bilingual education charged that it impeded assimilation, while proponents contended just the opposite. In California, that debate came to a head in 1998 with the passage of Proposition 227. The proposition, which affected an estimated 1.4 million English-language learners in the state's public schools, declared that all public schoolchildren must be taught "English by being taught in English." What are the main arguments for and against the initiative in this excerpt from a voter guide published by California's secretary of state before the election?

Proposition 227 Arguments (1998)

Argument in Favor of Proposition 227

WHY DO WE NEED TO CHANGE CALIFORNIA'S BILINGUAL EDUCATION SYSTEM?

- Begun with the best of intentions in the 1970s, bilingual education has failed in actual practice, but the politicians and administrators have refused to admit this failure.
- For most of California's non-English speaking students, bilingual education actually means monolingual, SPANISH-ONLY education for the first 4 to 7 years of school.
- The current system fails to teach children to read and write English. Last year, only 6.7 percent of limited-English students in California learned enough English to be moved into mainstream classes.
- Latino immigrant children are the principal victims of bilingual education. They have the lowest test scores and the highest dropout rates of any immigrant group.
- There are 140 languages spoken by California's schoolchildren. To teach each group of children in their own native language before teaching them English is educationally and fiscally impossible. Yet this impossibility is the goal of bilingual education.

COMMON SENSE ABOUT LEARNING ENGLISH

- Learning a new language is easier the younger the age of the child.
- Learning a language is much easier if the child is immersed in that language.
- Immigrant children already know their native language; they need the public schools to teach them English.

Source: http://primary98.ss.ca.gov/VoterGuide/Propositions/227.htm

- Children who leave school without knowing how to speak, read, and write English are injured for life economically and socially.

WHAT "ENGLISH FOR THE CHILDREN" WILL DO:

- Require children to be taught English as soon as they start school.
- Provide "sheltered English immersion" classes to help non-English speaking students learn English; research shows this is the most effective method.
- Allow parents to request a special waiver for children with individual educational needs who would benefit from another method.

WHAT "ENGLISH FOR THE CHILDREN" WON'T DO:

It will:

- NOT throw children who can't speak English into regular classes where they would have to "sink or swim."
- NOT cut special funding for children learning English.
- NOT violate any federal laws or court decisions.

WHO SUPPORTS THE INITIATIVE?

- Teachers worried by the undeniable failure of bilingual education and who have long wanted to implement a successful alternative—sheltered English immersion.
- Most Latino parents, according to public polls. They know that Spanish-only bilingual education is preventing their children from learning English by segregating them into an educational dead-end.
- Most Californians. They know that bilingual education has created an educational ghetto by isolating non-English speaking students and preventing them from becoming successful members of society.

WHO OPPOSES THE INITIATIVE?

- Individuals who profit from bilingual education. Bilingual teachers are paid up to $5,000 extra annually and the program provides jobs to thousands of bilingual coordinators and administrators.
- Schools and school districts which receive HUNDREDS OF MILLIONS of extra dollars for schoolchildren classified as not knowing English and who, therefore, have a financial incentive to avoid teaching English to children.
- Activist groups with special agendas and the politicians who support them.

Alice Callaghan
Director, Las Familias del Pueblo

Ron Unz
Chairman, English for the Children

Fernando Vega
Past Redwood City School Board Member

Rebuttal to Argument in Favor of Proposition 227

Several years ago, the 1970s law mandating bilingual education in California expired.

Since then local school districts—principals, parents and teachers—have been developing and using different programs to teach children English.

Many of the older bilingual education programs continue to have great success. In other communities some schools are succeeding with English immersion and others with dual language immersion programs. Teaching children English is the primary goal, no matter what teaching method they're using.

Proposition 227 outlaws all of these programs—even the best ones—and mandates a program that has never been tested anywhere in California! And if it doesn't work, we're stuck with it anyway.

Proposition 227 proposes

- A 180-day English only program with no second chance after that school year.
- Mixed-age classrooms with first through sixth graders all together, all day, for one year.

Proposition 227 funding comes from three wealthy men . . . one from New York, one from Florida, and one from California.

The New York man has given Newt Gingrich $310,000!

The Florida man who put up $45,000 for Proposition 227 is part of a fringe group which believes "government has no role in financing, operating, or defining schooling, or even compelling attendance."

These are not people who should dictate a single teaching method for California's schools.

If the law allows different methods, we can use what works. Vote NO on Proposition 227.

John D'Amelio
President, California School Boards Association

Mary Bergan
President, California Federation of Teachers, AFL-CIO

Jennifer J. Looney
President, Association of California School Administrators

10 Many Asian Americans were also part of the growing debate about bilingual education in the 1990s, especially in California. What does this source reveal about some of the complexities surrounding the issue of bilingual education?

The Lessons of Bilingual Education (1998)

These days, it's not clear whether Asian Americans support or oppose bilingual education, or even how much they care. Some polls have shown majorities as high as 70 percent in favor, but bilingual advocates question whether the sampling is large enough to be statistically significant. Among public officials, proponents include Garden Grove Councilman Ho Chung, and Westminster Councilman Tony Lam, as well as state Treasurer Matt Fong, who is seeking the Republican nomination for the U.S. Senate.

The education issue cannot be distorted by ethnic sensibilities or political opportunism," said Chung, a Korean American. "Children are our future. We have to educate them. We have to have one common language for everybody to be able to communicate."

However, Judy Chu, a Democratic candidate for the state Assembly from the Monterey Park–San Gabriel area east of Los Angeles, says the Unz initiative* would hurt kids.

"The massive dismantling of bilingual programs under Unz would do a great disservice to limited-English-proficient students in our area," said Chu, adding she isn't concerned that her stance could hurt her at the polls. "This is a very diverse area. Lots of people come from other countries." . . .

Leland Yee, a San Francisco supervisor and former San Francisco School Board member, said he opposes 227, but criticizes the political and educational establishment for doing a "terrible job" on behalf of limited-English-speaking children.

"The Unz Initiative says we can't have non-English primary language

*Proposition 227.

Source: Bill Wong, "The Lessons of Bilingual Education," *AsianWeek,* May 20, 1998. Reprinted by permission.

instruction. I can't accept that. But I can't accept business as usual "because policymakers have not exercised sufficient political will to hire enough qualified bilingual teachers and provide enough primary-language textbooks," Yee said.

"If I were the parent of a limited-English-proficient student, I would think twice about putting my kid into a bilingual class," he added. . . .

Have bilingual programs worked for Asian Americans? Experts say there haven't been enough studies done. On May 1, San Francisco school officials issued a study showing that bilingual students who completed the district's program did as well, if not better, in reading and math scores, grade-point average and attendance as students not in the program. Unz criticized the study for looking only at students who had completed the program and not at those who hadn't.

Absent broad, conclusive studies, Tammy Leung's experience, like that of many others, sheds insight. Leung immigrated to the United States from Hong Kong in 1978, when she was 15. She could read and write English, but couldn't speak it or understand it. She took bilingual classes at Oakland High, including core subjects taught in Cantonese and English.

"It worked for me," she said in barely accented English. "It gave me confidence when I did well in classes. It gave me a feeling I could do well in the United States."

Eventually, she got her bachelor's degree in nursing at San Jose State University and is now a registered nurse.

When asked how she thinks she would have done had she been placed in an English-only immersion program, she said, "I would have dropped out of school."

CONCLUSION

Perhaps you have come to the conclusion that the impact of multicultural curricula is not easy to assess. You may also have discovered that other students do not share your conclusion about the lessons to be drawn from late-twentieth-century battles over teaching of history in schools. One reason, ironically, is our own close proximity to the problem. As time passes it will be easier to evaluate the impact of multiculturalism in education, including the significance of its impact on the history taught in schools. With their own society as a reference point, historians will be able to trace the long-term influence of late-twentieth-century changes in school curricula that we cannot yet see.

Even the passage of time, though, will not solve another problem regarding any assessments of multiculturalism or its impact on the teaching of history. The final impartial judgment on multiculturalism or anything else of historical importance is like a desert mirage: The closer we seem to get, the further it recedes from us. First, as we have seen repeatedly in this volume, historians' views of the past are shaped by their own times. As circumstances change, so too do their interpretations. Moreover, much like your own conclusions about multicultural-ism's impact on education, historical analysis inevitably reflects the values of the historian. And history, as we have also seen, is shaped by the historian's as-sumptions about historical inquiry itself. Whether expressed or not, all histori-ans' work reflects views about the role of ideology in history, whether history is better written from the "bottom up" or "top down," and the relative importance of economic, political, demographic, or other factors in shaping the past. Thus, no matter how many years have passed, there will never be a last word on mul-ticulturalism's impact on American education or American society.

As this chapter clearly demonstrates, however, this does not mean that our historical interpretations do not matter. Conflicts over the assimilation of people from different cultures are as old as the American republic itself. So are the concerns of many Americans about what their children are taught in school, especially what they learn about their own nation's past. These issues are obvi-ously still with us. And because they affect us all, we all have a vested interest in how they are resolved. As this chapter also reminds us, debates about these issues often turn on the lessons from the past. Thus, assessments about multi-culturalism illustrate how those who interpret the past have the power to influ-ence policies today. Whatever future historians conclude about the impact of multiculturalism in the late twentieth century, then, one thing is certain: None of them will likely deny that late-twentieth-century conflicts over it stand as a powerful reminder about the importance of historical interpretation.

FURTHER READING

Dinesh D'Souza, *Illiberal Education: The Politics of Race and Sex on Campus* (New York: Free Press, 1991).

Gary B. Nash, Charlotte Crabtree, and Ross E. Dunn, *History on Trial: Culture Wars and the Teaching of the Past* (New York: Alfred A. Knopf, 1997).

David W. Stewart, *Immigration and Education: The Crisis and the Opportunities* (New York: Lexington Books, 1993).

Roberto Suro, *Strangers Among Us: How Latino Immigration Is Transforming America* (New York: Alfred A. Knopf, 1998).

Reed Ueda, *Postwar Immigrant America: A Social History* (Boston: Bedford Books, 1994).

NOTES

1. "Is America's Ethnic Revival a Fad Like Jogging?" interview with Stephan Thernstrom, *U.S. News & World Report,* November 17, 1980, p. 85.
2. Quoted in Philip Gleason, "Sea Change in the Civic Culture in the 1960s," in Gary Gerstle and John Mollenkopf, eds., *E Pluribus Unum?: Contemporary and Historical Perspectives on Immigrant Political Incorporation* (New York: Russell Sage Foundation, 2001), p. 132.
3. Quoted in Reed Ueda, "Ethnic Diversity and National Identity in Public School Texts," in Diane Ravitch and Maris A. Vinovskis, eds., *Learning from the Past: What History Teaches Us About School Reform* (Baltimore: Johns Hopkins University Press, 1995), p. 121.
4. Quoted in David L. Kirp, "The Battle of the Books," *San Francisco Chronicle,* Sunday *Image* section, February 24, 1991, p. 20.